INDIAN SERPENT-LORE

OR

THE NAGAS IN HINDU LEGEND AND ART

INDIAN SERPENT-LORE

OR

THE NAGAS IN HINDU LEGEND AND ART

BY

J. PH. VOGEL, Ph.D.

Professor of Sanskrit and Indian Archaeology in the University of Leydren, Holland, Late Superintendent, Archaeological Survey of India.

WITH THIRTY PLATES

GYAN

Published by

Gyan Publishing House
5, Ansari Road
Daryaganj, New Delhi-110002
Phone: 011-47034999, 9811692060
E-mail: books@gyanbooks.com

Distribution Network
gyanbooks.com
India, USA, Canada, UK, Australia, France

ISBN : 978-81-212-2526-7 (HB)
First Published, 1926

2nd Impression 2021

Printed at: Gyan Press, Delhi.

Indian Serpent-Lore
or
The Nagas in Hindu Legend and Art
Author: J. PH. Vogel

INDIAN SERPENT-LORE

OR

THE NĀGAS IN HINDU LEGEND AND ART

BY

J. PH. VOGEL, PH.D.,

Professor of Sanskrit and Indian Archæology in the University of Leyden, Holland,
Late Superintendent, Archæological Survey of India.

WITH THIRTY PLATES

ARTHUR PROBSTHAIN
41 GREAT RUSSELL STREET, LONDON, W.C.
1926

NĀGARĀJA OF AJAṆṬĀ

[Frontispiece

TO MY FRIEND AND TEACHER,

C. C. UHLENBECK,

THIS VOLUME IS DEDICATED.

PREFACE

IT is with grateful acknowledgment that I dedicate this volume to my friend and colleague, Professor C. C. Uhlenbeck, Ph.D., who, as my *guru* at the University of Amsterdam, was the first to introduce me to a knowledge of the mysterious Nāga world as revealed in the archaic prose of the *Paushyaparvan*.

In the summer of the year 1901 a visit to the Kuḷū valley brought me face to face with people who still pay reverence to those very serpent-demons known from early Indian literature. In the course of my subsequent wanderings through the Western Himalayas, which in their remote valleys have preserved so many ancient beliefs and customs, I had ample opportunity for collecting information regarding the worship of the Nāgas, as it survives up to the present day.

Other nations have known or still practise this form of animal worship. But it would be difficult to quote another instance in which it takes such a prominent place in literature folk-lore, and art, as it does in India. Nor would it be possible to name another country where the development of this cult can be studied during a period which may be estimated at no less than three millennia. During so vast a space of time the deified serpents have haunted the imagination of the people of Hind. But even more astonishing is the endless variety of aspect under which the Nāgas appear in Indian literature and art. We meet, on the one hand, with the primitive type of the reptile endowed with the magic properties which we are wont to associate with the dragon of Western fable. On the other hand, the Nāga frequently has the character of a water-spirit. Again, he may be able to assume any form he chooses, and commonly appears in human shape. In Brahmanical legend he may become a pious ascetic, in Buddhist lore he may even develop into a self-denying saint Very often these various types appear strangely blended.

In the present volume it has been my object to collect the legends relating to the Nāgas which are found in the Brahmanical and Buddhist literature of India. We do not pretend that in that gigantic body of literary tradition there may not be a Nāga story which has escaped our notice. The three chief repositories of serpent-lore—the Mahābhārata, the Jātaka Book, and the Rājataraṅgiṇī—have, at least, been fully utilized. But for the rest it is questionable whether much would have been gained by aiming at completeness. The stories here presented will certainly suffice to show the Nāgas in that great variety of aspect to which reference has been made.

As the story-tellers of ancient India were fond of indulging in repetition and detail, it appeared often unavoidable to curtail the narrative considerably. In doing so it has been our endeavour to retain something of the exotic flavour of the Eastern tale, and, in particular, to preserve any such features as may be of interest for our present subject. While freely utilizing existing translations we have not refrained from making such alterations as seemed to be called for either for the sake of philological accuracy or on account of the general style of the book. The sculptures reproduced in our plates have been partly selected for their æsthetic or archæological interest, partly because they illustrate the legends contained in the text.

My obligations for assistance rendered in various ways are numerous. For the supply of photographs to illustrate my book, I am much indebted to Sir John Marshall, Kt., C.I.E., M.A., Litt.D., Director-General of Archæology in India, and to the various officers of his Department; to Sir Aurel Stein, Kt., C.I.E., Ph.D.; to Mr. Ramāprasād Chanda, M.A., Officer in charge of the Archæological Section, Imperial Museum, Calcutta; to the Curators of the Provincial Museums at Lahore and Lucknow; to Mr. R. Narasimhāchār, late Director of Archæological Researches, Mysore State; to Mr. F. D. K. Bosch, Ph.D., Director of the Archæological Survey of Netherlands-India; to M. Louis Finot, Directeur de l'École Française d'Extrême-Orient, Hanoi; to Mr. C. Stanley Clarke, Curator Indian Section, Victoria and Albert Museum, South Kensington; to Mr. T. A. Joyce, of the British Museum, and to M. Delaporte, Conservateur, Musée du Trocadéro, Paris.

Among the persons who have helped me with information I wish to mention Mr. Dines Andersen, Ph.D., Professor of Pali in the University of Copenhagen; Rev. T. Grahame Bailey, Ph.D.; Mr. J. J. L. Duyvendak, Reader of Chinese in the University of Leyden; Rev. A. H. Francke, Ph.D.; Sir George Grierson, K.C.I.E., Ph.D., Litt.D., I.C.S. (ret.); Pandit Hīrānanda Sāstrī, M.A., M.O.L., Superintendent for Epigraphy; Mr. Sten Konow, Ph.D., Professor of Sanskrit in the University of Kristiania; Pandit Nityānanda, Srinagar, Kashmir; Babu Prayāg Dayāl, Curator Provincial Museum, Lucknow; M. J. Przyluski, Professeur à l'École des Langues Orientales, Paris; Mr. B. Sanjiva Rao, Principal Queen's College, Benares; Mr. H. A. Rose, I.C.S. (ret.); Mr. H. Lee Shuttleworth, I.C.S. (ret.); M. Philippe Stern, Musée Guimet, Paris.

My special thanks are due to Mrs. Kuenen-Wicksteed, and to my friend, Sir Thomas W. Arnold, C.I.E., Litt.D., Professor of Arabic in the University of London, for their great care in revising my manuscript.

J. PH. VOGEL.

CONTENTS

LIST OF PLATES

INTRODUCTION

AMONG the many strange tales which the companions of the great Macedonian conqueror brought home from the Land of the Five Rivers, those relating to serpents of gigantic size were not the least wonderful. Nearchos, the admiral of Alexander, according to Strabo,[1] expresses his surprise at the multitude and malignancy of the tribe of reptiles. " They retreat from the plains to the villages which do not disappear under water at the time of the inundations, and fill the houses. On this account, the people raise their beds to a great height from the ground, and are sometimes compelled to abandon their homes, through the presence of these pests in overwhelming numbers. In fact, were it not that a great proportion of the tribe suffered destruction by the waters, the country would be reduced to a desert. The minute size of some and the immense size of others are sources of danger ; the former because it is difficult to guard against their attacks, the latter by reason of their strength, for snakes are to be seen of sixteen cubits in length."

Onesikratos, whom Strabo [2] somewhat unfairly calls " the master fabulist as well as the master pilot of Alexander ", says that the king of Abhisāra (the hill tract south-west of Kashmir), as the envoys who came from him related, kept two serpents, one of which was 80 and the other 140 cubits in length. Other Greek writers mentioned that the natives used to hunt serpents among the Emōdoi mountains and rear them in caves.

Ælian,[3] too, in his account of India refers to " the bane of snakes ". He also speaks of the herbs which serve as antidotes against the bite of any snake and refers to the curious belief that a snake, if it kills a man, cannot creep into its underground home, " the earth refusing to receive it, and casting it out from her household, banishing it, so to speak, from her bosom."

" When Alexander was assaulting some of the cities in India," the same author [4] relates, " and capturing others, he found in many of them, besides other animals, a snake which the Indians, regarding as sacred, kept in a cave and worshipped with much devotion. The Indians accordingly with every kind of entreaty implored Alexander to let no one molest the animal, and he consented to this. Now when the army was marching past the cave, the snake heard the sound that arose (that kind of animal being very sharp both of hearing and sight), and hissed so loud and emitted such gusts of rage that every one was terrified and quite confounded. It was said to be seventy cubits long, and yet the whole of

[1] J. W. M'Crindle, *Ancient India as described in classical literature*, Westminster, 1901, pp. 51 ff.

[2] Ibid., pp. 34 f. [3] Ibid. .p. 140. [4] Ibid., p. 145.

B

it was not seen, but only its head that projected from the cave. Its eyes, moreover, are reported to have equalled the size of the large, round, Macedonian shield."

Apart from the exaggerated size attributed to certain Indian snakes (in which matter the Greeks, perhaps, relied too much on their Indian informants), these accounts may on the whole be accepted as based on fact. For our present purpose the last passage quoted from Ælian is of special interest, as it testifies to the existence of real serpent worship—the cult of the live animal—in the Panjāb during the fourth century B.C. Now, whereas genuine ophiolatry prevails up to the present day in Western and Southern India, it is found in Northern India only in the form of certain survivals which will be discussed in our concluding chapter. The name under which the snakes are still worshipped in India is the same by which we find the deified serpent regularly designated in ancient literature: Sanskrit *nāga* > modern *nāg*.

Regarding the origin and significance of Nāga worship, there prevails a very marked diversity of opinion. The views expressed by James Fergusson in his large book, *Tree and Serpent Worship* (1868, 2nd ed. 1873), have often been quoted, and have, no doubt, exercised considerable influence, but will hardly find any adherents among really competent scholars of the present generation. According to him the Nāgas were not originally serpents but serpent-worshippers—an aboriginal race of Turanian stock inhabiting Northern India, who were conquered by the warlike Aryans. Fergusson positively declares that neither the Aryans nor the Dravidians were serpent-worshippers, and, in order to maintain his thesis, he even asserts that "any traces of serpent-worship that may be found in the Vedas or earlier [*sic*] writings of the Aryans must either be interpolations of a later date or concessions to the superstitions of the subject races". Buddhism, which replaced serpent-worship, he qualifies as "little more than a revival of the coarser superstitions of the aboriginal races". Apart from these strange and baseless theories, Fergusson's book contains a fair amount of useful information about ophiolatry, as practised not only by the Indians but also among other nations of antiquity.

The distinguished German indologist, the late Professor Hermann Oldenberg, reckons the Nāgas to belong to that class of demoniacal beings which is best represented by the were-wolves. They appear, indeed, often in human shape, as is also the case with were-wolves, tiger-men, and swan-maidens. "We cannot conclude our account of the mythic animal world," Oldenberg says,[1] "without considering the relations which are believed to exist between animal and human existence. The conception of a substantial unity

[1] H. Oldenberg, *Die Religion des Veda*, 2nd ed. (1917), p. 81. The passage alluded to by Oldenberg occurs in the Pali canon of the Buddhist scriptures; it is the story of the snake that wished to become a monk. It will be found in our Chapter II; below, pp. 110 f.

between animal and man, which during the Vedic period is met with only in certain survivals, finds an expression in the belief in beings like were-wolves. Presumably, the "tiger-men" belong to this class, and certainly do the Nāgas, which seem to be men, but in reality are snakes. According to an ancient Buddhist text their serpent nature manifests itself on two occasions, namely, during sexual intercourse and in sleep."

The belief in lycanthropic beings existed no doubt in ancient India, as is evident from various passages in the *Ṛig-veda*, where they are designated by the general name of *Yātudhāna* and are often associated with Rākshasas. "Warding off the Rakshas and Yātudhānas, the god [Savitar] stood, praised night after night" (*R.V.*, i, 35, 10). Elsewhere Agni, the Fire-god, is invoked to destroy the Yātudhānas with his flames and with his arrows. From another interesting hymn (*R.V.*, vii, 104), addressed to the gods Indra and Soma, it appears that the Yātudhānas are sorcerers and witches, who during the night assume the shape of various animals, such as owls, dogs, wolves, eagles, and vultures. Snakes are not mentioned in this connexion. There seems, however, to exist a fundamental difference between beings of the were-wolf type and Nāgas. The former are conceived as human beings, possessed of uncanny powers, but leading their existence in the society of men. The Nāgas may occasionally assume human form, but they do not belong to the human world. Theirs is the Nāgaloka, wherever that mysterious realm of snakes may be located. They are decidedly unhuman (*a-mānusha*), and in Buddhist writings they are frankly classed among animals. In the legends they usually exhibit a bewildering blending of human and serpentine properties, they may even act entirely as human creatures, yet there can be no doubt that their real nature and form are those of the serpent. In the Nāga the animal element preponderates, at least, according to the earlier conceptions, whereas the were-wolves appear to be primarily conceived as human beings. Another point of difference is that the were-wolves are invariably dangerous and malignant; the Nāgas on the contrary, though easily moved to anger, are worthy of being propitiated, as their activity is, on the whole, beneficial to the welfare of man, especially in connexion with their power over the element of water.

It is this association with the water, so conspicuous a feature in Indian serpent-lore, which induced another distinguished scholar, Hendrik Kern, to propound that the Nāgas are essentially water-spirits.[1] According to Kern, they are to be regarded as personified forces of nature; in the first instance the snake-like coiling rain-clouds emitting flashes of lightning—the serpents of the sky—which are transported to the lakes and pools on earth

[1] Kern, *Over den vermoedelijken oorsprong der Nāga-vereering, Bijdr. tot de taal-, land- en volkenkunde van Ned. Indië*, vol. lxxii (1916), pp. 395 ff. Kern admits the possibility of real ophiolatry among the aboriginal population of Southern India.

and finally are "confounded" with real poisonous snakes. Kern's view, thus briefly formulated, is no doubt somewhat one-sided. It emphasizes at any rate a very important aspect of Nāga worship, viz. the close relationship between the Nāgas and the element which in a hot country like India is of such vital significance for human and animal existence. In many a legend the Nāgas are said to haunt lakes and ponds and the sources of rivers. They are beneficial givers of rain, but, if roused to anger, they send down destructive hail-storms, and ravage the produce of the fields.

Dr. C. F. Oldham, Brigade-Surgeon of the Indian Army, has offered a totally different explanation of Nāga-worship.[1] In his opinion the Nāgas were originally not demons, but people who claimed descent from the Sun and had the hooded serpent for a totem. Takshaśilā, the Taxila of the Greeks, he says, was the chief city of the Nāga people in the north of India. Takshaka was one of their chiefs. "It was on his return from a raid into the country of Takshaśilā that Janamejaya, the Bhārata rāja of Indraprastha, at the instigation of the Brāhman Uttaṅka, held his serpent sacrifice. The victims on this occasion were the Nāga prisoners taken in the raid, who were burned alive, with Brahmanical rites, as recorded in the Mahābhārata."

Mr. Oldham's interpretation of Nāga-worship has met with very little support.[2] In the absence of historical data, such an explanation is bound to bear a strongly subjective stamp. For our knowledge of the history of King Parikshit and King Janamejaya no sources are available, but the highly fantastic sagas preserved in the *Mahābhārata*. It is possible, even probable, that those sagas are ultimately based on historical fact, but an attempt to make out what that historical basis has been is likely to produce results as fantastic as these sagas themselves.

It is certainly worthy of note that some Nāga-kings (for the serpent demons, too, are monarchical, like most other classes of beings) bear names which are identical with those of certain royal personages in the Epic. Both in Brahmanical and Buddhist literature frequent mention is made of a Nāgarāja named Dhṛitarāshṭra. It will be hardly necessary to point out that the same name is borne by the father of the hundred Kaurava princes who are the opponents of the five Pāṇḍavas.[3] Another Nāga-king who figures in the Great Epic is

[1] C. F. Oldham, *The Sun and the Serpent* (London, 1905), pp. 30 f. and 57 f. Previously the same author had published a paper in the *Journal of the Royal Asiatic Society* for the year 1901, pp. 461 ff.

[2] Professor E. W. Hopkins, *Epic Mythology*, p. 23, appears also to be inclined to explain the Nāgas on a euhemeristic basis. "Garuḍas and Tārkshyas," he says, "may conceivably have been human chieftains of the Western coast, though they scarcely present as strong a claim to euhemeristic interpretation as do their natural foes the Nāgas." Cf. also p. 46, footnote.

[3] It must, however, be observed that the patronymic or metronymic of the serpent-demon Dhṛitarāshṭra, is Airāvata, a name by which he is frequently designated, whereas Dhṛitarāshṭra, the blind king of the Kuru race, is the son of Vyāsa by Ambikā, the widow of Vichitravīrya,

called Kauravya, which means " the scion of the Kuru race ". Other royal names applied to Nāgas are Dhanañjaya and Ambarīsha ; the former is a regular epithet of the Pāṇḍava hero Arjuna, and the latter name is borne by a king of the race of Ikshvāku, who figures in the legend of Śunaḥśepa according to the version found in the *Rāmāyaṇa*. In the *Tāṇḍya-mahābrāhmaṇa* (xxv, 15) there is a passage in which a Nāga Janamejaya together with other Nāgas is said to have performed a sacrifice. The name " Janamejaya " occurs also at the end of a list of Nāgas in the *Mahābhārata* (*Sabhā-p.*, ix, 10). We may add the instance of Nala, well-known as the hero of a famous episode in the Great Epic, but also mentioned in the Ceylonese chronicle *Mahāvaṁsa* as a Nāgarāja residing in Mañjerika.

It we might assume that in ancient India deceased rulers were sometimes worshipped in the form of snakes (a supposition which in itself seems quite plausible), this would present again a new aspect of serpent-worship. We possess, however, no proof either archæological or literary of such a custom. There certainly are legends about kings who were changed into snakes in consequence of a curse and as a punishment of their evil deeds. A well-known example is the story of Nahusha, an ancient king, who, after having been raised to the throne of Indra, in his presumption insulted the seven Sages, and, being cursed by Agastya, was doomed to live as a snake for ten thousand years.[1] 'The *Rājataraṅgiṇī* (i, 153–67) relates of a mighty monarch of Kashmir, Dāmodara by name, who wished to bring water to the plateau which still is known as Damdar Uḍar. Once hungry Brahmins came to him and begged for food, but the king said : " I do not give food until I have bathed. Take yourselves off (*sarpata*)." Then they cursed him : " Be thou a snake (*sarpa*)." And the chronicler adds : " Even to this day people recognize him by the steam of his breath, which the curse has made hot, as he rushes about in search of water far and wide on the Damdar Uḍar." [2] '

From the above it is evident that there exists a great divergence of opinion amongst scholars with regard to the character of the Indian serpent-demons. Yet it might be said that each of the authorities quoted is right in a certain sense. The mistake common to them all is that of taking one special feature of serpent-worship and making it the basis of interpretation. Now it is impossible to solve the problem in such a one-sided manner. The French scholar, Auguste Barth, has rightly laid stress on the complicated character

[1] Although the name of Nahusha occurs in lists of Nāgas, he is usually represented as a large serpent of the boa type (*ajagara*). His story is told at great length in the *Mahābhārata* (*Udyoga-p.*, x–xviii ; cf. also *Vana-p.*, clxxviii–clxxxi). The legend has been explained as a solar myth by J. S. Speyer, *Le Mythe de Nahusha*. *Actes du sixième congrès international des Orientalistes, tenu en* 1883 *à Leide*. Partie iii, section 2, pp. 81 ff.

[2] *Rājat.*, transl. Stein, vol. i, pp. 29 f. The popular legend of King Dāmodara, as Sir Aurel Stein observes, is still current in Kashmīr.

of Indian snake-worship. After a general survey of the Nāgas, he says [1]: "These brief indications are enough to show that the serpent religions of India form a complex whole, and such as is not accounted for by viewing it as a simple worship of deprecation. We can distinguish in it: (1) the direct adoration of the animal, the most formidable and mysterious of all the enemies of men; (2) a worship of the deities of the waters, springs, and rivers, symbolized by the waving form of the serpent; (3) conceptions of the same kind as that of the Vedic Ahi, and connected closely with the great myth of the storm and the struggle of light with darkness."

Professor Moritz Winternitz,[2] of Prague, likewise emphasizes the many-sided character of Indian snake-worship in the course of a very able and extensive article which certainly may be regarded as the most important contribution to our knowledge of the subject.

Before commencing our account of the historical development and various aspects of Indian snake-worship, there is one point more to be considered. Several writers, like Fergusson,[3] have put forward the opinion that Indian snake-worship was un-Aryan in its origin. According to them the Aryans adopted it from the Dasyus, the dark-skinned aborigines of the Peninsula. One of the chief arguments adduced in support of this view is the fact that in the *Ṛig-veda*, the earliest of the four Vedas, no reference to snake-worship is made. It should, however, be remembered that the *Ṛig-veda-saṃhitā* is a collection of some thousand hymns from which it is impossible to derive a complete idea of the civilization of those days.[4]

In the *Yajur-veda* and especially in the *Atharva-veda* serpent-worship is referred to unambiguously. The same is true of later Vedic literature.

In this connexion it should also be noted that the mythic snake-kings bear personal names which almost invariably are not Dravidian, but purely Aryan.[5] The very word *nāga*, by which the serpent demons are generally designated, is supposed to be related with the English word "snake", and consequently is Indo-Germanic in its origin.

If we wish to explain serpent worship, we must start from the animal itself,[6] which

[1] Auguste Barth, *The Religions of India* (1882), pp. 266 f.; *Oeuvres*, vol. i (1914), p. 230.

[2] Moritz Winternitz, *Der Sarpabali, ein altindischer Schlangencult, Mitteil. der anthropol. Gesellschaft in Wien*, vol. xviii (1888), pp. 25 ff. and 250 ff.

[3] *Vide* also L. von Schröder, *Indiens Literatur und Kultur in historischer Entwicklung* (1887), p. 377. But cf. M. Winternitz, op. cit., pp. 262 ff.

[4] H. Oldenberg, *Die Literatur des alten Indien* (1903), p. 23: "Leben und Denken der alten Inder spiegelte sich in dieser Liedermasse nur unvollständig wider."

[5] M. J. Przyluski informs me that in his opinion the prefix *ku-* found in the Nāga names *Kuṭhara, Kuhara,* etc., seems to point to a possible connexion with non-Aryan languages. The same scholar is inclined to assign an Austro-Asiatic origin to the name *Karkoṭa*, apparently meaning "the Crested One".

[6] Monier Williams, *Religious Thought and Life in India* (1883), p. 319.

among a primitive population is so apt to be regarded as a demonic being endowed with magical power. The snake is unlike other animals, owing to its peculiar shape and its swift and mysterious gliding motion without the aid of either feet or wings. In addition to these most conspicuous properties the snake possesses other strange features such as the power of fascination of its eye, its forked tongue (of which the *Mahābhārata* offers a mythic explanation), and the periodical casting of its skin which is referred to in Vedic literature. The serpent is, indeed, the uncanniest of all animals. Above all things it is the deadly poison of certain snakes that causes the whole species to be looked upon as demoniacal beings which are to be dreaded and to be propitiated. There is an Indian proverb which says : " Even a great man is not worshipped, as long as he has not caused some calamity : men worship the Nāgas, but not Garuḍa, the slayer of Nāgas." [1]

From modern statistics it is evident how great a mortality is caused by snakes among the native population of India. In the year 1919 more than 20,000 persons fell victims to snakes, whereas only 2,637 were killed by other animals. We may safely assume that at a time when a large part of the country was still covered with jungle the snake danger was even much greater than it is now. It will, therefore, cause no surprise that among " The Eight Dangers " enumerated in Buddhist writings we find " the danger from the disturbance of Nāgas " (*Nāga-saṃkshobha-bhaya*).[2]

Although we may safely assume that Indian ophiolatry had its first cause in the dread inspired by the poisonous reptiles, we find in the earliest sources the real serpents mentioned side by side with mythic snakes which haunt not only the earth, but also the sky and the upper region. To the native mind these imaginary monsters possessed no doubt as much reality, as the creeping things of the earth which constantly endangered their lives.

In this connexion let me quote the following passage from the *Yajurveda*.[3]

" Homage be to the snakes whichsoever move along the earth. Which are in the sky and in heaven, homage be to those snakes. Which are the arrows of sorcerers and of tree-spirits, and which lie in holes, homage be to those snakes. Which are in the brightness of heaven, which are in the rays of the sun, which have made their abodes in the waters, homage be to those snakes."

It is especially the *Atharva-veda* in which numerous interesting references to the snakes occur. It is well known that this Veda consists largely of magical spells. Several of them

[1] Otto v. Böhtlingk, *Indische Sprüche* [2] (1870), vol. i, p. 7, No. 39.

[2] *Lalitavistara* (ed. Lefmann), p. 442. The term Nāga may also be taken in the sense of " an elephant " In plastic representations of " the Eight Dangers " both the snake and the elephant are shown. Cf. Burg. *Buddhist Cave Temples* (1883), p. 51, pl. xxiii, fig. 3. It deserves notice that in the list of the *Lalitavistara* the Nāgas are mentioned between Devas and Yakshas, so that evidently snake-demons are meant.

[3] *Maitrāyaṇī-saṃhitā*, ii, 7, 15, ed. L. von Schröder, vol. i, p. 97.

are charms resorted to in order to avert the danger of snakes. The method followed is twofold. On the one hand, the object is to propitiate the snake-demons and to solicit their protection against their own tribe. On the other hand, charms are wielded against the snakes in order to counteract their magical power and, if possible, to destroy them. Very expressive is *A.V.*, vi, 56 [1]:—

"Let not the snake, O gods, slay us with our offspring, with our men ; what is shut together may it not unclose [2]; what is open may it not shut together ; homage to the god-people.

Homage be to Asita, homage to Tiraśchirāji, homage to Svaja [and] Babhru, homage to the god-people.

I smite thy teeth together with tooth, thy [two] jaws together with jaw, thy tongue together with tongue, thy mouth, O snake, with mouth."

The four terms *asita* ("black"), *tiraśchirāji* ("cross-lined"), *svaja* ("adder" ?), and *babhru* ("brown"), which occur in verse 2, are commonly explained as denoting certain extant species of snakes.[3] I feel inclined, however, to take them in the sense of personal names of snake-demons which apparently are associated with the four quarters of the sky. In the *Atharva-veda* such a group of four is often invoked, although under different names.

In *A.V.*, vii, 56, 1, we read of four serpents called Tiraśchirāji, Asita, Pṛidāku, and Kaṅkaparvan. In *A.V.*, v, 13, 5–6, we have first the names Kairāta, Pṛishṇa, Upatṛiṇya, and Babhru, and subsequently Asita, Taimāta, Babhru, and Apodaka. *A.V.*, x, 4, 13, gives four similar names, Tiraśchirāji, Pṛidāku, Śvitra, and Asita, but here they are used in the plural.

That the four serpents mentioned under somewhat varying names in the verses quoted were connected with the four quarters we conclude from the two hymns, *A.V.*, iii, 26 and 27. Both these hymns contain a homage to the gods of the quarters, but it is significant that the first of the two is also used as a serpent-incantation. In this hymn each quarter is represented by a group of gods—perhaps it would be better to speak of spirits—which are indicated as "missiles" (*heti*), "impetuous, eager ones" (*aviśyu*), "radiant ones" (*vairāja*), "piercers" (*pravidhyant*), "smearers" or "lickers" (*nilimpa*), and "helpers" (*avasvant*). Ralph Griffith was undoubtedly right in explaining this hymn as a charm to win the favour of the Serpents of all the regions under heaven. This becomes perfectly clear when we compare hymn 27, which we quote in full :—

[1] Cf. Whitney's translation, Harvard Oriental Series, vol. vii, first half, p. 323, and Ralph Griffith's transl., vol. i, p. 276.

[2] According to the commentator, the expressions "open" and "shut" refer to the snake's jaws.

[3] Heinrich Zimmer, *Altindisches Leben*, pp. 94 f.

1. Eastern quarter ; Agni the regent (*adhipati*) ; Asita the warden (*rakshitar*) ; the Ādityas the arrows : homage to these regents, homage to the wardens, homage to the arrows, etc.

2. Southern quarter : Indra the regent ; Tiraśchirāji the warden, the Pitaras the arrows : homage, etc.

3. Western quarter : Varuṇa the regent, Pṛidāku the warden, nourishment the arrows : homage, etc.

4. Northern quarter : Soma the regent, Svaja the warden, the thunderbolt the arrows : homage, etc.

5. Fixed quarter : Vishṇu the regent, Kalmāshagrīva the warden, the herbs the arrows : homage, etc.

6. Upward quarter : Bṛihaspati the regent, Śvitra the warden ; rain the arrows : homage, etc.

In this hymn we find the well-known conception of a group of divinities, here six in number, which are regarded as *dikpālas* or guardians of the several quarters of the Universe. But it will be noticed that these *dikpālas* have not yet been stereotyped into the fixed group of four or eight *lokapālas* of later Hindu mythology.[1] Now, side by side with each of the divine regents another supernatural being is invoked as the warden or protector of the region in question. That these secondary guardians are divine serpents is evident from their names, which to some extent agree with that group of four serpents met with in various passages of the *Atharva-veda*. We may surmise that the idea of four or six dragons guarding the corners of the world is more primitive than that of the anthropomorphic *lokapālas*. Quite possibly both the system of the guardian-gods and that of the elephants of the quarters (*diṅ-nāga*) are ultimately derived from the notion of the dragons of the sky which must have been still alive in the early period when the hymns of the *Atharva-veda* were composed.

In this connexion we may also quote a hymn of the *Black Yajurveda*,[2] in which likewise the six regions are associated with six divine regents and with an equal number of dragons, the names of which are identical with those of *A.V.*, iii, 27. The order in which they are given slightly differs, and Vishṇu as regent of the "fixed" quarter has been substituted by Yama, the King of the Dead. The second half of the Yajurvedic hymn agrees in substance with *A.V.*, iii, 26 ; here, too, the various quarters of the sky are denoted as the abodes of certain classes of spirits which bear obscure names similar to those used in

[1] E. W. Hopkins, *Epic Mythology*, pp. 149 ff.

[2] *Taittirīya-saṃhitā* (ed. A. Weber, *Indische Studien*, vols. xi–xii), v, 5, 10 ; transl. by Winternitz, op. cit., p. 48.

the *Atharva*. In connexion with the first half of the hymn in question there can be little doubt that these mysterious terms are used to indicate the tribes of serpents, of which the dragons of the sky are the overlords.

In Buddhist literature, too, we meet with a snake-charm or *paritta* of a very early date, in which four tribes of serpent-kings (*ahirāja-kulāni*) are mentioned.[1] It runs as follows :—

Virūpakkhehi me mettaṃ, mettaṃ Erāpathehi me, Chhabyāputtehi me mettaṃ, mettaṃ Kaṇhāgotamakehi cha, " I love Virūpakkhas, the Erāpathas I love, I love Chhabyāputtas, the Kaṇhāgotamakas I love."

Now it is noteworthy that Virūpakkha and Erāpatha are not only the names of two Nāgarājas, but in Buddhist mythology they figure also as the *lokapālas* of the Western and Eastern region respectively.

Another interesting parallel is afforded by two later Buddhist texts, the *Lalitavistara* and the *Mahāvastu*,[2] both composed in Sanskrit. The twenty-fourth chapter of the former work is devoted to the meeting of the Buddha with the two merchants, Trapusha and Bhallika, who offer him his first meal after the Bodhi. The chapter concludes with a benedictory hymn, in which the protection of the four quarters is invoked upon travelling traders. Now here each quarter is represented by a group of seven *nakshatras*, by one of the Buddhist *lokapālas* side by side with one of the following four Brahmanical *lokapālas* : Sūrya, Yama, Varuṇa, and Maṇibhadra. The Buddhist *lokapālas* are the well-known four 'Great Kings' or Mahārājas of Buddhist mythology: Dhṛitarāshṭra, Virūḍhaka, Virūpāksha, and Kuvera. The resemblance between this benedictory hymn and the ancient hymn of the *Atharva-veda* (iii, 27), quoted above, is very striking. The most remarkable point certainly is that here the ancient dragons of the quarters have been replaced by the four Mahārājas. Two of the latter, moreover, are designated by names which were originally borne by serpent-kings, as appears from the ancient *paritta* preserved in the Pali Canon.

In the charm from the *Atharva-veda* (vi, 56), quoted above, the snakes are twice invoked under the name of *devajana*, lit. 'god-people'. Elsewhere (*A.V.*, viii, 8, 15) they are named together with Gandharvas and Apsarases, Devas, Yakshas, or gnomes (*puṇyajana*), and Manes (*pitaras*). In another hymn (*A.V.*, xi, 9, 24) we meet with a similar enumeration of supernatural beings, comprising also tree-spirits (*vanaspati* and *vānaspatya*) and herbs (*oshadhi* and *vīrudh*).

[1] *Chullavagga*, v, 6 ; Oldenberg, *Vinaya Piṭakam*, vol. ii, p. 110 ; *S.B.E.*, vol. xx, p. 76 ; *Jātaka* (ed. Fausböll), vol. ii, p. 145, vs. 101 ; *The Jātaka*, vol. ii (transl. by Rouse), p. 101. The English translator, too, takes the words *Virūpakkha*, etc., as indicating kinds of snakes. Cf. also *The Bower Manuscript*, ed. R. Hoernle (Calcutta, 1897), part vi.

[2] *Lalit.* (ed. Lefmann), pp. 387–91 ; transl. Foucaux, pp. 322–5 ; *Mahāvastu*, vol. iii, pp. 305–10.

The *Gṛihyasūtras* contain an account of the 'Sarpabali', the annual rite which has the twofold purpose of honouring and warding-off the snakes. As the subject has been dealt with at great length by Professor Winternitz, we may refer the reader to his able article.[1]

Here it will suffice to state that the whole observance takes no less than four months. It is initiated on the full-moon of Śrāvaṇa, the first month of the rainy season, and concluded on the full-moon of Mārgaśīrsha, the first month of winter. During this period people sleep on bedsteads raised from the ground in order to protect themselves against their dangerous visitors. This custom, as we have seen above, was duly noted by Nearchos. The concluding ceremony is, therefore, designated by the Sanskrit word *pratyavarohaṇa*, meaning 'the descending or moving downwards'.

In the course of the observance a certain number of verses are to be recited, including the *yajus* from the *Maitrāyaṇī-saṃhitā*, which we have quoted above, verses addressed to the serpent-kings, and also a verse in which 'the White One' is invoked. This term denotes the mythical white horse which is frequently mentioned in the Ṛigveda: it was presented by the Aśvins to Pedu and, therefore, bears the name of Paidva: it is supposed to trample the serpents under its feet. According to Winternitz,[2] it is the Solar Horse.

In the *Gṛihyasūtras* the divine snakes are, on the one hand, divided into three groups pertaining to earth, sky, and heaven, to which sometimes those of the quarters are added as a fourth group. But, on the other hand, we find also the division according to the four quarters discussed above. In both cases the object evidently is to include all the serpents of the whole Universe.

The point I wish to note here is the time for which the serpent rite is prescribed: it is the rainy season. This circumstance is not very difficult to explain. It is during the rains that the snakes, driven out of their holes by the water, seek a refuge in the dwellings of men. At that time of the year the danger of snakes is greatest.

Does not this observation also help us to understand the close relationship which popular belief has established between the snake and the water? As we have seen above, Barth and Kern assume that it is the capricious shape of the clouds and the winding course of rivers and rivulets which would have led the popular imagination to identify them with serpents. I do not wish to deny the possibility of such a poetical vision, which can be exemplified by means of passages from Sanskrit literature. But the popular belief in question is perhaps to be accounted for not so much from such poetical conceptions as

[1] *Der Sarpabali, ein indischer Schlangencult. Mitteil. der Anthropologischen Gesellschaft in Wien*, vol. xviii (1888), pp. 25–52 and 250–64.

[2] Op cit., pp. 50 f.

from a quasi-rational relation which the primitive mind is wont to establish between two phenomena simultaneously observed. From the fact that the snakes regularly make their appearance at the commencement of the rainy season it may have been concluded that the advent of the rains was due to the magical power of those reptiles.

The great variety of words by which the snake is indicated in Indian literature bears also witness to the dread inspired by the silent creeping creature, the very mentioning of whose name was supposed to bring about its dangerous presence. We may note in the first place the curious expressions, 'the toothed rope' (*datvatī rajjuḥ*) and 'the putrid rope' (*pūtirajju*), which occur in the *Atharva-veda* and for which it would not be difficult to find parallels in various languages.[1] It is curious that similar terms have remained in vogue in India up to the present day. "Snakes," Mr. Crooke observes,[2] "should, of course, be addressed euphemistically as 'maternal uncle' or 'rope', and if a snake bites you, you should never mention its name, but say 'A rope has touched me'." There can be little doubt that the use of these expressions is due to taboo notions. In Pali we find the snake denoted by the words *dīgha*, 'long,' and *dīghajātika* ('of the long sort'), which must have a similar origin.[3] As regards the numerous synonyms found in epical and classical literature, it is not possible to decide in each case whether the word is due to taboo or may be regarded as a poetical conception. But we may safely assume that very often taboo notions underlie the poetical usage.

Several of those synonyms have reference to peculiar qualities either observed in the snake or merely ascribed to it by popular belief. For, apart from those strange properties actually observed in the animal, it will be seen that it has become the object of quite a cycle of still stranger superstitions not only in India but all over the world. In Europe this serpent lore is very prominent in mediaeval literature, especially in books dealing with natural history like the *Liber de Proprietate Rerum* by Bartholomæus Anglicus. In the works of poets of the Renaissance like Shakespeare those ancient popular beliefs still survive in many a poetical conceit or simile.

The way of a serpent upon a rock was one of the four things which were too wonderful for King Solomon (Prov. xxx, 19). "The serpent alone of all animals," Eusebius wrote, "without legs or arms or any of the usual appliances for locomotion, still moves with

[1] *A.V.*, iv, 3, 2; Bloomfield, *S.B.E.*, vol. xlii, p. 147, "the biting rope"; cf. p. 366, and *A.V.*, viii, 8, 2; Bloomfield, op. cit., pp. 117 and 582, "the rotten rope." Cf. *Jāt.*, vol. ii, p. 144, i, 22, *pūtirukkhantarā nikkhamitvā eko sappo.* Cf. *The Bower Manuscript*, p. 226, footnote 1.

[2] *Folk-lore of Northern India*, vol. ii, pp. 142 f.

[3] Skt. *dīrghajātya* occurs *Suparṇādhy.*, iii, 4. Cf. Charpentier, *Die Suparṇasaga*, pp. 216 f. The word *dīrghaprishṭha*, 'long-backed,' is found in some *kośas*, but not in literature.

singular celerity." In ancient India this peculiarity found expression in a number of synonyms by which the snake is designated in Sanskrit literature.[1]

The popular belief, however, that this most obvious observation is merely the result of delusion, and that, in other words, the snake is in possession of legs which are only visible to those of his own kind, is certainly typically Indian. It is not only implied by the term *gūḍhapād(a)* found in indigenous lexicons, but also by the proverb which says: "Only a snake can see a snake's legs." [2]

In the same manner the absence of external organs of hearing led to the strange conception that the snake could hear by means of his eyes; hence the term *chakshuḥ-śravas* ('hearing-by-sight', 'using its eyes for ears') applied to the snake.

The curious way in which the snake protrudes his tongue as if licking up the air may have led to the belief that the creature was content to feed on the wind. Hence the snake is not only called 'licker' (*leliha, lelihāna*) and 'double-tongue' (*dvijihva, dvirasana*), but also 'wind-eater' (*vāyubhaksha, vātāśin, pavanāśin, pavanabhuj, anilāśana, śvasanāśana, mārutāśana*). The poet Bhartṛihari [3] says that the Creator has ordained the wind as food for the snakes: like frugality, therefore, is recommended to the wise. The snake thus comes to be regarded as the paragon of asceticism, as is exemplified in the story of the virtuous Nāga Padmanābha which is told in the *Mahābhārata*.[4]

In mediaeval Europe the curious habit in question was associated in particular with the chameleon, which animal the naturalists of the Middle Ages regularly class among the 'serpents'. It was supposed that the mole lived on earth, the salamander on fire, the herring on water, and the chameleon on air.[5]

When Hamlet is asked by the king: "How fares our cousin Hamlet?" he answers: "Excellent, i' faith, of the cameleon's dish: I eat the air, promise-crammed: You cannot feed capons so."

The casting of the skin is another peculiarity of the snake which in India, like other

[1] The *Amarakośa* (i, 8, 6–8) contains no less than twenty-five synonyms for a snake, including the words *bhujaga, bhujaṃga, bhujaṃgama, bhogin, pannaga, uraga,* and *jihmaga,* which all have reference to the animal's peculiar way of moving. Most of these words are frequently met with in literature. Besides we have *urogama* (*Suparṇ.*, xv, 3) and *uraṅga* (*Bhāg. P.*, x, 16, 23), also *chakrin* and *kuṇḍalin.*

[2] *M.Bh.*, *Śānti-p.*, cciii, 13, and *Rām.*, *Sundara-k.*, xlii, 9. The word *gūḍhapāda* occurs *Hitop.*, i, verse 135.

[3] *Vairāgya-śat.*, 98 (ed. P. v. Bohlen, p. 70). Cf. *Pañchat* (ed. Kosegarten), p. 139, vs. 161. *Sūtrālaṅkāra* (ed. Huber), p. 254.

[4] Cf. below, pp. 84 f.

[5] Bartholomæus Anglicus says: Dicitur autem cameleon vivere solo aere sicut talpa ex terra et allec ex aqua et salamandra ex igne.

countries of the world, has drawn attention and is reflected in folk-lore. In a verse of the *Ṛigveda* (ix, 86, 44) the gushing stream of strained Soma is compared to a serpent creeping out of his slough. From a hymn of the *Atharva-veda* it is evident that the sloughs are carefully collected on account of the magical powers ascribed to them. The opening verse is rendered by Ralph Griffith as follows :—

"There on the bank those Vipers lie, thrice-seven, having cast their skins ;
Now we with their discarded sloughs bind close and cover up the eyes of the malicious highway thief."

Apparently the snake's skin is supposed to procure invisibility. According to Kauṭilya's *Arthaśāstra* (xiv, ch. iii), the skin of a snake filled with the ashes of a man bitten by a snake will cause beasts to be invisible.

The practice of casting its skin suggested longevity or even immortality in the snake, an idea which can also be traced in ancient India. The *Tāṇḍya-mahābrāhmaṇa* (xxv, 15) refers to a serpent sacrifice, celebrated by the snakes who thereby have gained a footing in the world. The officiating priests who are enumerated include some prominent Nāgarājas, namely Dhṛitarāshṭra-Airāvata and Takshaka, but also, as we have noticed above, Janamejaya. The text then says : "By this sacrifice, verily, the snakes have conquered death ; death is conquered by those who will perform this sacrifice. Therefore they cast off their old skin, and, having cast the same, they creep out of it. The snakes are Ādityas ; like unto the splendour of the Ādityas is the splendour of those who perform this sacrifice."

The casting of a snake's skin is a favourite simile found in Vedic and epic literature. It is especially applied to the freeing one's self from evil and to the liberation from mundane existence.

We read in a *Brāhmaṇa* text [1] : "They [the gods] smote away evil ; in accordance with their smiting away the serpents smote away evil ; having smitten away evil, they lay aside their old worn-out skin and continue with a new one. He smiteth away evil who knoweth this." An *Upanishad* [2] says : "Like a snake's skin, dead and cast off, lieth upon an ant-hill, likewise lieth this body ; but that which is bodyless, immortal, and life, is pure Brahman, is pure light." In the Great Epic [3] it is said : "Like a *ruru* deer droppeth its old horn and like a serpent leaveth its skin and regardless goeth its way, in like manner he that is liberated relinquisheth evil."

Medical properties are ascribed to the skins of black snakes,[4] but also to other parts

[1] *Aitareya-br.*, vi, 1 ; Keith's transl., p. 259.
[2] *Brihadaranyaka-up.*, iv, 4, 7. Cf. also *Praśnop*, v, 5, and *Kaush. Br.*, xviii, 7 ; Keith's transl., p. 448.
[3] *M.Bh.*, *Śānti-p.*, ccxix, 48.
[4] Julius Jolly, *Medicin* (*Grundriss der indo-arischen Philologie und Altertumskunde*), p. 57.

of the serpent. "Eating a serpent's flesh, or anointing with its fat, or applying part of its body to the wound, was a remedy against snake-bite among Greeks, Romans, Arabs, Jews, American Indians, Abipones, Thonga, and other races, and is also found in folk-medicine in many lands still—an example of the principle that like cures like." [1]

Whereas, on the one hand, the mere exhalation of the venomous serpent is supposed to cause blindness, we have, on the other hand, a fable of the *Pañchatantra* to exemplify how a blind man recovers his sight by the vapour issuing from pieces of a poisonous snake cooked in milk.[2]

The most dreadful and mysterious property possessed by certain species of snakes—the power of inflicting a sudden and almost instantaneous death—has also given rise to many superstitions. The destructive action of the poison resembles that of the all-devouring fire. Hence the snake belongs to those beings which are believed to possess in a high degree that magical energy which is indicated by the Sanskrit word *tejas* (= 'heat, fire').[3] The fire-like action ascribed to the Nāga's poison is exemplified by many a story included in the present volume. The Nāga Takshaka by his fiery bite reduces a banyan-tree to ashes and sets King Parikshit's one-pillared hall on fire.[4] According to an ancient legend preserved in the Pali Canon, the Buddha and the Nāga of Uruvilvā combat each other by means of their 'fire', until in the end the *tejas* of the former proves to be the more powerful.[5] The pool of the Yamunā infested by the Nāga Kāliya is described as overcast with a dense smoke caused by the poison-born fire, the surface of the water being hot with venomous flames. Even the birds of the sky did not approach it, and when grass fell in its water it was burnt by its heat.[6]

The fatal action of the snake's poison was exaggerated into the belief that the Nāga could cause harm by its mere breath or by its sight alone. It is often mentioned in the *Jātakas* that the Nāga can carry destruction by the fiery blast of his nostrils (*nāsavāta*, *nāsikāvāta*).[7] In the *Kharaputta-jātaka* the angry Nāga king sends four Nāga youths and orders them to enter King Senaka's bedchamber and destroy him like chaff by the breath of their nostrils. In the *Champeyya-jātaka* it is said that a Nāga could reduce a town to

[1] James Hastings, *Encycl. of Religion and Ethics*, vol. xi, p. 406.

[2] *Pañch.*, v, story 13 (Bombay ed., 1885, B.S.S., No. 1, p. 67).

[3] Snakes are said to be *atitejas*. Böhtlingk, *Ind. Spr.*, 3778 (1618) and 6902 (5192). Cf. *Jāt.*, vol. ii, p. 296, l. 14.

[4] See below, pp. 67 f.

[5] See below, pp. 107 f.

[6] Below, pp. 87 f.

[7] *Jāt.*, vol. ii, p. 295, 1, 24 (transl. p. 206); vol. iii, p. 16, i, 22 (transl. p. 11), p. 276, xi, 6–7 (transl. p. 175), and p. 418, i, 6 (transl. p. 251); vol. iv, p. 457, i, 9 (transl. p. 283), and vol. vi, p. 74, xi, 15–18 (transl. p. 42), p. 164, i, 25 (transl. p. 85), p. 171, xi, 18–19 (transl. p. 89).

ashes, whilst the hero of the *Bhūridatta-jātaka* asserts of himself : " I am a Nāga possessed of supernatural power and magical fire and difficult to overcome : in my wrath I could bite a prosperous country with my fire." [1]

The term *ahivātakaroga* (lit. 'snake-wind-disease') occurs in Buddhist literature to designate some disease, perhaps malarial fever, which in the Terai is believed to be due to snake's breath.[2]

In the *Sāma-jātaka* [3] it is related that the aged parents of Sāma, the hero of the story, once returning to the hermitage late in the evening, were surprised by a shower of rain, and sought shelter under a tree. Here they stood on an ant-hill which was inhabited by a poisonous snake. The snake, becoming aware of their presence, grew angry, and " smote them with the blast of his nostrils ", so that they both were struck blind and neither could see the other. In the *Parantapa-jātaka* [4] the Brahmin who has witnessed the king's murder pretends to have lost his sight by a similar cause. " O king," he says, " I am come back with my eyes lost ; I was standing by an ant-hill in a wood full of serpents, and the breath of some venomous serpent must have fallen on me."

In the Middle Ages the same belief was associated with the basilisk, who with his fiery breath was supposed to pollute the air so that no beast or plant could live in it. The basilisk or cockatrice, believed to be the hybrid of a cock and a snake, was moreover credited with the power of killing by its mere look. " Among all living creatures, there is none that perishes sooner than doth a man by the poyson of a Cockatrice, for with his sight he killeth him, because the beams of the Cockatrice's eyes do corrupt the visible spirit of a man, which visible spirit corrupted, all the other spirits coming from the brain and life of the heart are thereby corrupted, and so the man dyeth." [5] Shakespeare, in 'Romeo and Juliet', speaks of the " death-darting eye of cockatrice ", and in his 'Henry VI' (3rd pt., act ii, scene 2), Gloster, the later Richard III, exclaims : " I'll slay more gazers than the basilisk."

The belief that the snake can kill by means of its sight is likewise widespread. The Indian epics speak of serpents that are " poison-eyed ". In the Jātaka-Book the Nāga wife of King Brahmadatta says to her husband, when he invites her to follow him to his

[1] *Jāt.*, vol. iv, p. 460, i, 1 (transl. p. 285), and vol. vi, p. 171, i, 19 (transl. p. 89). In the original : *Nāgo ham asmi iddhimā tejasī duratikkamo ḍasseyaṃ tejasā kuddho phītam janapadam api.* Cf. *Mahāvastu*, vol. ii, p. 178, i, 4, and p. 182, l. 1.

[2] *Jāt.*, vol. ii, p. 79, l. 9, transl. vol. ii, p. 55.

[3] *Jāt.*, vol. vi, p. 74, transl. vol. vi, p. 42.

[4] *Jāt.*, vol. iii, p. 418, transl. vol. iii, p. 251.

[5] Topsell, *History of Serpents* (1658), pp. 677 and 681. Cf. Crooke, *Folk-lore of Northern India*, vol. ii, pp. 136 f.

royal residence: "We possess deadly poison, and we are easily displeased for a trifling matter, and the anger of a co-wife is a serious thing. If I see or hear anything and cast an angry look thereon, it will be instantly scattered like a handful of chaff; therefore I cannot go." It is for this reason that the Nāga heroes of certain Buddhist stories, in their wish to realize the ideal of forbearance and *ahiṃsā*, close their eyes when they see their enemy approaching them. The pious Nāga-king Champaka, seeing the snake-charmer, says to himself: "My poison is powerful, and if I am angry and send forth the breath of my nostrils, his body will be shattered and scattered like a handful of chaff; then my virtue will be broken. I will not look upon him." The same is related of the Nāgarāja Bhūridatta.[1]

The poet Bhartṛihari [2] says in one of his aphorisms that it is less dangerous to be struck by the eye of a serpent than by that of a woman; in the former case physicians and herbs are available, but in the latter case none.

The knowledge of poisons and antidotes (*Kalpa* or *Kalpasthāna*) is one of the eight chief subjects of Indian medical science. Suśruta, the Hippocrates of ancient India, says at the outset of his chapter on snake-poison [3]: "Innumerable are the famous Lords of Nāgas, headed by Vāsuki and beginning from Takshaka, earth-bearers, resembling the sacrificial fire in their splendour (*tejas*), who incessantly cause thunder, rain and heat, and by whom this earth with her oceans, mountains and continents is supported, and who in their wrath might smite the whole world by their breath and sight. Homage be to those. With them there is no need of the healing art. But of those of the poison fangs that belong to the earth and bite human beings I will enumerate the number in the appropriate manner and in the proper order."

The main remedies employed against snake-bite are herbs and charms, the secret of which is supposed to be in the possession of ascetics. But in the *Atharva-veda* (viii, 7, 23) the snakes themselves are mentioned among the animals that have a knowledge of medical herbs.

Curiously enough, the snake's poison is also credited with a healing virtue, especially in counteracting poison. "With poison I smite thy poison," we read in a verse of the *Atharva-veda* (v, 13, 4), used as a charm against venomous snakes. The episode of Bhīma's visit to the Nāga world illustrates that vegetable poison is 'killed' by animal poison, and in the famous tale of King Nala we find that the hero, when possessed of the evil spirit Kali, is freed by the bite of the Nāga Karkoṭa.[4] In this connexion we may also refre

[1] See below, pp. 152 and 159.

[2] *Śringāra-śataka*, 86, ed. P. von Bohlen, p. 34; transl. p. 95.

[3] Susruta, *Kalpasthāna*, iv, ed. Calcutta, 1835, vol. ii, p. 252. Suśrutas, *Ayurvedas: id est Medicinæ systema*, transl. F. Hessler (Erlangen, 1844), pp. 222 f.

[4] See below, pp. 80 f.

to a *jātaka*,[1] in which a physician tries to cure his patient by inducing the snake to suck its own poison out of the wound. But the snake refuses to do so.

An Indian proverb [2] says that snake-poison causes no harm to a snake. Whether this statement is based on fact or not, we may leave undecided. The idea, anyhow, did exist, and may easily have led to the belief that the snakes themselves produce an antidote against their own poison. In Europe, too, such a belief prevailed during the Middle Ages.

Here we may refer to a pretty legend contained in the *Harshacharita* [3] regarding a wonderful pearl necklace which was presented to the king by a holy man. The pearls of this jewel were born from the tears of the Moon-god, which had fallen down in pearl-oysters and become an antidote against all poisons, "in consequence of its having been produced from the moon, which is the ever-cooling fountain of ambrosia." This precious necklace came into the possession of Vāsuki, the King of Serpents, who presented it to Nāgārjuna during his stay in the Nether World (*Pātāla, Rasātala*). Nāgārjuna, in his turn, gave it to Sātavāhana, and in course of time it came into the hands of the holy teacher from whom King Harsha received it.

The remedy against snake-bite, as we have seen, is sought in the snakes themselves on the principle that like cures like. It will appear even more natural that people would seek protection with Garuḍa, the great enemy of the Nāgas. It is believed that serpents loose their poison at the mere sight of Garuḍa.[4] In the *Bhūridatta-jātaka* we read of a Suparṇa who gave a recluse a priceless spell and showed him the simples pertaining thereto. The anchorite in his turn imparted the spell to Ālambāyana, and the latter used it to capture the Nāga king, who was the Bodhisattva.[5]

Moreover, there exists a precious stone, named after Garuḍa—it is the emerald—which is credited with the power of destroying poison. Says the *Rājataraṅgiṇī* (iv, 331): "The danger of lightning is averted by the diamond; the ruby produces prosperity; various kinds of poisons, too, are counteracted by the emerald (lit. 'the stone of Garutmant')." In the same book (i, 58) we read of one of the early rulers of Kashmir that his arm "was adorned by the jewel sacred to Garuḍa".[6] May we assume that the emerald was worn as a prophylactic against snake-bite? The figure of Garuḍa, too, when

[1] *Jātaka*, vol. i, pp. 310 f.; transl. and vol. i, p. 168.

[2] *Ind. Spr.*, 3001.

[3] *Harshacharita* (Bombay, 1897), pp. 250 f.; transl. Cowell and Thomas, pp. 251 f.

[4] *Ind. Spr.*, 4558 (4655) = *M.Bh.*, *Anuśāsana-p.*, xxvi, 44. *Bhavanti nirvishāḥ sarpā yathā Tārkshyasya darśanāt, Gaṅgāyā darśanāt tadvat sarvapāpaiḥ pramuchyate.*

[5] See below, p. 158.

[6] *Rājat.* transl. Stein, vol. i, pp. 12 and 153.

introduced in bracelets and diadems of statues representing Bodhisattvas in royal attire,[1] may have been something more than a mere decorative device. A similar power was ascribed by Pliny to the agate.

A remedy against snake-bite which is still in vogue is the so-called 'snake-stone', which seems to be usually a piece of bone soaked in blood and repeatedly baked. It is supposed to have absorbent properties and to draw the venom out of the wound.[2]

After what has been remarked above, it will perhaps seem less strange that the snake, the most dangerous and deadliest of animals, comes to be looked upon as a harbinger of good luck and prosperity. Whereas, on the one hand, the sight of a snake is considered a bad omen, there exists, on the other hand, a widespread belief that the same animal has power to impart fecundity and remove barrenness. In the whole of Western and Southern India the cobra is worshipped up to the present day by women who are desirous of offspring. This practice we find also mentioned in literature. We read of the Nāga hero of a *jātaka* [3] that, after he had taken up his abode upon an ant-hill, the wayfarers and villagers began to worship him. "And people began to crave sons by his aid, having faith in him and doing him worship."

In Bāṇa's famous Sanskrit novel *Kādambarī* [4] it is related how Vilāsavatī, the Queen of Tārāpīḍa, the monarch of Ujjayinī, in her anxiety to obtain children, performs various auspicious rites. "In the celebrated pools of the Nāga tribes she dived and by circumambulation in sun-wise turn she worshipped the *pīpal* and other sacred trees to which honour was wont to be shown."

Nor will it be a matter of surprise that the snake is regarded as the tutelar deity of the house. "Each Vāstu or domicile," a Bengali author writes,[5] "is believed to have a representative snake, called the *Vāstu-sarpa*, which is regarded with great awe. If the *Vāstu-sarpa* is seen to abandon a house it is an unlucky omen, and the perpetuity of the house, the continuity of the race or family, is believed to be endangered." With reference to Southern India we may quote the Abbé Dubois. "If a snake happens to get into a house, far from turning out the inconvenient guest and killing it on the spot, they feed it

[1] *Mathurā Museum Catalogue*, Allahabad, 1910, p. 58, pl. x.

[2] W. Crooke, op. cit., vol. ii, p. 141.

[3] *Champeyya-jātaka*. See below, p. 152.

[4] *Kādambarī* (Bombay, 1896), p. 134; Miss C. M. Ridding's transl. (London, 1896), p. 56. In this connexion we may call attention to a passage in the *Avadāna-śataka* (ed. Speyer), vol. i, p. 195, enumerating various classes of deities which are resorted to by a childless man. The list is headed by the term *Rāmadevatā*. Would it be too hazardous a supposition to conjecture that this strange expression is really due to a misreading of *Nāgadevatā* ?

[5] *J.A.S.B.*, vol. xxxix (1870), p. 206. Also Crooke, op. cit., vol. ii, pp. 144 f.

plentifully and offer sacrifices to it daily. Hindus are known to keep deadly snakes for years in their houses, feeding and petting them. Even if a whole family were in danger of losing their lives, no one member would be bold enough to lay sacrilegious hands on such an honoured inmate." [1]

The benevolent household snake, according to Crooke,[2] represents the soul of some deceased ancestor which has taken up its residence there.

In ancient Egypt the snake was called 'the son of the Earth' or 'the life of the Earth'. According to Aelian (ii, 21), the Earth is the mother of dragons. We find the same association in ancient India. Kadrū, 'the Tawny One,' who, according to the well-known myth, becomes the mother of the thousand Nāgas, is a personification of the earth. The snake-mother is also called Surasā,[3] 'she of good flavour.' Hence in Sanskrit literature the snakes are often indicated by the metronymics *Kādraveya* and *Sauraseya* (the latter word being sometimes confounded with *Saurabheya*, meaning 'a descendant of Surabhi, *alias* a cow'). In the fifth canto of the *Rāmāyaṇa*,[4] which is devoted to the account of the exploits of Hanumant, the 'Nāga-mother', Surasā, appears in the shape of a Rākshasī in order to prove the strength of the monkey hero during his flight to Laṅkā. She suddenly rises from the ocean and threatens to devour Hanumant, who, through his cunning, escapes from her jaws. In this passage Surasā seems to have lost her original character as earth-goddess. There is, however, another passage in the *Rāmāyaṇa*,[5] which brings out the close connexion between the Earth and the Nāgas. It is the pathetic tale of the last Canto, which relates how Sītā, after having been re-united with Rāma and cleansed from all guilt, is swallowed by the earth. After Sītā's solemn oath the earth-goddess appears seated on an unrivalled throne which is carried on their heads by Nāgas "of boundless might and adorned with divine jewels". She receives Sītā in both her arms, instals her on the seat and thus returns with her to the Nether World (*rasātala*).

The conception of the snake as 'the son of the earth' is, no doubt, closely associated with the belief, familiar from the fairy tales of Greece and Germany, which regards serpents as guardians of buried treasures.[6] An example is given in the *Pañchatantra* in the fable of the hooded snake in the ant-hill who daily grants a gold piece to the poor Brahmin Haridatta.[7] Another instance from the same book is the story of the two snakes—the one

[1] *Hindu Manners, Customs, and Ceremonies*, 2nd ed. (1899), p. 648.
[2] Op. cit., vol. ii, p. 133.
[3] *M.Bh.*, *Ādi-p.*, lxvi, 70, and *Rām.*, *Araṇya-k.*, xiv, 28.
[4] *Rām.*, *Sundara-k.*, i, 137–60.
[5] *Rām.*, *Uttara-k.*, xcvii, 17–20.
[6] E. Küster, *Die Schlange in der griechischen Kunst und Religion*, p. 120.
[7] See below, chapter iv.

living in an ant-hill and the other in the intestines of a prince—who imprudently betray each his own weakness and thus meet their fate.[1] The one in the ant-hill guarded two jars full of gold. In Buddhist lore, too, the same trait occurs. We may quote the legend of the black serpent of Rājagṛiha who was subdued by the Buddha.[2] In this case the gold-guarding snake was no other than the previous owner of the treasure, who was a wealthy man, but so miserly ṭhat he did not even give a *bali* to a crow. In consequence he was reborn as a black serpent so poisonous that by his look alone he deprived people of their lives.

This superstition survives in the folk-lore of modern India. "It is a common Indian belief," Mr. Crooke observes,[3] "that when a very rich man dies without an heir he cannot take away his thoughts from his treasure, and returns to guard it in the form of a monstrous serpent. But after a time he becomes tired of his serpent life, and, either in a dream or assuming the human voice, he asks the persons living near the treasure to take it and offer him one of their dearest relatives in return. When some avaricious person complies with the serpent's wishes he gets possession of the wealth and the serpent then enters into some other state of existence."

It is only natural that the possession of riches is attributed in no less a degree to the Nāgas who have, as it were, a double claim to wealth in that they combine the nature of serpents with that of demigods. It is exemplified in certain *jātakas,* how the Nāgas, while inflicting terrible punishment upon the greedy, reward the virtuous by their bounty.[4] The Nāgarāja Champaka, after entertaining the king of Benares right royally for seven days, shows him the treasures of gold and silver and jewels heaped up in his mansion and bids him to take whatever he wishes.[5]

And in the *Rājataraṅgiṇī*[6] we have the pretty legend of Mahāpadma the Nāga of the great Vular lake, who promises the king of Kashmir a gold-mine on condition that the latter will save him from the machinations of the Dravidian sorcerer. But as the king fulfils this condition in a manner offensive to the Nāga's self-respect, he is shown only a mine of copper-ore.

Not only do the Nāgas boast of the possession of untold wealth in precious metal and stones, they are also the happy owners of various priceless objects—sometimes provided with magic virtue—which occasionally they bestow on their friends and favourites. When

[1] *Pañch.*, iii, fab. 10 (ed. Kosegarten), p. 183; *Pūrṇabhadra*, iii, fab. 11, ed. Hertel, pp. 208 f.; Schmidt's transl. p. 229. Benfey, *Pantschat.*, vol. ii, pp. 256 ff. (cf. vol. i, pp. 369 f.).

[2] *Avadāna-śataka*, vi, 1, ed. Speyer, vol. ii, pp. 289 ff.; Feer's transl. pp. 198 ff. Cf. Foucher, *Art gréco-bouddhique*, vol. i, pp. 453 ff. The same *motif* occurs in the *Sachchaṃkira-jātaka* (No. 73). *Jātaka*, vol. i, p. 323; transl., vol. i, p. 178.

[3] W. Crooke, op. cit., vol. ii, p. 135.

[4] Below, pp. 139 ff. [5] Below, p. 153. [6] Below, pp. 244 ff.

the Bodhisattva after his prolonged fast had received a golden vessel of milk-rice from the hands of Sujātā, it was the Nāga-daughter of the River Nairañjanā who brought him a jewelled throne. Seated on that throne, the Bodhisattva partook of his meal.[1] In the Jātaka Book we read of the Nāgarāja Bhūridatta who presented his Brahmin guest not only with divine garments and ornaments, but also with the jewel that grants all wishes.[2] The treacherous Brahmin was not, however, to enjoy these gifts for long, for in the sequel of the story it is related that, wishing to bathe, he took off the ornaments and laid them on the bank of the river, but at the very moment they returned to the Nāga-world. Exactly the same thing happened with the magical gem. It slipped out of the Brahmin's hand, and as soon as it fell it went into the ground and disappeared in the Nāgaloka. The fairy tales, too, mention magical objects in the possession of the Nāgas. In the *Kathāsaritsāgara* we hear of a wonderful lute which out of gratitude the Nāga Vasunemi, the eldest brother of Vāsuki, bestowed on king Udayana when the latter had redeemed him from a snake-charmer.[3]

This lute the Vatsa king used to capture wild elephants. Another story in the same collection [4] relates of a magician who, with the aid of Prince Mṛigāṅkadatta, undertakes to conjure a Nāga in order to acquire the matchless sword 'Beryl-beauty', which endows its owner with invincibility and with the kingship over the fairies. Among Buddhist fairy tales we may quote the story of Prince Sudhana,[5] in which the hunter Halaka, having saved the Nāga Janmachitraka, craves the infallible lasso as a reward. In this connexion we may also mention the Nāga-power granting elixir which Bhīma is made to quaff on his visit to the snake-world and the life-restoring jewel of Ulūpī, the Nāga-bride of Arjuna.[6]

Besides material objects endowed with magic properties, the Nāgas know magical spells which they impart to specially favoured mortals. In a *jātaka* (No. 386) the king Senaka receives from his Nāga-friend a charm which enables him to understand the language of animals. In a story of the *Kathāsaritsāgara* a hermit causes a prince to dwell for seven days in a serpent-lake and endows him with the magical spell 'mohinī' after he had endured during that time the bite of the snakes.[7]

The possession of treasures, magic gems, and spells is, of course, a characteristic which the Nāgas share with other classes of divine and semi-divine beings. The Nāgas are also praised for having accomplished wonderful works of art, especially in the days of

[1] See below, pp. 97 f. [2] Below, p. 157. [3] Below, pp. 176 f.
[4] Below, pp. 178 f. [5] Below, p. 186. [6] Below, pp. 73 and 77.
[7] *Kathās.*, xlvi, 121 ; Tawney's transl., vol. i, p. 440.

Nāgārjuna.[1] The Nāga Mahākāla is said, at the request of the Emperor Aśoka, to have produced colossal images of Gautama Buddha and of his two predecessors.[2]

In Buddhist tradition the serpent-demons are also represented as guardians of holy objects. It is related that after the Parinirvāṇa of the Buddha they, too, received a share of his holy relics. We may also quote the legend of the relic-shrine of Rāmagrāma, which was protected by the Nāgas against spoliation.[3] A Buddhist prophecy current in Ceylon holds that, when owing to the decline of the faith the relics of the Tathāgata will no longer receive due veneration, they will first be gathered together at the Ruwanwäli Dagaba at Anurādhapura, after which they will go to the Rājāyatana Dagaba in the Nāgaloka. Hence they will go to the Bodhi-tree of Gayā and here they will be consumed in a conflagration. Then all knowledge of the doctrine of the Buddhas will disappear.[4]

Besides the bodily remains of the Master, there are the relics of his Dharma-kāya, or ' Body of the Law ', namely the sacred texts. It happens that these spiritual treasures, too, are entrusted to the Nāgas. Did not they keep for many centuries the *Prajñāpāramitā*, that book so highly reverenced among the Northern Buddhists ? It had been revealed by the Buddha himself, but was too abstruse to be comprehended by his contemporaries. Only when Nāgārjuna, the great master of the Mahāyāna, had risen in the world, the Nāgas invited him to visit their mysterious realm in the ocean and delivered it to him.[5] Possibly it was the name ' Nāgārjuna ' which originally suggested this legend.

Whereas the Nāgas are, on the one hand, believed to be keepers and bestowers of wealth, they are, on the other hand, eager to rob precious things which they find in the possession of mortals. In the legend of Uttaṅka, which is told in the *Mahābhārata* in two different versions, it is the Nāga who seizes the ear-rings which the Brahmin hero of the story had obtained from the Queen as a present for the wife of his *guru.*[6] The same motif is employed by Kālidāsa in a pretty episode of the 16th canto of his *Raghuvaṃśa*[7] with reference to Kuśa the son and successor of Rāma. The poet relates how, while the king is bathing in the river Sarayu, the ' victory-imparting ' ornament which he had received from Agastya, slips from his arm and vanishes in the water. The fishers who are ordered to search the river-bed fail to trace it and conclude that it must have been seized out of greed by the Nāga Kumuda dwelling in a pool (*hrada*) of the river. When Kuśa, in his

[1] *Chitralakshaṇa*, transl. B. Laufer. Leipzig, 1913, pp. 189 f.

[2] Spence Hardy, *Eastern Monachism*, pp. 273 f. Cf. *Mahāvaṃsa*, v, 87–94.

[3] Beneath, pp. 127 f.

[4] Spence Hardy, op. cit., p. 429.

[5] L. A. Waddell, *Lamaism*, London, 1895, p. 11.

[6] See below, pp. 61 f.

[7] *Raghuvaṃśa*, xvi, 72–88. In the concluding stanza Kumuda is called the fifth son of Takshaka.

anger, aims his terrible Garuḍa arrow at the invisible Nāga, the waters of the flood suddenly part in violent motion and the serpent-king appears holding a beautiful girl by the hand. He informs Kuśa that this girl is his youngest sister, Kumudvatī by name, who, while playing with the ball noticed the precious gem, and out of childish curiosity had seized it. The Nāga not only restores the jewel to its rightful owner, but, at the same time, offers him the fair Kumudvatī in marriage. The offer is gladly accepted, and the king is united in wedlock with the Nāga princess. Owing to this matrimonial union, the poet concludes his tale, the Nāga king was freed of the fear of Garuḍa, while in the realm of Kuśa the danger of poisonous snakes subsided.

From Buddhist lore we may refer the reader to the episode of the golden bowl which, after having been used by the Buddha for his first meal following his Enlightenment, was seized by the Nāgarāja Sāgara.[1]

Whilst in the present instance the value of the bowl was not a little enhanced by its association with the Master, it cannot be a matter of surprise that the Nāgas also covet objects of a purely spiritual preciousness. We have seen that they are also supposed to be the guardians of such objects. In the Ceylonese chronicle *Mahāvaṃsa* it is narrated at great length how a branch of the Bodhi-tree was conveyed to Ceylon under the personal supervision of the nun Saṅghamitrā who was the daughter of the great Aśoka. When the ship with its priceless load fared forth into the sea, the waves of the ocean were stilled for a *yojana* all around, lotus-flowers of the five colours blossomed forth, and manifold instruments of music resounded in the air. Then the Nāgas practised their magic to win the branch of the Bodhi-tree, but Saṅghamitrā, through her supernatural power, assumed the form of a Garuḍa. "Terrified, the great Nāgas betook themselves to the saint with entreaties, and when they had escorted the great Bodhi-tree to the realm of the serpents and had worshipped it for a week by bestowing on it the kingship of the Nāgas and by manifold offerings, they brought it again and set it upon the ship." [2]

In the story of Uttaṅka, according to its earlier version,[3] the ear-rings of the Queen are seized by the Nāga, after they have been deposited on the ground. In the later version the hero of the story had tied the precious ear-rings in his antelope's hide. He climbs a *bilva*-tree to pluck the fruit after having hung the hide on a branch. But the hide containing the rings falls down, and as soon as they touch the ground "a snake of Airavata's race" seizes them and disappears in an ant-hill.

[1] See below, p. 97.

[2] *Mahāvaṃsa*, xix, 17–23; transl. G. Turnour (1889), p. 75; transl. W. Geiger and M. H. Bode (1912), pp. 129 f. In the corresponding passage of the *Dīpavaṃsa*, xvi, 8–29 (transl. Oldenberg, p. 193), the Nāgas are mentioned among the classes of beings which worship the Bodhi-tree on its way to Ceylon, but we read of no attempt on their part to seize it. Cf. also Spence Hardy, *Eastern Monachism* (1860), p. 326.

[3] Below, pp. 62 and 67.

In the *Bhūridatta-jātaka* we have noticed the same trait; here the jewels which originate from the Nāgas, vanish when they touch the ground and disappear into the Nāgaloka.[1] Plainly the earth is considered to be the depository of jewels and precious metals and the snakes which are the sons of the earth are the rightful owners of the treasures concealed in the womb of their mother.

Here we may also mention the curious belief that the hooded serpent carries a priceless jewel in its hood. Says Varāhamihira [2]: "The snakes of the lineage of Takshaka and Vāsuki, and the snakes roaming at will (*kāmaga*) have bright, blue-tinged pearls in their hoods."

The poets of the classical period [3] never grow tired of referring to this conceit, especially with regard to the world-serpent Śesha, the jewels on whose thousand heads illumine the Nether-world by their effulgence. In aphorisms too the jewel in the serpent's head affords a very favourite theme. Thus a maxim ascribed to the great Chāṇakya says [4]: "A villain is to be shunned, even if he were adorned with wisdom: Does not the serpent inspire terror, albeit he be embellished with a jewel?"

Spence Hardy,[5] after quoting this aphorism as belonging to a collection of a hundred proverbs current in Ceylon, adds the following: "This jewel is thought by the natives to be formed in the throat of the naya. It emits a light more brilliant than the purest diamond, and when the serpent wishes to discover anything in the dark it disgorges the substance, swallowing it again when its work is done. It is thought to be possible to obtain the jewel by throwing dust upon it when out of the serpent's mouth; but if the reptile were to be killed to obtain it, misfortune would certainly follow."

The snake-jewel is still a stock subject in Indian folk-tales.[6]

In the Western world a similar popular belief is met with. In antiquity it was associated with the dragon, as appears from the following passage which Benfey [7] quotes from Pliny: "Dracontites sive dracontia e cerebro fit draconum, sed nisi viventibus abscisso nunquam gemmescit, invidia animalis mori se sentientis. Igitur dormientibus amputant. Sotacus qui visam eam gemmam sibi apud regem scripsit, bigis vehi quaerentes tradit: et viso dracone spargere somnifica medicamenta atque ita praecidere. Esse autem candore translucido, nec postea poliri aut artem admittere."

[1] Below, p. 158.
[2] *Bṛihatsaṃhitā*, lxxxi, 25; Kern's *Verspr. Geschr.*, vol. ii, p. 100.
[3] *Raghuvaṃśa*, x, 7; xi, 59; xiii, 12; xvii, 63. *Rājat.*, iii, 58, 529; viii, 1528.
[4] *Ind. Spr.*, 2850 (1180); also 773 (288), 1958 (759), 6221 (2866), and 7022.
[5] *Eastern Monachism*, p. 316.
[6] W. Crooke, op. cit., vol. ii, pp. 143 f.
[7] *Pantschat.*, vol. i, p. 214 footnote.

During the Middle Ages it was not only the dragon who was credited with the possession of the marvellous snake-jewel, but also two other species of serpents, namely the aspis and the idros. Now, it is interesting that, whilst the dragon is closely allied to the Indian Nāga, the aspis is the North African counterpart of the hooded snake of India.[1]

It is well known that during the Renaissance it is the toad which was believed to carry a precious stone in its head. Possibly this belief was merely due to a misinterpretation of the name *batrachita* applied by Pliny to certain stones originating from Koptos. The name which was originally meant to denote the peculiar colour of the stone, may have given rise to the notion that it originated from the toad, which is described by Topsell as " the most noble kinde of Frog, most venomous and remarkable for courage and strength ".

That the toad was venomous was believed by Shakespeare and his contemporaries ; hence, no doubt, the notion that the toad-stone, when swallowed, was a certain antidote against poison. Toad-stones set in silver were preserved as precious amulets and may still be seen in collections of mediaeval jewels. Nowadays they are best known from the passage in Shakespeare's " As you like it " (Act ii, scene 1, 13–14).

> "Sweet are the uses of adversity,
> Which, like the toad, ugly and venomous,
> Wears yet a precious jewel in his head."

We have seen that in India the serpent is supposed to carry the jewel in its hood. It is well known that this so-called hood is peculiar to a certain species of snake which zoologists designate as Naja tripudians, but which among the European community of India is known by its Portuguese name as cobra or cobra di capello. The cobra is widely distributed : from Transcaspia to China and to the Malay Islands ; in the Himalayas it ascends to about 3,000 feet above the level of the sea. Very large specimens are said to attain more than six feet in length ; but a cobra of five feet is considered large.[2] When agitated they erect themselves upon the hinder third or quarter of their length, whilst they spread out the hood and sway the head and neck to the right and left, always in the attitude ready for striking. The hood is formed by the spreading and moving headwards of the ribs.

In Sanskrit the hood is designated by the words *phaṇa, phaṇā, phaṭa, phaṭā, sphaṭa, phuṭa,* and *darvī* (lit. ' a ladle, a spoon '). We find a reference to this hood (*darvi*) in a

[1] It is the Uræus serpent of ancient Egypt, the fire-spitting dragon, who is shown round the solar disk and round the diadem of the Pharao.

[2] Hans Gadow, *Amphibia and Reptiles* (*Cambridge Natural Hist.*, vol. viii, London, 1901), pp. 626 ff.

verse of the *Atharva-veda.*[1] In Kālidāsa's *Śakuntalā*[2] there is a stanza which says: "The fire flameth when the fuel is stirred, the serpent when assailed maketh a hood; commonly people show their greatness when stirred."

It is the cobra which under the name of *nāg* is worshipped up to the present day in large parts of India. The Nāga of Indian mythology and folk-lore is not really the snake in general, but the cobra raised to the rank of a divine being. From many a legend rendered in the present volume, it is evident that the Nāga in his animal form is conceived as the hooded snake. Muchilinda shelters the Buddha against the inclemency of the weather by spreading his hood over the Master's head. Śesha carries the earth on his thousand-fold hood. In the legend of Jīmūtavāhana, too, the hood is mentioned among the characteristics of the Nāga.[3]

The evidence of Indian art points to the same conclusion. The Nāga, represented either in a purely animal or in a semi-human shape, is always characterized by the snake-hood.

Besides the uncanny properties common to all snakes which have been surveyed above, and the sudden and terrible action of its poison, the cobra is conspicuous by its hood with its curious spectacle-marks, whence it is called 'brilslang' in Dutch and 'serpent à lunettes' in French. It will be no matter of surprise that the last-mentioned peculiarity has drawn special attention among the population of India so apt to attach prognostic significance to bodily marks (Skt. *lakshaṇa*) of men and animals. According to a familiar legend, which will be found beneath, the so-called spectacle marks are the footprints left by Kṛishṇa on the heads of the Nāga Kāliya.[4] After his victory the shepherd-god addressed the serpent: "When Garuḍa seeth my footprints marked on thy heads, that enemy of thy race will not assail thee."

It is said that according to a Buddhist legend the spectacle marks are a favour which the Buddha bestowed on the cobra that had sheltered him against the heat of the sun.[5] Here, too, the marks are said to provide a safeguard against the attacks of Garuḍa. This legend, which evidently originates from the ancient story of the Nāga Muchilinda, appears to be comparatively modern. I have not been able to trace it to any ancient source.

Sometimes the Nāgas are said to be adorned with the *svastika* or mystic cross, but in one passage of the *Harivaṃśa* it is said to be half a *svastika.*[6] At first sight this expression may seem strange, but in our opinion there can be little doubt that here, again, we must

[1] *A.V.*, x, 4, 13. Cf. above, p. 8.

[2] *Śakuntalā*, ed. Böhlingk, verse 158; Bengal recension (ed. Pischel), verse 185; Monier Williams, *Sakoontalā*, p. 173.

[3] See below, p. 171.

[4] See below, p. 89.

[5] Brehm, *Tierleben*, 4th ed., vol. v, p. 432.

[6] *Harivaṃśa*, 3934, 4433, 4440, 5185. *Vishṇu-purāṇa*, transl. Wilson, p. 146.

think of the so-called spectacle-mark, the shape of which may well be described as a *svastikārdha*, or 'half-svastika'. It is well known that the *svastika* is looked upon as a sign of good augury. Quite possibly it may have contributed to the sanctity of the animal which was supposed to bear it.

The favourite haunt of the cobra is the ant-hill (Skt. *valmīka*, Pali *vammīka*). This point, attested by naturalists, we find again and again in the ancient serpent-lore of India. In the epics the arrow piercing the body of the enemy is compared to a snake entering an ant-hill.[1] The fable of the snake (*nāgendra*) killed by ants illustrates that sometimes the abode in the ant-hill may become fatal to its occupant.[2] In the story of the three Brahmin brothers in the *Kathāsaritsāgara* [3] the youngest one, Viśvadatta, is ordered by his two malicious elder brothers (who wish to rid themselves of him) to level an ant-hill, but instead of a poisonous cobra, it turns out to contain a pitcher filled with gold.

The *Gāmaṇichaṇḍa-jātaka* (No. 257) [4] is the story of the fourteen riddles. The seventh conundrum is the riddle of the snake. "When I go out to get my food," the snake says, "I leave this ant-hill faint and famishing, and yet I fill the entrance hole with my body, and I get out with difficulty, dragging myself along. But when I come in again I feel satisfied and fat, yet I pass quickly through the hole without touching the sides. How is this?" The answer is: "Under the snake's ant-heap lies a large treasure-crock, and there he lives guarding it. So when he goes out, from greed for his treasure his body sticks fast; but after he has fed, his desire for the treasure prevents his body from sticking and he goes in quickly and easily."

In these ancient tales we find the ant-hill associated not only with the snake, but also with the treasure which the serpent is believed to guard. The same trait is met with in the two fables from the *Pañchatantra*, which we have mentioned previously: the one of the gold-granting snake and the poor Brahmin, and the other of the two serpents which betrayed each his own weakness. These snakes are fabulous beings which have the power of speech. Thus it is only natural that the mythical serpent-demons, too, are connected with the ant-hill. The great Nāga heroes of the *jātakas*, Champaka, Śaṅkhapāla, and Bhūridatta, each in his turn, select an ant-hill, on the top of which they lie down to keep the commandments of the Sabbath.

The close connexion between the sacred snake and the ant-hill will readily account for the special significance attached to the latter in popular worship. It is looked upon not

[1] *M.Bh.*, *Droṇa-p.*, cxxxvi, 15. *Rām.*, *Araṇya-k.*, xxix, 11 (ed. Gorresio, xxxv, 12).

[2] *Pañchat.* (ed. Kosegarten), iii, fab. 4, pp. 170 f., transl. Schmidt, pp. 215 f. Cf. *A.V.*, vii, 56, 7, *adanti tvā pipīlikā*.

[3] *Kathās*, xxxiii, 36–52; Tawney's transl., vol. i, p. 293.

[4] *Jātaka*, vol. ii, p. 303, ll. 8–16; transl., vol. ii, p. 211.

only as the venerated abode of the snake deity, but also as the entrance to the mysterious snake-world far below the world of men. We may again refer to the ancient story of Uttaṅka in its second version. In another passage of the *Mahābhārata* [1] the elephants of the four Quarters instruct Reṇuka that a *bali* must be deposited after sunset on an ant-hill. Although the sky-elephants (*diṅ-nāga*) are speaking, the *bali* is evidently meant for the Nāgas. Why after sunset ? Because the cobra avoids hot sunshine and hunts chiefly in the late afternoon and the evening.

Magic and medical properties are ascribed to the earth taken from a *valmīka*. Its use is recommended as an antidote against snake-poison ; and even an ablution in water which has run out of an ant-hill is believed to be beneficial.[2] In certain rites, too, the earth from ant-heaps is used.[3] In his chapter on the exploration of water-springs, Varāhamihira [4] frequently mentions ant-hills which in connexion with certain trees are believed to indicate the presence of water. It deserves notice that in this passage the ant-hill is indicated by various synonyms meaning 'the abode of snakes' (Skt. *ahi-nilaya, ahi-saṃśraya, sarpāvāsa*). Evidently it is as 'the abode of snakes' that it is believed to indicate the site of hidden springs.

Here we must also refer to the connexion which is believed to exist between the ant-hill and the rainbow. "The rainbow," Varāhamihira says,[5] "is formed by vari-coloured solar rays that, pressed by the wind, appear in the shape of a bow in a cloudy sky. Some Masters say that the rainbow arises out of the exhalations of the serpents of Ananta's family." The famous Indian astrologer, it will be observed, offers two different explanations : the one pseudo-physical and the other mythological. It is characteristic that he places them side by side, without rejecting either of the two.

Kālidāsa, too, in his *Meghadūta* (stanza 15) speaks of the 'bow of Indra' which issues forth from the top of the ant-hill. The scholiast Vallabhadeva, in commenting on this stanza, quotes an ancient tradition (*āgama*) which holds that the origin of the divine bow in the rainy season is the ant-hill, because it is 'pregnant of snakes' (*sarpagarbha*). Another commentator offers a somewhat different explanation. The rays shining forth from the jewels in the heads of the great Nāga Vāsuki penetrate into the sky from the Nether Regions through a fissure of the ant-hill, and coming in contact with the rain cloud, they assume the form of Indra's bow. This, too, is said to be an old tradition.[6]

[1] *M.Bh., Anuśāsana-p.*, cxxxii, 7–16.
[2] *Suśruta*, ii, p. 271, l. 3 ; transl. p. 228, l. 28. *M.Bh., Vana-p.*, lxxxiv, 7.
[3] *J.A.S.B.*, vol. xxxix, part i, p. 210.
[4] *Bṛihatsaṃhitā*, liv ; Kern, *Verspr. Geschr.*, vol. ii, pp. 27 ff.
[5] Op cit., xxxv, 1–2 ; Kern, *Verspr. Geschr.*, vol. i, p. 283.
[6] *Meghadūta*, ed. G. R. Nandargikar, Bombay, 1894, notes, p. 20.

It may be questioned whether the name Vālmīki, which is clearly a patronymic, may not derive its origin from the sanctity attached to the abode of the cobra.

In speaking of the connexion between the rainbow and the snake, Mr. Crooke remarks :[1] " It is possibly under the influence of the association of the snake, a treasure guardian, that the English children run to find where the rainbow meets the earth, and expect to find a crock of gold buried at its base."

Up to the present day the ant-hill performs, as it were, the function of a natural altar in the popular cult of the serpent. In our concluding chapter, which is devoted to modern serpent-worship, we shall be able to adduce abundant evidence. Here it will suffice to quote the Abbé Dubois, who says in his well-known book :[2] " Snake-worshippers search for the holes where they [the snakes] are likely to be found, and which more often than not are in the little mounds raised by the *kariahs*, or white ants. When they have found one they visit it from time to time, placing before it milk, bananas, and other food which the snake is likely to fancy."

The ant-hill, however, is only the visible entrance to the mysterious World of Serpents which is located in the Nether Regions, called Pātāla or Rasātala, far beneath the human world. This is the abode generally assigned to the Nāgas both in Hindu cosmogony and fable. When Takshaka is almost being seized by Uttaṅka, he assumes his serpent-form and escapes through a fissure in the earth to his subterraneous realm. It is in the Nether World (*Pātālatale*) that Takshaka's son Aśvasena hears the frightful tumult of the battle of Kurukshetra.[3] We find the same in Buddhist lore. When Piliyakkha, the cruel king of Benares, concealed in his ambush, watches the pious young hermit Śyāma approaching surrounded by the forest-deer, he says to himself: " All the time that I have been wandering here I have never seen a man before ; is he a god or a Nāga ? Now if I go up and ask him, he will fly up into the heaven if he is a god, and he will sink into the earth if he is a Nāga." [4]

According to the *Purāṇas* the Nether World is divided into seven regions extending downwards ten thousand *yoyanas* each. The names assigned to those divisions vary, but most descriptions agree in placing Pātāla lowermost. This nethermost abyss, however is not a place of darkness and terror, but an abode of delight and wondrous charm. The

[1] Op. cit., vol. ii, p. 144. In the Kuḷu valley the rainbow is called Buḍhī Nāgan or Nāgin, i.e. ' the old female snake '.

[2] *Hindu Manners*, p. 648 ; *Panjāb Notes and Queries*, vol. iii, 92, 59.

[3] See below, p. 79.

[4] *Jātaka*, vol. vi, p. 76, xi, 9–12 ; transl. vol. vi, p. 43. In the Sanskrit version (*Mahāvastu*, vol. iii, pp. 209 ff.) the king is called Peliyaksha.

muni Nārada, after his return from those regions to the skies, declared amongst the celestials that Pātāla was much more delightful than Indra's heaven. " What," exclaimed the sage [1] " can be compared to Pātāla, where the Nāgas are decorated with brilliant and beautiful and pleasure-shedding jewels ? Who will not delight in Pātāla, where the lovely daughters of the Daityas and Dānavas wander about, fascinating even the most austere ; where the rays of the sun diffuse light, and not heat, by day ; and where the moon shines by night for illumination, not for cold ; where the sons of Danu, happy in the enjoyment of delicious viands and strong wines, know not how time passes ? There are beautiful groves and streams and lakes where the lotus blows ; and the skies are resonant with the Koïl's song. Splendid ornaments, fragrant perfumes, rich unguents, the blended music of the lute and pipe and tabor ; these and many other enjoyments are the common portion of the Dānavas, Daityas, and snake-gods, who inhabit the region of Pātāla."

The very name of Bhogavatī, the town of the serpents, characterizes it as a place of pleasure (*bhoga* has the double meaning of a ' snake's coil ' and ' enjoyment ').

In the Pali literature the subterraneous mansion of the Nāga Kāla is indicated by the name of Mañjerika.[2]

Only few mortals have penetrated into the inaccessible Nāga world, like Uttaṅka, the young Brahmin, whom we have mentioned before. Yet it is said that there exist numerous entrances to the Nether World. In the story of King Bhūnandana, told in that great depository of fairy tales, the *Kathāsaritsāgara*, the king who wishes to marry a Daitya maiden is addressed by a Brahmanical ascetic in the following words : [3] " There are on this earth many openings leading to the lower regions, but there is a great and famous one in Kashmir made by Maya by which Ushā the daughter of Bāṇa introduced her lover Aniruddha into the secret pleasure-grounds of the Dānavas and made him happy there. And Pradyumna, in order to deliver his son, laid it open, making a door in one place with the peak of a mountain, and he placed Durgā there, under the name of Śārikā, to guard that door, after propitiating her with hundreds of praises. Consequently, even now the place is called by the two names of Peak of Pradyumna and Hill of Śārikā." The Hill of Śārikā is the Hari Parbat near Srīnagar, the capital of Kashmīr.[4]

Another entrance to Pātāla is the cave of Namuchi, which an ancient king of Kashmīr,

[1] *Vishnu-purāṇa*, transl. Wilson, p. 204. The fourth canto of the *Padma-purāṇa*, called *Pātālakhaṇḍa*, is devoted to a description of the Underworld.

[2] *Jātaka*, vol. i, p. 72, l. 14 ; *Buddhist Birth Stories*, p. 97 ; cf. *Jāt.*, vol. vi, p. 264, ll. 4–5, and Spence Hardy, *Eastern Monachism*, p. 274.

[3] *Kathās.*, lxxiii, 107–112 ; Tawney's transl., vol. ii, p. 197.

[4] Cf. *Rājat.*, transl. Stein, vol. ii, p. 446.

Raṇāditya by name, was believed to have entered " after passing through the waters of the Chandrabhāgā ". Having reigned three hundred years on earth, this monarch obtained the sovereignty over the Underworld (*Pātālaiśvarya*), the realm of the Daityas and Dānavas.[1]

" In the Sikandar, a tributary of the Son, is a deep waterhole, where no one dares to go. The water is said to reach down as far as Pātāla, or the infernal regions." [2]

Another favourite haunt of the Nāgas is the Ocean. In the Great Epic it is denoted as 'the Abode of the Nāgas' (*Nāgānām ālayam*).[3] It is well known that up to comparatively modern times both the mariners and scholars of the West believed the sea to be inhabited by strange monsters, which we find faithfully portrayed on early maps. The much more exuberant imagination of ancient India was no less prone to people the mysterious deep with every kind of demon and beast: *Asuras, Yakshas,* and *Rākshasas* mingle with gigantic *makaras* and sea-elephants.[4] In an early text of the Pali Canon the Buddha compares his doctrine and discipline with the Ocean. " There are," he says,[5] " in the great ocean eight astonishing and curious qualities, by the constant perception of which the mighty creatures take delight in the great ocean." Now the eighth and last of these astonishing qualities is " that the great ocean is the dwelling-place of mighty beings, among which are these—that is to say, the Timi, the Timiṅgala, the Timitimiṅgala, the Asuras, the Nāgas, and the Gandharvas. There are in the great ocean creatures so constituted that they stretch from one to five hundred leagues."

In Buddhist tradition both Varuṇa and Sāgara, really gods of the sea, have become converted into Nāgarājas. It is also significant that among the Buddhist *lokapālas*, or 'the four Great Kings', as they are commonly called, Virūpāksha, the ruler of the Nāgas, is the regent of the Western quarter which in Brahmanical mythology is assigned to Varuṇa, the Indian Neptune. Occasionally certain islands—Rāmaṇīyaka (in the *Ādi-parvan*) and Nāgadvīpa [6] (*Sussondi-* and *Valāhassa-jātaka*) are mentioned as dwelling-places of the snake-gods. In the *Sussondi-jātaka* (No. 360) the Isle of the Nāgas (Nāgadvīpa) has the specific name of 'Seruma-dvīpa', but, strange to say, it is described as the home not of the Nāgas, but of a Suparṇa or Garuḍa. In the *Kākāti-jātaka* (No. 327) we have a variant of the same story, but here the place of the Suparṇa is called Kebuka.

[1] *Rājat.*, iii, 468; Stein's transl., vol. i, p. 114.

[2] W. Crooke, op. cit., vol. i, p. 43.

[3] *M.Bh.*, *Ādi-p.*, xxi, 6; xxv, 4.

[4] *Jātakamālā* (ed. Kern), p. 89, i, 6; Speyer's transl., p. 126.

[5] *Chullavagga*, ix, 1. 3–4; *S.B.E.*, vol. xx, pp. 302 and 305.

[6] Pali: Nāgadīpa, which is also mentioned in the *Mahāvaṃsa*, xlii, 62, and lix, 12.

The Jātaka book speaks of "the Nāgas that dwell in the sea" (*samuddaṭṭhakanāgabhavane*) [1] and "the Nāgas that dwell in the mountains" (*pabbataṭṭhakanāgabhavane*). A passage in the Pali chronicles of Ceylon, which will be rendered beneath,[2] narrates how a dreadful war between those two tribes of Nāgas was averted by the timely intervention of the Buddha himself.

Sometimes we find distinct mountains mentioned as the abode of Nāgas. In the course of the description of the earth contained in the beginning chapters of the *Bhīshmaparvan* [3] the serpents and Nāgas are located on Mount Nishadha. A *jātaka* speaks of the Dardara (Pali *Daddara*) Nāgas, which live at the foot of Mount Dardara.[4] In Kashmir tradition the Nāga Nīla who is the sovereign of his tribe in that country, appears to be closely associated with Mount Dhanada. But his real abode is the spring of the Vitastā. Is the Nāga sometimes conceived as the spirit of the mountain ?

This much is certain, that mountains and trees haunted by Nāgas are of rare occurrence. Very common, on the contrary, is the popular conception that the Nāgas inhabit lakes, pools, rivers, and springs. It is not only attested by many an ancient legend, either Brahmanical or Buddhist, but still lives in Indian folk-lore up to the present day. "My children are of a watery nature," the Nāga-mother says to her royal husband in the first chapter of the *Bhūridatta-jātaka.*

Among the manifold allurements of the Serpent-world the Nāgakanyā or snake-maiden is not the least seductive. Strange though it may seem, the female counterparts of the snake-demons are invariably conceived as beings of great beauty. When Hanumant,[5] in search of Sītā, penetrates into the harem of Rāvaṇa, he sees "Nāga maidens with fair hips, and faces resembling the full moon". These had been ravished by the giant king of Laṅkā. It is high praise, indeed, when it is said of a mortal woman, like Ilā, the mother of Purūravas,[6] that she equals or surpasses the Nāgīs in beauty. King Brahmadatta, seeing the fair Padmāvatī, asks : [7] "Is she a *devakanyā*, a *nāgakanyā*, a *kinnarakanyā*, a *mānushī* ?" Pious Nāga princes like Śaṅkhapāla, Champaka, and Bhūridatta, find it difficult to perform the Sabbath-vow in the midst of the crowds of beauteous nymphs of the Nāgaloka.

By their great charms the Nāgīs are apt to rouse the passion of mortal men. Amorous and matrimonial alliances between representatives of both these classes of beings are often

[1] *Jātaka*, vol. vi, p. 158, l. 15, and p. 194, l. 6.

[2] See below, pp. 118 f.

[3] *M.Bh.*, *Bhīshma-p.*, vi, 51. The Nishadha mountains are the abode of other supernatural beings, such as Gandharvas and Vidyādharas. Cf. *Kathās.*, lxxxvi, 142 and 144 ; Tawney's transl., vol. ii, p. 291. According to *Kathās.*, civ, 80 (Tawney, vol. ii, p. 415), Nishadha is the name of a country in the Himālaya.

[4] *Daddara-jātaka.* Cf. below pp. 137 f.

[5] *Rām.*, *Sundara-k.*, xii, 21.

[6] *Rām.*, *Uttara-k.*, lxxxviii, 14.

[7] *Mahāvastu*, vol. iii, p. 157.

met with in Indian fable. The subject is nothing but a variety of that theme of fairy-tales in favour all over the world : the union between the mortal man and the immortal woman.[1] The Great Epic presents examples in the episode of Arjuna the Pāṇḍava hero and Ulūpī, the nymph of the Ganges, and the story of the ascetic Jaratkāru and his like-named bride, who was the sister of the Serpent-king Vāsuki.[2]

We have seen that Kālidāsa, too, in his *Raghuvaṃśa* has employed the *motif*; here it is Rāma's son and successor, Kuśa, who marries Kumudvatī, the youngest sister of the Nāgarāja Kumuda. Kalhaṇa in his *Rājataraṅgiṇī* has preserved the pretty Kashmirian legend of the love between the Brahmin Viśākha and Chandralekhā, the fair daughter of the Nāga Suśravas.[3] From Buddhist sources, too, we may quote examples. In the introductory chapter of the *Bhūridatta-jātaka*, we are told how a widow of the Nāga tribe wins the love of the exiled prince of Benares. The daughter born of their union, named 'Seaborn', is in her turn wooed by Dhṛitarāshṭra, sovereign lord of all Nāgas. Here we have the far less common *motif* of the superhuman husband and the human wife. It is true that in the present instance the wife is of mixed descent, her mother being a Nāgī, but in the narrative of her matrimony with the Serpent-king she figures entirely as the human bride so that her husband even strives to conceal his real nature from her. Another instance of such a match we find in the *Kathāsaritsāgara* : the poet Guṇāḍhya, the reputed author of the lost *Bṛihatkathā*, we are told, was the son of the Nāga-prince Kīrtisena by a Brāhmaṇī.

The Chinese pilgrim, Hiuen Tsiang, has preserved in his itinerary a local legend[4] of Udyāna, the present Swāt valley, on the north-west frontier of India. A prince of the Śākya clan escapes the massacre of his kinsmen by the fierce Virūḍhaka of Kosala, and seated on a wild goose, he flies through the air and arrives in the borderland of the North-West. Here he meets a Nāga girl with the inevitable result and, after marrying her, his father-in-law presents him with a sword which he uses to kill the king of the country and to take his place. There remained, however, one impediment to his happiness. Every time he went to rest by the side of his wife from her head there appeared the nine-fold Nāga crest. The husband, in disgust, waited till she slept and then cut off the serpent crest with his sword. In consequence the descendants of the royal pair were ever afflicted with headache.

Besides the kings of Udyāna, there were several other royal houses of ancient India which claimed a Nāga or Nāgī as their progenitor. The dynasty of Kashmīr which included

[1] W. Crooke, op. cit., vol. i, p. 45. In the *Paushya-parvan* the *purohita* of King Janemejaya is also said to have been born from a snake-mother.

[2] See below, pp. 74 f. and 59 f. [3] Below, pp. 241 ff. [4] Below, pp. 123 ff.

the famous Lalitāditya (eighth century) among its scions, was asserted to descend from the Nāga Kārkoṭa.[1] In later days the rulers of the neighbouring principality of Bhadarvāh (the 'Bhadrāvakaśa' of the *Rājataraṅgiṇī*) claimed descent from the serpent-king Vāsuki, who is still regarded as the guardian deity of the country, now a district of the Jammu-Kashmir State.[2]

The Rajas of Chutia (or Chhota) Nāgpur derive their origin from the Nāga Puṇḍarīka; in what manner this happened may be briefly related.[3] Puṇḍarīka, as the story says, once assumed the form of a Brahmin and repaired to the house of a certain *guru* at Benares to acquaint himself with the sacred scriptures. The learned instructor was so pleased with his pupil that he gave him to wife his only daughter, the beautiful Pārvatī. Unfortunately, the Nāga even in his human form could not rid himself of his double tongue and his foul breath. He begged his wife not to question him about the meaning of these unpleasant peculiarities, but once while they were making a pilgrimage to Purī she insisted on knowing the truth. He had to gratify her curiosity, but, having done so, he plunged into a pool and vanished from her sight. In the midst of her grief and remorse she gave birth to a child, but instead of rejoicing she prepared for herself a funeral pyre, wishing to become a *satī*.

At this juncture there appeared a Śakadvīpa Brahmin, bearing an idol of the Sun-god. His eyes fell on the new-born babe which was guarded by a huge hooded snake. It was Puṇḍarīka in his natural form. Addressing the Brahmin, he foretold that the child would become the Raja of the country to be called Nāgpur, that the Brahmin was to be his family priest and the idol his tutelaty deity. Then, confiding the child to the Brahmin, he again disappeared into the pool. In commemoration of this event the members of the ruling house of Chutia Nāgpur always wear a head-dress so arranged as to resemble a serpent coiled round with its head protruding over the wearer's brow. The seal of the Mahārāja and arms of the family show as a crest a cobra with a human face under its expanded hood, surrounded by the insignia of royalty.

Another instance of serpent origin is afforded by the ruling house of Maṇipur,[4] a feudatory state situated between Bengal and Burma. The peculiar god of the royal family is a species of snake called Pa-kung-ba, from which the Raja claims descent. When it appears it is coaxed on to a cushion by the priestess in attendance, who then performs certain ceremonies to please it. This snake appears sometimes, they say, of great size;

[1] *Rājat.*, iii, 529, Stein's transl., vol. i, p. 119.

[2] See below, pp. 250 f.

[3] We follow E. T. Dalton, *Descriptive Ethnology of Bengal*, Calcutta, 1872, pp. 165 f. Cf. Fergusson, *Tree and Serpent Worship*, p. 65, and Andrew Lang, *Custom and Myth*, second edition, pp. 80 f.

[4] *Ind. Ant.*, vol. vii, p. 43, and Fergusson, op. cit., p. 64.

when he does so it is indicative of his being displeased. So long as he remains of a diminutive form it is a sign of his being in good humour.

Bastar, the feudatory state in the south-east corner of the Central Provinces, is ruled by a Nāga dynasty, whilst most Gond chiefs in the same province likewise pretend to be descended from the Nāgavaṃśa.[1]

Not only royal and noble houses claim Nāga descent; a certain caste of Kāyasthas, or professional clerks, belonging to Bengal, derive their origin from no less a personage than the serpent-king Vāsuki.[2]

If, now, we turn our attention to Southern India, we find that according to the *Siṃhāsanadvātriṃśikā*, the semi-legendary king Sālivāhana of Pratishṭhāna was the son of the Nāga Ananta, with whose assistance he slew Vikramāditya of Ujjayinī.[3] It is curious that the first Lohara dynasty of Kashmir which derived its origin from Sātavāhana counted among its scions a king of the name of Ananta-deva (A.D. 1028–63).

Nāga descent was also assigned to the famous dynasty of the Pallavas which held sway on the coast of Coromandel from the fourth to the middle of the eighth century of our era. A curious legend preserved in Tamil poetry connects the origin of the Pallavas with the Choḷas, the ancient rulers of Coromandel: it relates that the first 'Toṇḍaiman' (i.e. Pallava) was the son of a Chola king by a female serpent-demon.[4] That this legend is of an early date is apparent from epigraphical records. But, whereas the inscriptions of the Pallavas are unanimous in recognizing Aśvatthāman, the son of the Brahmin warrior Droṇa, as the progenitor of their line, they do not agree with regard to the nature of his spouse and the name of the son born from their union. In the Pallava inscriptions she is called an Apsaras, but a Nāgī in those of the Ganga-Pallavas.[5]

It is curious that in Further India, too, we meet with royal clans which are believed to descend from a Nāgī ancestress. The most illustrious example is supplied by the Hindu or Hinduized dynasty, which in ancient times ruled the Khmer kingdom of Cambodia.[6] The origin of this kingly house was attributed to a Brahmin, named Kauṇḍinya, who first

[1] Auguste Barth, *Œuvres*, vol. i, p. 230.

[2] *J.A.S.B.*, vol. xxxix (1870), part i, p. 220.

[3] Weber, *Indische Studien*, vol. xv, p. 228.

[4] In the ancient Tamil poem *Maṇimegalai* the Nāgī is called Pilivaḷai, the daughter of the Nāga-king Vaḷaivaṇan (Airāvaṇa ?). Cf. Venkayya, *A.S.R.*, for the year 1906–7, pp. 220 f., and *B.E.F.E.O.*, vol. xi (1911), pp. 391 f.

[5] The Rāyakoṭa charter of Skandaśishya, edited by Dr. Hultzsch (*Ep. Ind.*, vol. v, pp. 49 ff.) calls her *dvijihvāṅganā*, a woman of the two-tongued (*alias* serpent) tribe. Another charter issued by Nandivarman III likewise refers to the Nāga ancestress of the Pallavas.

[6] *B.E.F.E.O.*, vol. iv (1904), p. 901, and vol. xi (1911), pp. 391 ff. M. Cœdès has pointed out that the Cambodian legend is in all probability due to Pallava influence.

fixed the site of the capital Bhavapura by throwing a lance which he had received from Aśvatthāman the son of Droṇa. The same Kauṇḍinya married Somā the daughter of the Nāga king, and it was after her that the dynasty became known as Somavaṃśa. In this connexion it is very curious that, according to a tradition recorded by a Chinese author of the thirteenth century, the king of Cambodia each night had carnal intercourse with a Nāgī.

In describing the capital of Cambodia, now represented by the famous ruins of Angkor Thom, that author says [1]: " In the palace there is a tower of gold, on the top of which the king sleeps. All the natives maintain that in this tower there is the spirit of a nine-headed serpent, who is master of the soil of the whole kingdom. It appears every night in the shape of a woman. At first the sovereign sleeps with her. Even the principal wives of the king dare not enter. He comes out in the second watch of the night and then he may sleep with his wives and concubines. If it happens that the spirit of the serpent does not appear, it means that the moment of the king's death has arrived. If the king fails a single night to come, some misfortune is sure to happen."

Finally, we may make mention of a Talaing tradition ascribing the origin of the first king of Thatōn to a dragon (i.e. a Nāga) mother.[2] The Talaings at one time formed a nation or a politically dominant tribe which ruled all Lower Burma from Bassein in the West to Maulmein in the East and away South to Tenasserim. They are now confined to the Thatōn and Amherst districts of Burma and to villages on the Menam and Meklawng rivers in Siam.

In the course of a valuable study,[3] M. J. Przyluski has pointed out that the story of the Nāgī ancestress is widely spread in the Far East. According to this scholar an earlier form of the motif is that of the fish-born princess, to which he ascribes an Austronesian origin.

The great importance of the Nāgas both in Buddhist and in Brahmanical lore is reflected in plastic and pictorial art. The legends show the Nāga sometimes as a mere animal, sometimes as a human creature, but generally human and animal properties are strangely blended. The same is the case with the Nāga as rendered in Indian art. We can in the main distinguish three iconographical types: first, the form of the serpent, usually many-headed; second, the human form universally characterized by means of the polycephalous serpent-hood; third, a combination of the two, the upper part of a human body being combined with the lower half of a snake's coils. Of these three forms, the one

[1] *B.E.F.E.O.*, vol. ii (1902), pp. 144 f.

[2] *J.R.A.S.*, for the year 1918, p. 126.

[3] J. Przyluski, *La princesse à l'odeur de poisson et la Nāgī dans les traditions de l'Asie Orientale, Études asiatiques*, 1925, pp. 322 ff.

last mentioned is comparatively rare; it does occur in Brahmanical sculpture, but in Buddhist art it is hardly ever employed.

The simplest and most primitive form in which the Nāgas appear in Indian art is the serpent form. But just as the gods are distinguished from mere mortals by the plurality of their arms, thus the divine serpents are many-headed. It is a characteristic of the Nāgas often insisted upon in literature. In art the number of heads varies, but is always uneven; it may be three, five, or seven. It cannot be a matter of surprise that a marked preference for the number five exists. In literature, too, the five-headed serpent is often mentioned a simile in the epics likens it to the human arm ending in the hand with its five fingers.[1]

In poetry a hundred or even a thousand heads are sometimes attributed to certain Nāgas (particularly to the World-serpent Śesha), but plastic art for obvious reasons must abstain from visualizing such extravagant numbers.

The Nāga in the semblance of a polycephalous serpent is of frequent occurrence on the earliest Buddhist monuments. The central architrave of the Eastern *toraṇa* of Sānchi[2] bears a well-known relief representing the worship of a sacred tree by forest animals. Now among the beasts of the jungle naturalistically treated we notice a five-headed Nāga side by side with his natural foe, the Garuḍa. On the same eastern gateway of Sānchi we have the scene of the Buddha subduing the venomous dragon in the fire-hut of the Kāśyapa brothers of Uruvilvā.[3] The presence of the Buddha, as is usual in the early school of Central India, is only indicated by a symbol—an empty seat—but the Nāga is plainly shown in the semblance of a five-headed cobra. (Plate IV.)

Among the reliefs of the Bharhut *stūpa*, which are earlier than those of Sānchi by about a century and must belong to the second century B.C., we also meet with this Nāga type, e.g. in a relief showing a five-headed serpent conversing with an ascetic who is seated in front of his hut—perhaps an illustration of the *Maṇikaṇṭha-jātaka*.[4] (Plate IIc.)

This primitive mode of representing the serpent-demon has been preserved up to the present day on the Nāgakals of Southern India which will be dealt with in the concluding chapter of the present volume.

Side by side with the theriomorphic Nāga the earliest monuments know the anthropomorphic Nāga, which, as we shall see, maintains a marked prominence in all the

[1] *Nalopākhyāna*, v, 5.

[2] Fergusson, *Tree- and Serpent worship*, pl. xv, 3.—Grünwedel, *Buddhist Art in India*, pp. 49 f., fig. 26.—A. Foucher, *La porte orientale du Stūpa de Sānchi*, pp. 73 f., fig. 3; *The Beginnings of Buddhist Art*, pp. 107 f., pl. vii, 2.

[3] Fergusson, op. cit., p. 143, pl. xxxii.—Grünwedel, op. cit., p. 62, fig. 35.—Foucher, op. cit., pp. 57 ff., fig. 5; *Beginnings*, pp. 97 f., pl. ix, 1.—V. A. Smith, *History of fine art in India and Ceylon*, fig. 47.

[4] A. Cunningham, *The Stūpa of Bharhut*, pl. xlii, fig. 1.

PLATE II.

(a) Nāgarāja of Bharhut.

(b) Medallion of Bharhut.

(c) Hermit and Nāga of Bharhut.

[To face p. 38

later stages of Buddhist art, not only in India proper, but also in Ceylon, Java, China, and Japan. The characteristic mark which distinguishes the human-shaped serpent-demon is the snake-hood surmounting his head-dress or surrounding his head. The number of snake-heads constituting the hood varies, but, as in the case of the theriomorphic Nāga, it is always uneven and commonly five. The female counterparts of the Nāgas (presumably in token of the inferiority of their sex) usually wear a crest consisting of a single serpent head. Among the archaic demi-gods who guard the gates of the Bharhut *stūpa* there is a Nāgarāja named Chakavāka (Skt. Chakravāka = Anas casarca) in the inscription, who, like his companion-doorkeepers, is standing, with his hands raised in adoration, in an attitude which indicates his devotion to the Buddha.[1] This Nāgarāja was in all probability a godling locally worshipped, his name not being known from elsewhere. He bears a human shape, but as if to remind us of his real nature, there is the five-fold snake-crest surmounting his head-dress. His feet are placed upon a rock in front of which we see a lake or pond full of lotus-flowers and enlivened by various aquatic animals. (Plate II*a*.)

Another Bharhut bas-relief, carved in the shape of a medallion, shows a Nāgarāja accompanied by two female chowrie-bearers. The Nāga is distinguished by the usual five-fold serpent-crest, but here the five snake-heads stand so wide apart as almost to present the appearance of a tree. The two Nāgīs show the hybrid form in which the upper part of a human body ends in the coils of a snake. (Plate II*b*.)

Among the Bharhut reliefs there is one, decorating the Prasenajit pillar, so-called, of the Southern Gate, which is of especial interest for our present subject. (Plate III.) It shows, as an inscription informs us, the Lord Buddha being worshipped by the Nāgarāja Airāvata or Elāpattra.[2] Here, too, the sculptor has abstained from portraying the Buddha, the presence of the Master being symbolized by an empty stone seat at the foot of a sacred tree. The Nāgarāja, on the contrary, is depicted not less than three times in accordance with the synoptic method of illustrating followed by the early school of Central India. First we see him as a five-headed serpent emerge from the lake which forms the background of the relief. Next he appears in a human form with a five-fold serpent-crest and accompanied by two Nāgīs each wearing a single snake-emblem. For the third time the Nāga-king is shown kneeling down in a devout attitude at the side of the stone seat under the tree, which, as we saw, indicates the Buddha's presence. Here, in consequence of a visual error of the sculptor, the crest of five snake-heads issues from the side and not from the back of his turban.

[1] Cunningham, op. cit., pl. xxi; Burgess, *Ancient Monuments*, pl. 24, No. 1.

[2] Cunningham, op. cit., pl. xiv. The inscription reads: *Erapato nāgarāja Bhagavato va[ṃ]date*, meaning "The Nāgarāja Erapata worships the Lord".

It can hardly be doubted that the iconographic type of the human Nāga with his serpent-crest was derived from the more primitive conception of the Nāga as a polycephalous snake. We may compare Egyptian art, in which theriomorphic gods and goddesses were shown in human form but provided with an animal head.

As in the Bharhut sculptures the figures of gods and men are nearly always shown facing, it is impossible to decide in what manner the snake crest was supposed to be attached to the body of the Nāga. It seems, indeed, that on this point opinions were divided. On the one hand the hood, as seems most natural, was thought to issue forth from the neck of the Nāga very much in the same manner as in the case of Ẓaḥḥāk, the wicked Arabian king of Persia, of whom the *Shāh Nāmah* narrates that Ahriman had kissed him on both his shoulders.[1] Consequently there grows a snake from each shoulder and these monsters are daily to be fed with the brains of two men. After a reign of a thousand years the tyrant is slain by Feridun.[1]

In a passage referred to above, the Chinese pilgrim, Hiuen Tsiang, relates the story of a king of Udyāna who had married a Nāga maiden. " Every time he went to rest by her side, from her head came forth the ninefold crest of the Nāga." The way in which the snake-crest is supposed to issue from the neck of the Nāga is illustrated by a Nāga figure seen from the back, which occurs among the frescoes of Ajaṇṭā.[2]

We find also, however, evidence of a different conception. Among the sculptures of Sānchi there are two reliefs which must represent the Nāgarāja Muchilinda sheltering the Buddha.[3] In each case the Nāga is seated in front of a tree and is attended by Nāgīs, all of whom have a single-headed snake at the back of their head. Now it is curious that in one of these two reliefs there is a female shown with her back turned towards the spectator, and, if we may trust the reproduction, it is a complete snake which appears to hang down from her back.

If, now, we turn to the Græco-Buddhist school which flourished in the north-west frontier province Gandhāra during the first centuries of the Christian era, we observe a distinct predilection for the Nāga of human form. It is only in the scene of the fire-spitting dragon of Uruvilvā tamed by the Buddha (of which numerous replicas exist in Gandhāra art) that the former is invariably shown in reptile shape.[4] (Plate IX*b*.) This is, indeed, quite

[1] In the saga of the *Shāh Nāmah*, here summarized, we have a reminiscence of the ancient Iranian myth of the dragon Aẑish Dahaka, which is killed by the hero Thrætaona. The two snakes growing from Ẓaḥḥāk' shoulders recall his original serpent nature.

[2] Grünwedel, op. cit., fig. 20. We have here also a very rare, if not unique, example of a Nāga with a two-fold serpent-crest.

[3] Fergusson, op. cit., pl. xxiv, figs. 1 and 2.

[4] A. Foucher, *L'art gréco-bouddhique du Gandhāra*, vol. i, figs. 224–7.

PLATE III.

ELĀPATTRA WORSHIPPING THE BUDDHA (BHARHUT).

[To face p. 40]

The Conversion of the Kāśyapas (Sānchi).

in accordance with the legend, as preserved in Buddhist literature. The Peshâwar Museum possesses, moreover, a bas-relief from Sahr-i-Bahlol, which according to M. Foucher, represents the Nāga king Elāpattra visiting the Buddha in the Deer Park near Benares. This sculpture shows a five-headed snake in front of the seat on which Buddha sits in the midst of the members of his congregation.[1] (Plate VIII*a*.) For the rest, however, in the numerous scenes relating to the conversion of Nāgas, these spirits of the waters are always portrayed in human form.[2] Usually they are shown issuing half-way from a fountain enclosure, the Nāga king wearing a multiplex snake-crest, whilst his consort has a single snake for an emblem. (Plate IX*a*.) It is curious that in some cases where they are seen in profile they clearly wear a complete snake attached, so it seems, to their head-dress, and curling down their back.[3] We have noticed the same peculiarity in a bas-relief of Sānchi.

A very favourite subject of Græco-Buddhist art refers to the hereditary feud between the Nāgas and Garuḍa.[4] The best-known specimen—the sculpture from Sanghao showing a Nāgī in the clutches of the giant-bird—appears to be an Indian adaptation of a masterpiece of Leochares, representing Ganymede carried off by the eagle of Zeus. In some cases a group of several Nāgas is shown being assailed by Garuḍa, some being seized and others falling prostrate in confusion. (Plate XV*a*, *b*.) It deserves notice that in all these sculptures the Nāga has the appearance of a human being. The plaques representing this subject, of which several specimens are known to exist, must once have formed part of the head-dress of statues in royal attire. The Lahore Museum has recently acquired a Bodhisattva head in which this decorative member has been partially preserved. It is interesting that the device in question, employed in exactly the same fashion, occurs also on a colossal Bodhisattva head from the Kaṅkālī Ṭīlā near Mathurā, now preserved in the Lucknow Museum. It seems highly probable that plaques of this kind wrought in precious metal were actually worn by persons of rank, perhaps not merely as ornaments, but also as a prophylactic against snake bite. We have seen above that the figure of Garuḍa is also found introduced into bracelets.

The country round Mathurā (Muttra), which is now so closely associated with the cult of the shepherd god Kṛishṇa, must once have been a great centre of Nāga worship.[5] A Sanskrit inscription preserved in the Lucknow Museum refers to a local serpent deity,

[1] *A.S.R.* for 1911–12, p. 105, pl. xxxviii, fig. 5.—Foucher, op. cit., vol. ii, p. 29, fig. 317.

[2] A. Foucher, op. cit., vol. i, figs. 194–6, 251, 270–5.

[3] *Ibidem*, figs. 273-5.

[4] Grünwedel, op. cit., pp. 108 ff., fig. 61.—Burgess, *Ancient Monuments*, pl. 113 and 115, fig. 1.—V. A. Smith, *History of Fine Art*, pp. 117 ff., figs. 70 and 70*a*.—Foucher, op. cit., vol. ii, pp. 32 ff., figs. 318–21.—Spooner, *Handbook to the Peshawar Museum*, p. 72.

[5] Cf. the author's paper *Nāga worship in ancient Mathurā* (*A.S.R.* for 1908–9, pp. 159 ff., pl. liii–lv).

named Dadhikarṇa, who appears to have had his own shrine not far from the Buddhist convent founded by King Huvishka in the year 47 of Kanishka's era. The remains of this royal foundation were excavated from the Jamālpur (or Jail) Mound in 1860.

Among the numerous Nāga images recovered in the Mathurā district the most valuable specimen is undoubtedly the inscribed statue from Chhaṛgaon, a village situated 5 miles almost due south of the city of Mathurā. (Plate V.) It is now preserved in the local Museum[1]. The spirited attitude of this image deserves special notice. The Nāga is shown standing with his right arm raised over his head as if ready to strike. The left hand is broken, but probably held a cup in front of the shoulder. The head is surmounted by a seven-headed snake-hood. From the well-preserved inscription incised on the back of the image it appears that it was set up at a water-tank in the fortieth year of the Kushāṇa era during the reign of King Huvishka.

The Chhaṛgaon statue represents the best and possibly one of the earliest specimens of a distinct class of Nāga images, of which numerous examples have come to light in the Mathurā district. (Plate VI*b*.) These icons still receive the worship of the rural population, but under a different name ; they are invariably designated as ' Dau-ji ' (meaning " the elder brother ") or ' Baldeo '.[2] Modern images of Baladeva, which are manufactured in such large numbers at Mathurā and Brindāban, are nothing but imitations of the ancient Nāga figures. How the images of the Nāgas came to be confounded by the villagers with effigies of Baladeva (or Balarāma), the elder brother of Kṛishṇa, it is not difficult to explain. Baladeva is believed to be an incarnation of Śesha, and we shall see that in Sanskrit literature, too, he is sometimes completely identified with his spiritual father, the World-Serpent.

From an iconographical point of view the ancient Nāga images of Mathurā exhibit certain features which deserve to be briefly noted. The hood of serpent-heads, here usually seven in number, assumes the appearance of a circular nimbus round the head of the deity. This development is, no doubt, due to the halo having been introduced by the Græco-Buddhist school as a neçessary adjunct of Buddha and Bodhisattva figures. In most Nāga images from Mathurā it is quite clear that the hood is not conceived as an excrescence springing from the back of the human frame. It forms part of a complete serpent whose coils are plainly visible both at the front and at the back of the sculpture. The artist, therefore, gave expression to the dual nature of the snake-demon by portraying a human being standing in front of a polycephalous serpent.

[1] *Mathura Museum Catalogue*, p. 88, No. C. 13.

[2] Cf. also the image of Balarāma found at Tumain in Gwalior State and reproduced *A.S.R.* for **1918–19**, part i, p. 22, pl. xiii*a*. This sculpture has been assigned to the second or third century A.D.

This mode of rendering the Nāga remained in vogue during the later phases of Indo-Buddhist art. A very fine specimen of a seated Nāga was found on the site of Nālandā in the course of excavations carried out in the cold season of 1920.[1] (Plate XIV.) This Nāga holding a rosary in his right and a vase in his left hand is shown sitting in an easy posture on the coils of a snake, whose windings are also visible on both sides of the figure, whilst a grand hood of seven cobra-heads forms a canopy overshadowing him. This image has been tentatively identified with the Buddhist saint Nāgārjuna, the master of the Mahāyāna. The sculpture, however, presents a type of Nāga images peculiar to the mediaeval art of India,[2] although it would be difficult to point out another specimen of equal artistic merit. In this connexion it is interesting to note that according to the Chinese pilgrims Nālandā was named after a Nāga.[3] Other instances may be quoted of Buddhist sanctuaries such as those of Sārnāth and Sankisa, which were at the same time (perhaps we may say, originally) dedicated to serpent worship.

If now we retrace our steps to the art of Amarāvatī, we find that here, too, the snake-hood surrounds the head of the Nāga in nimbus-like manner, but the treatment is much more graceful than at Mathurā. (Plates VII and X.) The snake-heads, usually seven in number, are shown separated from each other and slightly curved forward so as to form a most artistic headgear. Evidently the artist conceived the hood as being attached to the back or the neck of the serpent-demon. This is plainly visible in the Amarāvatī medallion (now in the British Museum) showing a Nāga king and his retinue worshipping a relic-casket. The Nāga-maidens grouped in varying attitudes around the throne on which the precious casket is placed, are distinguished by a single snake issuing from behind their heads.[4]

The Nāga figures which guard the entrance to the Buddhist sanctuaries of Ceylon are clearly derived from the anthropomorphic type of India proper. The earliest specimen found at Anurādhapura shows a close affinity to the Nāgas of Amarāvatī. The Nāgas of Ruwanwäli Dāgaba, which Mr. Vincent Smith assigns to the early centuries of the Christian era, must belong to a considerably later period.[5]

The same highly artistic treatment of the Nāga figure is met with in Gupta art. One

[1] *Annual Report A.S.I.*, Eastern (now Central) Circle for 1919–20, p. 38, pl. iii*a*.—*A.S.R.* for 1919–20, part i, p. 29, pl. xx*b*.

[2] We may adduce an inscribed Nāga image in the Calcutta Museum and a standing Nāgī from Sānchi (*A.S.R.* for 1912–13, part i, pl. ix*a*).

[3] Hiuen Tsiang, *Si-yu-ki* (transl. Beal), vol. ii, p. 167.—I-tsing, *Les religieux éminents* (transl. Chavannes), p. 93.

[4] Fergusson, op. cit., pl. lxii.—Grünwedel, op. cit., fig. 8.

[5] V. A. Smith, *Hist. of fine art*, p. 88, pl. xxi.—According to Mr. A. M. Hocart, the Nāga shown sub *b*. must belong to the Polonnaruva period, perhaps to the twelfth century A.D.

of the finest specimens known to exist is undoubtedly the beautiful group at Ajaṇṭā.[1] It shows a Nāgarāja, distinguished by a magnificent seven-fold snake-hood, sitting in an easy pose, and attended by his consort, likewise seated, and by a female attendant holding a fly-whisk (Frontispiece).

We may also compare the Gaja-Lakshmī of Cave XIV at Ellora. The goddess is seated on her conventional lotus-throne. The waters beneath are enlivened by some Nāgas issuing from amongst a mass of lotus-plants naturalistically treated ; they hold up treasure-vases which are perhaps meant as a tribute offered to the Goddess of Good Fortune.

Among the famous frescoes of Ajaṇṭā, too, there are several representations of Nāgas, particularly in Cave II. Here we meet with each of the three Nāga types described above ; we have not only the Nāga in his animal shape and the anthropomorphic snake-god canopied by a hood of seven serpent-heads, but also the third type, namely that of the Nāga, the upper part of whose body is human, while the lower part from the hips downwards is purely animal. A beautiful instance of the last-mentioned type is the well-known group of a Nāga and a Nāgī desporting themselves in the waves, from a wall-painting in Cave II.

This third type, which we might call the mermaid type, and which finds a still closer parallel in Hesiod's description of the serpent-goddess Echidna [2] is extremely rare in Indo-Buddhist art. In Brahmanical sculpture, on the contrary, it is not at all uncommon. Sometimes it occurs side by side with the anthropomorphic Nāga. This is, for instance, the case in the huge rock-carving of Māmallapuram (Plate XVIII), which is traditionally known as ' Arjuna's Penance ', but which, according to M. Victor Goloubew represents the Descent of the Gaṅgā.[3] Among the numerous figures which cover the left-hand rock we notice a couple of serpent-demons, shown in their usual human form and wearing a snake-hood. More prominent, however, are the Nāga and the Nāgī which occupy the cleft between the two rocks, and seem to rise from the Nether Regions. They are excellent specimens of the iconographic type in which the man and the reptile are blended into a phantastic being of lifelike appearance. Both carry a hood, which in the case of the male consists of no less than seven cobra-heads, whereas the female has to be content with a

[1] Havell, *The Ideals of Indian Art*, pp. 164 ff., pl. xxiv.—Coomaraswamy, *Viśvakarma*, pl. lxxii.

[2] Hesiod's *Theogonia*, verses 298 f. :

ἥμισυ μὲν νύμφην ἑλικώπιδα καλλιπάρῃον
ἥμισυ δ'αὖτε πέλωρον ὄφιν δεινόν τε μέγαν τε

Cf. E. Küster, *Die Schlange in der griechischen Kunst und Religion*, pp. 89 ff.

[3] Havell, op. cit., pl. xix.—Coomaraswamy, op. cit., pl. lxxiv.—*Ars Asiatica*, vol. iii, pl. xxix–xxxiv.

PLATE V.

(a) Front View. (b) Back.

NĀGA IMAGE OF CHHARGAON.

[To face p. 44

three-fold hood. The wonderful piece of sculpture to which these Nāgas belong is a work of Pallava art, and may be attributed to the seventh century of our era.

Another fine example of the mermaid type occurs on a bas-relief placed in one of the niches of the well-known temple of Deogaṛh in the Jhansi district of the United Provinces. The subject of this remarkable piece of sculpture is undoubtedly the legend of 'the Deliverance of the Lord of elephants' (*Gajendra-moksha*). In this legend, as known from literature, the aquatic monster from whose grasp the elephant is freed by Vishṇu is described as a crocodile. But in the Deogaṛh bas-relief it clearly assumes the shape of a Nāga, combining the human with the serpent form in mermaid fashion, and holding the feet of the elephant caught in the coils of its snake tail. The Nāga is accompanied by a Nāgī of similar appearance, but much smaller in size, both being moreover provided with the usual hood, which in the case of the male Nāga consists of seven cobra-heads.[1]

In the sculptures representing the Varāha or Boar incarnation of Vishṇu, which will be discussed beneath, the world-serpent Śesha and his female satellites are habitually shown in the manner here described, which so well renders the hybrid nature of the Nāga. We wish only to quote the large rock-carving of Udayagiri in Gwalior State.[2]

The type of the snake-tailed Nāga remains a favourite subject in mediaeval art, and is conspicuous on the temples of Orissa. It finds its finest expression in the wonderfully decorative motif of the amorous Nāga couple, the coils of whose serpent-bodies are interlaced in a singularly graceful fashion. Some good specimens may be seen in the Calcutta Museum.[3]

In the various countries of the Far East which have been influenced by Indian civilization we find the Nāga both in literature and in art.[4] As the religious art of China and Japan has largely undergone the influence of Gandhāra, it cannot be a matter of surprise that here the snake-kings are represented as men (in Chinese costume!) with a dragon issuing from the back of their neck. The Leiden Ethnographical Museum possesses a fine Japanese painting representing the Indian sea-god Varuṇa. He wears a crown surmounted by five dragon heads. The emblem is undoubtedly of Indian origin, but the general style of this excellent picture shows nothing Indian.[5]

[1] Burgess, *Ancient Monuments*, pl. 252.—For an inferior replica likewise from Deogaṛh, cf. *A.S.R.* for 1917–18, part i, p. 7, pl. *ib*.

[2] Burgess, op. cit., pl. 216 and 217.

[3] Anderson, *Catalogue*, part ii, p. 308.

[4] M. W. de Visser, "The Dragon in China and Japan," *Proceedings of the Royal Academy of Sciences at Amsterdam*, Philological section, New Series, vol. xiii, Amsterdam, 1913.

[5] The Japanese Varuṇa belongs to a group of twelve (Hindu) gods who are associated with the Zodiac. He is the god of the waters and the guardian of the West.

In the Khmer art of Cambodia, which probably derived its inspiration mostly from Southern and Eastern India, a very pronounced preference is shown for the theriomorphic Nāga. The many-headed serpent is employed as a decorative device in a manner quite unknown in India proper. Let us only quote the pair of enormous snakes, each carried by a row of fifty-four stone giants, which are placed outside the Gate of Victory of Angkor Thom. (Plate XXII.)

In the Isle of Java, on the contrary, it is the human-shaped Nāga which was received with especial favour. On the main monument of the island, the great *stūpa* of Borobudur, the Nāga is invariably shown in its human form (Plates XII and XVI), even in those scenes in which the legend clearly required an animal-shaped creature. The most striking example is the well-known episode of the serpent-king Muchilinda sheltering the Buddha under his hood against the inclemency of the weather. From the Buddhist scriptures it is perfectly clear that Muchilinda, in order to perform his benevolent and pious act, appears as a serpent, whereas only when his services are no longer required he assumes human form.[1] Yet the Hindu-Javanese artist even here adheres to the principle of representing his Nāgas as human beings, their serpent nature being merely indicated by the snake-hood. The way in which this emblem is treated in the ancient art of Java is worthy of note. The snake-heads, usually five and sometimes three in number, and always shown separately, surmount the head-dress in crest-like manner, but never assume the appearance of a halo such as became the fashion on the Indian continent from the time of the Kushāṇa dynasty onwards. The snake-crest of Hindu-Javanese art finds perhaps its nearest parallel in that of the Nāgarāja of Bharhut, and though it may be rash to conclude that the one was directly derived from the other, there is good reason to assume that the type of the anthropomorphic Nāga was introduced into Java at a very early date. It is very curious that in a later stage of Javanese art, when the Hindu influence gradually makes way for the truly Indonesian inspiration, the Nāga in its animal form becomes more and more prominent. A most interesting example is afforded by the so-called Nāga monument of Panataran in Eastern Java, which may be attributed to the middle of the fourteenth century. (Plate XXIII.) It is decorated with nine figures carrying four huge serpents, the heads of which protrude at the four corners of the building. This curious edifice was no shrine dedicated to the worship of the Nāgas, but in all probability served the purpose of a store-house of the temple requisites. In the Isle of Bali such a store-house is called a *kĕhun*.

[1] See below, pp. 102 f.

CHAPTER I

THE NĀGAS IN THE GREAT EPIC

WE should turn our attention in the first place to the opening book of the *Mahābhārata*, called *Ādi-parvan*, which is singularly rich in myths and sagas relating to the Nāgas. They are grouped around the story of the serpent sacrifice instituted by King Janamejaya, the Pāṇḍava ruler of Hastināpura.

Here we meet with the myth of the origin of the Nāgas: they are the sons of Kadrū ('the Tawny One'), who is a personification of the Earth.[1] Her sister Vinatā ('the Bent One'), the goddess of Heaven, became the mother of two sons: Aruṇa, the charioteer of the Sun-god, and Garuḍa, who was appointed to be the carrier of Vishṇu. The enmity between the Nāgas and their cousin, Garuḍa, is a favourite theme in Indian literature and art.

The two sisters, Kadrū and Vinatā, so the story continues, laid a wager, which the former won by fraud. Those of her sons who had refused to be partners in the fraud, the Serpent-Mother cursed; they were to perish in the fire of King Janamejaya's holocaust. The immediate cause of this serpent sacrifice was the violent death of Janamejaya's father, Parikshit, who, while engaged in hunting, had imprudently insulted a Brahmanical ascetic who had taken a vow of silence and consequently gave no answer to the king's questions. Incensed by anger, Parikshit flung a dead snake round the shoulders of the hermit, who, however, remained unmoved. But his youthful son, on learning the insult that had been offered to his aged father, struck the king with his curse; on the seventh day from thence Takshaka, the lord of snakes, was to lead him to the abode of Yama, the god of death. In spite of all precautions taken by the king, the Brahmin's curse took effect. On the seventh day, the sun having almost set, the king ate some fruit in which Takshaka lay hidden in the shape of a little worm. Suddenly the Nāga assumed his real form, enveloped his victim within his coils, and bit him. The burning poison of the dragon caused the palace to be consumed in a blazing fire, and Parikshit fell as if struck by lightning.

It was at the instigation of the Brahmin Uttaṅka that Parikshit's son, Janamejaya,

[1] In other sources the Serpent-mother is called Su-rasā (lit. 'the Well-flavoured One'), a name which likewise must refer to the Earth. She is one of the daughters of Daksha. The snakes as her offspring are called Sauraseya. Cf. *Rām.*, *Sundara-kāṇḍa*, i, 137 ff., and *Vishṇu-Purāṇa* (transl. Wilson), p. 149.

resolved to take revenge on Takshaka for the death of his father. Uttaṅka had a personal grudge against the serpent-king, as is related at length in the *Paushya-parvan*, that remarkable chapter composed in very archaic prose. Takshaka, in the shape of a mendicant, had robbed him of a pair of ear-rings, a present from King Paushya's queen, and when Uttaṅka pursued him and was about to seize him, he re-assumed his own form and vanished through a fissure in the earth. The Nāgaloka, whither Uttaṅka then penetrated with the help of Indra, we find described as a delightful abode abounding in magnificent palaces and pleasure-houses. We may call special attention to the ancient hymn of praise addressed by Uttaṅka to the Nāgas 'that have Airāvata for their king' and which are likened to 'streaming thunderclouds accompanied by lightning and urged by the wind'.

As regards the serpent sacrifice so called, Professor Winternitz, in the course of an able paper,[1] has pointed out that it has the character of a magical incantation. Interesting parallels of such a 'Bannzauber' he quotes from the folklore of the Alps (Tyrol), Denmark, and the Pyrenees. "The recollection of such ancient magical rites," he remarks in conclusion, "has been preserved in the sagas in which we find the power of the sorcerers exaggerated to such an extent that the snakes are conceived as hurling themselves into the magic fire." A mythological interpretation of the serpent sacrifice Professor Winternitz does not admit.

The numerous Nāga stories contained in the *Ādi-parvan* and in the further cantoes of the *Mahābhārata* are given below. As the gigantic poem undoubtedly incorporates elements of varying date, it is evident that the snake sagas too must belong to different periods. In those which may be reckoned among the earlier portions of the Epic, it will be seen that the Nāgas mainly appear in their original serpent character. This is true in particular with regard to the cycle of the serpent sacrifice contained in the *Ādi-parvan*. Here the Nāgas are pre-eminently mordacious serpents, Takshaka, who plays such a prominent part in these legends, being their most typical representative. By his fiery bite a banyan-tree is reduced to ashes. But more powerful than the venomous serpent-demon is the Brahmanical priest skilled in magic and incantations.

In certain cases the Nāga's bite may be beneficial; it acts as an antidote. This we find in an episode from the boyhood of Bhīmasena and in the well-known tale of King Nala who, being possessed by the evil spirit Kali, is freed by the bite of the Nāga Karkoṭaka.

[1] M. Winternitz, *Das Schlangenopfer des Mahābhdrata* in *Festschrift "Kulturgeschichtliches aus der Tierwelt" des Vereins für Volkskunde und Linguistik in Prag zum zwölften Jahrestag seines Bestandes* (Prague, 1905), pp. 68–80.

The Nāgas may assume various forms. Takshaka appears at one time as a naked mendicant, at another as an old Brahmin, and on a third occasion as a little worm. But his proper shape is that of a snake. They may adopt yet other forms besides those of men and beasts. When the disobedient snakes, having been cursed by their mother, held council to frustrate the serpent sacrifice, some of them said: "Let us change ourselves into thunderclouds and quench the sacrificial fire by means of showers of rain." In one of the cantoes in which the battle of Kurukshetra is described, we read of a Nāga Aśvasena (he is the son of Takshaka) who in the shape of an arrow enters the quiver of Karṇa in order to take revenge upon Arjuna.[1]

In one of those cantoes which appear to belong to the younger strata of the Great Epic we meet with a Nāga who vastly differs in character from the venomous serpents of the *Ādi-parvan*. At the conclusion of the largely didactic *Śānti-parvan* there is the story of a wise and virtuous Nāga who lived on the bank of the Gomatī and who was wont to draw the one-wheeled chariot of the Sun-god. It is curious here to find a Nāga in the service of Sūrya, whereas in the ancient myths the Sun is hostile to the Nāgas, whose element is the water, and whose season is the time of the rains. No less surprising is it to find this Nāga, Padmanābha, urging his Brahmin guest to embrace the ascetic life, and himself embodying as it were the priestly ideal of the pious hermit.

It would, however, be rash to infer that the type of the pious Nāga exclusively belongs to a later period of a more advanced culture. In the ancient myths of the *Ādi-parvan* we encounter such a Nāga: it is Śesha, who among the Nāgas is the same as Vibhīshaṇa is among the Rākshasas. When the Nāgas had been cursed by their mother, Kadrū, it was Śesha who secluded himself from his brothers and practised austerities. Then Brahmā granted him a boon and Śesha chose that his mind might ever rejoice in righteousness, tranquillity and asceticism. Pleased with such great devotion, Brahmā enjoined him to carry the earth.

It is quite possible that originally Śesha was a less patient and peaceful creature than he is pictured in the *Mahābhārata*. This we may, perhaps, infer from the way he is mentioned in an earlier text, the *Suparṇādhyāya*,[2] where Śesha is called upon to beat the tops of the mountains. But, unfortunately, the passage in question is not very clear.

The Origin of the Nāga Race [3]

In the Age of the Gods there were two sisters, Kadrū and Vinatā by name exceeding beautiful, who were the fair daughters of Prajāpati. Their husband, the sage Kāsyapa, in his

[1] In *Droṇa-parvan*, lxxxi, 10-11, divine weapons (bow and arrows) appear as two fiery Nāgas.

[2] *Suparṇādhy*, v, 3.—Cf. Jarl Charpentier, *Die Suparṇasage* (1922), pp. 226 f.

[3] *M.Bh.*, *Ādiparvan*, xvi.

contentment, granted each of them a boon. Kadrū chose that she might become the mother of a thousand Nāgas, all of equal splendour, but Vinatā asked for two sons more powerful than those of her sister. In the course of time Kadrū brought forth a thousand eggs and Vinatā two. These eggs were carefully guarded in vessels of liquid, and, when five hundred years had elapsed, the thousand Nāga sons of Kadrū came forth. Then the other sister, not yet seeing her issue appear, grew sore ashamed, and in her longing for offspring she brake one of the two eggs. But the time not being full, the son who was thus born was possessed with only the upper half of his body, the lower part being unformed. (It was Aruṇa who became the charioteer of the Sun-god.) In his wrath, he cursed his mother, and spake: "As, owing to thy greed thou hast made me deformed of body, therefore, O mother, for five hundred years thou shalt become the slave of her with whom thou hast contended." He added that her other son would free her from his curse, if only she would patiently await the time of his birth for another five hundred years. At last her second son was born: the giant-bird Garuḍa, who preys on snakes. As soon as he was born, leaving his mother, he flew up in the sky in order to seize the food which had been ordained for him by the Creator.

THE WAGER OF KADRŪ AND VINATĀ [1]

[After narrating in the next three chapters the well-known myth of the Churning of the Ocean, the poet proceeds to relate in what manner the curse pronounced by Aruṇa over his mother was fulfilled. Among the wonderful things which were produced when the gods and demons churned the ocean was the white horse Uchchaiḥśravas.]

On learning this, Kadrū spake to her sister Vinatā: "Of what colour is the horse Uchchaiḥśravas? good lady, say it quickly." Quoth Vinatā: "White is that king of steeds, or what deemest thou, fair sister? Say thou too his colour and let us lay a wager." Answered Kadrū: "Black-tailed I deem the horse, O sweetly smiling one. Come and bet with me: may she that loses be the slave of her that wins."

Thus, having made this pact, both went home, saying: "We shall see to-morrow." But Kadrū, who wished to play false, gave order to her thousand sons: "Append ye yourselves quickly to that steed in the semblance of tail hairs black as antimony, so that I may not be a slave." Those who refused the snake-mother cursed: "When the Serpent sacrifice of King Janamejaya, the wise son of Pāṇḍu, taketh place, the pure god of fire will consume you." [2] Brahmā, the Creator, hearing the curse pronounced by Kadrū, rejoiced

[1] *M.Bh.*, *Ādi-parvan*, xx–xxiii.

[2] In the Grantha redaction three verses are added, in which the Nāga Kārkoṭaka promises to assist his mother.

together with the hosts of gods. For he saw that the snakes were great in number and that owing to their deadly poison they caused great danger and dismay to other creatures.

He summoned Kāśyapa and spake to him: "Thou must in no manner be wrathful, because those mordacious serpents, swelling with poison, which were generated by thee have been cursed by their mother. For the destruction of the snakes at the sacrifice hath been ordained by Fate from the very beginning." Thus saying, the Creator gave to the great Kāśyapa the knowledge of antidotes against snake poison.

In the meanwhile, those among the Nāgas who were obedient to their mother did as she had bidden them. When at daybreak Kadrū and Vinatā flew over the ocean, they beheld on the further shore the horse Uchchaiḥśravas white-coloured like the rays of the moon, but black-tailed. Thus Kadrū made Vinatā her slave, and the latter, being vanquished by her sister, was sorrow-stricken at her pitiable plight.

The Rape of the Soma by Garuḍa[1]

Once upon a time Kadrū, the mother of the snakes, ordered her sister to carry her to the abode of the Nāgas, situated in the womb of the sea. Vinatā was obliged to obey the command, and Garuḍa, at his mother's bidding, carried the Nāgas thither. But as in his flight he came too close to the sun, the snakes were scorched by the heat and fainted. The snake-mother Kadrū then took refuge with Indra and lauded him as the god of rain, thunder, and lightning, and as the chief among the gods. And the Lord of the fallow steeds, moved by her prayer, overcast the whole sky with masses of dark-coloured thunderclouds, and gave order to the clouds: "Cause ye nectar-like rain to flow." The clouds, flaming with lightning and incessantly roaring in the sky, let loose abundant water. The Nāgas felt the utmost joy, while Indra rained, and with their mother they reached the island of Rāmaṇīyaka.

This island, fashioned by Viśvakarman himself, and surrounded by the waters of the ocean, is covered with forests abounding in sundry flowers and fruits. It is adorned with charming abodes, with lotus-ponds, and heavenly lakes of limpid water. Fanned by pure winds carrying celestial perfumes, it is bedecked with lofty sandal trees which are haunted by birds and bees and pour down a shower of blossoms. The Nāgas, refreshed by the showers of rain and by the dew trickling down from the flowers, rejoiced in this place of delights, but after some time they spake to Garuḍa: "Carry us to some other island exceeding lovely and of pure water, for thou in thy flight seest many lovely lands, O Bird." Garuḍa wondered why he should have to do the bidding of the

[1] *M.Bh.*, *Ādi-parvan*, xxv–xxxiv.

snakes, and his mother told him how she had been deceived by her sister. Then Garuḍa asked the Nāgas: "What am I to bring or to know or what deed of valour am I to accomplish whereby I may be freed from slavery? Speak the truth, ye serpents (lit. lickers)." The Nāgas answered: "Do thou seize the nectar, then thou shalt be freed from slavery, O Bird."

Now Garuḍa was very hungry and asked his mother for food. Vinatā said: "In the womb of the ocean lieth the land of the Nishādas.[1] There thou wilt find thousands of Nishādas. Eat them and fetch the nectar." She warned him not to devour a Brahmin, for a twice-born Brahmin is not to be killed in any manner. Having received the blessing of his mother, Garuḍa stretched out both his wings and flew up in the sky. By the wind of his wings he blew up dense clouds of dust, caused the water of the ocean to dry up, and shook the mountain-rooting trees. The Nishādas, being confused by the wind and the dust, entered his wide-opened beak, and he devoured thousands of them.

After this meal he met his father Kāśyapa, who inquired after his health and asked whether there was plenty for him to eat. Then Garuḍa declared that his hunger was not yet appeased. Kāśyapa told him that in the heaven of the gods there was a lake in which an elephant and a tortoise, both of gigantic size, were fighting each other in consequence of a feud dating from a previous existence. These two animals he might seize and satisfy his hunger therewith. Garuḍa, having received his father's blessing, betook himself to that lake and seized the giant elephant with one talon and the giant-tortoise with the other Then he flew up in the sky and looked round for a place where he might devour them at his ease. Among the many gigantic trees which grow on the shore of the ocean he noticed the *Rauhiṇa*-tree, surpassing them all in size. The *Rauhiṇa*-tree spake to him: "Here I have a large branch 100 leagues in length. Alight thou on this branch and eat thy prey, the elephant and the tortoise." But when Garuḍa touched the branch with his talons it broke. Then he perceived that the Vālakhilyas [2] were clinging to that branch. Afraid of harming these holy men, Garuḍa did not dare to drop the branch of the giant-tree, but seizing it with his beak and holding the elephant and the tortoise in his clutches he flew about. At last his father saw his perplexity and showed him a high mountain where he could safely let down his burden and devour his prey at ease.

The story proceeds to relate at great length in what manner Garuḍa succeeded in winning the Soma after having vanquished the gods, extinguished the fire which

[1] The Nishādas are aborigines living in the Vindhya mountains. According to the Purāṇas, the first Nishāda was born from the thigh of King Vena. This progenitor of the race is described as black, dwarfish in stature, and flat-nosed. Cf. *Vishṇu Purāṇa*, transl. Wilson, pp. 100 f., footnote 4.

[2] A class of ascetics believed to feed on the rays of the sun.

surrounded it, and overcome the two poison-eyed snakes which guarded it. Even Indra, the chief of gods, was not able to withstand him, for when he hurled his terrible weapon, the thunderbolt (*vajra*), at the king of birds, the latter only dropped one of his feathers. Moved by his opponent's valour, Indra offered him a boon and Garuḍa chose that henceforth the Nāgas might become his food. Indra now concluded friendship with Garuḍa and the latter invoked the god's help in order to deceive the Nāgas in his turn. He told the Nāgas that he had brought them the nectar, but that they should bathe and prepare themselves before partaking of the heavenly food. This they did, but as soon as Garuḍa had placed the nectar on a litter of *kuśa* or *darbha* halms, it was seized by Indra, who carried it away to heaven. Thus, Garuḍa had fulfilled his task, and obtained the freedom of his mother and himself. But the snakes, on returning from their bath, found the nectar gone. All they could do was to lick the sharp *kuśa* blades to which some of the precious substance still adhered. The result was that from that day the snakes became double-tongued, and the *kuśa* grass obtained its purifying virtue by its contact with the nectar.

The myth of the rape of the nectar by the eagle which we have summarized above from the *Mahābhārata*, is repeatedly referred to in the hymns of the *Ṛigveda* (esp. iv, 26 and 27). Owing to the incoherent form in which the passages in question have come down to us, it is impossible to say in what exact shape the myth was then known. There is some reason to assume that in its more original form the eagle, like another Prometheus, brought down the *soma* from heaven, not at the request of the snakes, but on behalf of mankind, so that mortal man might use it in his sacrificial rites.

In the Ṛigvedic hymns extolling the winning of the *soma* no mention whatever is made of the story of Kadrū and Vinatā. It may have been in existence independently, but it is not until the period of the *Yajurveda* that it appears in literature, and here we find it combined with the myth of the rape of the *soma*. It will be unnecessary to review the different combined versions occurring in Yajurvedic scriptures, the fullest of which is that of the *Śatapatha-brāhmaṇa* (iii, 6, 2, 2 ff.).[1] Here the story is, of course, told in the dry style peculiar to this class of sacerdotal writings.

Of far greater interest is the rendering (here, too, the two myths are combined) found in an ancient epic poem known as the *Suparṇādhyāya* which must belong to the period of the *Brāhmaṇas* and earlier *Upanishads*. There can be little doubt that the version found in the *Ādi-parvan* of the Great Epic was drawn from this earlier poem in its original form. In the main both these versions closely agree in substance, whereas they greatly differ in form, the *Suparṇādhyāya* being mostly composed in *trishṭubh* stanzas which assume the

[1] Also *Taittirīya-saṃhitā*, vi, 1, 6, 1, and *Kāṭhaka*, xxiii, 10.

character of a dialogue. The contents, too, however, offer a few points of difference which deserve to be noticed.

The two sisters Kadrū and Vinatā (the former is sometimes called Aditi, and the latter Suparṇī, Śaunakī, and Śuṅgā) are identified with earth and heaven. It is said that they had assumed the shape of a female eagle (*suparṇī*) and of a female snake (*nāgī*). At a sacrifice of the gods they commit a fault and Kadrū loses one of her eyes. Hence, she is called " one-eyed " (*kāṇā*). The two sisters marry the sage Tārkshya.[1]

The birth of Aruṇa and Garuḍa is told in the same manner as in the Epic, but no reference is made to the birth of the Nāgas. It is, however, evident that Kadrū is the " Mother of Serpents " (*sarpamātar*). The passage relating to the wager is not very clear. Here, too, mention is made of a white horse and its tail, but no Nāgas come in. As regards the subject proper of the poem, the rape of the nectar, we find a number of guardians of the *soma* mentioned by name—evidently at least some of them Nāgas. Finally, it may be mentioned that the feather dropped by Garuḍa, when struck by Indra's thunderbolt, breaks into three pieces, from which peacocks, two-headed snakes, and mongooses are said to take their origin.

The *Suparṇādhyāya* has been made the subject of exhaustive studies, most recently by the Swedish scholar, Dr. Jarl Charpentier.[2] This author arrives at the conclusion that the story of Kadrū and Vinatā must originally have been an ancient animal saga (" Tiersage "), in which the chief actors were the snake and the eagle, or more correctly the mother of snakes and the mother of eagles who were identified with earth and heaven.[3] These two laid a wager as to which of them could see farthest. If that is so, it may be considered as the earliest specimen of an animal saga preserved in the world's literature.

The story, as Dr. Charpentier points out, belongs to that class of folk-tales which may be called " the wagering animals ", in which generally the animal least likely to win the wager does win it by taking recourse to deceit. The best-known example of such a story is the fable of the race between the hare and the tortoise. In the *Suparṇādhyāya* the two sisters are still described as animal-shaped, whereas in the *Mahābhārata* they have become quite anthropomorphic.

In both these poems we find the story of the snake-mother and the eagle-mother closely connected with the ancient myth of the rape of the nectar by Suparṇa. Thus, the

[1] In classical literature the name Tārkshya is used to indicate Garuḍa.

[2] Jarl Charpentier, *Die Suparṇasage*, Uppsala-Leipzig, 1922. In the course of this study the author deals with the works of previous writers.

[3] This early identification, supported by the names Kadrū (" Tawny ") and Vinatā (" Bent "), has been accepted by most modern scholars. M. Barth, however, in his *Religions of India*, p. 265 (*Œuvres*, vol. i, p. 229), takes Kadrū to be the personified Darkness, which can hardly be correct.

story was extended and the plot laid by the victorious sister was finally frustrated by a counter-plot (*pratimāyā M.Bh.* i, 34, 22), in which the son of the deceived sister was the chief actor. The Nāgas who have assisted their mother Kadrū in deceiving Vinatā are in their turn deluded by Vinatā's son.

In this manner the ancient myth has assumed a moral element which in all probability was originally strange to it. In its epic form it also serves to explain why Garuḍa feeds on the Nāgas. It is a favour bestowed on him by Indra as a reward for his courage, and, besides, the deceit practised by the Nāgas offers sufficient justification.

Incidentally the epic version also accounts for the split appearance of the snake's tongue and thus falls under a widely spread category of folklore which accounts for some conspicuous feature in a certain species of either man, beast, or plant.

The Dutch author, Abraham Roger(ius), in his well-known book [1] on the religion of the Brahmins of the Coromandel Coast gives a version of the ancient myth (perhaps the earliest account of it in a European language), in which not only the split tongue of the snakes is accounted for, but also the white colour of the beak and neck of Garuḍa. This peculiarity, it is said, is due to his having carried the *soma*. It is clear that this additional trait was not invented by Rogerius, but was told him by his Brahmin informants.

In this connexion it should be remembered that in the South of India the Garuḍa of legend is identified with a real bird, the Malabar eagle. "Its body is covered with glossy feathers of a bright chestnut colour ; its head, neck, and breast are whitish." Thus, it is described by the Abbé Dubois.[2] Are we, then, to assume that the Garuḍa of Indian mythology—the giant-bird which covers the sky and eclipses the light of the sun—is a conception ultimately derived from a bird of comparatively small size, and, moreover, of so timid a nature that even a hen defending her chickens can easily put it to flight ? However improbable such an assumption may seem at first sight, it would not be difficult to quote other instances of fabulous and deified animals of equally humble origin. In one respect, at any rate, the Garuḍa of nature agrees with the Garuḍa of legend : it is the deadly enemy of snakes. "It wages perpetual war," the Abbé Dubois says, "upon lizards, rats, and especially snakes. When it espies one of the last-named, it swoops down upon it, seizes it in its talons, carries it up to an enormous height, and then lets it drop. Following swiftly, it picks it up again, killed, of course, by its fall, and flies off with it to some neighbouring tree where it may be devoured at leisure."

[1] Abrahamus Rogerius, *De open-deure tot het verborgen Heydendom*, ed. by W. Caland. The Hague, 1915, pp. 100 ff. The author calls the two sisters 'Kaddrouwa Winneta' and 'Diti' !

[2] Abbé J. A. Dubois, *Hindu manners, customs, and ceremonies*, transl. by H. K. Beauchamp, 2nd ed., Oxford, 1899, pp. 646 f.

The enmity between the Garuḍa and the Nāgas which finds its mythical explanation in the ancient fable of Kadrū and Vinatā, the rival sisters, has provided an inexhaustible theme for Indian story up to the present day. We shall often have occasion to revert to it in these pages.

The great collection of stories, entitled *Kathāsaritsāgara*—a Sanskrit work of a comparatively late date, but said to be based on an early work composed in Prakrit—contains a version of the combined myth in condensed form.[1] It is inserted there in the edifying tale of Jīmūtavāhana, being introduced in order to explain the havoc wrought by Garuḍa in the Nāga world. On the whole, the tale as told by Somadeva agrees in substance with the story of the *Ādi-parvan*. There is, however, one point of difference which deserves to be mentioned. The colour not of the steed Uchchaiḥśravas but of the Sun's horses, is the matter disputed by the two sisters, and Kadrū, bent on winning, "induced her sons, the snakes, to defile the horses of the Sun by spitting venom over them." This trait in itself would not appear to be of much importance, as variations of this kind may easily occur in different redactions of the same story, especially when separated by so vast a space of time as is the case here. But it is very curious that in the old-Javanese version of the *Ādi-parvan* we meet with the same trait that the Nāgas blacken the horse (here Uchchaiḥśravas) by means of their poison.[2]

In this connexion we may mention that the Rape of the Soma by Garuḍa is illustrated in a remarkable series of nine sculptured panels which decorate the back of the Javanese temple Chandi Kĕdaton.[3]

A few words may be added with regard to the curious episode of the elephant and the tortoise which are seized and devoured by the Garuḍa. It has been conjectured that possibly there is some connexion between this episode, which occurs also in the *Suparṇādhyāya*, and the story of the Deliverance of the Lord of Elephants or *Gajendramoksha(ṇa)*, known from later epic literature.[4] It seems, indeed, plausible that the ancient savage folk-tale illustrating the wonderful strength of the giant-bird Garuḍa has developed into an edifying legend, meant to magnify the supreme god Vishṇu.

Near the Trikūṭa, the story runs, there is a large lake, 100,000 *yojanas* in length, wherein lived a crocodile (*graha*), who once seized an elephant, chief of the herd. After having fought for 1,000 divine years, the elephant, being caught in dreadful snares,

[1] *Kathāsaritsāgara*, xxii, 181–201, Tawney's transl., vol. i, pp. 182 f.

[2] *Adiparwa, Oudjavaansch prozageschrift*, uitgeg. door Dr. H. H. Juynboll, The Hague, 1906, p. 35.

[3] These sculptures have been first identified by Dr. Brandes and were subsequently fully discussed by Dr. P. V. van Stein Callenfels. *Oudheidkundig Verslag* for the year, 1921, pp. 21 ff., with four plates illustrating the nine panels.

[4] *Bhāgavata-purāṇa*, viii, ch. 2–3.

recited a *stotra* in honour of Vishṇu. Then the supreme god, mounted on Garuḍa, appeared and rescued the elephant. The elephant and the crocodile were in reality two Gandharvas, Hāhā and Hūhū by name, who had been cursed by the Muni Devala.

The story is illustrated in a sculpture which adorns the northern niche of the famous Gupta temple of Deogaṛh, but it is very curious that the adversary of the 'lord of elephants' adopts here the form of a Nāga with sevenfold snakehood. This Nāga, who shows the usual combination of a human figure and a serpent, has caught the feet of the elephant in his coils, while his hands are folded in adoration. He is accompanied by a Nāgī in the same posture. Evidently they are shown in the act of worshipping the four-armed god Vishṇu whom we notice mounted on Garuḍa and hovering above the two opponents.[1]

The Myth of Śesha the World Serpent[2]

Eldest among the children of Kadrū was the Nāga Śesha who detached himself from his brethren and sought refuge in penance. Brahmā noticed him emaciated by asceticism and wearing the matted hair and bark garment of a recluse. Quoth Brahmā : "What doest thou, Śesha ? By thy hard penance thou causest distress to mankind. Tell me the wish that dwelleth in thy heart." Śesha answered : "My brethren are all slow of understanding, so I cannot endure to stay with them. For this I crave thine approval. Constantly they hate each other like enemies, and they do not suffer Vinatā and her son. Him they loathe, although he is greater in strength owing to the boon conferred by our father, great Kāśyapa. Therefore, I have undertaken these austerities so that, freed from this body, I may not sojourn with them hereafter." Brahmā counselled him not to grieve over the fate of his brothers, and allowed him to choose a boon. Then Śesha spake : "This is the boon which I choose, O grandfather. May my mind ever delight in righteousness, tranquillity and asceticism." Said Brahmā : "I am pleased, Śesha, with thy self-control and peace of mind. But act thou according to my word for the welfare of all creatures. This movable Earth with her rocks and woods, with her seas, villages, groves, and towns, hold her firmly, O Śesha, so that she may be immovable." Śesha consented and the Earth made him an opening, which he entered, in order to support her from beneath. From that time onward Śesha at the command of Brahmā carries the sea-girdled Earth on his head, encompassing her with his endless coils.

[1] Cunningham, *ASR.*, vol. x, p. 107. Burgess, *Ancient Monuments*, pl. 252. For a replica of inferior style also found at Deogaṛh, vide *ASR.* for 1917–18, part i, p. 7, pl. *ib.*

[2] *M.Bh.*, *Ādi-parvan*, xxxvi.

How the Nāgas held Council [1]

It was under the auspices of their King Vāsuki that the Nāgas assembled in order to devise means whereby they might escape the cruel fate awaiting them at the Serpent sacrifice of King Janamejaya. Vāsuki, on opening the proceedings, declared : " For every kind of curse there exists a ' counter-check ' (*pratighāta*), but for those who are cursed by their mother no deliverance can be found anywhere." Yet they must endeavour to prevent the sacrifice from being performed. The counsels put forward by the assembled Nāgas were manifold. Some of them proposed that they might change themselves into Brahmins and beg the king not to allow the sacrifice to take place. Others, proud of their learning, gave advice that, after having assumed the shape of the king's ministers, they might convince him that the intended oblation was fraught with great evil both here and hereafter.

The following expedient also was propounded : " Let one serpent be deputed to bite the high-priest (*upādhyāya*) versed in the ritual of the Serpent sacrifice; for without him the holocaust could not be accomplished. Would it not even be advisable to kill in a similar manner all the priests who know the ritual ? " These suggestions, however, were discarded by the righteous and compassionate among the Nāgas who pointed out that the murder of Brahmins was a course in no case commendable. Then it was proposed that, when the sacrificial fire had been kindled, they might become thunder-clouds and quench the fire by showers of rain. It would also be possible at night to steal the ladles and other sacrificial implements and thus cause an obstacle. Or, peradventure, they could defile the prepared viands. A more violent measure it would be to appear at the sacrifice in hundreds and thousands and bite all present. Another expedient would be to carry off King Janamejaya, while bathing, or kill him by means of a poisonous bite. Were he dead, the root of all evil would be cut off. The last proposed scheme was considered by the Nāgas to be final, but it did not meet with the approval of Vāsuki, who said it would be better to propitiate their father Kāśyapa.

At last the Nāga Elāpatra declared that it was useless to oppose the will of the gods. It had, however, been ordained that there would be an escape from the danger threatening the snakes. Brahmā himself had assured the gods that only the wicked among the Nāgas were to perish ; the righteous among them would be saved through the intervention of Āstīka, the son of the sage Jaratkāru by a Nāga-maiden, likewise named Jaratkāru, the sister of the serpent-king Vāsuki.

This joyful news greatly comforted the assembled Nāgas, and Vāsuki ordered his

[1] *M.Bh.*, *Ādi-parvan*, xxxvii–xxxix.

attendants carefully to watch the sage Jaratkāru so that the serpent-king might offer him his sister in marriage, as soon as the time had come.

The Hermit Jaratkāru and the Snake-maiden Janatkāru [1]

Jaratkāru had adopted the ascetic life, and he wandered over the whole earth, visiting holy places and passing his days in abstinence and chastity, so that he might gain supreme bliss in the world to come.

But one day he beheld some *pitaras* or ancestral spirits hanging, head downwards, above a precipice and clinging to a clump of grass, of which only one halm still remained. And this halm was being gnawed by a rat. When the hermit, moved by compassion at their deplorable plight, questioned these dismal ghosts as to whether he could save them from their imminent fall by offering a portion and even the whole of his *tapas* or ascetic merit, he found to his dismay that they were the spirits of his own ancestors. As he, their only descendant, had adopted the ascetic's life and had chosen to die without offspring, they were threatened with being plunged into Hell, as soon as the oblations due to the Manes should cease. The rat whom he saw gnawing at the bundle of grass, their only support, was all-devouring Time who was about to destroy him too—the last halm on which their deliverance depended. No portion, not even the whole of his *tapas*, could save them. He must take a wife and beget offspring. This was the only means by which their future bliss could be secured.

Jaratkāru consented to their wish. He was willing to take a wife, but he made the condition that the maiden whom he was to marry should bear the same name as he and should be bestowed on him as an alms. Besides, he did not wish to support her. When, after long wanderings, he failed to find a bride on account of his advanced age, in despair he betook himself to the wilderness and called out to all beings, moving and unmoving and invisible, to grant him a maiden whom he could marry on the three conditions stated. The watchful Nāgas heard his lamentation, and reported to their sovereign Vāsuki what they had heard. At once the King of Snakes took his sister, beautifully adorned, and offered her to the old hermit as an alms. On learning that she, too, bore the name of Jaratkāru, and receiving the assurance that after their marriage they were to be supported by her brother, the Sage consented. They entered a room which the Serpent King had prepared for them in his palace. After they had been duly wedded, Jaratkāru warned his wife that, in case she were to give him any cause of displeasure, he would leave her immediately.

The young Nāga-bride, indeed, did all she could to please her irritable old husband. But one evening, while he was sleeping with his head in her lap and the solemn time for the

[1] *M. Bh.*, *Ādi-parvan*, xlv–xlviii. In an abridged form the story is told in xiii–xv.

twilight devotion had come, she knew not what to do. If she roused him from sleep, his anger was sure to be kindled. If she allowed him to sleep on, the time for the twilight devotion would pass. At last she decided to awaken him, but what she had dreaded happened. So greatly incensed was the old hermit that he at once resolved to abandon his newly wedded wife, and to re-assume the ascetic life. Great was the dismay of the Nāga-bride, especially because she had not yet brought forth the son who was to save the serpent-tribe from destruction. What would her brother say, seeing that her husband had left her before this aim of their union had been fulfilled ?

On this point, however, Jaratkāru re-assured her: "There is (*asti*)," he declared, "O fair one, in thy womb a son, resembling the Fire-god, who will be a sage great in righteousness and will master all Vedic lore." Having said this, Jaratkāru went away and again practised severe austerities as before. When the time had come, his Nāga spouse gave birth to a son, resembling a child of the gods, who was to remove the fear of both his father and mother. On account of the parting word of his father, "There is (*asti*)," he became known by the name of Āstīka.

The story of the two Jaratkārus belongs to that well-known type of fairy tales in which, two persons—the one human and the other superhuman—being united in marriage, their union comes to an abrupt end when a condition previously made by one of the two parties is broken by the other. In India the best-known story of this class is the ancient myth of Purūravas and Urvaśī, which can be traced back to the period of the *Ṛigveda*.

From Western literature let us only quote the mediæval folk-tale of the fair Melusyne whom the noble Raymondin met at the "Fontayne of Soyf" and to whom he was wedded on condition that on Saturday he should leave her alone without inquiring into her doings. After some happy years of married life, his suspicion having been roused, he broke his promise and "he sawe Melusyne within the bathe unto her navell in forme of a woman kymbyng her heere, and from the navel downward in lyknes of a grete serpent, the tayll as grete and thykk as a barell and so long it was that she made it to touche oftymes, while that Raymondin beheld her, the rouf of the chambre that was right hye." [1] This description of Melusyne, it will be observed, agrees very closely with the appearance of the snake-maidens of Indian folklore.

Now, it is only natural that generally it is the being of a higher order (either the bridegroom or the bride) who makes the condition. At first sight this does not seem to be the case here, as it is the hermit Jaratkāru who formulates three conditions to which he

[1] *Romances of Chivalry told and illustrated in facsimile*, by John Ashton, popular ed., London, 1890, p. 53.

adds a fourth one at the time when the bride is actually bestowed on him. It should, however, be remembered that in Brahmanical estimation a *Muni* like Jaratkāru, rich in *tapas*, is a person far superior to a simple Nāga girl, whom he condescends to marry. He is, therefore, in a position to impose conditions, and the difference of age counts for little.

The Brahmin Uttaṅka and the Serpent-king Takshaka

[The story of the Brahmin Uttaṅka whom the Serpent-king robbed of the ear-rings which he had begged from the queen as a teacher's fee and who penetrated into the Snake world where he recovered them with the help of Indra and Agni is told twice in the *Mahābhārata.* In the first place it forms part of that remarkable chapter which is known as the *Paushya-parvan*, and which is composed in very archaic prose interspersed with a few verses, its style resembling that of the *Brāhmaṇas.* The other version occurs in the *Áśvamedhika-parvan*, the 14th canto of the Great Epic, and is entirely in verse. The story as given in the *Paushya-parvan* may be summarized first.[1]]

The Brahmin Veda had three disciples ; one of them, Uttaṅka by name, had given abundant proof of a right understanding of his duties towards his master. When Uttaṅka had accomplished the study of the Vedas in the house of his *guru* he wished to go home, and asked his master what fee he might give him for his teaching, so as to go free from debt. The master left the choice of a teacher's fee to his wife and the latter begged Uttaṅka to obtain for her the ear-rings of the queen, the consort of King Paushya, so that she might be able to wear them herself at a religious festival which was to take place on the fourth day.

Having thus been addressed by the teacher's wife, Uttaṅka started out. On his way he saw a bull of exceeding size, and, mounted thereon, a man likewise of exceeding size. This man spoke to Uttaṅka : " O Uttaṅka, eat the ordure of this bull." Uttaṅka first hesitated, but when the giant had told him that his master had done so before, he obeyed the strange command.

The manner in which he obtained the ear-rings from Paushya's queen need not be related here in detail. Let us only mention that the queen, when handing over the ear-rings, warned Uttaṅka to be upon his guard against the serpent-king Takshaka. " The serpent-king Takshaka," she said, " desireth these ear-rings sorely." But Uttaṅka told her not to be uneasy, as Takshaka would not be able to cause him any hurt. Thus taking the ear-rings, he started home.

Now [2] on his way he saw a naked mendicant approaching, at every moment visible

[1] *M.Bh., Ādi-parvan*, iii.

[2] The following portion of the story we render in literal translation.

and again invisible. Then Uttaṅka laid the ear-rings on the ground and proceeded to perform an ablution.

Meanwhile, the mendicant rapidly drew near and, seizing the ear-rings, ran away. Uttaṅka, having performed his ablutions and paid homage to the gods, pursued him with great speed. As the mendicant was not far off Uttaṅka seized him. But on being seized, he abandoned that shape, and, assuming his real shape as Takshaka, suddenly entered a large hole in the earth, and having entered it, he went to his own abode, the World of Snakes. Then Uttaṅka remembered the words of the queen, and he followed Takshaka. He tried to dig out the hole with his stick, but he could not. While he was thus toiling Indra saw him. He, Indra, sent his thunderbolt, saying: "Go thou and offer aid to that Brahmin." Then the thunderbolt entered the stick and split the hole asunder. Uttaṅka followed it through the same hole, and having entered, he beheld the World of Snakes—unbounded, filled with hundreds of palaces, pavilions, turrets and pinnacles, and covered with various places of play and prodigy. There he extolled the Nāgas in these stanzas:—

"They that have Airāvata [1] for their king—the Snakes, shining forth in battle—are like unto thunderclouds impelled by lightning-attended wind. Being fair-shaped and multiform and wearing variegated ear-rings withal, they glow in the upper sky like the Sun—those scions of Airāvata.

"Many are the dwellings of the Nāgas on the northern bank of Gaṅgā: those great serpents, too, that dwell yonder I include in my praise. Who would wish to move in the army of the sunbeams without Airāvata? Eighty-eight hundreds and twenty thousands [in number], the foremost among the Snakes start, when Dhṛitarāshṭra moveth them.

"Whether they creep near him or whether they have gone a far way, I have paid homage to those whose eldest brother is Airāvata.

"That King of Nāgas, Takshaka,[2] whose dwelling was formerly in Kurukshetra and in the Khāṇḍava [Forest] I lauded for the sake of the ear-rings.

"Takshaka and Aśvasena, the two constant companions, dwelled in Kurukshetra along the river Ikshumatī.

[It is] the last-born [brother] of Takshaka, known by the name of Śrutasena, who dwelled in Mahadyuman,[3] desiring the leadership of the Nāgas; to that great one I must ever pay homage."

[1] It appears from *A.V.*, viii, 10, 29, that Airāvata is the patronymic of the Nāgarāja Dhṛitarāshṭra.

[2] Cf. *M.Bh. Ādi-p.*, ccxxvii, 4. "Takshaka, the powerful Nāga king, was not there when the [Khāṇḍava] forest was being burnt, for he had gone to Kurukshetra." Aśvasena is the son of Takshaka. See infra., p. 73.

[3] Said to be the name of a *tīrtha*.

When he, though thus exalting the Nāgas, did not obtain the ear-rings, he beheld two women who were weaving a weft which they had fixed upon a well-woven warp.[1] And in that warp there were black and white threads. And he saw a twelve-spoked wheel which was being turned round by six youths. And he saw a man and a horse beautiful to behold. These all he extolled with the following sacred stanzas :—

> " Here three-hundred-and-sixty are attached to the fixed, yet ever moving wheel of four-and-twenty knots, and six youths turn it round. This multiform warp two women are weaving, while constantly turning the threads black and white, unweariedly turning all creatures and the created worlds. [Hail to Indra] who is the bearer of the thunderbolt and the protector of the world, who hath slain Vṛitra and Namuchi, the great god who donneth his black garments and who severeth truth from untruth in the world, who bestrideth his vehicle—which is the ancient steed Vaiśvānara [2] born from the waters—hail to him, the Lord of Creation, the Lord of the Triple World, the Destroyer of Castles."

Then that man spake to him : " I am pleased with this thy praise. What favour shall I do unto thee ? " He answered : " May the Nāgas come into my power." The man spake to him again : " Blow this horse from behind." Then when the horse was being blown, flames of fire attended with smoke spouted forth from all the openings of his body. Thereby the World of Snakes was filled with dense smoke. Then Takshaka, dismayed and frightened by the heat of the fire, took the ear-rings and, suddenly coming forth from his dwelling, said to Uttaṅka : " Be pleased to take these ear-rings."

Uttaṅka took them from him.

Uttaṅka's further adventures may be briefly related. With the aid of the gods he came back just in time to hand over the ear-rings to his master's wife, so that she might wear them on the festive day. His master then explained to him which personages he had met.

The two women were Dhātar and Vidhātar. The black and white threads which they were weaving were the nights and the days. The twelve-spoked wheel was the year with its three-hundred-and-sixty days, and the six youths who were turning it round were the six seasons. The man was Parjanya, and his horse the Fire-god Agni. The giant whom Uttaṅka had met first was Indra, and the bull on which he was seated was Airāvata, the lord of Nāgas. The ordure of the bull which he had eaten was nectar, and it was owing to the virtue of this food that he had escaped alive from the World of the Snakes.

After having taken leave from his *guru*, Uttaṅka went his way to Hastināpura, the residence of King Janamejaya. Incensed at the vexation caused him by Takshaka, he was

[1] Cf. *R.V.*, i, 164, 48. [2] The fire-god Agni.

resolved to chastise the great Serpent with the aid of the king. He appeared at the court, and in glowing verses he urged Janamejaya to take revenge upon Takshaka. For it was he who by his fiery bite had caused the death of the king's father, Parikshit.

The metrical version of the story of Uttaṅka and the Snakes, which is found in the 14th canto of the *Mahābhārata*,[1] differs in several respects from the older prose version of the *Paushya-parvan*. Here Uttaṅka is said to be a Brahmin of the race of Bhṛigu who has his hermitage in the midst of the Maru desert. Kṛishṇa comes to visit him, and from his guest he craves the favour that at his bidding clouds will appear in the desert and pour down refreshing rain. " Up to this day," the poet says, " such clouds rain in the desert and are known as ' Uttaṅka's clouds ' (*Uttaṅka-megha*)." The story of Uttaṅka's visit to the snake-world is as follows :—

Uttaṅka lived for a very long time in the house of his *guru* Gautama. So great was his obedience that his master did not wish to send him home, as he had done in the case of his other disciples. Uttaṅka himself, in his zeal to serve his master, did not notice that he had become old and grey, until one day he broke down under the burden of a heavy load of fuel which he had fetched for the sacrificial fire. Then he shed hot tears, and when his *guru* asked him the cause of his grief he complained that hundreds and thousands of *brahmachārins* had been allowed to return home. He alone was retained and had grown old in his master's service. Gautama then restored his youth, offered him his daughter in marriage, and gave him leave to go. Uttaṅka now wished to pay his teacher's fee, and Gautama's wife, Ahalyā, being asked, told him to obtain for her the jewelled ear-rings of Queen Madayantī, the consort of King Mitrasaha Saudāsa. Now Saudāsa, in consequence of a curse, had become a cannibal, and when Uttaṅka appeared before him, he welcomed him as his proper food. Uttaṅka, however, proffered his request and promised to return, after he should have obtained the ear-rings. He did obtain the jewelled rings, after the Queen had explained to him their miraculous power and warned him to guard them against Nāgas and other demons who are eager to possess them. The snakes, she said, would seize the jewel when it was put down on the ground.

Uttaṅka started on his journey back to his master's hermitage. He had carefully tied the precious ear-rings in his antelope's hide. Now after some time he became hungry and when he saw a *bilva*-tree laden with fruit, he climbed it and began plucking the fruit, after having hung the antelope's hide on one of the branches. Unfortunately the hide containing the rings fell down. As soon as they touched the ground a snake born from the race of Airāvata seized them and disappeared in an ant-hill. In vain Uttaṅka tried with

[1] *M.Bh.*, *Āśvamedhika-p.*, liii–lviii.

the aid of his stick to dig a way to the snake-world. Thirty-five days he toiled, hot with anger and impatience, until the earth could no longer stand the unbearable shocks, and began to quake violently. Then Indra, mounted on his chariot, came that way and saw him. He took pity on the Brahmin and explained to him that it would be quite useless to attempt to dig a way to the Snake-world, which was at a distance of many thousands of *yojanas*. Uttaṅka answered that, if he did not succeed in penetrating into the Snake-world and get back the ear-rings, he would die on the very spot. Then Indra ordered his thunderbolt to enter the stick, and the earth, split asunder by the strokes of the thunderbolt, opened a way to the World of Snakes. Along that road Uttaṅka entered the Snake-world stretching for many thousands of *yojanas*. It was surrounded with numerous walls made of gold and adorned with jewels and pearls. He saw water-tanks with crystal flights of steps and rivers of pure water. He saw many trees haunted by flocks of various birds ; and he saw the gate of that world which is five *yojanas* in width and a hundred *yojanas* high. But although he had penetrated into the Serpent-world, Uttaṅka was at a loss to know how to recover the stolen ear-rings. Then there appeared a horse which had a tail of black and white hair, a copper-coloured muzzle, and eyes of the same colour that seemed to flame forth in splendour. This horse spake to him : " Blow me from behind, then thou shalt recover the ear-rings which the son of Airāvata will bring thee. Do not feel any disgust in this matter, my son, as thou hast performed the same act in the hermitage of Gautama." Then Uttaṅka learned that the horse was the *guru* of his *guru*, namely the Fire-god Agni, whom he had worshipped in the hermitage of his master and who now on that account was ready to assist him. He did as he had been told. At once flames of fire broke forth from every pore of the steed, and a dense smoke struck terror throughout the serpent world. The snakes, headed by Vāsuki, uttered loud lamentations. Their dwellings obstructed by clouds of smoke became invisible, like woods and mountains shrouded by mist. The snakes, their eyes reddened with smoke, appeared, being tormented by the heat of the fire and wished to know what Uttaṅka desired. They worshipped him with hands joined in adoration, threw themselves down before him, and implored his pardon. And after thus honouring him they brought him the divine ear-rings. Then Uttaṅka, having circumambulated Agni, returned to the hermitage of Gautama and told his master all that had happened to him.

The story of Uttaṅka, as told in the *Āśvamedhika-parvan,* must be a later version than that of the *Paushya-parvan.* It is significant that in this later version Uttaṅka is associated with Kṛishṇa, who reveals himself to him in his divine majesty, as he had done before to Arjuna. It is generally assumed that those passages in which Kṛishṇa is extolled as the supreme deity belong to the final diaskeuasis of the Great Epic. We notice, further, that the part of Uttaṅka's *guru* has here been usurped by Gautama, the husband of Ahalyā. But no reference is made to the legend of Ahalyā's adultery with Indra, which forms an episode of the *Rāmāyaṇa,* and is often alluded to in Brahmanical literature. In the present story Gautama and Ahalyā are represented as a happy couple. It is curious that in the later version of the story, Uttaṅka is brought face to face with the man-eating king Saudāsa, whose story is known from different sources both Brahmanical and Buddhist. It may safely be assumed that this combination of the two tales was an afterthought.

Finally, it should be noticed that in the secondary form of the tale the snake which steals the ear-rings is not Takshaka, but a 'scion of Airāvata'. At the same time Vāsuki is referred to as the chief of the Nāgas.

How King Parikshit was killed by the Nāga Takshaka [1]

Parikshit had succeeded his grandfather, the great Pāṇḍava Arjuna as ruler of Hastināpura, his father Abhimanyu having been killed in the battle of Kurukshetra. Once when the king was hunting the wild boar, the hyaena, and the buffalo in the forests round his capital, it happened that a deer hit by his arrow escaped alive. As this was considered a bad omen, the royal hunter eagerly searched in the jungle for the wounded animal. At last, exhausted and tormented by thirst, he came upon a holy man, Śamīka by name, who was practising asceticism in the wilderness. The king questioned him as to whether he had seen the wounded deer, but the *muni*, having adopted a vow of silence, made no answer. This roused the anger of the king, and, as he happened to see a dead snake lying there, he picked it up with the curved end of his bow and flung it round the neck of the ascetic. The holy man, having completely subdued his passions, paid no heed to the offence, and the king returned to the capital.

Now the *muni* had a son, Śṛiṅgin by name, of a very violent temper and difficult to propitiate. The young man was absent when the incident occurred, but he heard from one of his comrades in what manner his aged father had been insulted by the king. At once he flew into a passion, and, taking water into his hand, he pronounced this terrible curse: "Because that sinful king, despising the twice-born and bringing disgrace upon the race of Kuru, hath hung a dead snake on the shoulders of my aged father while engaged in austerities, therefore the Lord of Snakes, Takshaka, that poisonous serpent filled with magic potency, and urged on by the power of my word, will lead him on the seventh day to the abode of Yama, the god of death."

[1] *M.Bh., Ādi-p.*, xl–xliii. An inferior rendering of the same story is found in *Ādi-p.*, xlix–l. In the *Bhāgavata* i, xviii, 24–50, the first portion of the saga is related, but here Parikshit has become a devout Vaishṇava. For a modern version current in the folklore of Central India, cf. *Ind. Ant.*, vol. xxviii (1899), pp. 193 ff.

When Śriṅgin told his father, in what terrible manner he had taken revenge for the insult offered by the king, the aged ascetic rebuked his son for his rashness. As, however, the word of a Brahmin is never spoken in vain, the curse pronounced could not be revoked. All that could be done was to warn the king of the danger which threatened him. The aged ascetic dispatched one of his disciples, Gauramukha by name, to Hāstinapura. On hearing the evil-boding message King Parikshit was not a little alarmed, but the consciousness of the sin committed caused him greater torment than the prospect of his imminent death. When Gauramukha had gone he held council with his ministers and devised all possible means for his own safety. He caused a palace to be built resting on one pillar, and, seated therein, he discharged his kingly duties. Physicians and Brahmins versed in spells were in attendance, and healing herbs were held in readiness. Careful watch was kept, so that not even the wind could enter the King's abode.

When the seventh day had come, the Sage Kāśyapa started on his way to minister unto the king. He had heard that on that day Takshaka would lead the king to the abode of Yama, and he wished to heal him, when bitten by the Lord of Snakes, so as to gain both merit and wealth. On the way he was met by Takshaka, who, having assumed the shape of an old Brahmin, asked him whither he was going and what he wished to do. Said Kāśyapa : " Takshaka, chief among serpents, will to-day burn by his fire King Parikshit, sprung of the race of Kuru. I go quickly, my friend, to heal him, when bitten by that Lord of Snakes, whose fire is like unto that of Agni." Then Takshaka said : " I am that Takshaka, O Brahmin, I shall burn the Ruler of the Earth. Turn back, for thou canst not heal whatsoever hath been bitten by me." Kāśyapa answered : " I shall heal the King, when he hath been bitten by thee ; such is my purpose, strengthened by the power of my knowledge." [1]

Takshaka spake : " If thou hast power to heal that which hath been bitten by me, then quicken this tree bitten by me, O Kāśyapa. Show the uttermost power of thy spells and exert thyself : this banyan-tree I shall bite before thine eyes, O best of twice-born." Quoth Kāśyapa : " O Lord of Snakes, bite this tree, if such be thy desire. I shall quicken it, when bitten by thee, O Serpent."

Then Takshaka bit the banyan-tree, and the tree, bitten by the snake and pervaded by his poison, flamed up on every side. Again the Lord of Snakes challenged the Brahmin to revive the tree, which had been turned into ashes. But Kāśyapa gathered the ashes into a heap. First he produced a sprout, then two leaves, then twigs and branches, and thus

[1] As has been mentioned before, Brahmā has endowed Kaśyapa, the progenitor of the *gotra* of the Kāśyapas, with the knowledge of antidotes against snake-poison (*vishaharī vidyā*). Cf. supra, p. 51.

brought the whole tree back to life. Said Takshaka: "No great marvel is it that thou, O best among twice-born, canst destroy the poison of me and my kind. Desirous of what profit doest thou go thither? Whatsoever fruit thou wishest to win from that best of princes, I shall give thee that fruit, however difficult to attain. As the King hath been overwhelmed by a Brahmin's curse, and the days of his life are exhausted, therefore O priest, the success of thy exertions is doubtful. Yea, thy shining glory, which is renowned in the three worlds, will be darkened like the hot-rayed sun, bereft of its splendour." Then Kāśyapa made answer: "Desirous of wealth I go thither; do thou give it to me, O Serpent. Then I will turn back, having obtained it as my own substance." Said Takshaka: "As much wealth as thou desirest from the king, and even more than that, I will give thee. Turn back, O best of Brahmins." Then Kāśyapa, recognizing through his divine insight that the king's span of life was at its end, turned back, and Takshaka pursued his journey to Hāstinapura.

On the way he learned that the king was being protected by means of poison-killing spells and charms. So it was necessary for him to use a stratagem. He caused some of his Nāgas to assume the appearance of hermits and charged them in that semblance to go to the royal court and offer fruit, water, and *darbha* grass to the king. King Parikshit graciously accepted the gift, and, after the feigned ascetics had been dismissed, he spake to his assembled ministers and friends: "Now eat with me these sweet fruits which have been brought by the hermits." Then, urged on by Fate and by the word of the *muni*, he began to eat the fruits. Now in the fruit which the king himself had taken there was a little worm black-eyed and copper-coloured. The king took it, and, addressing his ministers, he spake: "The sun is setting; now there is for me no fear of poison. May the word of the *muni* become true and let this worm, having become Takshaka in name, bite me. Thereby, forsooth, I shall have escaped the curse." Thus speaking and applying the worm to his neck, he laughed loud, bereft of his senses at the approach of Death. Even while he still laughed, the King was seized by Takshaka—for it was he who was concealed in the fruit. Takshaka, the Lord of Snakes, enveloped the king in his coils, and, roaring with a mighty sound, he bit the ruler of the earth. Seeing the king encircled by the Nāga, and hearing that awful sound, the ministers, in utter dismay, wailed loud and fled in all directions. Seized with terror, they saw the prodigious Nāga, the King of Serpents, moving through the air and drawing, as it were, a red line in the sky. The house, being enveloped by the fire which was produced by the poison of the Serpent, broke forth in flames and the King fell, as if stricken by lightning.

The Serpent Sacrifice [1]

When King Janamejaya had learnt from his ministers the ghastly tale of his father's death he resolved to take revenge upon Takshaka and his tribe. He vowed that he would celebrate a serpent sacrifice, and inquired from his priests whether they knew any rite by which Takshaka could be compelled to throw himself in the sacrificial fire. The Brahmins answered him that they did know the rites of the serpent sacrifice which of old had been instituted by the gods for the sake of the king himself and which could be performed by him alone. Then King Janamejaya deemed his revenge certain, and ordered the sacrificial implements to be brought.

The priests, after measuring off the place for sacrifice as prescribed in the ritual, consecrated the king so that he might gain the desired object of the oblation. But while the *sūtradhāra* was preparing the place of sacrifice, he noticed certain signs which betokened that the great rite would not be brought to an end owing to the interference by a Brahmin. The King, therefore, issued strict orders to the doorkeeper that on no account was any unknown person to be admitted. Now the priests proceeded to perform the rites of the serpent sacrifice, and, when they had kindled the sacrificial fire, the snakes were seized with terror. Compelled by the powerful spell, the serpents came from every side, quivering and hissing and curling round one another with head and tail, and hurled themselves into the blazing flames. They were white, black, and dark blue, old and young, and they produced sounds of various kinds. Some were a mile in length, others not larger than a cow's ear. Some were swift like steeds, and others huge-bodied like unto elephants. In hundreds and thousands, in myriads and millions, they were drawn irresistibly towards the fire, in which they found a certain death. Thus the curse pronounced upon her disobedient sons by Kadrū, the Mother of Snakes, was fulfilled.

Now Takshaka, as soon as he learnt that King Janamejaya had been consecrated for the sacrifice, had sought shelter in the abode of Indra. He entreated the chief of the gods to afford him protection and to save him from destruction. Indra spake to him : "Thou needest not be afraid, O Takshaka, Lord of Snakes, of this serpent sacrifice. Brahmā hath been propitiated by me before on thy behalf ; therefore thou needest not fear. Dispel the fever from thy mind."

Thus comforted, the best of snakes dwelt joyfully in the abode of Indra. But the Serpent King Vāsuki was seized with dismay and grief, when he saw his retinue steadily waning, as the Nāgas were tumbling incessantly into the sacrificial flames. Fear fell upon him, and with trembling heart he spoke to his sister : " My limbs, O fair one, are burning,

[1] *M.Bh.*, *Ādi-p.*, xlix–lviii.

and I distinguish no longer the regions of the sky. I sink under the burden of bewilderment and my heart quaketh. My sight wandereth sorely and my heart is torn asunder. Now, truly, shall I too fall unwillingly into the blazing fire. For this sacrifice of Parikshit's son is held because the King strives after our destruction. Surely I, too, shall have to go to the abode of the Lord of the Dead. Now the occasion hath come wherefore thou, my sister, hast been betrothed by me to Jaratkāru. Save us and our kin. Āstīka, indeed, O thou best among serpent-dames, will ward off this holocaust. So Brahmā himself hath told me. Therefore, beloved sister, speak thou to thy dear son, who, though young in years, is honoured by the aged, and entreat him, who knoweth the Veda well, for the deliverance of me and my servants."

Then Jaratkāru, the sister of the serpent king, summoned her son and told him how Kadrū had cursed her children, and how she herself had been given in marriage to the hermit Jaratkāru so that her son born from their union might save the Nāgas from dire destruction. This Brahmā himself had declared when, after the churning of the ocean, Vāsuki had begged the gods for their protection as a reward for his help in the winning of the nectar. Thus called upon now to fulfil that purpose of her marriage, her son, Āstīka, at once consented. He went to his maternal uncle and, imparting to him, as it were, new life, he spake to him : "" I shall save thee, O Vāsuki, Chief of Serpents, from that curse, O great being. It is the truth that I am speaking to thee. Be thou of good comfort, O Nāga ; for thou needest not be afraid. I shall strive, O king, that thou mayest gain bliss. My voice hath never uttered an untruth, even when I have spoken without restraint, far less in serious matters. I shall go to King Janamejaya, who hath been consecrated for the sacrifice, and I shall propitiate him with auspicious words, O my uncle, so that the sacrifice of the king may cease. Put thy faith wholly in me, O Lord of Snakes, great in understanding ; thy mind will not be disappointed in me." In this manner Āstīka comforted his uncle, while taking on himself the fever of his heart. Then he went quickly and reached the place of Janamejaya's great sacrifice, which was full of priests, resembling the sun in splendour. But when he wished to enter he was kept back by the doorkeepers. Then Āstīka extolled the king of unbounded glory, he lauded the sacrificing priests and the other Brahmins who were present, and, last of all, he praised Agni, the god of Fire. King Janamejaya he extolled above all the ancient rulers of the earth who had made themselves famous by their hecatombs.

Highly pleased by Āstīka's praise, the king spake to the assembled Brahmins: " Although a youth, this one speaketh like an old man ; not a youth, but an old man he is deemed by me. I wish to give him a boon ; concede it to me, O ye priests." But the sacrificing priests declared that a Brahmin, though he be young, must indeed be honoured by kings, yet first of all Takshaka must be compelled to approach the fire. When they informed the king that Takshaka had sought shelter in the abode of Indra, and that the god had promised him protection, Janamejaya, incensed in wrath, urged them to cause not only Takshaka but Indra himself to fall in the sacrificial fire. Induced by the royal word, the sacrificers exerted themselves to the utmost and used their most powerful spells. Then Indra himself, mounted on his celestial chariot, appeared in the sky, praised by all the gods and followed by thunderclouds and by spirits of the air and hosts of heavenly nymphs. Takshaka had concealed himself within the folds of Indra's mantle, and trembled with fear. The priests again cited the Nāga by means of their powerful charms. Even Indra, seeing that holocaust, was seized by terror, and, leaving Takshaka to his fate, he returned to his celestial abode. When Indra had gone, Takshaka senseless with fear, was drawn irresistibly by the power of the *mantras* towards the blazing flames.

The priests spake to the king: "Here cometh Takshaka speedily into thy power, O king. The mighty roar is heard of him roaring with terrifying sound. Abandoned by the Bearer of the Thunderbolt, verily the Nāga tumbleth from the celestial vault, his body dropping by the magic spells. Whirling through the air, he cometh bereft of his senses, the Lord of Snakes, hissing his violent hissings."

Now King Janamejaya, deeming his aim fulfilled, spake to Āstīka: "O worthy youth, I grant thee a boon deserving of thy unbounded greatness. Choose, and whatsoever wish there dwelleth in thy heart I will give it thee, even though it were ungivable." Then, at the very moment when Takshaka was about to fall in the fire, Āstīka answered: "If thou givest me a boon, it is this I choose, O Janamejaya. Let this thy sacrifice cease, and may the snakes be saved." Upon these words the son of Parikshit, not overpleased, said to Āstīka: "Gold, silver, and kine and whatsoever else thou likest, let me give thee that as a boon, O priest, but let not my sacrifice cease." Āstīka answered: "Gold, silver, and kine I do not choose from thee, O king. May this thy sacrifice cease: hail to the race of our mother." In vain the king endeavoured to persuade Āstīka to choose some other boon, until at last the assembled priests advised the King: "Let the Brahmin attain his wish." Thus Takshaka was saved.

[Āstīka obtained as a boon from the Nāgas that the recital of his story shall free men from the danger of snakes.]

How the Boy Bhīmasena was Healed of Poison by the Nāgas[1]

After the five sons of Pāṇḍu had received the sacraments prescribed by the Veda, they grew up in their ancestral home together with the sons of Dhṛitarāshṭra. When

[1] *M.Bh.*, *Ādi-p.*, cxxviii, 14–cxxix.

playing with their cousins they excelled in all boyish games. In running, seizing a prize, eating and wrestling, Bhīmasena, the second of the five brothers, overcame all the sons of Dhṛitarāshṭra. With little effort he alone gained the mastery over them all. He seized them by the hair, and pulling them down by force, he dragged them along the ground so that they screamed as their knees, heads, and shoulders were bruised. When they were bathing he clasped his arms round ten boys at the same time, and plunging into the water kept them under, not letting them go until they were almost dead. When they had climbed a tree to pluck the fruit Bhīmasena kicked the tree so violently that it shook and the frightened boys came tumbling down together with the fruit. In their sports and exercises they could never overcome "Wolf-belly". Thus contending with his cousins, Bhīma acted not in malice, but Duryodhana, the eldest son of Dhṛitarāshṭra, on seeing Bhīmasena's irresistible strength, showed his evil mind. In his infatuation and greed of power he conceived the thought: "This 'Wolf-belly', the middle-born son of Kuntī, who standeth first in strength, must be overcome by deceit. As long as he liveth and is in possession of his great strength and courage he alone contendeth with us all. Now when he is asleep in the urban garden we will throw him into the Ganges. Then after laying hands upon his younger brother and upon the first-born Yudhishṭhira and throwing them into custody, I shall rule the earth."

Having thus resolved, the evil Duryodhana constantly looked for an opportunity to foil the noble Bhīma. In a garden on the bank of the Gaṅgā he caused beautiful pavilions and tents to be erected, and had all kinds of dainty food prepared by skilled cooks. Then he invited his cousins to amuse themselves with "water-sport" together with his brothers at that delightful spot. Yudhishṭhira accepted the invitation, and both Kauravas and Pāṇḍavas drove out from the city mounted on chariots and elephants. Having reached the garden they disported themselves in the shade of the blossoming trees and in the water. But while they were partaking of the food which had been prepared for them, the evil-minded Duryodhana, "having nectar in his tongue but a dagger in his heart," stealthily threw *kālakūṭa* poison in the meat which he himself served up for Bhīma. The latter, being without any suspicion, took the food, and Duryodhana, that basest of men, inwardly laughing, deemed his object attained. At the end of the day, when they were tired of their sports, they all went to sleep. But the powerful Bhīma, who had exerted himself more than the others and was overcome by fatigue, fell asleep in a pavilion built over the bank of the river, where he could enjoy the fresh wind. Now his body, which was pervaded by the poison, became stiff and motionless like a corpse. Then Duryodhana bound him with bonds made of creepers and dropped him into the river. Being insensible, the son of Pāṇḍu sank to the bottom of the water, where he came down heavily in the abode of the Nāgas, threatening to crush the little Nāga children. Then a number of very venomous Nāgas gathered and bit Bhīma violently with their large poison-clotted fangs. But when he was bitten by them, the *kālakūṭa*-poison, being vegetable, was killed by the serpent's poison, being animal (*sthāvaraṃ jaṅgamena*).[1] The fangs of those snakes, even where they bit the vital parts, did not pierce his skin, so massive was that broad-chested youth. Then the son of Kuntī woke up, tore his fetters asunder, and smote the snakes so that several were killed. Those that escaped repaired to Vāsuki, and spake to the King of Snakes, who equals Indra : " That man, O Lord of Nāgas, having been bound, was cast into the water, and it seemeth to us that he must have drunk poison. We found him insensible, but as soon as he had been bitten by us he woke up, and, having recovered consciousness, he tore his fetters and smote us. Thou must know this man of long arms." Then Vāsuki, followed by the Nāgas, went and saw the long-armed Bhīma of terrible prowess. Āryaka, too, the great-grandfather[2] of Pṛithā (Kuntī) saw him, and, recognizing him as the daughter's son of his daughter's son, he embraced him and pressed him to his bosom. Then the Lord of Nāgas, the glorious Vāsuki, was well pleased and spake to Āryaka : " What favour shall I do unto him ? Shall I give him great wealth, a multitude of jewels and other riches ? " But the Nāga answered : " What boots him a multitude of wealth ? Let the boy drink elixir from the cup which containeth the strength of a thousand Nāgas. Give him as much as he can drink." Vāsuki consented, and Bhīma, seated facing east, drank the elixir under the benediction of the Nāgas. He quaffed the cup in one draught, the powerful son of Pāṇḍu, and in the same manner he quaffed eight cups more. Then the long-armed Bhīmasena rested on a divine couch of ivory provided by the Nāgas, and took his ease, that Tamer-of-his-Foes.

On the eighth day the son of Pāṇḍu awoke from his sleep, the elixir having been completely digested, so that now he was possessed of immeasurable strength. The snakes carefully waited upon him and spake to him : " As thou, long-armed hero, hast drunk the powerful elixir, therefore thou art now possessed of the strength of a myriad of Nāgas and wilt be irresistible in battle. Go thou now to thy house, having bathed in celestial water. Thy brothers suffer pain without thee, O Bull among the Kurus." Then he bathed, the long-armed hero, and put on white garments and a wreath, and after performing in the abode of the Nāga auspicious rites, become great of strength by means of poison-killing herbs of exquisite fragrance, he partook of most excellent viands given by the Nāgas. Honoured by the Snakes and hailed with benedictions, the hero, bedecked with celestial ornaments,

[1] Cf. Suśruta, *Āyurveda* (Calcutta, 1835–6), vol. ii, p. 251, l. 10 ; *sthāvaraṃ jaṅgamaṃ caiva dvividhaṃ viṣam ucyate.*

[2] It is not clear whether Āryaka is supposed to be Kuntī's grandfather or great-grandfather.

took leave of the Nāga, and with joyful mind departed from the World of Serpents (*Nāgaloka*)—that Tamer-of-his-Foes. Being thrown up from the water by the Nāga, the lotus-eyed son of Pāṇḍu was placed again in the same woodland and the Nāgas disappeared before his eyes.

Then Bhīmasena returned to his home, where he was received with great joy by his mother and his brothers, who had suffered great anxiety on his account. When afterwards his malicious cousin tried again to poison him by means of *kālakūṭa* poison, it had no effect whatsoever on him and he absorbed it without harm.

Arjuna and Ulūpī [1]

When the long-armed Arjuna, the glory of the Kauravas, went forth, he was followed by many great Brahmins versed in the knowledge of the Veda, by mendicants and other holy men. Attended by these and many other companions, the son of Pāṇḍu went forth like Indra surrounded by the Maruts. He saw beauteous woods and lakes and rivers and seas and countries and holy places of pilgrimage. Thus he reached Gaṅgādvāra and there he made his halting-place. Now listen to the wonderful deed that the best of the Pāṇḍus there accomplished, he the pure of heart. While the son of Kuntī and the Brahmins were halting there, the priests proceeded to offer up the fire-sacrifice. When the sacrificial fires had been kindled and were blazing on both river-banks, Gaṅgādvāra was rendered exceeding beautiful by that throng of virtuous and holy men, who were piously making their ablutions. Arjuna, that Bull among the Pāṇḍavas, also descended to the River Ganges. When, after performing his ablutions and satisfying the ancestral spirits, he wished to come up from the water and to perform the fire-sacrifice, the long-armed hero was drawn away into the water by the Nāga king's daughter Ulūpī, moved by love. There in the highly praised abode of the Nāga Kauravaya, the devout son of Pāṇḍu saw a fire. There he accomplished the sacrifice, Arjuna the son of Kuntī, and the Fire-god, being worshipped by him with sacrifice undauntedly, was pleased. After having accomplished the fire-sacrifice, the son of Kuntī turned to the daughter of the Nāga king and spake, almost laughing: "What rashness is this, O shy one, which thou hast done, O fair one? And what country is this, O thou of good fortune, and who art thou and whose daughter?" Ulūpī answered: "Born in the race of Airāvata is the Serpent, highty Kauravya. Of him I am the daughter,[2] O king, a serpent-maiden Ulūpī by name. When I saw thee, O Tiger among men, come down to the river for thy ablutions, I became moved by Kandarpa, the god of love. Me, pining with love for thy sake, O son of Kuru, and not wishing any

[1] *M.Bh.*, *Ādi-p.*, ccxiv.

[2] Elsewhere (*Virāṭa-p.*, ii, 14) Ulūpī is called the sister of Vāsuki.

other man, thou must now make glad by giving thyself to me, O guiltless one." Said Arjuna: "The King of Justice (Yudhishṭhira) hath enjoined upon me to practise chastity during a period of twelve years, and I am not my own master. Yet I am anxious to fulfil thy wish, O creature of the waters. No untruth whatsoever hath ever been spoken by me at any time. Let me then act in such manner, O Serpent-maid, that I may speak no untruth and yet fulfil thy wish, and at the same time not neglect my duty." Ulūpī said: "I know why thou wanderest over the earth and why thy elder brother hath enjoined thee to practise this life of chastity. When you married the daughter of Drupada you made a pact that whosoever of you should visit her while belonging to another should be condemned to practise chastity in the wilderness for twelve years. Thou hast, therefore, been banished for the sake of Draupadī and thou hast acted righteously. But thou must also protect the afflicted, O long-eyed one, and in protecting me thou actest righteously. For it is right that thou shouldst save my life by answering my love. If thou refusest my love, thou wilt cause my death. By granting me life, O long-armed one, thou wilt practise the highest righteousness. I have turned towards thee for protection, O best of men, for thou ever givest shelter to the distressed and helpless. Now I came for protection and I cease not to weep for grief. Out of love I entreat thee: fulfil then my wish and grant my desire by giving thyself to me."

Thus addressed by the daughter of the Lord of Serpents, the son of Kuntī, for the sake of righteousness, did as she bade him. The glorious hero spent that night in the abode of the Nāga, and, when the sun had risen, he left the palace of Kauravya; and when he had returned with her to Gaṅgādvāra, the good Ulūpī left him and went to her own dwelling, after bestowing upon him a gift, that he should always be invincible in the water, and all creatures of the water should be in his power.

In the *Bhīshma-parvan* [1] it is related that Arjuna had a son, Irāvant, born from the daughter-in-law of the Nāgarāja.[2]

Being without offspring, she had been given by Airāvata (to Arjuna ?), her [first] husband having been killed by Suparṇa. Arjuna took her for his wife, as she was overpowered by love. Thus Arjuna's son was born *parakshetre*. This son grew up in the Nāgaloka guarded by his mother, but was rejected by his maternal uncle [3] out of hostility towards his father Arjuna. He went to Indraloka on learning that Arjuna was

[1] *M.Bh.*, *Bhīshma-p.*, xc.

[2] The Comm. says that the Nāgarāja is Airāvata. But *Ādi-p.*, ccxiv, 18, she calls herself the daughter of Kauravya, who is born in the race of Airāvata. Cf. also *Āśvam-p.*, lxxxi, 23.

[3] The Comm. says that this *pitṛivya* is Aśvasena, but Jacobi in his Index (s. Ulūpī) calls her "Witwe Aśvasena's". Aśvasena is mentioned in the *Paushya-parvan* as the son of Takshaka.

there. There he saluted his father and made himself known: "I am Irāvant, may it please thee; I am thy son, O Lord." Arjuna embraced his son and led him into Indra's palace. He asked Irāvant to render him assistance at the time of battle, and Irāvant consented. Therefore he appeared at Kurukshetra.

After having shown great prowess, he was killed by the Rākshasa, Alambusha Ārshyaśṛiṅgi. Both used *māyā*. Irāvant was surrounded by Nāgas, the race of his mother. He himself assumed the shape of the serpent Ananta. But Alambusha assumed the shape of a Suparṇa and devoured the Nāgas. Then he slew Irāvant with the sword. His head with diadem and ear-rings fell.

In the *Āśvamedhika-parvan*,[1] the Serpent-daughter Ulūpī again appears.

Arjuna had a son, named Babhruvāhana, by Chitrāṅgadā the daughter of Chitravāhana. After her father's death, he succeeded him as king of Maṇipūra. Now, when Yudhishṭhira had resolved to perform a horse-sacrifice or *aśvamedha* and Arjuna at the head of an army was following the sacrificial horse, he happened to come to Maṇipūra. As soon as Babhruvāhana learnt that his father had arrived, he came to meet him courteously. But Arjuna taunted him, saying that he showed great ignorance of the laws of chivalry (*kshatradharma*), as he received his father thus meekly, where he ought to have opposed the intruder arms in hand. Now, while Babhruvāhana stood hesitating, the Serpent-daughter Ulūpī, understanding what was happening, split the earth and made herself known to Babhruvāhana in the following words: "Learn thou that I am thy mother, Ulūpī the Serpent-daughter. Do according to my word, O son; it shall be the supreme law for thee. Fight thy father who is all eager for fighting. For in that manner he will undoubtedly be pleased with thee." Thus urged by his mother, Babhruvāhana made ready for battle. He girded on his golden armour, donned his glittering helmet, and mounted his good chariot hung with a hundred quivers and drawn by horses swift as thought. Raising his standard—a golden lion—he went forth to fight the son of Kuntī. First he ordered his men to seize the sacrificial horse, and Arjuna, seeing the horse seized, rejoiced in his heart at his son's prowess. Then there was a terrible encounter between father and son. At last Babhruvāhana hit his father in the heart with one of his sharp-pointed arrows. Arjuna fell, but Babhruvāhana, seeing his father slain by his own hand, fell into a swoon. Then Chitrāngadā, seeing that both her husband and her son had fallen, appeared on the battlefield weeping and trembling. She spake to Ulūpī: "Lo, Ulūpī, our husband lying slain in battle by my son because of thee." She implored her to bring Arjuna back to life and declared that she would seek death by fasting unless she saw her

[1] *M.Bh.*, *Āśvam-p.*, lxxix–lxxxi.

husband restored to life. Then Babhruvāhana recovered consciousness, and seeing his mother seated near his father's body, he broke out in lamentations, and solemnly averred that he, too, would die by starvation.

Now Ulūpī thought of the life-restoring jewel which is the ultimate resort of the Snakes. She took it and said to Babhruvāhana : " Stand up, my son, and grieve not. Arjuna hath not been conquered by thee. Invincible by man he is and likewise invincible by the gods and even by Indra. It is a magical illusion which I have shown for the sake of the Lord of men, thy glorious father. Anxious to know the strength of thee, his son, in battle had he come. Therefore, son, thou hast been urged by me to fight. Do not reproach thyself with even the slightest sin. He is a holy being, a great spirit primeval, eternal and imperishable. Not even Indra can conquer him in battle, O son. This celestial jewel I have brought, O Prince of men, which ever brings dead Nāga chiefs back to life. Place it on the breast of thy father, and thou wilt see the son of Kuntī restored to life." Babhruvāhana did as she bade him. Being touched with the jewel, Arjuna arose as from a long sleep and embraced his son.

Seeing Ulūpī and Chitrāṅgadā on the battlefield, he was seized with wonderment. Then the former explained to him that all had happened for his own welfare. As he had caused Bhīshma to be slain contrary to the laws of chivalry, he had loaded himself with heavy sin and would certainly have gone down to hell, had this sin not been previously expiated. Moreover, the Vasus had cursed him, but they had also indicated this means of atonement, that Arjuna should be slain by his own son. This having now come to pass, his sin had been expiated.

Arjuna rejoiced greatly and invited Babhruvāhana to be present at the great horse-sacrifice together with his two mothers.[1]

In the last canto but one of the Great Epic [2] it is related how the five Pāṇḍavas and their spouse Draupadī leave Hastināpura to become hermits. The citizens and the women of the palace accompany them some distance and then return to the city. The serpent-daughter Ulūpī entered the Gaṅgā and Chitrāṅgadā went to Maṇipūra, whilst the other ' mothers ' remained with the young king Parikshit.

Arjuna and Aśvasena, the Son of Takshaka [3]

Agni, the Fire-god, had often attempted to devour the Khāṇḍava Forest; but Indra protected it, because it was inhabited by his friend, the Nāga Takshaka. Whenever Agni

[1] It is mentioned (lxxxviii, 2) that Chitrāṅgadā and Ulūpī (*Kauravyasyātmajā*) appear at the horse-sacrifice and greet Pṛithā and Krishṇā (i.e. Draupadī).

[2] *M.Bh., Mahāprasthānika-p.*, i, 27.

[3] *M.Bh., Ādi-p.*, ccxxiii–ccxxvii.

endeavoured to burn it down, Indra sent heavy showers of rain. At last Brahmā granted the Fire-god his wish, but when Agni had set the wood on fire, the creatures who lived therein exerted themselves to the utmost to extinguish the flames. Elephants in hundreds and thousands quickly carried water in their trunks and poured it upon the conflagration. Many-headed Nāgas in the vicinity of the fire sent forth a mass of water from their heads. In the same manner other creatures combated the fire with the aid of various implements. Seven times the fire broke forth in flames, seven times it was quenched.

Then the angry Agni betook himself again to Brahmā and complained that his exertions were all in vain. Brahmā, having pondered a while, declared that the Fire-god would succeed, if he secured the help of Nara and Nārāyaṇa who had been born on earth as Arjuna and Kṛishṇa. When again Agni had set the forest on fire, they would ward off all the forest-creatures, yea, even Indra himself. Now Agni solicited the assistance of the two heroes. Arjuna declared that they were willing to help him, but in an undertaking of such magnitude the use of divine weapons was indispensable. Agni, therefore, procured the bow Gāṇḍīva with two inexhaustible quivers, as well as the divine chariot with the white horses and the monkey standard. Armed with such superhuman weapons, they would be able to fight the Rākshasas, Piśāchas, Daityas, and Nāgas who haunted the Khāṇḍava Forest.

Now the Fire-god assumed his fiery shape and began to burn down the Forest. Enveloped by flames, it resembled Mount Meru struck by the rays of the radiant sun. The creatures of the wood tried to escape in all directions, but Arjuna and Kṛishṇa, having taken their stand on both sides of the forest, slaughtered them by hundreds and thousands. The flames rose to the heaven and caused dismay among the celestials. Then, Indra, warned by the gods, went forth to save the Khāṇḍava Forest, and, covering the sky with a multitude of chariots of various forms, he, the Lord of the gods, began to rain. The clouds, urged on by the king of the Devas, poured down heavy showers on Khāṇḍava. But owing to the terrible glow the rain-drops dried up in the air and did not even reach the conflagration. The angry Indra again and again sent down masses of water from huge clouds and the forest looked terrible, enveloped in fire, rain, and smoke and filled with thunder and lightning.

While Indra was thus pouring down, Arjuna warded off the water by means of a shower of arrows shot from his heavenly bow. The whole Khāṇḍava Forest he enveloped with his darts, like the Moon shrouding it in mist. No living being could escape, as the sky was obscured by the arrows of Arjuna. Now Takshaka, the Serpent-king great in strength, was not there, when the wood was burning, for he had gone to Kurukshetra. Aśvasena, the powerful son of Takshaka, was there; he laboured fiercely to escape from the fire.

He could not go out, obstructed by Arjuna's bolts; his mother, the Serpent-daughter, saved him by swallowing him. First she gulped down his head, and while still swallowing his tail, she rushed out wishing to save her son. In her course the son of Pāṇḍu pierced her head with a sharp arrow and Indra saw her. Wishing to save him, the Bearer of the Thunderbolt stunned the son of Pāṇḍu by a squall of wind and in the meantime Aśvasena escaped.

Seeing this terrible guile, Arjuna, deceived by the Nāga, cursed in his wrath the crooked serpent: "Thou shalt be without a support." [1]

At the time when the great battle of Kurukshetra had been raging for several days, there was a terrible encounter between Arjuna and Karṇa, the great hero of the Kauravas.[2] Now, as by the violent shocks caused by chariots, horses, and elephants the earth split asunder, the Nāga Aśvasena sleeping in the Nether World (*Pātāla*) woke up. He was the same who had escaped from the conflagration of the Khāṇḍava Forest. Remembering his former feud with Arjuna, the angry Serpent appeared on the surface of the earth, and, seeing his enemy engaged in a frightful contest with so dangerous an adversary as Karṇa, he thought: "Now hath the time come to revenge my injuries upon the evil-minded son of Kuntī."

Thus thinking, he assumed the shape of an arrow and entered the quiver of Karṇa. At that moment Arjuna and Karṇa were covering the sky with showers of arrows, so that the light of the day was obscured. Now Karṇa laid on his bow that terrible, foe-slaying, flaming arrow, snake-mouthed and polished, which he had kept for a long time for the son of Kuntī and put away in sandal powder resting in a quiver of gold. When the Nāga-arrow was placed on the bow the whole sky broke forth in flames, frightful thunderbolts fell down in hundreds, and the gods which guard the quarters of the sky uttered cries of lamentation.

Karṇa himself did not know that the Nāga had entered the arrow by the power of magic (*yoga-balena*). The arrow shot from the bow-string by Karṇa's hand blazed like fire, while it pierced the air. But Kṛishṇa,[3] seeing that flaming bolt, quickly pressed down the chariot with his foot without effort, so that it sank somewhat into the earth and the moon-light-coloured horses fell on their knees. At this deed loud shouts of exultation resounded in the sky, heavenly voices were heard, and a shower of celestial flowers fell down. The arrow struck Arjuna's diadem decorated with gold and jewels, and the priceless head-ornament—Brahmā himself had made it for Indra and Indra had given it to Arjuna, when he wished to slay the demons—fell on the earth, like the sun setting with ruddy disk.

[1] The scholiast appears to be uncertain about the purport of the word *apratishṭha* (lit. "without a support"), for which he offers a twofold explanation: "without shelter" and "without posterity".

[2] *M.Bh.*, *Karṇaparvan*, xc, 12-54.

[3] Kṛishṇa is Arjuna's charioteer.

The Nāga, after wholly consuming Arjuna's golden diadem by its fiery poison, wished to return to the quiver; but on being perceived by Karṇa, he spake: "Thou hast shot me without aiming, Karṇa; so I have not been able to cut off Arjuna's head. Now quickly shoot me again after aiming well, and I shall slay him who is thy enemy and mine." Being thus addressed, Karṇa, the charioteer's son, spake: "Who art thou, terrible of shape?" The Nāga answered: "Know that the son of Kuntī hath done me great wrong and that my feud with him sprang from the murder of my mother. Were even the Bearer of the Thunderbolt his protector, he must go to the dwelling of the King of the Dead." But Karṇa said: "Not by resorting to another's strength, O Nāga, does Karṇa strive for victory in battle. I will not twice place the same arrow, O Nāga, even though I had to slay a hundred Arjunas." The Nāga king, incensed by these words, now strove himself to kill the son of Kuntī and assumed his own form. Then Kṛishṇa spake to Arjuna in the midst of the battle: "Slay the great Serpent with whom thou art in feud." Arjuna asked: "Who is this Nāga who freely cometh to Garuḍa's mouth?" Quoth Kṛishṇa: "It is he whose mother thou hast slain, when in the Khāṇḍava Forest thou nourishedst the Fire-god and she had concealed his body so that, flying through the air, they seemed one form. Now he, remembering that feud, seeketh thee, indeed, for his own destruction. Look how he cometh like a flaming meteor, dropping from the sky." Then Arjuna, turning round in anger, pierced with six pointed arrows sharp-edged the Nāga who came flying across the air; with pierced body he dropped to the earth.

King Nala and the Nāga Karkoṭaka [1]

When King Nala, being possessed by an evil spirit, had abandoned Damayantī, his wife, he saw a great conflagration burning in the dense forest. There in the midst of the flames he heard the voice of some being, saying loudly again and again: "Come hither, Nala, quickly!" "Fear not!" With these words Nala entered into the midst of the fire and saw a Nāga-king lying coiled up in the shape of an ear-ring. This Nāga lifted up his folded hands and trembling he spake to Nala: "Know, O King, that I am the Nāga Karkoṭaka. Once I mocked the great sage Nārada, that mighty ascetic, and, incensed with wrath, he hath cursed me, saying: 'Stay thou fixed to the spot like a tree, until Nala shall come and take thee away from here. Then thou wilt be freed from the curse which I have pronounced.' Owing to this curse I am unable to move a single step. Thou must save me and I will show thee the way to great felicity. I shall be thy friend; there is no Serpent that equals me. I shall not be heavy in thy hand; take me quickly and go." Having thus spoken, the Lord of Nāgas made himself small, even to the size of a thumb,

[1] *M. Bh.*, *Vana-parvan*, lxvi (= *Nalopākhyāna*, xiv).

and Nala took him and proceeded to a place free from the fire. Having reached an open spot which had been spared by the scorching flames, he wished to let the Nāga go, but Karkoṭaka spake again: " Go on a few paces, counting thy steps, O king of Nishadha. Then I shall bring thee supreme felicity, O long-armed man. Then, as he had begun to count his steps the Nāga bit him at the tenth pace,[1] and, as soon as he had been bitten, his own shape disappeared. Seeing himself thus changed, Nala stood in amazement; the Nāga he saw restored to his own form. Then the Nāga Karkoṭaka said, comforting him: " I have changed thy form so that people shall not know thee. That demon on whose account thou art afflicted with great grief, O Nala, owing to my poison will grievously dwell in thee. As long as with his poison-stricken limbs he leaveth thee not, so long, O great king, he will dwell in thee grievously. Since he hath afflicted thee, who art innocent and without guilt, O Lord of men, I will make him moan with rage and will be thy protection. Thou wilt have no fear, O Tiger among men, from tusked and fanged animals nor from foes nor from those that know sacred texts. Thou wilt feel no pain caused by the poison, O king, and in battle, O Chief of kings, thou wilt ever be victorious. Now go thou hence, O king, to the fair city of Ayodhyā and present thyself there to King Ṛituparṇa, saying: 'I am Bāhuka, the charioteer.' For the king possesseth great skill in the game of dice, and he will give thee the secret of dice-playing in exchange for the secret science of horses. That illustrious scion of Ikshvāku's race will become thy friend. When thou art once versed in dice, thou wilt be blessed with great felicity. Thou wilt be united with thy spouse—set not thy mind to grief—and thou wilt regain both thy realm and thy two children: this I speak to thee in truth. Shouldst thou wish to see again thy own form, O Lord of men, thou must remember me and put on this garment. Clad with this garment, thou wilt recover thy own form."

Thus speaking, Karkoṭaka gave him celestial robes. After having thus directed Nala, the King of Nāgas vanished out of sight.

Mātali, the Charioteer of Indra, in search of a Son-in-law[2]

Mātali, the charioteer of Indra, had an only daughter, named Guṇakeśī, who was renowned for her beauty. When the time had come to give her in marriage, Mātali pondered: " How difficult it is for persons of lofty mind and exalted position to have a grown-up daughter. When she is to be married it causeth trouble in three families—in that of her father, in that of her mother, and in that of her future husband." As he could

[1] Nala says *daśa*, " ten," which means also " Bite! "
[2] *M. Bh., Udyoga-parvan*, xcvii–cv.

not find a bridegroom worthy of his daughter either among gods or men, on a certain night he consulted his wife Sudharmā and resolved to go to the Nāga-loka in search of a son-in-law. " Among gods and men," he said, " I can find no bridegroom who equalleth her in beauty. Surely there will be one among the Nāgas." Then Mātali, after solemnly taking leave of his consort by circumambulating her and smelling his daughter's head, set out for the earth.

Now on his way he happened to meet the great sage, Nārada, who asked him : " Where art thou going, O charioteer, either on thy own business or on some errand of thy master Indra ? " Then Mātali gave him the whole account of his purpose in travelling, whereupon Nārada said : " Let us go together. I have set out from heaven, in order to visit Varuṇa, the god of the waters. I will show thee the whole world and explain everything. Then we shall be able to choose a bridegroom, O Mātali." When they had descended to the earth, they first visited the Lord of the waters, who received Nārada and Mātali with all the distinction befitting their rank. Graciously dismissed by Varuṇa, they wandered through the Nāga-loka and Nārada gave his companion an account of all the beings that live inside the earth and of all the wonders which belong to the realm of Varuṇa. In the centre of the Nāga-loka he showed him Pātāla, the town inhabited by Daityas and Dānavas. There they saw the four elephants which support the earth : Airāvaṇa, Vāmana, Kumuda, and Añjana, the sons of Supratīka. Nārada asked Mātali whether among the inhabitants of Pātāla there was any whom he wished for his son-in-law. But Mātali answered : " There is no one here that pleaseth me : go quickly somewhere else."

Then Nārada guided him to Hiraṇyapura, 'the Golden City' of the Daityas and Dānavas, which was fashioned by Viśvakarman himself. He showed him the mansions of gold and silver, adorned with manifold jewels. But when he asked Mātali whether he wished here to select a bridegroom for his daughter, the charioteer of Indra replied : " Divine Sage, I would do nothing to displease the celestials. Now there is a constant feud between the Devas and the Dānavas. How can I approve of a matrimonial alliance with our opponents ? Let us go elsewhere, I may not visit the Dānavas."

Next they came to the world of the Suparṇas, who are the descendants of Garuḍa, and feed on the Nāgas. On account of their cruel nature they are called Kshatriyas and do not rise to the rank of Brahmins, for they destroy their own relatives. Nārada enumerated the chief among the Suparṇas.

As Mātali did not wish to make a choice here, they proceeded to Rasātala where dwelleth Surabhi, the nectar-born mother of the cows. Out of a jet of her milk which came down on the earth the Milk Ocean took its origin. She is the mother of the four heifers who protect the four quarters.

They continued their journey and Nārada said: "This is Bhogavatī, the town governed by Vāsuki, which is equal to Amarāvatī, the town of Indra, the Lord of the gods. Here stayeth the Nāga Śesha, who ever by his *tapas* beareth up the mighty earth. He of great strength, and adorned with divine ornaments, resembleth in shape a white mountain, while carrying a thousand heads with flaming tongues. Here dwell free of care, the sons of Surasā, the Nāgas manifold of shape and adornment. Numbered in thousands, all strong and fierce by nature, they are marked with jewels, *svastikas* and wheels and wear the auspicious emblem of the water-jar (*kamaṇḍaluka*). Some have a thousand heads, and others five hundred; some have a hundred heads and others are three-headed. Some have twice-five heads and others are seven-faced. With the huge coils of their large bodies they can encompass even a mountain. There are many thousands, myriads and millions of Nāgas which all belong to one race. Hearken: the chief among them I will name." Nārada then enumerated the chief among the Nāgas, beginning with Vāsuki, Takshaka, Karkoṭaka, and Dhanañjaya. "These and many others," he said, "are reckoned to be the sons of Kaśyapa. Lo, Mātali, whether here there be any one who pleaseth thee for thy son-in-law."

Mātali looked attentively at one and seemed pleased. He asked Nārada: "From what race is he descended who standeth in front of Kauravya Āryaka and who is so full of splendour and so beautiful to behold? Who are his father and mother? Of which race is he, as it were, the great standard? By his devotion, firmness, beauty, and strength he seemeth to me to be worthy of becoming the husband of Guṇakeśī."

Nārada, seeing Mātali thus pleased at the sight of Sumukha, related his greatness, birth and deeds. Quoth Nārada: "It is the Nāga prince Sumukha born from the race of Airāvata. He is honoured as the son's son of Āryaka and the daughter's son of Vāmana. His father, a Nāga Chikura by name, O Mātali, was slain by the son of Vinatā not very long ago." Then Mātali, rejoicing in his heart, spake to Nārada: "He, best among Serpents, pleaseth me for a son-in-law, my friend. Exert thyself in this matter. I am pleased with him and I wish to give my dear daughter to that Nāga, O holy man." Thereupon Nārada addressed Āryaka, the Serpent-king, saying: "This is the charioteer and dear friend of Indra, hight Mātali, pure, virtuous, and of good demeanour, full of prowess, and strength. He hath a daughter, renowned under the name of Guṇakeśī, who is unequalled in beauty. After having diligently searched the three worlds, he hath chosen Sumukha, thy son's son, to be the husband of his daughter. If it pleaseth thee likewise, O best of Snakes, thou must quickly make up thy mind, Āryaka, to accept his daughter. Although he be bereft of his father, we have chosen him on account of his virtue and out of high esteem for thee and for Airāvata. Mātali is anxious to come and bring himself his daughter. To this thou must give thy consent."

Then Āryaka, both distressed and delighted, made answer: "In no way, O great Sage, do I disparage thy words. Besides, who would not welcome a union with the companion of Indra? But I hesitate on account of the weakness of our case. My son, who shaped this youth's body, O thou of great splendour, was devoured by the son of Vinatā, and therefore we are afflicted with grief. Now Garuḍa hath said that after a month he will come back and eat Sumukha, too. This is sure to happen, and on that account my joy hath vanished on account of Suparṇa's word."

Then Mātali and Nārada took Sumukha to Indra and it happened that at the same time Vishṇu had come to visit the Lord of the gods. When Nārada had related the whole case, Vishṇu said to Indra: "Give thou him nectar and make him equal to the gods. Let Mātali and Nārada and Sumukha through thy favour obtain the boon which they desire." But Indra, remembering the prowess of Garuḍa, said to Vishṇu: "Thou mayest give it him." Then Vishṇu spake: "Thou art the Lord of the whole world, moving and unmoving. Who dareth to render ungiven what hath been given by thee?" At last Indra granted the Nāga longevity (*āyus*), but he did not make him partake of the nectar. Sumukha joyfully accepted the boon granted by the Lord of the gods, and having married Guṇakeśī, he returned home.

The Gleaner

Story of the wise and virtuous Nāga Padmanābha who drew the one-wheeled chariot of the Sun-god[1]

In the excellent town Mahāpadma on the right bank of the Gaṅgā there lived a Brahmin, Dharmāraṇya by name, who excelled in moral conduct and sacred knowledge and diligently discharged his family and religious duties. But, although his mode of life was blameless in every respect, he felt unsatisfied and was troubled in his mind with grave doubts as to the ultimate goal of human existence. While thus vexed by perplexity, he was once visited by another Brahmin, a man of concentrated mind. By the sweetness of his speech this visitor soon won his confidence so that he resolved to make his guest a partner of his uncertainty. "I have begotten sons," he said to him, "and thus I have fulfilled the duty of an Aryan householder, O excellent priest. Now I wish to obey the Supreme Law; which is the road thither, O twice-born one?"

"Since the period of life aiming at offspring as its fruit is passed for me, I now wish to gather provender for the journey to the next world. In the midst of the ocean of transmigration I strive to reach the opposite shore and this is the thought that hath arisen in my mind: whence shall I obtain the barque called the good Law?" The guest answered

[1] *M. Bh.*, *Śānti-parvan*, ccclii–ccclxv. P. Deussen and O. Strauss. *Vier philosophische Texte des Mahābhāratam*, pp. 862 ff.

hat he himself was overwhelmed by the same embarrassment. So many and manifold were he means of salvation adopted by sundry people that it was extremely difficult to decide vhich was the road leading to the supreme goal. As the Sacred Law seemed to open so nany doors, his mind was agitated like a shredded cloud moved by the wind. He, therefore, ıdvised his host to betake himself for council to a wise and virtuous Nāga king, named ?admanābha, who lived in the Naimisha forest on the bank of the Gomatī,[1] in a town ıamed after the Nāgas. He described this Nāga as naturally prone to ablutions and fond ›f studying, accomplished in austerities and abstemiousness, and of superior moral conduct, ıs pious in his sacrificial works, a master of liberality, forbearing, of excellent demeanour ınd good character, truthful, free from envy, gifted with complete self-control, subsisting ›n leavings, affable in speech, gracious, honest and of great eminence, mindful of benefits, ıot quarrelsome, rejoicing in the welfare of other beings, and born of a race as pure as the vaves of the Gaṅgā.

Next day the Brahmin, after having taken leave of his guest, set out for the abode of he Nāga. When, after long travel, he reached the indicated spot, he was courteously eceived by Padmanābha's consort, to whom he explained the object of his visit. Then the ıousewife of the Nāga informed him that her husband had absented himself from his home or a month in order to draw the chariot of the Sun-god and that he was expected to eturn after seven or eight days. The Brahmin resolved to await Padmanābha's arrival, ınd withdrew to a sandbank in the river Gomatī, where he sat without taking any food. Then the Nāgas, the relatives of the serpent-king, became anxious about the Brahmin vho was sitting there in a solitary spot day after day without taking food. They came to ıim in great numbers and begged him to partake of their hospitality, offering him roots, ruit, and leaves. But he declined, saying that it was his firm intention to fast until the eturn of Padmanābha, their king.

At last the king of the Nāgas returned to his abode after having been dismissed by Vivasvant, the Sun-god. When his consort had washed his feet and duly honoured him, ıe questioned her whether during his absence she had discharged her duties with regard to he gods and the guests. Then his wife told him that a Brahmin had arrived seven days ›efore, and that this visitor had entreated her to bring her husband to his presence as soon ıs he should return home. So she prompted her husband to show himself to the guest. The Nāga king was vexed that a human being should have summoned him. "Among gods, lemons, and divine sages," he said, "we Nāgas, the descendants of Surasā,[2] possess great

[1] The river Gumti which flows by Lucknow and joins the Ganges at Sayyidpur below Benares.

[2] Another name of Kadrū, the mother of Snakes, who is identified with the earth. The Bombay edition ıas *saurabheyās*, for which *sauraseyas* is to be read (ccclx, 3–4). Cf. above, p. 20.

strength and speed. As givers of boons, we and our followers should receive the homage especially of men." His wife, however, succeeded in allaying his anger by reminding him of his royal duty. He declared that his surly temper was not due to pride, but was an innate fault of his race. It was owing to this defect in particular, he said, that the Nāgas laid themselves open to blame. He, however, fully recognized that there was no greater evil than wrath, and in order to demonstrate this truth, he quoted the examples of Rāvaṇa and Kārtavīrya. Now, hearing the words of his wife, he had subdued anger, that enemy of austerities and destroyer of felicity. Indeed, he extolled himself as fortunate in possessing such a virtuous consort.

The Nāga then betook himself to the Brahmin and graciously questioned him with regard to his wishes. Said the Brahmin : " Thou goest to draw in thy turn the one-wheeled chariot of Vivasvant. If thou hast seen there anything marvellous, tell me." The Nāga answered : " The exalted Sun is the abode of sundry marvels and from him do proceed all beings that are revered in the three worlds. In his thousands of rays, like birds in the branches of trees, there dwell and nestle the blessed saints together with the deities. From him goeth forth the mighty wind, which spreadeth in the sky ; what marvel greater than this ? Distributing that wind, out of love for the welfare of all creatures, he sendeth forth water during the rainy season ; what marvel greater than this ? Standing in the middle of his disk, the Lord, shining with supreme splendour looketh down on mankind ; what marvel greater than this ? During eight months with his bright beams he re-absorbeth again in due time the moisture which he hath sprinkled down ; what marvel greater than this ? In his splendour reposeth the supreme Soul, he bringeth forth all seeds and supporteth the earth withal together with movable and immovable things. In him is the many-armed god, the eternal Purushottama who hath neither beginning nor end ; what marvel greater than this ? Now hear from me the one marvel of marvels, which in the stainless ether hath been seen by me from the abode of the Sun.

Once at midday, when the source of light scorched the worlds, there came forth a splendour equal unto that of the Sun. Illuminating all the worlds with the effulgence of its own light, that splendour hastened towards the Sun, cleaving as it were the sky. Like a burnt oblation this luminary spread radiance by means of its rays, and, indescribable in form, it seemed a second sun. At the moment when it had come near, Vivasvant, stretched forth both hands, and the being also, eager to respond to his homage, held out the right hand. Cleaving as it were the sky, that splendour entered the ray-encircled Sun and in a moment it became united with the God of Light.

Among those who had witnessed this wonderful scene there arose a doubt which of the two was the Sun-god on his chariot and which the other. " Who is that being," they questioned Sūrya, " which hath ascended the heaven like unto a second sun ? " Then Sūrya answered : " It is not the god who is companion to the Wind (namely, the Fire), nor a demon, nor a Nāga ; it is a sage who hath fulfilled the vow of living by gleaning and who hath gone to heaven. He was a pious priest, living on roots and fruit, eating withered leaves, and subsisting on water and wind. That pious priest praised Śiva by means of Vedic hymns and strove to reach the Gate of Paradise ; therefore he hath gone to the highest heaven. Free from attachment, and without desire, that priest subsisted ever on gleanings and was intent on the weal of all beings, O ye Snakes. Neither gods nor Gandharvas, nor demons nor Nāgas surpass those beings which have reached the highest goal."

The Brahmin Dharmāraṇya, having heard this wonderful tale, felt his doubts removed, and, as he had gained the object of his visit, he took leave of the Nāga who in vain urged him to postpone his departure. On parting he informed the Nāga that he, too, had resolved to assume the vow of living by gleaning as he recognized that the ascetic life was the surest road to gain supreme bliss after death.

How Kṛishṇa overcame the Nāga Kāliya [1]

Once upon a time the youthful Kṛishṇa of lovely appearance, tending his herd of cows and calves, roamed about the beauteous woods of Braj. He was at the age when boys are wont to wear their hair in side-locks called crow's wings. Being dark of complexion and having donned fine raiment, yellow like the filament of the lotus, he resembled a rain-cloud at the time of twilight. His well-rounded arms, ever revered by the immortals, were busy with staff and rope in tending the calves. His radiant face encompassed by flowing locks, was as a full-blown lotus-flower surrounded by swarms of bees. Adorned with a wreath of various flowers of the wood, which shone like the stars in heaven, and dark-coloured like a cloud in the rainy season, he appeared like the month of Nabhasya [2] embodied. Singing and playing by turns, he roamed about, now blowing through a leaf agreeable to the ear, now piping his lovely cow-herd's reed. Thus, Kṛishṇa wandered with his companions through the cool and shady forests which resounded with the shrill cries of the wild peacocks and re-echoed the thunder of the clouds. Flowing with fresh water and refreshed by cool winds, the forest-ranges exhaled the sweet perfumes of the blossoming trees.

[1] *Harivaṃśa*, 3592–3702 (lxviii–lxix). A less prolix version of the legend is found in the *Bhāgavata-purāṇa*, canto x, 1st half, xvi.

[2] Nabhasya is the ancient name of the second month of the rainy season. Cf. R. Sewell and S. B. Dikshit, *The Indian Calendar*, p. 24.

At last he reached the banks of the fleetly flowing Yamunā where the trees were adorned with creepers and the wind was cool through contact with the waves. He beheld the river covered with lotus-flowers and enlivened by the sounds of cranes, geese, and ducks—the broad river-bed intersected with numerous water-channels, forming a multitude of sandy islands.

While wandering along this beauteous river, Kṛishṇa beheld a pool of great depth and vast extent like an ocean with unstirring waters. Bare it was of water-born creatures and abandoned by water-haunting birds. Difficult of access it was, as its banks were full of snake-infested holes. Over it there hung a smoke caused by poison-born fire ; and its surface was hot with venomous flames. Its water was undrinkable alike for men and beasts, wanting to quench their thirst. Even the birds of the sky did not approach it, and when grass fell in its water it was burnt by its heat.

When Kṛishṇa saw this vast pool at the distance of but one *kos* to the north of Braj, he thought : " In this large pool the fierce lord-of-snakes, whose name is Kāliya, and who resembleth a pile of black antimony, hath plainly taken up his abode. He hath given up his dwelling in the ocean,[1] thus have I heard, out of fear of the king of birds, snake-eating Suparṇa. By him this whole ocean-speeding Yamunā hath been defiled, and out of fear of the snake-king no one dareth to inhabit this country. This wood abounding in various trees, being guarded by the satellites of the serpent-king, is untouchable like poisoned food which hath the appearance of being without poison. Therefore, I must chastise this king of serpents, so that the stream with its gracious waters may be enjoyed by the people of Braj and that they freely may frequent all its holy sites. For this reason am I dwelling as a cowherd in this land of Braj that I may subdue the wicked that traverse the road of evil."

After these words, Kṛishṇa, having tightly fastened his girdle, nimbly ascended to the top of a *kadamba*-tree and from that tree he threw himself into the middle of the pool. So heavy was his fall that the water gushed up with a jerk and by the noise the great abode of the serpents was shaken. Then the angry Snake, the king of serpents Kāliya, red-eyed with wrath, rose from the pool, resembling a mass of dark clouds. Lifting up his five awful heads, while his five mouths with quivering tongues spat flames and hissed like fire, he filled the whole pool with his huge coils of fiery lustre. By the blaze of his fury the whole

[1] According to the *Bhāgavata* (x, i, 16, 63), the original home of Kāliya was the island Ramaṇaka. It is further on related (x, 1, 17, 1, 2–12) why Kāliya had taken refuge in the pool of the Yamunā. After having presumptuously partaken of the offerings which the Nāgas were obliged to give to Garuḍa, the latter had assailed him. Thereupon Kāliya had fled to the said pool where he was safe against danger owing to the curse pronounced by Saubhari.

water grew seething hot; and the river Yamunā, frightened as it were, recoiled, while from his jaws filled with flames, there came forth an angry blast.

On seeing Kṛishṇa in the pool playing in childish sport, the serpent-lord blew from his mouth flames and smoke, so that the trees which stood near along the banks were in a moment reduced to ashes. There rushed out other huge snakes—his sons and wives and servants—spitting dreadful poison-engendered fire. These serpents caught Kṛishṇa in their coils so that his feet became entangled and he stood motionless as a mountain. Then they bit him with their sharp fangs frothy with poison, but the hero did not die.

In the meanwhile, the frightened cowherds hastened to Braj, lamenting with voices choked with tears.[1] They told Nanda how Kṛishṇa in his folly had dived into the pool and was in imminent danger of being killed by the snakes. With tottering steps the aged cowherd and his wife Yaśodā, attended by young and old, betook themselves to the pool and they all stood on the bank weeping and wailing. But Balarāma cried out to his brother, Kṛishṇa: "O Kṛishṇa, thou long-armed one, quickly subdue the serpent-king who assaileth thee with his poison. Our kinsfolk, deeming thee a mere mortal, lament piteously, mistaking thee, O Lord, for a human being."

On hearing these words uttered by Rohiṇī's son, Kṛishṇa stretched forth both his arms and burst asunder the snake's coils which fettered him. With both his feet he jumped on the huge body of the serpent that issued from the pool, and, suddenly mounting on the large central head of the monster, he danced. Then, being crushed by Kṛishṇa, the serpent dropped his heads, and while a flood of blood poured from each mouth, he spake:[2] "In my folly, O Kṛishṇa, I have shown this anger. Tamed by thee and deprived of my poison, I have come into thy power, O fair-faced One. Therefore command me; what shall I, together with my wives, offspring, and kinsmen, do, or to whom shall I submit? I pray thee; grant me my life." On seeing the serpent with his five-fold head bent down, Kṛishṇa made answer: "An abode in the waters of Yamunā I allow thee not. Go thou to the ocean with thy wives and kinsmen. If anyone of thy sons or servants shall be seen here again either in the water or on the land, I will surely kill him. May this water henceforth be blessed. Go thou to the ocean. When Garuḍa seeth my foot-prints marked on thy heads,[3] that enemy of thy race will not assail thee."

[1] In the *Bhāgavata* (x, 1, 16, 12–13) it is related that Nanda and the cowherds of Gokula were warned of Kṛishṇa's danger by evil portents.

[2] According to the *Bhāgavata* (x, 1, 16, 33–39) the wives of Kāliya intercede with Kṛishṇa in favour of their wicked husband.

[3] The foot-prints left by Kṛishṇa on the hood of the Nāga are no doubt the spectacle marks of the cobra. Cf. *J.A.S.B.*, vol. xxxix (1870), part i, p. 220. Cf. above, p. 27.

The mighty dragon, humbly receiving these words, left the pool before the eyes of the cowherds, and vanished from their sight. After the vanquished snake had gone the cowherds stood amazed and reverently circumambulated Kṛishṇa. Then they spake to Nanda, his foster-father: "Blessed art thou and highly favoured in having such a son. Henceforward in all distress Kṛishṇa will be the refuge of the cowherds, the kine, and the cow-pen. The waters of Yamunā, frequented by holy men, have now become wholesome; and our cattle will now for ever freely graze on her river-banks. Verily, we are rustics that we did not recognize Kṛishṇa as a great being, like fire hidden in the fold."

Thus wondering and lauding the imperishable Kṛishṇa, the multitude of cowherds returned to the cow-pen, like the gods to the heavenly garden of Chitraratha.

The triumph of the divine Kṛishṇa over the evil dragon of the Yamunā presents a subject eminently suited to plastic representation. Sculptural renderings, however, are extremely rare. Among the numerous images of deities decorating the 'Rath of Dharmarāja', one of the five rock-cut temples of Māmallapuram on the Coast of Coromandel, there is a two-armed male figure defeating a three-headed Nāga whose snake-tail he holds with both hands. If we are correct in identifying this group with Kṛishṇa vanquishing the Kāliya Nāga, it would be the earliest example known in the history of Indian art. The *raths* of Māmallapuram belong to the seventh century.[1] Another sculptured representation is said to exist on the wall of the pillared walk round the central shrine in the great Kailāsa temple at Ellora.

Metal images of Kāliyamardana-Kṛishṇa are not uncommon in the South of India. A very fine specimen from Kāttu-Edayāru in the South Arcot district is preserved in the Madras Museum. It shows the youthful Kṛishṇa dancing on the five-fold head of the Nāga, the end of whose tail he has seized with his left hand—a graceful and well-balanced composition.[2]

In pictorial art, too, the subject is met with. Dr. A. K. Coomaraswamy has published a very attractive picture in his collection, which presents a very vivid rendering of Kṛishṇa's exploit[3]. The divine hero of blue complexion, as usual, and wearing an orange-coloured garment round his loins has seized with both his hands the white-bellied, black serpent, whose heads (to the number of fourteen) he is trampling under foot. Seven Nāgīs—half

[1] *A.S.R.* for the year 1910–11, p. 50.

[2] Gopinatha Rao, *Elements of Hindu iconography* (1914), vol. i, pp. 212 f., pl. lxiv. Krishna Sastri, *South Indian Images* (1916), pp. 38 f., fig. 26.

[3] *Burlington Magazine*, vol. xx (1912), p. 315, pl. i, and *Rajput Painting*, pl. liii. Another miniature picture showing this scene is preserved in the Munich Ethnographical Museum. Vide *Münchener Jahrbuch der bildenden Kunst*, vol. xiii (1923), pp. 82 f.

woman, half snake—approach him from both sides, reverently imploring him to grant them the life of their lord, whilst the river-bank is occupied by the wailing crowd of cowherds and milk-maids, among whom grey-bearded Nanda and his wife Yaśodā are most prominent. Evidently the anonymous maker of this picture has followed the version of the *Bhāgavata-purāṇa.* This cannot be a matter of surprise, if we remember the immense popularity of this book, especially of the tenth canto in its Hindī translation, entitled *Prem Sāgar.*

The spot on the river-bank of Kṛishṇa's victory is still pointed out at Mathurā; it is known as Kālimardan Ghāṭ, and an annual festival called Nāg Līlā is celebrated there with a procession of boats. The date is Kārtik sudi 14.[1]

How Akrūra beheld the World of Serpents[2]

[When Kaṃsa, the cruel king of Mathurā, had learned that his nephews, Kṛishṇa and Baladeva, were still among the living, he resolved to entice them to the capital so that he might get them into his power and bring about their destruction. He, therefore, deputed Akrūra (who was Kṛishṇa's paternal uncle) to the cowherds of Braj with the order that they should bring the annual tax in kind due to the king. On receiving the royal command, the cowherds headed by Nanda collected the customary tribute consisting of kine and buffaloes, milk and clarified butter, and made ready to betake themselves to the king.]

Kṛishṇa and Baladeva went, too, mounted on the same car as their uncle Akrūra. When they had reached the bank of the river Yamunā, Akrūra spake to his nephew, Kṛishṇa: "Hold thou the chariot back, my dear, and take good care of the horses. Give them grass and tarry a moment until I return. In this pool of the Yamunā I will worship the lord of snakes by means of divine *mantras*;[3] for he is the sovereign of the whole world. I will bow down to the mysterious deity who is the cause of the Universe, and whose head is adorned with the blessed *svastika* cross,[4] the thousand-headed snake Ananta, clad in a dark blue garment, who is a devotee of Vishṇu. The poison which cometh forth from the mouth of that regent of justice, I will drink it all nectar-like, as if I were an immortal being. On seeing that two-tongued one who is marked with the *svastika* and adorned with glory, the meeting of snakes will be for our welfare. Do ye two stay and together await my return, until I come back from the pool of the lord of snakes." Then Kṛishṇa

[1] F. S. Growse, *Mathurā a District Memoir,* 2nd ed. (1880), p. 248.

[2] *Harivaṃśa,* 4388–4460 (lxxxiii). The episode is also related in the *Bhāgavata,* x, 39.

[3] The *Bhāgavata mantras,* according to the commentator Nīlakaṇṭha are certain verses from the *Ṛig-veda* (v, 52, 17).

[4] The Nāgas are sometimes said to be marked with the sign of the *svastika*. Cf. above, pp. 27 f.

answered joyfully: "Go thou quickly, righteous one, we cannot continue our journey without thee."

Now Akrūra dived down in the pool of the Yamunā and in the Nether Region (*Rasātala*) he beheld the World of Snakes. In the middle thereof he saw the thousand-headed lord of the serpents who carried a plough in one hand and whose frame was supported by a mace. His lofty banner was a golden fan-palm. He was of white complexion and was wrapped in a dark-coloured garment. He wore a single ear-ring and, being intoxicated, he slept.[1] He was seated at his ease on the shining seat formed by the mass of his coils. Long-armed was he, his breast was covered with a wreath of golden lotus-flowers and his limbs were anointed with red sandel. He was worshipped by the chief among the Nāgas, headed by Vāsuki. The two Nāgas, Kambala and Aśvatara, holding chowries were fanning the deity who was seated on the seat of justice. The other snakes, Karkoṭaka foremost, attended him and laved their monarch by means of golden jars. Seated in his lap was Vishṇu, dark like a thundercloud, and wearing a yellow garment, his breast adorned with the *Śrīvatsa*.

When Akrūra came up from the water, he saw Kṛishṇa and Baladeva sitting in the car as before, but when he dived again in the flood he observed them in their divine shape.

At last he returned, and Kṛishṇa questioned him as to what wonderful sight he had seen in the Snake-world, which had made him tarry so long. Akrūra answered him: "What wonder can there be in the movable and immovable world beyond thee? Such a rare wonder hath been seen by me, O Kṛishṇa, that even now I still seem to see and enjoy it. For I have met here the wonder of all the worlds in visible form, and a greater wonder, O Kṛishṇa, I cannot see. Come, let us go to the town of King Kaṃsa before yet the light-diffusing Sun hath sunken down at the end of the day."

[1] In the *Bṛihatsaṃhitā*, lviii, 36, the image of Baladeva is described in the following terms: "Baladeva must be made having a plough in his right hand, with eyes lively from drink, and wearing a single ear-ring. His complexion is fair, like a conch shell, the moon, or lotus-fibre."

CHAPTER II

THE NĀGAS AND THE BUDDHA

IF we survey Buddhist literature, we find that in the legends relating to the life of Śākyamuni the Nāgas play as prominent a part as in Brahmanical lore. In those writings, however, they appear to us in an aspect essentially different from that presented by the Great Epic. There is a marked tendency in Buddhist tradition to emphasize and exemplify by many edifying tales the fact that the ancient gods, even Brahmā and Śakra, were inferior and subservient to the great Sage of the Śākya tribe. The same applies to the Nāgas. The dreaded serpent-demons are generally represented as devout worshippers of the Buddha. It is true that often they have to be converted : they start by being fierce and rebellious. But as soon as they have come under the holy influence of the Master they, too, become pervaded by his all-penetrating gentleness and abandon their savage habits. They accept his doctrine and forsake the doing of harm to other creatures. Neither gods nor men nor animals can resist the holy influence of the Blessed One : thus the Nāgas too, who in reality combine the nature of these three classes of beings, are won by his word.

One of the earliest snake stories preserved in Buddhist scripture relates the contest of the Buddha with a savage serpent in the fire room of the Kāśyapa brothers of Uruvilvā. During the whole night the Buddha and the Nāga fight one another with the magic fire (*tejas*) which they emit from their persons. At last the fire of Buddha proves stronger than that of the snake, and the latter is caught in Buddha's alms-bowl. In this ancient story the Nāga, apart from his magical property of spitting flames, is nothing but a snake. He possesses no human quality, and has neither a name nor the power of speech. In the numerous sculptural renderings of this scene we find the Nāga invariably represented as a snake—usually many-headed to indicate his demoniacal nature.

A Nāga of this type, however, is exceptional in Buddhist writings. Usually the human qualities predominate, and the Nāga even becomes a human being possessed with those moral virtues which are specially commended in the teachings of the Saṅgha.

Side by side with the tale of the fire-spitting dragon of Uruvilvā there is the legend of Muchilinda, the Nāga king, who sheltered Buddha during seven days against rain and wind by spreading his snake-hood like a canopy over the Master's head.

Another curious story contained in the *Vinaya-piṭaka* (one of the three main divisions of the Pali canon) is that of the Nāga who assumed human shape and was ordained as a Buddhist monk, in order to be released from his serpent-birth. But his true nature having been disclosed in his sleep, the unfortunate Nāga was expelled from the monastery by the Buddha himself. In this legend we find the idea, often expressed in Buddhist literature that the Nāga is an inferior and degenerate being, whose snake-birth is a consequence of his evil *karman*.

These three snake-stories from the Pali *Tripiṭaka*, however different in their presentation of the Nāga, have one point in common, which, although negative, deserves to be noted. In none of them the Nāga is a being dwelling in the waters of the earth or endowed with special power over the waters of the sky. It is certainly curious that the great Nāga Muchilinda, instead of withholding the showers of rain which threaten the Buddha with discomfort, has to sit up for a whole week and to use his body as an umbrella.

We have noticed above that the close connexion of the Nāgas with the watery element is very marked in the myths and legends of the *Mahābhārata*. The same feature we find in another important source of Nāga lore, namely, the narratives of the Chinese pilgrims, those fervent Buddhists, who undertook the long and dangerous journey to India to visit the sacred relics in the holy land of their Faith. Fa-Hien (A.D. 399–414) was the earliest of these pious palmers, but it is especially the great Hiuen Tsiang (A.D. 629–45), whose itinerary contains a wealth of legendary lore regarding the Nāgas. The Chinese writers usually refer to the Nāgas under the name of 'dragons', and it cannot be doubted that the character of the dragon, as it appears in the folklore and literature of China, is partly derived from the Indian conception of the Nāga.[1]

The narratives of the Chinese pilgrims are separated from the Pali canon, which we have referred to above, by a space of many centuries. If compared with the earliest Buddhist scriptures which originated in India, they show a remarkable growth of legend. Now it is interesting to note that in the legends preserved by the Chinese pilgrims the Nāgas figure pre-eminently as water-sprites, dwelling in rivers, lakes, and ponds and controlling atmospheric changes. It is not their poisonous bite which renders these Nāgas dangerous adversaries (in fact, they seem entirely to have forsaken the use of their fangs!) but it is their power to raise hail-storms, to cause floods, and thus to devour the crops of the fields. "All my sustenance comes from the fields of men," are the words spoken by the Nāga Apalāla.

Several of the legends contained in the account of Hiuen Tsiang's travels belong to Gandhāra, the borderland on the right bank of the Indus, and the surrounding mountain tracts. We possess a curious proof of the prevalence of snake-worship in that district in

[1] M. W. de Visser, "The Dragon in China and Japan," *Proc. Royal Academy of Amsterdam, Phil. Section*, New Series, vol. xiii (Amsterdam, 1913), introduction.

the inscription of Kāla darah,[1] in which a certain Theodoros, the son of Dati, records the construction of a cistern 'in honour of all snakes'. The donor, as may be inferred from his name, must have been a Greek or, at least, a man of Greek descent. The inscription is dated the 20th day of the month of Śrāvaṇa of the year 113. It is significant that Śrāvaṇa is the first month of the rainy season.

The Birth of the Bodhisattva

We have said above that the Nāgas figure very prominently in the legend of the Buddha's life. From his birth until his final extinction they show him their reverence. In the *Lalitavistara* we read that, when Queen Māyā had given birth to the future Buddha in the Lumbinī Garden, there appeared the two Nāgarājas, Nanda and Upananda, who, standing in the air, "half-bodied," and producing two streams of water cold and warm, bathed the Bodhisattva.[2] The same legend is told by Hiuen Tsiang, but in a duplicated form.[3] On his visit to the Lumbinī Garden, the pilgrim saw "a *stūpa* built by King Aśoka on the spot where the two dragons bathed the body of the prince." And after having narrated how the new-born Bodhisattva made seven paces in each direction, he adds: "Moreover, two dragons sprang forth, and, fixed in the air, poured down, the one a cold and the other a warm water stream from his mouth, to wash the prince. To the east of this *stūpa* are two fountains of pure water, by the side of which have been built two *stūpas*. This is the place where two dragons appeared from the earth. When the Bodhisattva was born, the attendants and household relations hastened in every direction to find water for the use of the child. At this moment two springs gurgled forth from the earth just before the queen, the one cold, the other warm, using which they bathed him."

Both these forms of the legend, which also occur in the *Mahāvastu*,[4] are represented in Buddhist art. We possess a bas-relief from Amarāvatī divided into four compartments of which one evidently refers to the miraculous birth of the Bodhisattva in the Lumbinī Garden.[5] Māyā is shown standing in the traditional attitude under the tree, while at her side the four deities hold up a long piece of cloth to receive the invisible child. In the adjoining compartment two females, one carrying a kerchief marked with the sacred foot-

[1] G. Bühler, *Ind. Ant.*, vol. xxv (1896), pp. 141 ff., and *Wiener Zschr. f. d. Kunde des Morgenlandes*, vol. x (1896), pp. 55 ff. E. Senart, *J.A.*, 9th Series, vol. xiii (1899), pp. 531 ff.

[2] *Lalitavistara* (ed. Lefmann), vol. i, p. 83, 11, 21–2; cf. also p. 93, 11, 3–4. Foucaux, vol. i, pp. 78 and 85. Cf. *Buddhacarita*, i, 27, 35, and 38. Cowell, pp. 5 and 7.

[3] *Si-yu-ki* (transl. Beal), vol. ii, pp. 24 f. Watters, *On Yuan Chwang*, vol. ii, p. 14. Cf. Fa-Hien, *Record* (transl. Legge), p. 67.

[4] *Mahāvastu* (ed. Senart), vol. ii, p. 23, ll. 4–7, and p. 24, ll. 17–20.

[5] Fergusson, *Tree and Serpent Worship*, p. 232, pl. xci, 4. A very similar piece of sculpture is reproduced by Burgess, *Amarāvatī*, pl. xxxii, 2.

prints and the other holding a parasol over it, hasten towards a cistern from which issues a male figure, the hands joined in adoration. There can be little doubt that this figure represents not the King Śuddhodana in his bath, as Fergusson conjectured, but a Nāga in his cistern. In the art of Gandhāra it is the usual way of representing such spirits of the water. In the present instance the Nāga does not seem to be provided with his usual emblem, the snake-hood.

Clearer still, though far less graceful, is the treatment of this scene in the Mathurā school of sculpture.[1] Here the Nāgas, Nanda and Upananda, recognizable by their halo of serpent-heads, appear from two masonry wells which conceal the lower half of their body. (Plate VI*a*.) They raise the joined hands towards a small nude figure which represents the Bodhisattva standing on a kind of pedestal in the centre. Some musical instruments floating in the air, are, no doubt, intended to indicate the heavenly music which was heard at the blessed time of the future Buddha's birth.

In sculptures of the Gupta period, found at Sārnāth, the other form of the legend has found plastic expression.[2] The two Nāgas suspended in the air " half-bodied ", to use the phrase of the *Lalitavistara*, empty their water-jars over the head of the infant Buddha, who is shown standing on his lotus. According to the synoptic method of illustrating peculiar to sculptures of this period (it is also usual in the early school of Central India), the scene of the Nāgas, Nanda and Upananda, administering to the Bodhisattva his first bath is here combined in one panel with the other scenes relating to the Nativity.

It can be no matter of surprise that Chinese artists, in rendering the scene of Buddha's birth, have paid special attention to the part played by the Nāgas on the occasion of that great event. It is found on one of the silk banners which were recovered by Sir Aurel Stein from the treasure cave of the ' Thousand Buddhas ' at Tun-Huang.[3] It is described by that author in the following terms : " The newly born Bodhisattva stands in a golden laver, raised on a stand between two palm-trees. Their tops are lost in a curling mass of black cloud, and in this there appear, ranged archwise, the heads of the ' nine dragons of the air ' gazing down on the infant with open mouths. A well-known Buddhist tradition makes Nāgas or divinities of the thunderclouds, i.e. ' Dragons ' in Chinese eyes, perform the laving of the New-born. The descent of the water, which their mouths are supposed to pour forth, is not actually represented here. Five women stand round, one holding a towel ".

[1] *Annual A.S.I.*, for 1906–7, pp. 152 f., pl. liiia.

[2] *Cat. Sārnāth Museum*, p. 183, No. C (*a*) 1 ; pl. xix*a*, and p. 186, No. C (*a*) 2 ; pl. xx.

[3] Aurel Stein, *The Thousand Buddhas*, pp. 52 f., pl. xxxvii, and *Serindia*, vol. iv, pl. lxxiv, central banner. Cf. also Fa-Hien's *Record* (transl. Legge), pl. ii, where nine dragons are seen spitting streams of water from the clouds ; the two springs are shown in front.

(a) Infant Bodhisattva adored by Nāgas (Mathurā).

(b) Nāga image of Kukargām.

[To face p. 96

In his account of the Lumbinī Garden, the Chinese pilgrim Hiuen Tsiang notes a great stone pillar which had been erected by order of King Aśoka to mark the hallowed spot of Śākyamuni's nativity. Originally it was crowned with the figure of a horse. But a malicious dragon struck the pillar with a thunderbolt so that it broke in twain.[1] The lower portion of the shaft was rediscovered in 1896 near the village of Rummindei, in Nepal territory. It still bears the record of Śākyamuni's birth engraved in very clear characters by order of the Emperor Aśoka. The horse-capital noticed by the pilgrim has not come to light again.

On a subsequent important occasion in the Bodhisattva's career we find the pair Nanda and Upananda mentioned again together with some others of their tribe. When the moment of the Great Renunciation or *Mahābhinishkramaṇa* was drawing near, various deities solemnly declared their intention of assisting the future Buddha in his great undertaking. The Nāgarājas Varuṇa, Manasvin, Sāgara, Anavatapta, Nanda, and Upananda spoke: "And we in order to do homage to the Bodhisattva will produce a cloud of benzoin (*kālānusāri*) and we will shower a rain of sandal powder which is the essence of snakes." [2]

The River Nairañjanā

Far more important than Śākyamuni's natural birth is his spiritual birth (in Buddhist scripture it is indicated by the name of Saṃbodhi or Mahābodhi), whereby he became the Buddha, 'the Enlightened One'. That great event which according to tradition took place under the sacred fig-tree of Gayā, has become the nucleus of numerous legends which are favourite subjects of literature and art.

It is related in the *Lalitavistara* [3] that, when Sujātā, the daughter of the village headman of Uruvilvā, had offered the Bodhisattva a golden vessel of milk-rice after his long fast, he went towards the 'river of Nāgas', the Nairañjanā, to refresh his limbs. After his bath he wished to sit down on a sandbank in the river, and the Nāga-daughter who inhabits the Nairañjanā brought him a jewelled throne. Seated on this throne, the Bodhisattva partook of the food which Sujātā had offered him and after finishing his meal, he cast the golden bowl carelessly into the water. Sāgara, the Nāgarāja, seized it at once and wished to carry it to his abode. But Indra, assuming the shape of Garuḍa and holding the *vajra* in his beak, endeavoured to rob the Nāga of his precious treasure. As he did not succeed by force, he re-assumed his own form and begged the bowl from the Nāga. Having thus obtained it, Indra took the bowl to the heaven of the thirty-three gods and instituted

[1] *Si-yu-ki*, vol. ii, p. 25. Watters, *On Yuan Chuang*, vol. ii, pp. 14 f.

[2] *Lalit.* p. 204, ll. 9–12. Foucaux, vol. i, p. 179 (also p. 193).

[3] *Lalit.* pp. 269 f.; cf. *Mahāvastu*, vol. ii, p. 302; *Nidānakathā*, p. 70.

an annual 'festival of the bowl', which, as the author assures us, was still celebrated in his days. The precious throne upon which the Buddha had sat, was preserved by the Nāga-daughter as an object of worship.

Among the series of a hundred-and-twenty sculptured *tableaux* on the Borobudur which illustrate the legend of the Buddha's life as described in the *Lalitavistara*, no less than five panels are devoted to the episode of the Nairañjanā (Nos. 85–9).[1] First we see how the Bodhisattva, while holding the bowl received from Sujātā in his right hand, approaches the bank of the Nairañjanā where he is received by four divine personages including apparently a Nāga, who, kneeling down, pay him homage with hands joined in adoration. Then he is shown standing in the midst of the waves, while celestials and *ṛishis* adore him from the clouds and shower down divine flowers and ornaments. Having finished his bath in the river, the Great Being is approached by the Nāga maiden, who is the Naiad of the Nairañjanā. Kneeling down in a peculiar attitude, she offers her present, the throne, which occupies the centre of the panel (No. 87). On the other side of the throne there are three more kneeling figures of female Nāgas, evidently her attendants. Each of them is characterized by a three-fold serpent-crest. In the next *tableau* the Bodhisattva is seated cross-legged on the throne and stretches out his right hand in the direction of the Nāgī who is still kneeling with two attendant Nāgīs, and seems to witness his meal. In the fifth and last panel (No. 89) referring to this episode the future Buddha is still shown seated on his throne in nearly the same attitude as in the preceding scene. Here, however, the position of the right hand is slightly different, evidently to indicate that he has cast away the bowl, after having finished his meal. The Nāgarāja, who is recognizable by his snake-hood, is shown twice, first in the act of reverently receiving the bowl which has been sanctified by the Master, and a second time seated in his watery palace and handing over the precious object to Indra. The latter is the ordinary type of a royal personage, but is distinguished by his attendant, seated behind him, who wears a peculiar head-dress in the shape of an elephant's trunk. From this we may infer that the satellite in question is meant to portray Indra's elephant Airāvata, who here assumes human shape.

The Bodhisattva Extolled by the Nāga Kālika

The Bodhisattva's progress from the river Nairañjanā towards the sacred tree is described as a triumphal march in which a host of heavenly beings accompany him. The Nāgarāja Kāla or Kālika also comes forth and in a hymn of praise foretells his approaching

[1] C. M. Pleyte, *Buddha-legende*, pp. 123–6. N. J. Krom, *Barabudur*, vol. i, pp. 188 ff.; plates, series 1*a*, pl. xliii–xlv.

enlightenment. Aśvaghosha in his *Buddhacharita*[1] relates this incident in the following words :—

Then Kāla, the best of Serpents, whose majesty was like unto that of the lord of elephants, having been awakened by the unparelleled sound of the Buddha's feet, uttered this praise of the great Sage, being sure that he was on the point of attaining supreme knowledge : " Inasmuch as the earth, pressed down by thy feet, O Sage, resoundeth repeatedly, and inasmuch as thy splendour shineth forth like the sun, thou shalt assuredly to-day enjoy the desired fruit. Inasmuch as rows of birds fluttering in the sky offer thee reverential salutation, O lotus-eyed One, and inasmuch as gentle breezes blow in the sky thou shalt certainly to-day become the Buddha." Being thus extolled by the best of Serpents, and having taken some pure grass from a grasscutter, he, having made his resolution, sat down to obtain perfect knowledge at the foot of the great holy tree.

The *Lalitavistara* and tbe *Mahāvastu,* in rendering this episode, indulge in their usual prolixity, and the latter text presents it in several repetitions[2]. In both these books the hymn of Kāla covers a couple of pages. In the *Lalitavistara* it is the wondrous effulgence radiating from the Bodhisattva's person which awakens the Nāgarāja in his subterraneous abode ; in the *Mahāvastu* it is the quaking of the earth and in the *Nidānakathā* the sound of the golden bowl presented by Sujātā, which the Bodhisattva had cast into the river and which, reaching the palace of the Nāga king, struck against the bowls used by the three previous Buddhas on a similar occasion. According to a later tradition, preserved in Chinese sources, the Nāga through the effect of his bad *karman* was born blind, but when the Bodhisattva, while proceeding to the Bodhi-tree, passed his abode, his eyes were suddenly opened.[3]

The texts, however much they may differ in detail, all agree in the importance they evidently attach to the prophecy pronounced by the Serpent-king, which has the character of an Act of Truth. We may, therefore, expect to find the episode of the Nāga Kāla also rendered in plastic art.

On a profusely sculptured railing pillar of Amarāvatī there is indeed a bas-relief (Plate VII*a*), which must refer to this incident in the Buddha's career.[4] It occupies the space immediately above the central rosette, and is divided into three compartments by two vertical lines, a feature commonly noticed on the Amarāvatī pillars. Let us quote Fergusson's description : " In the centre a flight of Hansas or sacred geese are winging their

[1] *Buddhacharita,* xii, 113–16 (we quote Cowell's translation) ; *S.B.E.*, vol. xlix, pp. 135 f.

[2] *Lalit.*, vol. i, pp. 281–5. *Mahāvastu,* vol. ii, pp. 265, 302, 304, 308, 398, 400.

[3] Hiuen Tsiang, *Si-yu-ki* (transl. Beal), vol. ii, p. 132. Watters, *Travels,* vol. ii, p. 134. Cf. *Lalit.*, p. 281, l. 21, *ekāntaṃ tamasākulam mama gṛihaṃ prāgdushkṛitaiḥ karmabhiḥ.*

[4] Fergusson, *Tree and Serpent Worship,* p. 190, pl. lviii.

way across what appears to be a lake, between two trees. A hand issues from the right-hand tree, with two circular objects in it, and the geese under it look as if falling dead on the shore, but it may be they are only flying downwards. On the sand are five impressions of the sacred feet, there were probably originally eight,—and two birds, apparently peacocks, are somewhat indistinctly seen strutting on the sand. On the left hand are several women presenting flowers in pots, and on the right hand the Nāga Rāja with his seven-headed snakehood, and behind him his three wives, over each of whose heads may be seen the single-headed snake, which always marks them."

Fergusson's identification of this scene with the *Nachcha-jātaka* (the well-known story of the peacock wooing the daughter of the royal gold-goose) may be safely discarded. The footprints afford a sure indication that the subject of this relief is not a *jātaka*, but an event of the Buddha's last existence. They symbolize his bodily presence. Now one pair of footprints is shown in the lower left-hand corner and the other pair in the corresponding right-hand corner of the central space ; both are turned towards the right. The intention of the artist is perfectly clear ; the Buddha is crossing the water, and this water is not a lake, as Fergusson supposed, but must be the river Nairañjanā. In the passage quoted above from the *Buddhacharita*, the Nāga Kāla mentions " lines of birds fluttering in the sky ", which offer reverential salutations to the Buddha. The other Sanskrit texts are much more explicit on this point ; they enumerate various kinds of birds, including geese and peacocks which pay homage by performing the *pradakshiṇā* ; in other words, in their flight they encircle the Buddha, keeping him on their right side.[1] Now this is exactly what the geese in our relief are doing, and this explains the curious position of the leader of the flock, who looks " as if falling dead on the shore ". The two peacocks, too, it will be noticed, have their right side turned towards the single-footprint immediately above them, which indicates the Buddha crossing the river. As to the mysterious hand which, according to Fergusson, issues from the right-hand tree on the river-bank (on the photograph it is hardly discernible) we may compare a stanza of the *Buddhacharita*, which says that the Bodhisattva, slowly coming up the bank of the Nairañjanā, was supported as by a hand by the trees on the shore, which bent down the ends of their branches in adoration.[2] On reaching the opposite shore, he is greeted by the Nāgarāja, in whom we recognize Kāla uttering his prediction of the approaching Enlightenment. His being accompanied by three Nāgīs is in concord with the *Lalitavistara*.[3] For in this text we read that

[1] *Lalit.*, vol. i, p. 283, l. 6. *Mahāvastu*, vol. ii, p. 264, l. 16 ; p. 265, l. 6 ; p. 266, l. 19 ; 267, l. 6.

[2] *Buddhach.* xii, 105, *bhaktyāvanataśākhāgrair dattahastas taṭadrumaiḥ*.—Cowell, p. 135.

[3] *Lalit.*, p. 284, l. 11 ; p. 285, l. 16. Cf. also p. 281, ll. 12–13. *Kāliko nāgarājas tasyāṃ velāyāṃ tasya parivārasya purataḥ sthitvemā gāthā abhāshat.*

(*a*) KĀLIKA LAUDING THE BUDDHA (AMARĀVATĪ).

(*b*) JĀTAKA OF THE NĀGA CHAMPAKA (AMARĀVATĪ).

[*To face p.* 100

Suvarṇaprabhāsā ("Gold-shine"), the chief consort (*agramahishī*) of the Nāgarāja Kālika surrounded by a throng of Nāga-maidens in splendid array, lauded the Bodhisattva in a laudatory hymn and showered a rain of jewels and flowers on him as he went. Whether the group of flying female figures in the left-hand compartment are also *Nāga-kanyās*, it is difficult to decide. But the vases of lotus-flowers they carry are obviously meant as an offering to the Great Being.

The proposed identification is confirmed by the scene portrayed in the central medallion immediately beneath. It shows a group of women paying reverence to the invisible Bodhisattva symbolized by the Bodhi-tree.[1] As two of them carry a bowl, there can be little doubt that they represent the village girls of Uruvilvā, headed by Sujātā and her servant Uttarā. The huts around must be the dwellings of the village.

In the Græco-Buddhist art of Gandhāra, the episode of the Nāga Kāla paying homage to the Bodhisattva is often rendered.[2] Whilst its mode of illustrating this scene is much clearer and more direct, the Gandhāra school rendering this scene entirely lacks the mysterious charm of the Amarāvatī sculpture. The central figure is the person of the Bodhisattva, who, being on his way to the Bodhi-tree, is shown standing. He is faced by the Nāga Kāla, who is usually accompanied by his chief queen, Suvarṇaprabhāsā. Both the Nāga and the Nāgī, who are distinguished by their snake-hood, issue forth from an elegant fountain enclosure which conceals the lower half of their bodies. The enclosure has the appearance of a 'Buddhist' railing of the well-known type. It is provided with a gargoyle emitting a stream of water, so as to indicate that here it serves to enclose a sacred spring.

In the account of Aśoka's pilgrimage to the places hallowed by the presence of the Master, it is said that he also visited the spot where the Nāgarāja Kālika had extolled the Bodhisattva, when the latter was on his way to the Bodhimūla.[3] After the Nāga had shown himself to the king and answered his query as to the appearance of the Buddha, Aśoka ordered a *chaitya* to be made. Presumably this *chaitya* consisted of a stone railing of the pattern familiar in Buddhist art.

On a fragmentary Gupta sculpture from Sārnāth, representing the main events of Śākyamuni's life, we find a panel in which various scenes relating to 'the Great Renunciation' are combined. On the left side of the spectator the Bodhisattva is seen facing a Nāga who wears a five-fold snake-hood. It has been surmised that this Nāga is

[1] The tree in the central medallion is clearly not a mango, as Fergusson supposed, but an *aśvattha* (Ficus religiosa), in other words, the Bodhi-tree.

[2] A. Foucher, *Art gréco-bouddhique*, vol. i, pp. 383–9; figs. 194–6; and vol. ii, fig. 400. Burgess, *Ancient Monuments*, pl. 99.

[3] *Divyāvadāna*, pp. 392 f.

the Nāgarāja Kālika.[1] The identification appears acceptable as at his side we recognize the presentation of the bowl of milk-rice by Sujātā. The treatment is remarkable for its succinctness.

Among the series of 120 sculptures of the Borobudur which illustrate the *Lalitavistara*, the 91st panel portrays the legend of the Nāga Kālika paying reverence to the Bodhisattva.[2]

How the Serpent-King Muchilinda sheltered the Lord Buddha [3]

[It is related in the beginning of the *Vinaya-piṭaka* that the Lord Buddha, after attaining Enlightenment, spent some weeks in meditation at various places in the neighbourhood of the Bodhi-tree. At the end of the second week he betook himself to the Muchilinda-tree, and sat cross-legged at the foot of that tree during seven days, enjoying the bliss of emancipation.]

Now at that time a great cloud appeared out of season, and for seven days it was cloudy weather attended with rain and a cold wind. Then Muchilinda,[4] the serpent-king, issued from his abode, and enveloping the body of the Blessed One seven times with his coils, kept his large hood spread over the Master's head, thinking to himself: "May no cold touch the Blessed One, may no heat touch the Blessed One, may no gnats, flies or creeping things, no wind or heat come near the Blessed One."

Now at the end of those seven days the serpent king Muchilinda, seeing the sky clear and free from clouds, loosened his coils from the body of the Lord, and, changing his own appearance into that of a Brahmin youth, stood before the Blessed One, raising his joined hands and did reverence to him.

In the *Nidānakathā* [5] the story of Muchilinda sheltering Buddha against wind and rain is told in a few lines immediately after the episode of the Tathāgata's temptation by the daughters of Māra. According to this version the temptation took place in the fifth week, and the meeting with Muchilinda apparently in the sixth week after the Bodhi. It is said here that Buddha, when enveloped seven times by the coils of the snake-king, enjoyed the bliss of salvation as if he had been resting in a shrine (*gandhakuṭī*).

The well-known Sanskrit text *Lalitavistara* [6] gives an evidently later version of the legend. Here Buddha is protected not only by the serpent-king Muchilinda, but also by

[1] *Sārnāth Museum Catalogue*, p. 187, pl. xx.

[2] Pleyte, *Buddha-legende*, p. 129. Krom. *Barabudur*, vol. i, p. 192. Plates: series 1*a*, pl. xlvi.

[3] *Mahāvagga*, i, 3. *Vinaya Piṭakam* (ed. Oldenberg), vol. i, p. 3. *S.B.E.*, vol. xiii, p. 80. *Buddhism in translations*, p. 86.

[4] Pali Muchalinda.

[5] *Jātaka* (ed. Fausböll), vol. i, p. 80. Rhys Davids, *Buddhist Birth Stories*, p. 109.

[6] *Lalit.*, vol. i, pp. 379 f. Foucaux, part i, p. 316.

a number of other Nāgarājas, who have come from the East, South, West, and North. They all envelop the Buddha with their coils and form a canopy over his head by means of their crests, so that, when thronged together, they resemble Mount Meru. According to this rendering, it was the fifth week after the Bodhi, whereas the temptation by the three daughters of the Evil One had taken place in the fourth week.

In the *Mahāvastu* [1] the story is briefly related. Here it is said that Buddha spent the fourth week after the Enlightenment in the dwelling of the Nāgarāja Kāla and the fifth one in that of the Nāgarāja Muchilinda. Then there arose a " cloud out of season " and the Nāga protected him against the rain during a week in the manner described above.

It is a point of some interest that in the earliest version of this legend which is preserved in the Pali canon mention is made of a Muchilinda-tree which is not spoken of in the later sources. Evidently there is some connexion between the Nāga Muchilinda and the tree of the same name under which the Buddha was seated. May we perhaps assume that in the ancient story the Nāga was conceived as a tree-spirit ? Such an assumption is all the more plausible as in a Buddhist birth-story we read of a huge banyan-tree which is haunted by Nāgas.[2]

The scene of the Nāga sheltering Buddha lends itself admirably for plastic rendering. Yet in the art of India proper the examples of this subject are but few in number. Earliest in date is a piece of sculpture from Sānchi [3] which on two faces is carved with a series of panels. It must have belonged to one of the pillars of the southern gateway, and is now preserved in the local museum. The upper panel of the front face shows the Muchilinda-tree decorated with garlands. On both sides we notice a garland-carrying *kinnara* hovering in the air. The Buddha's presence is only indicated by an empty seat in front of the tree. In the foreground the Nāgarāja in the shape of a human being wearing a five-fold snake-hood is seated on what appear to be rocks. On both sides of him two of his queens are shown sitting on wicker stools and behind them there are female attendants holding *chowries*. The Nāgīs, as usual, have only a single snake-hood. It is interesting that in agreement with the early Pali version of the story, Buddha's seat is placed under a tree. It has the appearance of a sacred tree.

In the art of Amarāvatī we find the subject treated in an entirely different fashion. Here the person of the Buddha is portrayed sitting cross-legged on the folds of the serpent

[1] *Mahāvastu* (ed. Senart), vol. iii, pp. 300 f. Cf. *Buddhacharita*, xv, 49–53.

[2] *Mahāvāṇija-jātaka*, No. 493 of the great Pali-collection. In *Lalit.*, i, p. 11, l. 1, the *muchilinda* and *mahāmuchilinda* occur in an enumeration of various trees.

[3] *Cat. of Sanchi Museum*, p. 21, No. A. 15, pl. viii. The panel is reproduced from a drawing by Fergusson, *Tree and Serpent Worship*, pl. xxiv, fig. 1. The same plate shows a bas-relief from the Western *toraṇa* in which the same subject is found treated in greater detail, the Nāga king being attended by a band of female musicians.

whose many-headed hood is visible around his halo.[1] This highly artistic manner of rendering the subject although not really in agreement with textual tradition (for there the Nāga is said to have enveloped Buddha with his coils), is but seldom met with in the later art of India proper. We can quote only one example of mediocre workmanship from Sārnāth.[2] On the other hand, the *motif* has found great favour in the art of Further India, whither, according to so good a judge as M. Foucher, it was introduced from Amarāvatī.[3] We reproduce a very fine specimen from Cambodia in Plate XVII.[4]

We may note parenthetically that the figure of Buddha sheltered by the Nāga found in Buddhist sculpture has its counterpart both in Brahmanical and Jaina art. In the former there is the group of the god Vishṇu supported by the World-serpent Śesha. The usual presentation of this subject is to show the four-armed god reclining on the snake as on a couch, but in the cave temples we meet with a few cases in which Vishṇu is seated on the top of the snake's coiled-up body, whilst its hood is extended like a canopy over his head.

With regard to the art of the Jainas, it should be noted that the Tīrthaṃkara Pārśvanātha (who is the last but one in the series of twenty-four Saviours) is distinguished by a snake-hood.[5] To this peculiarity we shall have occasion to revert in the sequel. According to a Jaina legend it was the Yaksha (!) Dharaṇendra who spread his many hoods over the head of the Arhat during a violent storm. In all probability this story was modelled after the earlier legend of Muchilinda.

Among the sculptures of Borobudur we find a panel (No. 101) devoted to the legend of Muchilinda.[6] Here the Buddha is shown seated cross-legged on a lotus-throne inside a *maṇḍapa*. At the side of this pavilion the Nāga king, overshadowed by the royal umbrella, kneels down before the Lord. He has a following of five Nāga satellites—three male and two female—carrying offerings and wearing like their ruler a head-dress surmounted by snake-heads. The rendering of the scene, as found on the Javanese monument, differs conspicuously from that met with in Indian art. The reason is that at Borobudur the Nāgas are always pictured in purely human shape, apart from the snake-hood. It was, therefore, clearly impossible for the artist to follow the legend more closely.

[1] Fergusson, *Tree- and Serpent-worship*, pl. lxxvi. Burgess, *Amarāvatī*, pl. xxxi, 7. Cf. also Burgess, *Buddhist Cave Temples*, pl. xxvii.

[2] *A.S.R.* for 1904–05, p. 85, pl. xxx *b*. *Sārnāth Museum Catalogue*, p. 247.

[3] Foucher, *Art gréco-bouddhique*, vol. ii, p. 628, fig. 521.

[4] The original is preserved in the Musée du Trocadéro at Paris. Cf. the interesting remarks by M. G. Coedès, *Bronzes khmèrs* (*Ars Asiatica*), pp. 33 ff., pl. xxi–xxiii, 2.

[5] G. Bühler and J. Burgess, *On the Indian sect of the Jainas* (London, 1903), pp. 63 f.

[6] Pleyte, *Buddha-legende*, p. 144. Krom. *Barabudur*, vol. i, pp. 200 f. ; plates : series 1*a*, pl. li. The heads of the two Nāgī attendants are damaged, but we may assume that they, too, were originally distinguished by the usual serpent emblem.

Three more panels belonging to the Buddha legend sculptured on the Borobudur may here be briefly noticed. In the sacred texts it is related that on his way from Uruvilvā to Benares (where he was going to preach the Good Law) Buddha halted at Gayā, where he was hospitably received by the Nāgarāja Sudarśana. This episode (which is only briefly mentioned in the Sanskrit books) we find pictured in great detail in the 111th panel of the Buddha series. On one side the Master is seated on a throne under a canopy. A Nāga carrying a parasol stands on his left. The remainder of the panel is occupied by a crowd of more than twenty Nāgas and Nāgīs, partly sitting and partly standing. Evidently they are Sudarśana and his followers who are bringing dishes of food for the acceptance of their exalted guest.[1]

In describing the Buddha's further journey to Benares, stage after stage, the *Mahāvastu* and the *Buddhacharita* speak of yet another Nāga king, named Kamaṇḍalu, who entertained him in like manner at Lohitavastuka.[2] This episode, however, is not rendered in the Buddha series of Borobudur, which throughout follows the *Lalitavistara*.

In the last *tableau* but one of the series (No. 119) we see the Buddha being bathed in a lotus tank by his first five converts previous to his famous sermon in the Deer Park of Benares. It is curious that, besides the Buddha and his five attendants in monks' dress, the panel contains four satellites which their head-dress proves to be Nāgas, or, rather, two Nāga couples, one standing on the proper left and the other seated on the proper right. Neither the *Lalitavistara* nor any other text known to us refers to the presence of such beings on this great occasion.[3] Perhaps the artist introduced them here as auspicious participants or as the spirits of the pond in which the Buddha bathed. Or are we to assume that they refer to the legend of Elāpattra which we will now narrate ? The standing Nāga holds a parasol and his female companion lotus-flowers whilst the seated Nāga clasps what appears to be a censer, and his consort folds both hands in the attitude of adoration.

The Nāgarāja Elāpattra Questions the Buddha [4]

[The following story is known from Tibetan and Chinese sources. It also occurs in the *Mahāvastu* under the title ' Questions of Nālaka ', but in so confused and abrupt a form that we have preferred to follow the version found in the two Tibetan Lives of Buddha.]

[1] *Lalit.*, vol. i, p. 406, l. 18. Foucaux, p. 338. *Mahāvastu*, vol. iii, pp. 324 ff. *Buddhacharita*, xv, 92. Cowell, p. 169. Pleyte, *Buddha Legende*, p. 154. Krom, *Barabudur*, vol. i, p. 207 ; plates : series 1*a*, pl. li.

[2] *Mahāvastu*, vol. iii, pp. 327 f. *Buddhacharita*, xv, 96. Cowell, p. 170.

[3] *Lalit.*, vol. i, p. 410, ll. 1–2. Foucaux, p. 341. *Mahāvastu*, vol. iii, p. 329, l. 16. Pleyte, op. cit., p. 160. Krom, op. cit., vol. i, p. 211 ; plates : series 1*a*, pl. lx.

[4] *Mahāvastu*, vol. iii, pp. 383 ff. *Buddhacharita*, xvii, 3. Schiefner, *Lebensbeschreibung*, pp. 248 f. Rockhill, *Life*, pp. 46 f. Beal, *Romantic Legend*, pp. 279 f.

While the future Buddha still dwelt in the Tushita heaven, he had pronounced two enigmatical stanzas, which no one but the Master himself could explain. There lived at that time a Nāga king, called Suvarṇaprabhāsa, who saw in the palace of Vaiśravaṇa a copy of these mysterious verses, incised on a stone slab. He took it to his friend, Elāpattra, the Nāga of Takshaśilā, who recognized in it a saying of Buddha. On the advice of Suvarṇaprabhāsa, the Nāgarāja Elāpattra assumed the form of a young Brahmin (*māṇava*), and went round the cities of India promising a *lakh* of gold to anyone who could interpret the enigma pronounced by the Lord. So at last he reached Benares where the people advised him to consult Nālaka, the nephew of the Sage Asitadevala.[1] Nālaka, not being able himself to solve the problem, promised to procure the Nāga the desired answer within seven days. Having found out that a Buddha had arisen in the world and that he was abiding in the Deer Park of Ṛishipatana near Benares, he told Elāpattra. Then Elāpattra reflected: "Should I appear in my present shape as a Brahmin, the other Brahmins who have not accepted the Law will cause me harm. If I appear in my own form the other Nāgas will be wroth with me. So I will go to the Lord in the semblance of a *chakravartin* or universal monarch." But the Lord Buddha rebuked him for his deceit and ordered him to assume his natural shape. When Elāpattra confessed that he feared the anger of his fellow-Nāgas, the Lord appointed Vajrapāṇi to protect him. Thereupon the Nāga Elāpattra became a serpent of such gigantic size that his tail was still in his palace at Takshaśilā, while his seven-hooded head was seen at Benares. And now, whenas he questioned the Buddha about the future, the Lord made answer that he should await the arrival of Maitreya who would reveal it to him. Whereupon the Nāga disappeared.

According to the Chinese version of the story, there follows a dialogue between Buddha and the Nāga, in the course of which the latter asks in what manner he may acquire a store of merit whereby he might be reborn as a *Deva* or as a man.[2] Being instructed by the Lord in the Law, Elāpattra began to weep, and Buddha asked him why he did so. On this Elāpattra rejoined: "I remember in days gone by, that I was a follower of Kāśyapa Buddha, and because I destroyed a tree called 'Ila' I was born in my present shape, and was called 'Elāpattra'. Then this same Kāśyapa told me that after an indefinite period when Śākya Buddha came into the world, that I should again receive a human shape, and so by becoming a disciple attain final deliverance, and it is for this reason I weep."

Then Elāpattra, having taken refuge in the Buddha, the Law and the Church departed.

[1] Asitadevala is the *ṛishi* who shortly after the birth of the Bodhisattva, foretells his future greatness.

[2] The *Mahāvastu*, more logically, makes the Nāga inquire into the meaning of the incomprehensible stanzas which had moved him to wander to Benares.

(*a*) Kālika lauding the Buddha (Amarāvatī).

(*b*) Jātaka of the Nāga Champaka (Amarāvatī).

[*To face p.* 100

When the Chinese pilgrim Fa-Hien [1] visited the Deer Park of Benares, he noticed among the many sacred monuments of that place a *stūpa* erected on the spot where the dragon Elāpattra had asked Buddha : " When shall I be freed from this Nāga body ? "

Hiuen Tsiang in the course of his very detailed account of the Deer Park does not mention this particular memorial, but on his visit to Takshaśilā he saw the very place which was supposed to be the abode of the Nāga in question.

There exist two Græco-Buddhist sculptures which M. Foucher [2] has identified with the meeting of Buddha and Elāpattra in the Deer Park at Benares. The one which was found at Karamār and is now preserved in the Lahore Museum, shows the Nāga kneeling with folded hands at the side of the Buddha who is accompanied by Vajrapāṇi. Behind the kneeling Nāga there is a fountain from which a Nāgī (?) appears in an attitude of adoration. The important point, according to M. Foucher, is that both the Buddha and his satellite Vajrapāṇi are shown seated. It must, however, be admitted that there is some reason to challenge the proposed identification. The supposed Elāpattra assumes here neither the shape of a *chakravartin* nor that of a gigantic seven-headed snake. He does not even wear the usual serpent emblem. Nor is there any indication of the scene being laid in the Deer Park.

In the case of the other sculpture (Plate VIII*a*), which was excavated at Sahr-i-Bahlol by Sir Aurel Stein, and is now in the Peshāwar Museum, the identification seems to be far more probable. Here the Buddha sits in the midst of five shaven monks, four of whom are seated on either side of him, whilst the fifth one is standing behind his right shoulder, Vajrapāṇi occupying the corresponding position to the left. The number of five is significant, in all probability they are the first five converts of the Deer Park. The Nāga is shown twice ; first in royal dress and snake-hood, standing with both hands joined in the attitude of adoration, and the second time as a five-headed snake in front of Buddha's seat. No doubt the objection could be made that it is a snake of very modest size, but it was clearly impossible for the artist to portray a serpent whose body stretched from Taxila to Benares !

How the Lord Buddha subdued the fiery dragon of Uruvilvā [3]

[After the Lord Buddha had preached his first sermon in the Deer Park of Benares he returned to Uruvilvā which had been the scene of his spiritual struggle and victory.]

[1] *Record* (transl. Legge), p. 96.

[2] Foucher, *Art gréco-bouddhique*, vol. i, pp. 505 ff., fig. 251, and vol. ii, p. 29, fig. 317. The second sculpture was first published in the *A.S.R.* for 1911–12, p. 105, pl. xxxviii, fig. 5.

[3] *Mahāvagga*, i, 15, *Vinaya Piṭakam*, vol. i, pp. 24 f. ; *S.B.E.*, vol. xiii, pp. 118 ff.

At that time there lived at Uruvilvā three Brahmanical ascetics, the brothers Kāśyapa, who were the chiefs of several hundreds of hermits. The Lord, having gone to the hermitage of Uruvilvā-Kāśyapa (such was the name of the first brother) spake to him : "If it be not disagreeable to thee, Kāśyapa, let me spend one night in the room where thy sacred fire is kept." "It is not disagreeable to me," Kāśyapa answered, "but there is a savage serpent-king of great magical power, a dreadfully venomous snake; let him do no harm to thee." The Buddha repeated his request a second and a third time, and at last Kāśyapa gave way.

Then the Lord entered the fire-hut, made himself a couch of grass, and sat down cross-legged, keeping the body erect and surrounding himself with watchfulness of mind. The Nāga, seeing that the Lord had entered, became irritated and sent forth a cloud of smoke. Then the Lord thought: "What if I were to leave intact the skin and flesh and bones of this Nāga; but were to conquer the fire which he will send forth, by my fire."

Now the Lord effected the appropriate exercise of miraculous power and sent forth a cloud of smoke. Then the Nāga, being unable to master his rage, sent forth flames and the Lord, converting his body into fire, sent forth flames, so that the fire-room looked as if it were burning and blazing.

At the end of that night, the Lord, leaving intact the skin and flesh and bones of that Nāga, and conquering the Nāga's fire by his fire, threw him into his alms-bowl and showed him to Urivilvā-Kāśyapa, saying: "Here thou seest the Nāga; his fire hath been conquered by my fire." Then Kāśyapa thought: "Truly the Great *Śramaṇa* possesseth high magical powers and great faculties, in that he is able to overcome that savage serpent-king. He is not, however, as holy a man as I am."

Quite a succession of miracles were needed before Kāśyapa of Uruvilvā and his followers acknowledged the spiritual superiority of the Buddha and became members of his community. The number of these miracles, the Pali text says, amounted to three thousand five hundred, but among those which are related, Buddha's contest with the fiery dragon stands first. Evidently it was considered an exploit of the highest import that the magic fire produced by the Buddha had proved more powerful than that of the savage Nāga.

This is also emphasized in the *Mahāvastu*.[1] Here the taming of the serpent in the fire-room (*agniśaraṇa*) is the last and crowning miracle by which the Kāśyapas and their followers are finally induced to acknowledge the superiority of the Buddha. We have the ancient legend here presented to us in an evidently later and more developed form.

[1] *Mahāvastu*, vol. iii, pp. 428 ff.

According to this later version the *jaṭilas*, on seeing the fire-room all ablaze by the Buddha's *tejas*, exerted themselves to quench the conflagration and to save Gautama. In the stanzas following the passage in prose it is related that the Nāga, after having been released by the Buddha, assumed human form, fell at the Master's feet and humbly craved his forgiveness.

The victory of the Buddha over the wicked Nāga in the fire-hut is represented in a well-known bas-relief on the eastern gateway of Sānchi.[1] Here, too, as was usual in the ancient school of Central India, the person of the Buddha is not shown. His presence is probably indicated by the stone seat in the fire-hut—a domed, open pavilion supported on pillars—which occupies the centre of the panel. Flames of fire indicative of the Buddha's *tejas* are seen bursting forth from the horse-shoe bays in the roof. Over the seat the five-headed hood of the snake is plainly visible. In the group of three *jaṭilas*—characterized as such by their matted hair (*jaṭā*) and their garments of bark (*valkala*)—we may in all probability recognize the three Kāśyapa brothers before and after their conversion.[2] For the rest the panel is filled with all that belongs to an Indian hermitage. In the foreground we notice a hut thatched with leaves, in front of which a bearded ascetic is seated on a bundle of grass (*brishī*). Apparently he is engaged in doing penance, as indicated by the band passed round his knees and loins (*paryaṅka-bandha*). Another hermit stands facing him. At the side of the hut flows the river Nairañjanā enlivened by aquatic birds and lotus-plants. Anchorites are seen drawing water, bathing in the company of buffaloes and an elephant, or practising *tapas* with both arms raised (*ūrdhvabāhu*). The background is occupied by a variety of fruit-bearing trees with monkeys busy in the foliage.

In the art of Amarāvatī we find the episode rendered in very much the same manner, although not with an equal wealth of detail.[3] Here the presence of the Buddha in the fire-hut is indicated by a pair of footprints over which appears the five-fold head of the Nāga. The hut is surrounded by a group of six hermits seated with hands raised in adoration. In the background three trees, a deer, and two boys complete the picture.

Numerous examples of the scene of the Buddha's victory over the Nāga of Uruvilvā

[1] Fergusson, *Tree- and Serpent-worship*, pp. 143 f., pl. xxxii. Grünwedel, *Buddhist Art in India*, pp. 61 ff., fig. 35. A. Foucher, *Beginnings of Buddhist Art*, pp. 97 f., pl. ix, 1. The above account differs in some details from previous descriptions of this sculpture. The Nāga is certainly represented with five, not with seven heads as stated by Fergusson and Grünwedel. M. Foucher thinks that the three ascetics visible to the left of the foreground are in the act of filling their pitchers in order to quench the supposed conflagration. This incident is indeed represented in Gandharan Art.

[2] Such a repetition of the same personages in one panel is quite in agreement with the practice of the early Buddhist school of sculpture. The ascetics grouped on the right side of the fire-hut are in any case shown paying reverence to the invisible Buddha, as is manifest from their raising their joined hands in token of adoration. This gesture is the *añjali* of Indian literature.

[3] Fergusson, op. cit., p. 208, pl. lxx.

are met with among the Græco-Buddhist sculptures of Gandhāra. Here the person of the Buddha has been introduced and is usually represented standing in the midst of the Brahmanical anchorites. Mr. Hargreaves draws my attention to the great number of examples in the Peshāwar Museum. " These are not in the form of reliefs," he writes, " but show on a pedestal a standing Buddha, turning half-left to a very small Kāśyapa and a *brahmachārin* standing by his left foot.[1] No. 608 of the Lahore Museum undoubtedly came from such a representation. I fancy we have a dozen of these in Peshāwar. When the little figure of Kāśyapa and his attendant are lost (as very frequently happens), there remains a standing Buddha image slightly turned to the left. One wonders why this subject was so popular."

The Lahore Museum contains some more sculptures relating to the same subject.[2] They show Buddha seated cross-legged inside the hut, the flames surrounding his body indicating his *tejas* or magical fire, by which he subdued the malicious Nāga. The latter has the appearance of a simple snake either winding up against the wall of the hut or curled up at the feet of the Master. The *jaṭilas* outside the hut exert themselves to extinguish the supposed conflagration, as is related in the *Mahāvastu*. On one sculpture discussed by Professor Grünwedel this episode of the legend is separately treated in a very convincing manner. On another fragment in the Lahore Museum (No. 2345) Buddha is shown presenting the snake in the alms-bowl to the eldest Kāśyapa. On the whole the sculptors of Gandhāra have succeeded well in rendering the gaunt figures of the Brahmanical ascetics. Throughout the Nāga is shown in the aspect of a snake, although polycephalous in the earlier examples from Sānchi and Amarāvatī. This is in close agreement with the ancient legend of the Pali *Tripiṭaka* in which the anonymous Nāga in the fire-room preserves to the end the character of an animal.

How a certain Nāga was ordained as a Buddhist Friar[3]

At that time there was a certain Nāga who was ashamed of having been born as a serpent. Now this Nāga thought: " By what expedient could I become released from being born as a serpent, and quickly obtain human nature ? " Then this Nāga thought: " These Buddhist friars lead indeed a virtuous, tranquil, and holy life; they speak the truth; they keep the precepts of morality, and are endowed with all virtues. If, then, I could obtain admittance among the Buddhist friars, I should be released from my serpent birth, and quickly obtain human nature."

[1] *A.S.R.* for 1909–10, pp. 57 ff., pl. xx, figs. *a*, *b*, and *c*; and 1911–12, p. 113.

[2] Foucher, *Art gréco-bouddhique*, vol. i, pp. 447 ff., figs. 224–6, and vol. ii, figs. 435 and 461. Grünwedel, *Buddhist Art*, pp. 126, ff., fig. 78. Burgess, *Ancient Monuments*, pl. 131. *A.S.R.*, 1907–8, p. 139; pl. xlv*d*.

[3] *Mahāvagga*, i, 63. *Vinaya Piṭakam* (ed. Oldenberg), vol. i, pp. 86 ff. *S.B.E.*, vol. xiii, pp. 217 ff.

Now this Nāga, having assumed the shape of a youth, went to the *Bhikshus*, and asked for admittance to the Order; and the Friars granted him admittance to the Order and ordained him. At that time the Nāga dwelt together with a certain *Bhikshu* in the last cell of the Jetavana Monastery. Now this Friar, having arisen in the night, when the dawn was at hand, was walking to and fro in the open air. When the *Bhikshu* had left the cell, the Nāga deemed himself safe from discovery and fell asleep in his natural shape. The whole cell was filled with the snake's body: his coils bulged out of the window.

Then the *Bhikshu* thought: "I will go back to the cell," opened the door, and saw the whole cell filled with the snake. Seeing which he was terrified and cried out. The *Bhikshus* ran up and said to him: "Why didst thou cry out, friend?" "This whole cell, friends, is filled with a snake; the coils bulge out of the window." Then the Nāga was awakened by the noise and sat down on his seat. The *Bhikshus* said to him: "Who art thou, friend?" "I am a Nāga, reverend Sirs." "And why hast thou done such a thing, friend?" Then the Nāga told the whole matter to the *Bhikshus*; the *Bhikshus* told it to the Blessed One.

Thereupon the Blessed One, having ordered the fraternity of the *Bhikshus* to assemble, addressed the Nāga: "Ye Nāgas are not capable of spiritual growth in this doctrine and discipline. However, Nāga, go thou and observe fast on the fourteenth, fifteenth, and eighth day of each half-month, thus wilt thou be released from being born as a serpent and quickly obtain human nature." Then the Nāga became sad and sorrowful, and went away.

Quoth the Blessed One: "There are two occasions, O *Bhikshus*, whereon a Nāga, having assumed human shape, sheweth his true nature; when he hath sexual intercourse with a female of his species, and if he thinketh himself safe from discovery. Let an animal, O *Bhikshus*, that hath not received the ordination, not receive it; if it hath received it, let it be expelled."

How the Elder Svāgata subdued the Nāga of the Mango Ferry[1]

At that time the Lord Buddha, having wandered through the Chedi country, went to Bhadravatikā. Now the cowherds, the goatherds, the ploughmen, and the wayfarers saw the Blessed One coming from afar, and, seeing the Blessed One, they spake: "Let the Blessed One, please, not go to the Mango Ferry; at the Mango Ferry, please, in the hermitage of the Jaṭila there dwelleth a Nāga of great magical power, a dreadfully venomous snake; let him do no harm to the Blessed One."

When they had said this the Master remained silent. A second and a third time they repeated their warning, and the Master remained silent. Now, while wandering and begging his food the Blessed One gradually came to Bhadravatikā and there he sojourned.

[1] *Suttavibhaṅga, pāchittiya*, li. *Vinaya Piṭakam*, vol. iv, pp. 108 ff.

Now the Elder Svāgata went to the hermitage of the Jaṭila of the Mango Ferry, and, having come there, he entered the fire-hut, made himself a couch of grass, and sat down cross-legged, keeping the body erect and surrounding himself with watchfulness of mind. The Nāga, seeing that the Elder Svāgata had entered, became irritated and sent forth a cloud of smoke. The Elder Svāgata, too, sent forth a cloud of smoke. Then the Nāga, being unable to master his rage, sent forth flames, and the Elder Svāgata, too, converting his body into fire, sent forth flames. And after having conquered the fire of the Nāga by his fire, the Elder Svāgata went to Bhadravatikā.

Now the Blessed One, after abiding as long as it pleased him at Bhadravatikā, went on to Kauśāmbī. The lay-members of Kauśāmbī had heard of the encounter between the Elder Svāgata and the Nāga of the Mango Ferry. The Blessed One, wandering and begging his food, gradually came to Kauśāmbī. When the lay-members of Kauśāmbī came to meet the Master, they repaired to Svāgata, saluted him, and said: "Tell us what is rare and acceptable to thee and we will provide it." When they had said this the Wicked Six [1] spake to the lay-members of Kauśāmbī: "Sirs, to friars 'pigeon' spirits (*kapotikā*) are as rare as they are acceptable, these ye may provide." So the lay-members of Kauśāmbī provided 'pigeon' spirit at every house and, seeing the Elder Svāgata come on his round of alms, they spake to him: "Let the Reverend Svāgata, please drink 'pigeon' spirit." When the Elder Svāgata had drunk 'pigeon' spirit, house by house, and he walked out of the town, he fell prostrate at the city gate. Then the Blessed One, coming out of the town with a large number of friars, saw the Elder Svāgata prostrate at the city gate, and, seeing him, he said to the friars: "Take Svāgata, friars." So the friars did: they took Svāgata to the convent and laid him down with his head towards the Master. But the Elder Svāgata turned round so that he came to lie with his feet towards the Master. Then the Blessed One said to the Friars: "Was not, Friars, Svāgata formerly respectful and obedient to the Buddha?" "Yes, so please you." And, Friars, is Svāgata now respectful and obedient to the Buddha?" "No, not he, so please you." "Did not, Friars, Svāgata encounter the Nāga of the Mango Ferry?" "Yes, he did, so please you." "And, Friars, is Svāgata now able to encounter a Nāga?" "No, not he, so please you." "Well now, Friars is it proper to drink that which when drunk stealeth away a man's senses?" "It is not, so please you." "It is improper, Friars, unsuitable, unworthy of a monk, it is unbefitting and to be avoided." Then the Blessed One laid it down as a precept that the drinking of intoxicants was an offence requiring confession and absolution.

[Evidently the story of the Elder Svāgata and the Nāga of the Mango Ferry is a partial

[1] The "Six" are a group of notoriously mischievous friars who are always represented as defying the rules of the Order.

imitation of the legend of Buddha's victory over the wicked serpent in the fire-room of the Kāśyapas. In the passage relating the contest with the Nāga there is often verbal agreement.

The story of Svāgata in a slightly modified version also forms the introduction to the *Surāpāna-jātaka*.[1] Here it is said that the Elder Svāgata not only mastered the Nāga-king, but also confirmed him in the Refuges and the Commandments !]

The Great Miracle of Śrāvastī [2]

In the town of Rājagṛiha, the capital of Magadha, there lived six heads of heretical sects who refused to acknowledge the superiority of the Buddha. They were loath to notice that they no longer commanded the respect of the wealthy citizens nor enjoyed the amount of alms they used to receive previous to the Master's appearance. So they communed together and resolved to make a great display of their supernatural powers in order to convince the multitude of their mastership. As Bimbisāra, the king of Magadha, was known to be a staunch supporter of the Buddha, they proceeded to Śrāvastī and there challenged the Bhagavat. The latter at once declared himself willing to accept their challenge, for he well knew that it was one of the ten duties imposed on all Buddhas to make a great display of their magical faculties in order to confound the heretical teachers. Moreover, Śrāvastī was the place predestined to be the scene of that Great Miracle.

The day fixed for the performance having arrived a large crowd of spectators assembled in the plain between the city of Śrāvastī and the Jetavana Garden, the favourite sojourn of the Buddha. The King Prasenajit himself came driving out of his palace in great pomp and took his royal seat to preside over the proceedings. At the invitation of the king, Buddha showed a series of miraculous manifestations which could leave no doubt to his supremacy. He rose into the air and caused flames of fire and streams of water to gush forth alternately from the upper and lower parts of his body. These preliminary miracles, however, he declared to be within the power of all his disciples.

Then Buddha conceived a mundane thought.[3] The gods hastened to execute it: Brahmā took a place on his right and Śakra on his left. The two Nāgarājas, Nanda and Upananda, created a golden lotus of a thousand leaves and of the size of a cart-wheel

[1] *Jātaka* (No. 81), vol. i, pp. 360 ff. Cambridge transl., vol. i, pp. 206 f. In a later and more extended form the same legend, under the title *Svāgatāvadāna* is the thirteenth story of the *Divyāvadāna* (ed. Cowell and Neil, pp. 167 ff.).

[2] *Divyāvadāna*, xii, *Prātihāryasūtra*, pp. 143 ff. E. Burnouf, *Introduction à l'histoire du buddhisme indien*, pp. 162 ff. According to Tibetan tradition Sākyamuni accomplished his Great Miracle in the sixteenth year of his ministry. Rockhill, *The Life of the Buddha*, p. 79.

[3] A mundane thought, viz. a thought within the comprehension of gods, men, and animals as opposed to a thought beyond the understanding of such beings.

with a jewelled stalk. On the corolla of this lotus-flower the Buddha seated himself in the attitude of meditation. Above this lotus he caused another lotus to appear on which likewise a Buddha was seen in the same position ; and thus in front, behind, and at the sides. By such magical multiplication of his own form he peopled the sky with a multitude of Buddha figures who seemed to walk, to stand, to sit, and to lie down. From these Buddhas there issued forth flames, flashes of lightning, and streams of water. Some of them put questions and others answered them.

When after this wonderful display Buddha had retaken his seat, he spake : " The fire-fly only shineth as long as the sun hath not risen ; but when the sun hath risen the light of the insect is no longer seen. Thus the sophists speak as long as no Buddha hath appeared ; but now that the Buddha hath spoken in the world, neither a sophist nor his disciple hath anything to say."

The heretical teachers were, in sooth, so utterly confounded, that, being invited by King Prasenajit to show their magical powers, they remained silent.

For the numerous sculptural and pictorial representations of the Great Miracle of Śrāvastī which are found in the art of Bharhut, Gandhāra, Ajaṇṭā, Sārnāth, etc., we may refer the reader to the able paper devoted by M. Foucher to the subject.[1] The point which here interests us particularly is the part played in Buddha's magical manifestation by the two Nāgas, Nanda and Upananda, whom we have already met in connexion with Śākyamuni's nativity. In the sculptures which refer to the Great Miracle we usually find them on both sides of the lotus-flower on which the Buddha is seated in the preaching attitude surrounded by more or less numerous magical counterparts of himself. In the examples from Gandhāra they are mostly shown issuing half-way from the water, whereas in the cave temples they are usually represented holding with both hands the stalk of the lotus-flower on which the central Buddha figure is enthroned. It is curious to note that gradually this *motif* of the *padmāsana* or 'Lotus-throne' supported by a pair of Nāgas develops into a mere decorative device. We notice it in bas-reliefs which evidently are not meant to illustrate the miracle of Śrāvastī at all. An instance may be quoted from Javanese art. (Plate XI.) The outer walls of the Chandi Měndut, the Buddhist temple found in the vicinity of the Borobudur, are decorated each with three sculptured panels.[2] The central

[1] A. Foucher, *Journal asiatique*, Jan.–Feb., 1909, and *The beginnings of Buddhist Art* (1917), pp. 147 ff. Cf. also Grünwedel's *Buddhist art in India* (1901), p. 108, fig. 60. *Cat. Sārnāth Museum*, p. 191, No. C (*a*) 6. pl. xxi, p. 192, No. C (*a*) 7, and p. 194, No. C (*a*) 15.

[2] B. Kersjes and C. den Hamer, *Tjandi Měndoet* (1903), p. 15, pl. xvii. According to the authors the two figures supporting the lotus are a Nāga and a Nāgī. Cf. also *B.E.F.E.-O.*, vol. ix (1909), p. 45 ff. N. J. Krom, *De Bodhisattwa's van den Měndut. Bijdragen*, vol. lxxiv (1918), pp. 419 ff. (esp. pp. 425 ff.). A. Foucher, *Beginnings*, p. 262 ff., pl. xliv.

panel of the south-western face shows a four-armed deity with two attendants, each seated on a conventional lotus-flower. Now the stalk of the lotus supporting the central figure is clasped by two Nāgas with triple snake-hood whose lower limbs are hidden by the waves from which the lotuses are supposed to rise. The position of these two Nāgas, it will be noticed, agrees exactly with that of Nanda and Upananda in Indian sculptures illustrating the Miracle of Śrāvastī, but in the present instance the deity occupying the central place appears to be a goddess, who may be either Chundā or Tārā.

How the Nāgarājas Kṛishṇa and Gautamaka came to hear the Good Law[1]

[The following episode forms part of the *Pūrṇāvadāna*, the second story of the *Divyāvadāna*.]

Now Dārukarṇi, Stavakarṇi, and Trapukarṇi, having collected excellent solid and liquid food, and having arranged the seats, announced to the Blessed One by means of a messenger that it was time, saying: "It is time, Sir, the food is prepared, wherefore we now await the Master's pleasure." At that time the two Nāga kings, Kṛishṇa and Gautamaka, abode in the great ocean. They reflected: "The Blessed One preacheth the Law in the town of Sūrpāraka;[2] let us go and hear the preaching of the Law." Thereupon with a retinue of five hundred Nāgas and producing five hundred rivers, they went forth to the town of Sūrpāraka.

Now it is a property of the Buddhas, the Blessed Lords, that they are ever watchful. The Lord reflected: "If those two Nāga kings, Kṛishṇa and Gautama, should come to the town of Sūrpāraka, they will obstruct the collecting of alms."

Then the Lord spake to the reverend Mahāmaudgalyāyana: "Receive thou Mahāmaudgalyāyana, special alms for the Tathāgata. And for what reason? There exist, Mahāmaudgalyāyana, five kinds of special alms. Which are those five? Food for an n-coming friar, for an out-going friar, for one who is sick, for him who attendeth the sick, and for one who meeteth with an obstacle. But in the present case the Blessed One is dealing with an obstacle.

Now the Lord accompanied by Mahāmaudgalyāyana betook himself to the Nāga kings Kṛishṇa and Gautamaka. And being come, he spake: "Consider, O Nāga kings, do ye not obstruct the collecting of alms in the town of Sūrpāraka." Whereupon the two Nāga kings made answer: "In such placid mood, O Lord, are we come that it would not be possible for us to cause harm even to a little worm or ant, far less to the folk inhabiting,

[1] *Divyāvadāna* (ed. Cowell and Neil), pp. 50 ff. Burnouf, *Introduction*, pp. 269 f.

[2] Sūrpāraka (or Sūpāraga, as it is called in the Pali Jātaka Book) was an important port on the west coast during the Buddhist period of Indian history. The village of Sopāra, near Bassein, north of Bombay, still preserves the ancient name.

the town of Sūrpāraka." Thereupon the Blessed One preached the Good Law in such manner to the Nāga kings, Kṛishṇa and Gautamaka, that, on hearing it, they turned themselves to the Buddha as a refuge, and to the Good Law and to the Community and they eke accepted the moral precepts.

The Blessed One began to make preparations for his meal. Each Nāga bethought himself: "May the Blessed One drink the water offered by me!" Then the Lord thought: "If I should drink the water offered by only one Nāga there will be a division amongst them. Therefore I must devise some expedient." Thereupon the Blessed One bespake Mahāmaudgalyāyana: "Go thou, Mahāmaudgalyāyana, where the five hundred rivers mingle, therefrom bring me a full bowl of water." "Yea, Lord," quoth Mahāmaudgalyāyana, giving ear to the Blessed One, and having drawn a full bowl of water where the five hundred rivers mingle, he repaired again to the Lord. Being come, he offered a full bowl of water to the Blessed One. And the Lord took it and drank.

[The episode rendered above is only another example of the piety shown by the Nāgas and of their eagerness to hearken to the Good Law. The main point of interest is that here we meet with the twins Kṛishṇa and Gautama(ka), whose names in their Pali form also occur in the ancient charm against poisonous snakes which is preserved in the *Tripiṭaka.*[1] In the present story they figure as Nāga kings dwelling in the Western Ocean.]

How the Lord Buddha crossed the River Gaṅgā with the aid of the Nāgas[2]

[From the beginning of the third *avadāna* found in the *Divyāvadāna* we quote the following episode.]

When the king of Magadha, Ajātaśatru the son of the Lady of Videha, had caused a bridge of boats to be constructed for the sake of his parents, the Lichchhavi nobles of Vaiśālī constructed a bridge of boats for the sake of the Lord Buddha. Now the Nāgas reflected: "We are debased creatures. What if we enabled the Lord to cross the river Gaṅgā by means of a bridge formed by our hoods?" And they made a bridge formed by their hoods.[3] Then the Blessed One spake to the friars: "Whosoever of you, Friars, in order to travel from Rājagṛiha to Śrāvastī, chooseth to cross the river Gaṅgā by the bridge of boats made by the king of Magadha, the son of the Lady of Videha, let him do so. And whosoever of you, Friars, chooseth to cross by the bridge of boats made by the Lichchhavi nobles of Vaiśālī, let him do so. But I, together with the Friar, the venerable Ānanda, shall cross the river Gaṅgā by the bridge formed by the hoods of the Nāgas." Then some crossed

[1] Cf. above, p. 10.
[2] *Divyāvadāna* (ed. Cowell and Neil), pp. 55 f.
[3] In the legend of Gūgā the snakes of Vāsuki form a bridge across a lake to enable the hero's wedding procession to pass. Cf. *Ind. Ant.*, xxvi, p. 54.

by the bridge of boats made by the king of Magadha, Ajātaśatru, the son of the Lady of Videha, and others by the bridge of boats made by the Lichchhavi nobles of Vaiśālī. But the Lord, together with the reverend Ānanda crossed by the bridge formed by the hoods of the Nāgas. Now at that time a certain lay-member spake the following stanzas :—

> Behold the men who cross the floating waves,
> making a solid path across the pools—
> Whilst the vain world tieth its basket rafts—
> these are the wise, these are the saved indeed.
> Buddha, the Blessed Lord, hath crossed the stream,
> the Brahmin standeth on the river bank.
> Where Buddha's *bhikshus* through the water wade,
> the Brahmin's pupils tie their fragile craft.
> A well, forsooth, it were of slight avail
> in lands producing water plentiful.[1]
> Having cut off the root of evil lust,
> what further quest needeth a man to make ?

In the *jātakas* it sometimes happens that the *gāthās* do not exactly fit in with the prose narrative in which they have been inserted. The reason is that the verses are the original and essential part, to which the story in prose has been added as a kind of commentary. The same appears to be the case in the episode quoted above from the *Divyāvadāna*.

The first of the three *gāthās* is also found in a very early Pali text, the *Mahāparinibbānasutta*. There it is narrated that the Buddha through his miraculous power crossed the river Ganges, while the common folks were busy seeking for boats and rafts of wood, and some made rafts of basket-work.[2]

For our purpose the main point of interest of the story is the notion of the Nāgas forming a bridge for the Buddha to enable him to pass the river. A similar incident is related in the *Mahāvastu* in a passage called *Chhattravastu*, " the legend of the Parasols." [3] There it is said that there were four bridges of boats thrown across the Gaṅgā, the first by king Bimbisāra of Magadha, the second by the 'inner' people of Viśālā, the third by the 'outer' people of Viśālā,[4] and the fourth by the Nāgas of the Gaṅgā, named Kambala and Aśvatara.

Each of the four parties was anxious that Buddha should use his particular bridge. Then Buddha, while crossing the river, performed a miracle : he made it appear as if he had crossed each of the four bridges. Thus the four parties concerned were all satisfied.

[1] The same simile occurs *Bhagavadgītā*, ii, 46. Cf. P. E. Pavolini's paper in *Album Kern* (Leiden, 1903), pp. 141 ff.

[2] *Mahāparinibbānasutta*, i, 34. *S.B.E.*, xi, pp. 21 f. Also *Udānam*, viii, 6 (*P.T.S.*, p. 90).

[3] *Mahāvastu*, vol. i, pp. 262 f.

[4] Perhaps the 'inner' Vaiśālakas are the townspeople of Vaiśālī and the 'outer' Vaiśālakas the country people.

Now, when Buddha crossed the river, King Bimbisāra honoured him by means of five hundred parasols. So did the people of Vaiśālī. When the Nāgas of the Gaṅgā, Kambala and Aśvatara, noticed this, they, too, produced five hundred parasols. Their example was followed by the Yakshas, the Guardians of the Quarters, the Thirty-three Gods, the Tushita gods, the Brahmakāyika gods, and the Śuddhāvāsa gods. Consequently the whole sky was covered with thousands of parasols. But Buddha created a magical semblance of his own person under each parasol, and it appeared to each of all those divine beings that the Lord was walking under his particular parasol.

The Nāgarājas Girika and Vidyujjvāla banished by King Bimbisāra [1]

[The following legend is found in a Life of Buddha written in Tibetan.]

In Rājagṛiha, the capital of the kingdom of Magadha, there lived two Nāgarājas, Girika and Vidyujjvāla by name, who were wont to repair daily to the Lord Buddha in the semblance of householders and pay him homage. When on a certain day they did reverence to the Law of the Buddha and not to king Bimbisāra who happened to be present, the latter became wroth and ordered his ministers to banish them from the realm. Joyfully the two Nāgas betook themselves to the ocean. Subsequently the water in Rājagṛiha diminished, on account of the drought the crop failed, and the country was stricken with famine. Then king Bimbisāra questioned the Blessed One, whether the two Nāgas had perished. " Have they not been banished by thee, O King ? " the Buddha answered. Reminded in this manner, the King spake : " If only they would appear again in my presence, I would hold out my hands, and crave their forgiveness, so that no evil may befall this country." At the command of the Lord, the two Nāgas immediately repaired to the Veṇuvana Convent. The King craved their pardon, the which was granted on the condition that he would erect two Nāga dwellings and offer sacrifice during six months.

How Mahodara and Chūlodara, the Nāga Kings of Ceylon, were reconciled by the Buddha [2]

Now the most compassionate teacher, when dwelling at the Jetavana [3] in the fifth year of his Buddhahood, saw that a war, caused by a gem-set throne, was like to come to pass between the Nāgas Mahodara and Chūlodara, uncle and nephew, and their followers. And he, on the Sabbath day of the waning moon of the month Chitta in the early morning,

[1] Schiefner, *Lebensbeschreibung Çākyamuni's*, p. 272. For a somewhat similar story regarding the Nāgarājas Nanda and Upananda, *vide B.E.F.E.-O.*, vol. vi (1906), pp. 8. f.

[2] *Mahāvaṃsa*, i, 44–70 ; Geiger's transl., pp. 5 ff. Also *Dīpavaṃsa*, ii, 1–51 ; Oldenberg's transl., pp. 124 ff. In the present legend the Pali forms have been retained.

[3] The famous Buddhist convent near Śrāvastī.

took his sacred alms-bowl and his robes, and from compassion with the Nāgas sought the Nāga-dīpa.[1]

This same Nāga Mahodara was then a king, gifted with miraculous power, in a Nāga kingdom in the ocean covering half a thousand *yojanas*. His younger sister had been given in marriage to the Nāga king on the Kaṇṇāvaḍḍamāna Mountain ; her son was Chūlodara. His maternal grandfather had given to his mother a splendid throne of jewels, then the Nāga had died and therefore this war of nephew and uncle was threatening ; and the Nāgas of the mountains, too, were armed with miraculous power.

A tree spirit, named Samiddhi-sumana, took a *rājāyatana*-tree standing in the Jetavana, his own fair habitation, and holding it like a parasol over the Buddha, attended him to Nāga-dīpa. (That very spirit had been, in his latest birth, a man in Nāga-dīpa. On the spot where afterwards the *rājāyatana*-tree stood he once saw Pachcheka-Buddhas[2] taking their meal, and at the sight his heart was glad and he offered branches to cleanse their alms-bowl. Therefore he had been reborn as a tree spirit in the pleasant Jetavana Garden, and his tree stood at the side of the main gate.[3])

Hovering in mid-air above the battlefield, the Buddha called forth dread darkness over the Nāgas. Then comforting those who were distressed by terror, he once again spread light abroad. When they saw the Blessed One, they joyfully did reverence to the Master's feet. Then the Vanquisher preached to them the doctrine that begets concord, and both Nāga kings gladly gave up the throne to the Buddha. When the Master, having alighted upon the earth had sat down and had been refreshed with celestial food and drink by the Nāga kings, the Lord established in the Three refuges [4] and in the Moral Precepts [5] eighty scores of Snake-spirits, dwellers in the ocean, and dwellers of the mainland.

The Nāga king, Maṇiakkhika of the Kalyāṇī river,[6] the maternal uncle of the Nāga Mahodara, who aforetime at the Buddha's first coming to Ceylon had heard the true doctrine preached, had then accepted the Three Refuges and the Five Precepts. Now, having come thither to take part in the battle, he besought the Buddha : " Great is the compassion that thou hast shown unto us, O Master ! Hadst thou not appeared, we had all been consumed to ashes. May thy compassion light especially upon me in that thou shalt come yet again to my dwelling, O thou peerless One." When the Lord had consented by his silence,

[1] Apparently the north-western part of Ceylon.

[2] Buddhas who do not preach the law.

[3] The *koṭṭhaka* is the main entrance gate giving access to the grounds of the monastery. Cf. *Chulla-vagga*, vi, 3, 8.

[4] The Buddha, his doctrine and his community.

[5] The five Moral Precepts, which are binding on all Buddhists, are abstention from destruction of life, theft, adultery, lying, and from the use of intoxicating liquors.

[6] Name of a river, which falls into the sea near Colombo.

he planted the *rājāyatana*-tree [1] on that very spot as a sacred memorial, and the Lord of the Worlds gave over the *rājāyatana*-tree and the precious throne to the Nāga kings to do homage thereto. " In remembrance that I have used these, do homage to them, ye Nāga kings ! This, well-beloved, will bring to pass blessing and happiness for you."

When the Blessed One had uttered this and other exhortation to the Nāgas, he the compassionate saviour of all the world, returned to the Jetavana.

[The Chronicle next relates how Buddha, three years later, visited the Nāga Maṇiakkhika, as he had promised.]

The Nāga Gopāla appointed the Guardian of the Buddha's shadow [2]

[To the south-west of the town of Nagar in the Kābul valley, so the Chinese pilgrim Hiuen Tsiang relates, a deep torrent rushes from a high point of the hill. The mountain sides are like walls ; on the eastern side of one is a great cavern, deep and profound, the abode of the Nāga Gopāla. The entrance leading to it is narrow ; the cavern is dark ; the precipitous rock causes the water to find its way in various rivulets into this cavern. In old days there was a shadow of Buddha to be seen here, bright as the true form, with all its characteristic marks. In later days men have not seen it so much. What does appear is only a feeble likeness. But whosoever prays with fervent faith, he is mysteriously endowed, and he sees it clearly before him, though not for long.]

In old times, when the Buddha abode in the world this dragon Gopāla was a cowherd[3] who provided the king with milk and cream. Having on one occasion failed to do so, and having received a reprimand, he proceeded in an angry temper to a neighbouring sanctuary, and there made an offering of flowers, with the prayer that he might become a destructive dragon for the purpose of afflicting the country and destroying the king. Then, ascending the rocky side of the hill, he threw himself down and was killed. Forthwith he became a great dragon and occupied this cavern, and then he intended to go forth and accomplish his original wicked purpose. When this intention had arisen within him, the Buddha, having investigated his object, was moved with pity for the country and the people about to be destroyed by the dragon. By the power of his mind he came from mid-India to where the dragon was. When the dragon saw the Buddha, his murderous purpose was stayed, and he accepted the precept against killing, and vowed to defend the true Law ; he

[1] The *Dīpavaṃsa* speaks here of the Khirapāla-tree.

[2] Hiuen Tsiang, *Si-yu-ki* (transl. Beal), vol. i, pp. 93 ff. T. Watters, *On Yuan Chwang's Travels in India*, vol. i, pp. 184 and 193 ff. The earlier pilgrim Fa-Hien also speaks of the cavern of Buddha's shadow which he locates half a *yojana* to the south of the city of Nagarahāra, but he makes no mention of the Nāga Gopāla. Ibid., p. xxxv, and Fa-Hien's *Record of Buddhistic Kingdoms* (transl. Legge), p. 39. Cf. J. Przyluski, *J.A.* (1914), pp. 514 f., and 565 ff.

[3] The noun *gopāla* means ' cowherd '.

requested the Buddha to occupy this cavern evermore, that his holy disciples might ever receive his (the dragon's) religious offerings.

The Buddha replied: "When I am about to die, I will leave thee my shadow, and I will send five *Arhats* to receive from thee continual offerings. When the true law is destroyed this service of yours shall still go on; if an evil heart riseth in thee thou must look at my shadow, and because of its power of love and virtue thy evil purpose will be stopped. The Buddhas who will appear throughout this æon will all, from a motive of pity, entrust to thee their shadows as a bequest."

Outside the gate of the 'Cavern of the Shadow' there are two square stones; on one is the impression of the foot of the Buddha with a wheel-circle beautifully clear, which shineth with a brilliant light from time to time. On either side of the 'Cavern of the Shadow' there are several stone chambers; in these the holy disciples of the Buddha reposed in meditation.

The Nāga Apalāla subdued by the Buddha [1]

[To the north-west of the town of Maṅgalapura, the capital of Udyāna, so the Chinese pilgrim Hiuen Tsiang relates, we enter a great mountain range and arrive at the fountain of the Nāga Apalāla. This is the source of the river Suvāstu (modern Swāt) which flows to the south-west.]

This Nāga, in the time of Kāśyapa Buddha, was born as a man and was called Gangi(?). He was able, by the subtle influences of the charms he used, to restrain and withstand the power of the wicked dragons, so that they could not afflict the country with violent storms of rain. Thanks to him the people were thus able to gather in an abundance of grain. Each family then agreed to offer him, in token of their gratitude, a peck of grain as a yearly tribute. After a lapse of some years there were some who omitted to bring their offerings, on which Gaṅgi in wrath prayed that he might become a poisonous dragon and afflict them with storms of rain and wind to the destruction of their crops. At the end of his life he was reborn as the dragon of this country; the flowings of the fountain emitted a white stream which destroyed all the products of the earth.

At this time, the Buddha Śākyamuni, of his great pity guiding the world, was moved with compassion for the people of this country, who were so singularly afflicted with this calamity. Descending therefore supernaturally he came to this place, desiring to convert the violent dragon. When Buddha's companion, Vajrapāṇi, took his thunderbolt and

[1] *Si-yu-ki* (transl. Beal), vol. i, pp. 122 f. T. Watters, *On Yuan Chwang's travels in India*, vol. i, p. 228 ff. The Nāga Apalāla is also mentioned, *Divyāvadāna*, p. 348, l. 20, and p. 385, l. 3, where it is said that his taming took place about the time of the Buddha's Parinirvāṇa. A somewhat different version of the legend occurs in the Vinaya of the Mūla-Sarvāstivādin school. Cf. J. Przyluski, *J.A.* (1914), pp. 510 ff.

smote the mountain side, the dragon-king, terrified, came forth and paid him reverence. Hearing the preaching of the law by Buddha, his heart became pure and his faith was awakened. The Buddha forthwith forbade him to injure the crops of the husbandmen. Whereupon the dragon said: "All my sustenance cometh from the fields of men; but now, grateful for the sacred instruction I have received, I fear it will be difficult to support myself in this way; yet pray let me have one gathering in every twelve years." The Buddha compassionately permitted this. Therefore, every twelfth year there is a calamity from the overflowing of the White River.

It can be no matter of surprise that the local legend of the Swāt Valley forms a favourite theme in the Græco-Buddhist art of Gandhāra.[1] The best examples known are certainly those pediments in which the scene of Buddha's victory over the malignant Nāga of the Swāt river has been chosen to occupy the main panel. (Plate IX*a*.) The subdivision of sculptures of this kind is Indian in its origin, as it can be traced back to the decoration found above the entrance of the early cave-temples. But the details both of the illustrated scenes of Buddha's life and of the decorative accessories clearly betray Hellenistic influence. The Buddha, exceeding the other figures in size, invariably occupies the centre of the panel. He is turned toward a group formed by the frightened Apalāla, accompanied by one or more of his Nāgīs. The Nāgarāja is shown either standing at Buddha's side or rising from the waters of the source of which he is the presiding deity. In most cases he, as well as his female companions, raise their joined hands in token of reverence towards the Master. Over the group of Apalāla and his followers we notice Vajrapāṇi smiting the rock with his thunderbolt or 'adamantine club', as the Chinese pilgrim calls it.

On the other side of the Buddha we usually see Vajrapāṇi represented a second time in his ordinary function as the constant satellite of the Master, together with one or two monks. The Mission House at Peshāwar is in possession of a very good and well-preserved specimen of such a pediment in which Buddha is followed by two personages in secular dress, one of whom takes something out of a vessel held by the other. Possibly they are the representatives of the population of Udyāna who are bringing the Nāga king the tribute in grain to which he will henceforth be entitled. The second Vajrapāṇi and the monk are partly visible on both sides of the halo surrounding Buddha's head.

The finest example of a pediment of the kind here described is undoubtedly the beautiful sculpture now preserved in the Calcutta Museum.[2] It was excavated at Loriyān

[1] A. Foucher, *L'art gréco-bouddhique du Gandhāra*, vol. i, pp. 544 ff., figs. 270–5. *A.S.R.* for 1906–07, p. 159, pl. lv. D. B. Spooner, *Handbook of the sculptures in the Peshāwar Museum*, pp. 26 f., pl. facing p. 53.

[2] Foucher, op. cit., fig. 271. Grünwedel, *Buddhist Art in India*, fig. 58.

(*a*) Apalāla subdued by the Buddha (Gandhāra).

(*b*) Buddha in the fire-hut of the Kāśyapas (Gandhāra).

[*To face p.* 122

Tangai, and, therefore, must once have served to adorn one of the numerous Buddhist sanctuaries in the very Swāt valley with which the legend of the Nāga Apalāla is so closely associated.

THE ŚĀKYA YOUTH WHO MARRIED A SNAKE-MAIDEN AND BECAME KING OF UDYĀNA [1]

[In the country of Udyāna, which nowadays is known as the Swāt Valley, on the north-west frontier of India, the Chinese pilgrim Hiuen Tsiang mentions a 'dragon' lake about 5 miles in circuit—the water pure as a bright mirror—situated on the crest of the mountain. In connexion with this lake he relates the following story.]

When Virūḍhaka, the fierce king of Kosala, marched against Kapilavastu and exterminated the noble Śākya race whereof the Buddha had been born, four of the tribe resisted the advance. These were driven away by their clansmen, and each fled in a different direction. When one of these Śākyas, being worn out by travel, sat down to rest in the middle of the road, there appeared a wild goose which alighted before him, and because of its docile ways, he at last mounted on its back. The goose then flying away, took him to the side of this lake: here he went to sleep under the shadow of a tree.

At this time a young Nāga maiden was walking beside the lake, and suddenly espied the Śākya youth. Fearing that she might not be able otherwise to accomplish her wish she transformed herself into a human shape and began to caress him. The youth, because of this, awoke affrighted from his sleep, and addressing her said: "I am but a poor wanderer worn out with fatigue; why then showest thou me such tenderness?" In the course of events the youth, becoming deeply moved, besought her to consent to his wishes. "My father and mother," quoth she, "require to be asked and obeyed in this matter. Thou hast favoured me with thy affection, but they have not yet consented." The Śākya youth rejoined: "The mountains and valleys surround us with their mysterious shades; where, then, is thy home?" She said: "I am a Nāga maiden belonging to this pool. I have heard with awe of thy holy tribe having suffered such things, and of thy being driven away from home to wander hither and thither in consequence. I have fortunately been able as I wandered, to administer somewhat to thy comfort, and thou hast desired me to yield to thy wishes in other respects, but I have received no commands to that effect from my parents. Unhappily, too, this Nāga-body is the curse following my evil deeds in a former existence." The Śākya youth answered: "One word uttered from the bottom of the heart and agreed to by us both and this matter is ended." Said she: "I respectfully obey thine orders; let whatsoever may follow." Then the Śākya youth spake: "By the power of my accumulated merit let this Nāga woman be turned into human shape." The woman

[1] *Si-yu-ki* (transl. Beal), vol. i, pp. 128 ff.

was immediately so converted. On seeing herself thus restored to human shape she was overjoyed, and gratefully addressed the Śākya youth thus: "By my evil deeds, I have been compelled to migrate through evil forms of birth, till now happily, by the power of thy religious merit, the body which I have possessed through many æons hath been changed in a moment. My gratitude is boundless, nor could it be expressed even if I wore my body to dust with frequent prostrations. Let me but acquaint my father and mother; I will then follow thee and obey thee in all things."

The Nāga maiden then returning to the lake addressed her father and mother, saying "Just now, as I was wandering abroad, I lighted upon a Śākya youth, who by the power of his religious merit succeeded in changing me into a human shape. Having formed an affection for me, he desireth to marry me. I lay before you the matter in its truth."

The Nāgarāja was rejoiced to see his daughter restored to human form, and from a true affection to the holy tribe he gave consent to his daughter's request. Then coming up from the lake, he expressed his deep gratitude to the Śākya youth, saying: "Thou hast not despised creatures of other kinds, and has condescended to those beneath thee I beseech thee come to my abode, and there do thou receive my humble services."

The Śākya youth having accepted the Nāgarāja's invitation, went forthwith to his abode. Upon which all the family of the Nāga received the youth with extreme reverence, and desired to delight his mind by an excess of feasting and pleasure; but the youth, seeing the dragon forms of his entertainers, was filled with affright and disgust, and he desired to depart. The Nāgarāja detaining him, spake: "Of thy kindness go not away. Do thou occupy a neighbouring abode; I will prevail to make thee master of this land and obtain for thee lasting fame. All the people shall be thy servants, and thy dynasty shall endure for successive ages."

The Śākya youth expressed his gratitude, saying: "I can hardly expect thy words to be fulfilled." Then the Nāgarāja took a precious sword and placed it in a casket covered with a white camlet, very fine and beautiful, and then he said to the Śākya youth: "Now of thy kindness go thou to the king and offer him this white camlet as a tribute. The king will be sure to accept it as the offering of a distant person; then, as he taketh it, draw thou forth the sword and kill him. Thus thou wilt seize his kingdom. Is this not excellent?"

The Śākya youth, receiving the Nāga's directions, went forthwith to make his offering to the king of Udyāna. When the king was about to take the piece of white camlet, the youth took hold of his sleeve, and pierced him with his sword. The attendant ministers and the guards raised a great outcry and ran about in confusion. The Śākya youth, waving his sword, cried out: "This sword that I hold was given me by a holy Nāga wherewith to punish the contumelious and subdue the arrogant." Being affrighted by the divine warrior, they submitted, and gave him the kingdom. Whereupon he corrected abuses and established order ; he advanced the good and relieved the unfortunate ; and then with a great train he advanced towards the Nāga palace to acquaint him with the completion of his undertaking ; and then taking his wife he went back to the capital.

Now the former demerits of the Nāga girl were not yet effaced, and their consequences still remained. Every time he went to rest by her side from her head came forth the nine-fold crest of the Nāga. The Śākya prince, filled with affright and disgust, finding no other plan, waited till she slept, and then cut off the dragon's crest with his sword. The Nāga girl, alarmed, awoke and said : " This will bring no good hereafter to thy posterity ; it will inevitably afflict slightly me during my life, and thy children and grandchildren will all suffer from pains in the head." And so the royal line of this country are ever afflicted with this malady, and albeit they are not all so continually, yet every succession brings a worse affliction.

After the death of the Śākya youth his son succeeded him under the name of Uttarasena.

According to the account of Hiuen Tsiang,[1] this king Uttarasena obtained a share of the relics of Buddha. When the division of the precious relics was taking place, he arrived after the other claimants, and, as he came from a frontier country, he was treated by them with slight respect. After obtaining a portion of the relics he returned to his country and erected a *stūpa* on the eastern bank of the Suvāstu (Swāt) river, to the south-west of the capital. This relic *stūpa* which the Chinese pilgrim visited in the course of his travels, is probably the same monument which may still be seen near the village of Barikot in the Swāt valley.[2]

The Nāgas obtain a share of the Buddha's holy relics[3]

In the early Pali text describing the Great Decease it is related that the Buddha died between the twin *sāl* trees of Kuśinagara in the country of the Mallas. After his body had been cremated, the rulers of the neighbouring clans and countries, seven in number, sent messengers to claim part of the holy relics of the Master. At first the Mallas were unwilling to concede to these requests, for they said : " The Blessed One died in our village domain. We will not give away any part of the remains of the Blessed One." Then a certain Brahmin, Droṇa by name, spake : " The Buddha was wont to teach forbearance. It is unseemly that over the division of his remains there should arise a strife." So with the approval of

[1] *Si-yu-ki* (transl. Beal), vol. i, pp. 126 f. T. Watters, op. cit., vol. i, p. 236

[2] Foucher, *Art gréco-bouddhique* vol. i, p. 74, fig. 16.

[3] *Mahāparinibbāna-sutta* (ed. Childers), pp. 68 ff., S.B.E., vol. xi, p. 131 f.

the Mallas of Kuśinagara, the Brahmin Droṇa divided the relics of the Buddha into eight parts. These were entrusted to the rulers of the various clans and countries, and each of them raised in his own place a *stūpa* or relic-tower over the sacred remains. Among the clans which thus obtained a portion of the Buddha's relics were the 'Koliyas' of Rāmagrāma.

In this earliest account of the Buddha's Nirvāṇa no mention whatsoever is made of the Nāgas, but at the end of the Pali book we find a few verses which evidently are a later addition. According to the commentator Buddhaghosa, they were added by Theras in Ceylon.

> Eight measures of relics there were of Him of the far-seeing eye,
> Of the best of men. In India seven are worshipped,
> And one measure in Rāmagrāma, by the kings of the serpent race.
> One tooth, too, is honoured in heaven, and one in Gandhāra's city,
> One in the Kālinga realm, and one by the Nāga race.

There is, indeed, a later tradition which holds that not only the human worshippers of the Master, but also the Devas and the Nāgas which had served him with an equally fervent devotion, obtained part of his relics. This tradition is preserved in the itinerary of Hiuen Tsiang,[1] for in the account of his visit to the reputed site of the Buddha's Nirvāṇa, we read: "Anavatapta the Nāga also, and Muchilinda and Elāpattra also, deliberated and said: 'We ought not to be left without a bequest; if we seek it by force, it will not be well for you!' The Brahmin Droṇa said: 'Dispute ye not so.' Then he divided the relics into three portions, one for the Devas, one for the Nāgas, and one remnant for the eight kingdoms among men. This addition of Devas and Nāgas in sharing the relics was a source of great sorrow to the kings of men."

The evidence of plastic and pictorial art confirms the conclusion that the story of the Nāgas sharing in Buddha's relics is due to a comparatively late development of the cycle of legends surrounding the Great Decease. Among the numerous Indian sculptures of the Nirvāṇa we do not know of any specimen in which Nāgas are shown among the mourning figures surrounding the Master's couch. In Chinese and Japanese pictures, on the contrary, where representatives of all classes of beings are thronging around the dying Buddha, we find the 'dragon-kings', too, mixing among the spectators.[2]

On the accompanying plate (X*b*) we reproduce a singularly elegant medallion from Amarāvatī which may be regarded as an illustration of the above legend.[1] The centre is

[1] *Si-yu-ki* (transl. Beal), vol. ii, p. 41. Watters, op. cit., vol. ii, p. 42.

[2] Grünwedel, *Buddhist Art*, p. 123, fig. 76.

[3] Fergusson, *Tree- and Serpent-worship*, p. 197, pl. lxii. Grünwedel, *Buddhist Art*, fig. 8. Cf. Burgess, *Amarāvatī*, pl. xxxiv. The original is in the British Museum.

occupied by a richly decorated throne on which a relic casket is placed. Behind it stands a Nāgarāja between two *chowri*-bearers, who, like their master, are characterized by the snakehood forming, as it were, a nimbus around their heads. A very elaborate canopy is visible above these three personages. The rest of the medallion is filled with a great number of figures, belonging no doubt to the serpent-king's court. Of those in the background only the heads are shown. On both sides of the throne there is a graceful group, each of two female figures, of which those to the left are shown in the act of taking garlands from a tray held by a dwarf. These four, as well as the seven females kneeling in varied attitudes of devotion in front at the foot of the throne belong to the Nāga race, as is evident from the snake which in each case will be seen issuing from their backs or surmounting their heads.

The Stūpa of Rāmagrāma guarded by the Nāgas[1]

[Among the countries visited by the Chinese pilgrim Hiuen Tsiang was also that of Rāmagrāma, which he describes as waste and desolate.. The towns were decayed and the inhabitants few.

To the south-east of the old capital, the pilgrim says, there is a brick *stūpa*, in height less than 100 feet. Formerly, after the Nirvāṇa of the Buddha, a previous king of this country, having obtained a share of the *śarīras* of his body, returned home with them, and to honour these relics he built this *stūpa*. Miraculous signs are here displayed, and a divine light from time to time shines around.]

By the side of the *stūpa* there is a clear lake. A dragon at certain periods cometh forth and walketh here, and changing his form and snake-like exterior, circumambulateth the *stūpa*, turning to the right to pay it honour. The wild elephants come in herds, gather flowers, and scatter them here. Impelled by a mysterious power, they have continued to offer this service from the first till now.

In former days, when King Aśoka, dividing the relics, built *stūpas*, after having opened the *stūpas* built by the kings of the seven countries, he proceeded to travel to this country, and put his hand to the work of opening this *stūpa*, too. But the dragon, apprehending the desecration of the place, changed himself into the form of a Brahmin, and going forward he bowed down before the royal elephant and spake: "Mahārāja, thy feelings are well affected to the law of Buddha, and thou hast largely planted good seed in the field of religious merit. I venture to ask thee to stop thy car awhile and condescend to visit my dwelling." The king replied: "And where is thy dwelling? Is it near at hand?" Said the Brahmin: "I am the Nāga king of this lake. As I have heard that the great king

[1] *Si-yu-ki* (transl. Beal), vol. ii, pp. 26 ff. T. Watters, *On Yuan Chwang's travels*, vol. ii, pp. 20 ff. The site of Rāmagrāma which must have been somewhere between the Lumbinī Garden and Kuśinagara, has not yet been identified.

desireth to build a superior field of merit, I have ventured to ask thee to visit my abode." The king, receiving this invitation, immediately entered the dragon precinct, and sitting there for some time, the Nāga advanced towards him and said: "Because of my evil *karman* I have received this Nāga body; by religious service to these *śarīras* of Buddha I desire to atone for and efface my guilt. Oh, that the king would himself go and inspect the *stūpa* with a view to worship." King Aśoka, having seen the character of the place, was filled with fear and said: "All these appliances for worship are unlike anything seen amongst men." "If it be so," the Nāga rejoined, "Oh that the king would not attempt to destroy the *stūpa*!" The king, seeing that he could not measure his power with that of the Nāga, did not attempt to open the *stūpa* to take out the relics. At the spot where the dragon came out of the lake is an inscription to the above effect.

In the neighbourhood of this *stūpa* is a monastery with a very few friars attached to it. Their conduct is respectful and scrupulously correct; and one novice manageth the whole business of the community. When any monks come from distant regions, they entertain them with the greatest courtesy and liberality; during three days they keep them in their society, and offer them the four necessary things.[1]

The old tradition is this: Formerly there were some friars who agreed to come together from a distance, and to travel to worship this *stūpa*. When they had arrived they saw a herd of elephants, coming and departing together. Some of them brought on their tusks shrubs, others with their trunks sprinkled water, some of them brought different flowers, and all offered worship to the *stūpa*. When the friars saw this they were moved with joy and deeply affected. Then one of them, giving up his full orders, vowed to remain here and offer his services continually to the *stūpa*, and expressing his thoughts to the others, he spake: "I, in sooth, considering these remarkable signs of abounding merit, count as nothing my own excessive labours during many years amongst the monks. This *stūpa* having some relics of Buddha, by the mysterious power of its sacred character draweth together the herd of elephants who water the earth around the bequeathed body of the Saint. It would be pleasant to finish the rest of my years in this place, and to obtain with the elephants the end at which they aim." They all replied: "This is an excellent design; as for ourselves, we are stained by our heavy sins; our wisdom is not equal to the formation of such a design; but, according to thine opportunity look well to thine own welfare, and cease not thine efforts in this excellent purpose."

Having departed from the rest, he repeated his earnest vow, and with joy devoted himself to a solitary life during the rest of his days.

[1] The four requisites (Pali *chatupachchayaṃ*) of a Buddhist monk are clothing, food, bedding, and medicine.

In the above account of Rāmagrāma Hiuen Tsiang relates two local legends in connexion with the ancient *stūpa* which was believed to contain an eighth part of the Buddha's corporeal relics. The first story tells us of the relic shrine being guarded by the Nāgas, and consequently being the only one of the eight original *śarīra-stūpas*, which was left undisturbed by king Aśoka. According to the other story, the sacred monument, having become desolate, was taken care of by the wild elephants.

Both these legends are also found in the itinerary of the earlier pilgrim, Fa-Hien.[1] Now, if we remember that the term 'Nāga' has the double meaning of a serpent-demon and an elephant, we may safely assume that the second story has developed out of the first one, the word '*Nāga*' having been taken in its other sense. It may be noted that the episode of the *stūpa* guarded by the Nāgarāja is also found in the *Divyāvadāna*.[2]

In early Buddhist sculpture we find the legend of the deserted relic-shrine of Rāmagrāma portrayed in the two versions which are preserved in the itineraries of the Chinese pilgrims. The lowermost architrave of the eastern *toraṇa* of Sānchi bears on its inner face a very fine relief showing a *stūpa* which is worshipped by a herd of wild elephants.[3] These animals, carrying bunches of lotus-flowers in their trunks, approach the sacred monument from both sides. It is very tempting to see in this sculpture an illustration of the legend which we have rendered above. Upon the central architrave of the southern gateway [4] we find the other version of the legend depicted in a very convincing manner. On the proper right side of the panel the serpent-demons are shown in their watery home, surrounded by forest-trees, the lower part of their body concealed by the waves. Then we see the Nāgas approaching with their offerings the *stūpa*, which occupies the place of honour in the centre of the *tableau*. The male Nāgas, as usual, are distinguished by means of a five-headed snake-crest, whereas their female counterparts exhibit but a single cobra issuing from behind their head. On the other side of the sacred monument a royal cortege consisting of horsemen, a chariot, and mounted elephants is drawing near. We may assume that the personage standing on the chariot (he is attended by a *chowrie*-bearer) represents the great king Aśoka.

The *stūpa* worshipped by the Nāgas (viz. the serpent-demons) is a very favourite subject in the art of Amarāvatī. Sometimes the entrance to the sacred precinct is guarded by a five-headed snake.[5] This appears to be the simpler form of rendering the subject. But

[1] Fa-Hien's *Record* (transl. Legge), pp. 68 ff.

[2] *Divyāvadāna*, p. 380.

[3] Fergusson, *Tree- and Serpent-worship*, pl. xv, 4. Cf. pl. lxxxvii, 5.

[4] Fergusson, op. cit., pl. vii. Foucher: *La porte orientale de Sanchi*, pp. 29 f.; *Beginnings of Buddhist art*, pp. 109 f.

[5] Burgess, *Amarāvatī*, pl. xxxii, 5; xxxix, 3; and xliv, 2. Cf. Fergusson, op.cit., pl. xci, 1 and 2.

instances of a more elaborate treatment are not wanting. On a well carved slab (Plate X*a*) we see a *stūpa* guarded by Nāgas in animal form, but polycephalous, three being arranged round the body of the building, while others interlaced cover its dome.[1] Besides these, there are six Nāgas human in appearance, but distinguished as such by their snake-hood, who pay reverence to the relic-shrine. Two of them carrying offerings are shown hovering in the air. Two are standing on each side of the relic-shrine, and two female Nāgas are kneeling. It is a peculiar feature of this sculpture—noticed also in other specimens rendering the same subject—that here the *stūpa* is not crowned either by a single parasol or by the more usual row of superposed parasols, but carries quite a multitude of those emblems of royalty. This curious crowd of umbrellas, somewhat resembling a growth of mushrooms was noticed by Fergusson, who calls it " a curious ebullition of Hindu fancy ". Possibly it has a direct bearing on the legend here portrayed, and is meant to indicate the abundant resources in paying worship by which the Nāgas exceed mere mortal devotees We may refer the reader to the legend of the parasols related above. (p. 118.)

Finally we wish to note an early piece of sculpture (from its style it may be assigned to the Kushāṇa period) which was excavated at Sārnāth in 1905 and is now preserved in the local museum.[2] In this sculpture we find both the legends of Rāmagrāma, as it were, combined. It shows a *stūpa* being worshipped by a wild elephant with an offering of lotus-flowers and at the same time protected by some triple-headed serpents which form a garland round its dome.

The tooth-relic of the Buddha entrusted to the Nāgas [3]

[In the course of his account of the capital of Kashmīr, the Chinese pilgrim Hiuen Tsiang relates the following legend.]

About 10 *li* to the south-east of the new city and to the north of the old city,[4] and on the south of a great mountain, is a convent with about 300 priests in it. In the *stūpa* attached to the convent is a tooth of Buddha in length about an inch and a half, of a yellowish-white colour; on religious days it emitteth a bright light. In old days the Kritīya[5] race having destroyed the Law of Buddha, the priests being dispersed, each one selected

[1] Burgess, op. cit., pl. xl, 2. Cf. also Fergusson, op. cit., p. 237, pl. xcviii.

[2] *A.S.R.*, for 1904–05, p. 89, fig. 12. *Cat. of the Sārnāth Museum*, pp. 200 f., No. C (*b*) 9; pl. xxiii *b*.

[3] *Si-yu-ki*, (transl. Beal), vol. i, pp. 158 f. T. Watters, op. cit., vol. i, p. 279.

[4] The old capital of Kashmīr stood on the site of the village of Pāndrenthan which still retains in its modern form the ancient name of Purāṇādhishṭhāna, i.e. " the old capital ".

[5] The Kritīyas, according to Hiuen Tsiang, were a race of low-caste people said to be descended from the alien menials employed in the Buddhist monasteries, who gradually had gained great ascendency in Kashmīr and were bitterly opposed to the Buddhist religion.

PLATE X.

(a) STŪPA WORSHIPPED BY NĀGAS (AMARĀVATĪ).

(b) RELIC-CASKET WORSHIPPED BY NĀGAS (AMARĀVATĪ).

(To face p. 14).

his own place of abode. On this occasion one *Śramaṇa*, wandering throughout the Indies to visit and worship the traces of the Holy One and to exhibit his sincere faith, after a while came to hear that his native country was pacified and settled. Forthwith he set out on his return, and on his way he met with a herd of elephants rushing across his path through the jungle and raising a trumpeting tumult. The *Śramaṇa*, having seen them, climbed up a tree to get out of their way ; then the herd of elephants rushed down to drink at a pool and to cleanse themselves with the water ; then surrounding the tree they tore it up by the roots and forcibly dragged it to the ground. Having got the *Śramaṇa* they put him on the back of one and hurried off to the middle of a great forest where was a sick elephant swollen with a sore and lying on the ground. Taking the hand of the priest it directed it to the place of the hurt where a rotten piece of bamboo had penetrated. The *Śramaṇa* thereupon drew out the splinter and applied some medicinal herbs, and tore up his garment to bind the foot with it. Another elephant taking a gold casket, brought it to the sick elephant, who, having received it gave it forthwith to the *Śramaṇa*. The *Śramaṇa* opening it, found inside it the Buddha's tooth. Then all the elephants surrounding him, he knew not how to get away. On the morrow, being a fast-day, each elephant brought him some fruit for his midday meal. When he had finished eating, they carried the priest out of the forest a long way, and then they set him down and, after salutation paid, they each retired.

The *Śramana* coming to the western borders of the country, crossed a rapid river ; while he was so doing the boat was nearly overwhelmed, and the men consulting together, said : " The calamity that threatens the boat is owing to the *Śramaṇa*, he must be carrying some relics of the Buddha, and the dragons have coveted them."

The master of the ship, having examined his goods, found the tooth of the Buddha. Then the *Śramaṇa*, raising up the relic, bowed his head, and called to the Nāgas, and said : " I now entrust this to your care ; not long hence I will come again and take it." Then declining to cross the river, he returned to the bank and departed. Turning to the river he sighed and said : " Not knowing how to restrain these Nāga creatures hath been the cause of my calamity."

Then going back to India, he studied the rules of restraining dragons, and after three years he returned towards his native country, and having come to the riverside he built and established there an altar. Then the Nāgas brought back the casket containing the Buddha's tooth, and gave it to the *Śramaṇa* ; the *Śramaṇa* took it and brought it to this monastery and henceforth worshipped it.

CHAPTER III

THE NĀGAS IN THE JĀTAKAS

THE great Pali collection of birth-stories, i.e. tales relating to the previous existences of the Buddha, yields as rich a harvest of Nāga lore as does the *Mahābhārata,* that vast repository of Brahmanical legend. Here, too, the serpent-demons appear under greatly varying aspects. In dealing with the *Jātaka* book we must distinguish between those stories which are Buddhistic in origin and spirit and those (probably the large majority) which are in reality fables, fairy tales, ballads, and romances converted into birth-stories and adapted by the Buddhist preachers for the purpose of pious edification. It is in these ancient folk-tales that the Nāga has sometimes preserved its original character of a fabulous serpent. This is the case with the fable of the Nāga and the birds (*Ghatāsana-jātaka*), the introduction to the *Bakabrahma-jātaka*, and the amusing tale of 'the Nāga of the Mango Ferry' which we have rendered in the preceding chapter. In these stories the Nāga is essentially a snake, not, however, a mere animal of the serpent species, but a dragon of a particularly dangerous and fierce kind, and, moreover, possessed of magical properties, such as the power of spitting flames.

This primitive aspect of the Nāga is, however, as exceptional in the *Jātaka* collection, as it is rare in the legends relating to the Buddha's final existence which we have discussed in the preceding chapter. As a rule the Nāga of the *Jātakas* is a harmless and almost helpless creature, not only in conflicts with his powerful foes of old, the Garuḍa and the magician, but even when abused by the street urchins of Benares, as we read in the *Daddara-* and *Kharaputta-jātakas*. The hereditary enmity between the Nāga and his winged adversary the Garuḍa or Suparṇa (as he is also called) is often brought in. We are told in the story of Bhūridatta that as a general rule a captured Nāga looks at a crowd for two reasons, to see whether any Suparṇa or any kinsman is near : if they espy a Suparṇa they do not dance for fear ; if a kinsman, they do not dance for shame. When assailed by a Garuḍa, their only chance of escape is sudden flight, unless they prefer to resort to such a curious stratagem as we hear of in the *Paṇḍara-jātaka*. The danger threatening the snake tribe on the part of their voracious enemy has, moreover, increased not a little, since out of the single Garuḍa of Brahmanical literature there has sprung, if we are to believe Buddhist tradition, a whole tribe of such giant-birds. Their favourite haunt is the forest of silk-cotton-trees on the shores of the Southern Ocean.

This is an early notion, as appears from the *Suparṇādhyāya* (XXXI, 1), where the Garuḍa is said to have made his large nest in the *śālmali*-tree in the mountains. The *śālmali* (Pali: *simbali*, Hindi: *semal*) or silk-cotton-tree is the *Bombax malabaricus* or *Salmalia malabarica*, a stately tree with red blossoms.[1]

The *Uraga-jātaka* supplies us with an edifying story in which a holy hermit in a truly Buddhistic spirit brings about a reconciliation between a Nāga and a Suparṇa. The recluse was no other than the future Buddha.

A not less cruel and implacable opponent is the snake-charmer who, by means of magic spells (*mantra*) and drugs (*aushadha*) exercises an irresistible power over the Nāga. Some of the *jātakas* summarized beneath dwell at great length on the ruthless practices adopted by such wizards to reduce even the most powerful serpent-king to a state of utter helplessness, their motive being of no higher order than mere greed of lucre.

Now it is true that the harmlessness which in these Buddhist stories is so conspicuous and astonishing a feature in the usual presentation of the ancient snake-demons is mostly conceived as being a self-chosen virtue. It is the outcome of self-abnegation and spiritual striving, Great Nāga kings, we are repeatedly told, like Bhūridatta, Champaka, and Śaṅkhapāla, might easily turn on their human tormentors and destroy them with the blast of their nostrils—yea, they could annihilate even a whole town or country—but they renounce the use of their power to harm. They prefer to keep the commandments, and, when they see the wicked snake-charmer drawing near to ill-treat and capture them, they even close their eyes, the look of which alone would be a deadly weapon.

Thus in those birth-stories which are really Buddhistic in spirit we meet with the type of the pious Nāga who realizes the highest ideals of forbearance and self-sacrifice. Strange though it may seem, the poisonous and uncanny were-serpent of old has developed into a Buddhist saint. In fact, he is no other than the Great Being which in after-times is to become Gautama Buddha, the saviour of the world.

Such is the case with the three remarkable birth-stories named respectively after their Nāga heroes Champaka, Śaṅkhapāla, and Bhūridatta, each of whom is identified with the future Buddha. These three *jātakas* in an abbreviated form occur also in the *Chariyāpiṭaka*; here they belong to that group of ten birth-stories which serve to illustrate how the Bodhisattva possessed the highest perfection of *śīla*, i.e. morality or the keeping of the moral precepts. The three stories in question bear a marked similarity to one another:

[1] *Koṭisimbali-jātaka* (No. 412) and *Bhūridatta-j* (No. 543), section iv. Cf. Grünwedel, *Buddhistische Studien*, pp. 26 ff., fig. 34. On the *Suparṇādhyāya* see Jarl Charpentier, *Die Suparṇasage*, pp. 274 f.

in substance they are identical, though differing in detail.[1] First we have an introduction in which the circumstances of the Bodhisattva's snake-birth are set forth. In the *Champeyya-* and *Saṅkhapāla-jātakas* the Bodhisattva's birth in the snake-world is caused by a distinct aspiration conceived in a previous existence. But the Nāga in each case soon becomes weary of the sensual enjoyments of the Nāgaloka: he wishes to observe the Sabbath-vow in order to obtain a good rebirth.[2] Now as in the snake-world his pious purpose is difficult to fulfil owing to the allurements of the fair Nāga damsels, he goes to the world of men and, lying down on the top of an ant-hill, he makes a vow by which in a truly Buddhistic spirit he offers his body to any one who may care to take it. In the *Chariyāpiṭaka* this vow is expressed in the formula: "Whosoever wanteth my skin, my hide, my flesh, my sinews, or my bones, it is given to him: let him take it."

In the *Saṅkhapāla-jātaka* the Nāga king is caught by a gang of sixteen low-caste men, who carry him to their home to eat his flesh, but on the way he is released by Aḷāra, a householder from Mithilā. The grateful serpent-king entertains his rescuer during a year in the Nāgaloka.

In the *Champeyya-* and *Bhūridatta-jātakas* the Bodhisattva is caught by a snake-charmer who makes him dance and thereby gains much money. The captured snake must give a great performance in the presence of the king of Benares, but in the meanwhile his relatives have learnt of his sad fate. In the story of Champaka it is his faithful wife Sumanā, warned through a magic pond, at whose entreaties the king pays ransom and obtains his release.

In the *Bhūridatta-jātaka* the mother of the captive Nāga-prince sees an evil dream and his eldest brother Sudarśana goes to the rescue together with his half-sister Archimukhī, the latter in the shape of a frog. The snake-charmer, challenged and defeated by Sudarśana at the royal court of Benares, receives his due punishment, whereas the wicked Brahmin who had betrayed Bhūridatta is pardoned. The story ends with an eloquent sermon preached by Bhūridatta to denounce Brahmanical superstition.

In these and other *jātakas* we meet, on the one hand, with the Buddhist conception that Nāgas are inferior beings and that consequently snake-birth is to be regarded as the

[1] The author of the prose narrative also seems to observe a certain connexion between those three birth-stories, where he supplies us with a curious piece of information regarding the size of the Nāga-Bodhisattva in each of these snake-births. "Now in this (viz. the Champeyya) Birth the Bodhisattva's body was thick as a plough-head, in the Bhūridatta Birth thick as a thigh, in the Saṅkhapāla Birth as big round as a trough-canoe with an out-rigger." *Jātaka*, vol. iv, p. 456, l. 27; Cambridge transl., vol. iv, p. 283. Cf. also *Jāt.*, vol. v, p. 163, l. 19.

[2] In the *Bhūridatta-j.*, the hero of the story, after having seen Śakra's paradise with its hosts of heavenly nymphs, wishes to be reborn as a *deva*!

outcome of an evil *karman*.[1] On the other hand, we find the old popular notion of the marvellous attractions of the Nāga world which remind us of the account of the Brahmin Uttaṅka's visit to the Nether regions told in the *Paushya-parvan* of the *Mahābhārata*. But what in the Great Epic is only briefly indicated, is here discanted upon in a series of glowing verses, singing the splendours of the mysterious snake-world—palaces glittering with gold and precious stones, gardens rich in flowering and fruit-bearing trees, and, above all, crowds of fair damsels, a world of sensual enjoyment, denied to the common mortal and only to be won by special exertions and acts of piety.

A few picturesque stanzas I may be allowed to quote from the Cambridge translation ; it is Śaṅkhapāla who speaks :—

What charming spots in my domain are seen,
Soft to the tread and clothed in evergreen !
Nor dust nor gravel in our path we find,
And there do happy souls leave grief behind.

Midst level courts that sapphire walls surround
Fair mango groves on every side abound,
Whereon ripe clusters of rich fruit appear
Through all the changing seasons of the year.

Amidst these groves a fabric wrought of gold
And fixed with silver bolts thou mayst behold,
A dwelling bright in splendour, to outvie
The lightning flash that gleams athwart the sky.

Fashioned with gems and gold, divinely fair,
And decked with paintings manifold and rare,
'Tis thronged with nymphs magnificently dressed,
All wearing golden chains upon their breast.

The evident relish which these Buddhist poets experience in extolling the attractions of the Nāgaloka seems somewhat hard to reconcile with the austere spirit of early Buddhism. But do we not find the walls of the monasteries of Ajaṇṭā covered with many a similar scene of sensual enjoyment, in which female beauty is most conspicuous ? Yet 'the Book of Monastic Discipline' contains the injunction, ascribed to the Buddha himself, that the decoration of the convents should be restricted to a few floral or foliated devices.

We have still to note two *jātakas* in which the Nāga is not identified with the future Buddha, but with one of his principal disciples. In the *Mahāpaduma* he is Ānanda and in the *Sīlānisaṃsa* he is Śāriputra In both these stories the serpent-king figures as the helpful deity who in each case saves the hero from disaster and death. In the *Mahāvānija-* and *Jarudapāna-jātaka*, both of which agree in exemplifying the evil resulting from excessive

[1] This idea we find also illustrated in the *avadāna* of Subhūti who had been reborn five hundred times as a Nāga on account of his evil disposition and because he used to call the *bhikshus* 'serpents'. *Avadāna-śataka*, xci (ed. Speyer, vol. ii, p. 132 ; cf. transl. Feer, p. 370). Another instance is afforded by the *Uposhadha avadāna*, *Avadāna-śat.*, lix (ed. Speyer, vol. i, p. 338 ; cf. transl. Feer, p. 228).

greed, the Nāga assumes the lofty office of a just deity saving those in danger and chastising the wicked. In these two stories the virtuous caravan-leader, who keeps himself free from the covetousness of his companions, is rewarded by the Nāga king with abundant treasure. In other *jātakas*, too, the Nāgas are described as guardians and distributors of wealth, including objects with magical properties such as ' the gem that granteth all wishes ' which figures in the *Bhūridatta-jātaka*. It is, no doubt, an ancient trait that this jewel as soon as it touches the earth (viz the special domain of the snakes) suddenly disappears and returns to the snake-world from whence it came.

The *jātakas* contain not a few similar features of early snake-lore, such as the Nāga's power of assuming all kind of forms, even that of a seafaring-ship But, on the whole, it must be admitted that under the influence of Buddhist ideals the character of the ancient serpent demons has become strangely altered and has acquired an ethical value which certainly it did not possess in a more primitive stage.

The Nāga and the Birds [1]

Once upon a time a flock of birds had taken up their abode in a large tree which stretched its leafy branches over the waters of a lake. All these birds, roosting in the boughs, let their droppings fall into the waters below. Now that lake was the abode of Chanda, the Nāga king, who, being wroth at this fouling of the water, resolved to take vengeance on the birds and burn them out. So one night when they were all roosting along the branches, he set to work to drive them away : first he made the waters of the lake to boil, then he caused smoke to arise, and thirdly he made flames dart up as high as a palm-tree.

Seeing the flames shooting up from the water, the king of the birds cried : " Water is used to quench fire ; but here is the water itself on fire. This is no place for us ; let us seek a home elsewhere."

So saying he flew off with such of the birds as followed his advice ; but the disobedient birds, who stopped behind, all perished.

Now the king of the birds was the Bodhisattva.

The birth-story rendered above we find illustrated among the frescoes of the Ku-byauk-kyi Pagoda at Pagan, the ancient capital of Burma [2] The panel is somewhat damaged, and, owing to its small size, the details are not quite clear. But apparently the angry Nāga is shown in the shape of a snake.

[1] *Ghatāsana-jātaka* (No. 133), *Jātaka*, vol i, pp. 471 f., Cambridge transl, vol i, pp. 290 f.

[2] *A.S R.* for 1912–13, pp. 95 and 118 ; plate lx, fig. 57 (the last panel of the sixth row).

The Foolish Raftsmen and the angry Nāga [1]

[The *Bakabrahma-jātaka* contains a dialogue between the Buddha and a deity of the *Brahmaloka*, in which the latter's false doctrines with regard to his heavenly abode being eternal and permanent are exposed by a reference to his previous existences. In one of those former lives, of which the Buddha reminds him, he had saved a man whose boat had been seized by a Nāga in the river Gaṅgā. Of this incident the commentary gives the following interpretation.]

At that time he lived as an ascetic on the bank of the river Ganges. Some men tied two or three rafts together, erected a flowered pavilion on the top, and so they travelled, eating and drinking, to the house of some relative. Now the rest of the liquor they had drunk and the remnants of rice, fish, and betel they had eaten and chewed, they dropped into the Ganges. Then the Nāga king of the Ganges became enraged, saying to himself: "These men defile me with their leavings. Let me seize them all and drown them in the Gaṅgā." He made himself as large as a dhoney,[2] split the water, and expanding his hood, he came for them. When they saw the Nāga king, those men, frightened with the fear of death, made with one accord a great noise. The ascetic, hearing the sound of their wailings and recognizing the state of wrath of the Nāga king, said to himself: "Let them not perish before my eyes." Quickly by his magic power he made himself into a Suparṇa. When the Nāga king saw him, he was seized with the fear of death and vanished in the waves. So these men were saved.

The Story of Dardara, the exiled Nāga [3]

In the Himālaya region at the foot of Mount Dardara there is the abode of the Dardara Nāgas. Their king was Sūra-dardara who had two sons, Great Dardara and Small Dardara. The latter was passionate and cruel, and went about abusing and striking the Nāga maidens. The Nāga king, on hearing of his cruelty, gave orders for his expulsion from the Nāga world. But Great Dardara begged his father to forgive him, and saved his brother from expulsion. A second time the king was wroth with him, and again he was induced to forgive him. But on the third occasion the king said: "Thou hast prevented me from expelling this ill-behaved fellow; now both of you get you gone from this Nāga world, and live for three years at Benares on a dunghill."

With these words he drove them forth from the Nāga world and they went and lived at Benares. When the village boys saw them looking for their food in a ditch bounding

[1] *Bakabrahma-jātaka* (No. 405), commentary. *Jātaka*, vol. iii, p. 362. Cambridge transl., vol. iii, p. 220.

[2] A dhoney is a trough-shaped canoe with an out-rigger to steady it. Cf. Childers' *Pali Dictionary*, i, v., *doni*, and R. Mookerji, *Hist. of Indian shipping*, pp. 251 f. and pl. facing p. 252.

[3] *Daddara-jātaka* (No. 304). *Jātaka*, vol. iii, pp. 16 f., Cambridge transl., vol. iii, pp. 10 f.

the dunghill, they struck them and threw clods and sticks and other missiles at them, crying out: "What have we here—water-snakes with big heads and tails like needles?" and uttered other words of abuse.

Small Dardara, by reason of his fierce and passionate nature, being unable to put up with such disrespect, said: "Brother, these boys are mocking us. They know not that we are venomous serpents. I cannot stand their contempt for us. I will destroy them by the breath of my nostril."

And then, addressing his brother, he repeated the first stanza:—

O Dardara, who such an insult could bear?
"Ho, frog-eating stick-i-the-mud," they cry:
"To think that these poor harmless creatures should dare
A serpent with poisonous fang to defy."

On hearing his words Great Dardara uttered the rest of the stanzas:—

"An exile driven to a foreign shore
Must of abuse lay up a goodly store;
For where his rank and virtues none can know,
Only the fool his pride would care to show.
He who at home a 'shining light' may be,
Abroad must suffer men of low degree."

So they dwelt there for three years. Then their father recalled them home. And from that day their pride was abated.

How King Senaka received a charm from a Nāgarāja [1]

Once upon a time there reigned in Benares a king, named Senaka, who was friendly with a certain Nāgarāja. The latter once left the Nāga world and ranged the earth seeking food. The village boys seeing him said: "This is a snake," and struck him with clods and other things. The king, going to amuse himself in his garden, saw them, and being told they were beating a snake, said: "Don't let them beat him, drive them away," and this was done. So the Nāga king kept his life, and when he went back to the Nāga world he took many jewels, and coming at midnight to the king's bedchamber he gave them to him, saying: "I owe my life to you," so he made a friendship with the king and came again and again to see him. He appointed one of his Nāga girls insatiate in pleasures, to be near the king and protect him, and he gave the king a charm, saying: "If ever thou seest her not, repeat this charm."

One day the king went to the garden with the Nāga girl and was disporting himself in the lotus-tank. The Nāga maid, seeing a water-snake, quitted her human shape and made

[1] *Kharaputta-jātaka* (No. 386). *Jātaka*, vol. iii, pp. 275 ff. Cambridge transl., vol. iii, pp. 174 ff. *Jātaka Tales*, pp. 259 ff. Grünwedel, *Buddhistische Studien*, pp. 23 ff.

PLATE XI

NĀGAS SUPPORTING LOTUS-FLOWER (CHANDI MENDUT, JAVA)

[To face p. 138

love with him. The king, not seeing the girl, said : " Where is she gone ? " And repeated the spell ; then he saw her in her misconduct and struck her with a piece of bamboo. She went in anger to the Nāga world and when she was asked : " Why art thou come ? " she said : " Thy friend struck me on the back because I did not do his bidding," showing the mark of the blow.

The Nāga king, not knowing the truth, called four Nāga youths and sent them with orders to enter Senaka's bedchamber and destroy him like chaff by the breath of their nostrils. They entered the chamber at the royal bed-time. As they came in, the king was saying to the queen : "Lady, knowest thou where the Nāga girl hath gone ? " " King, I do not." " To-day when we were bathing in the tank she quitted her shape and misconducted herself with a water-snake. I said : 'Don't do that,' and struck her with a piece of bamboo to give her a lesson ; and now I fear she may have gone to the Nāga world and told some lie to my friend, destroying his good-will to me."

The young Nāgas, hearing this, turned back at once to the Nāga world, and told their king. He, being moved, went instantly to the king's chamber, told him all and was forgiven ; then he said : " In this way I make amends," and gave the king a charm giving knowledge of all sounds."

[The rest of the story is irrelevant.]

The Story of the Greedy Merchants [1]

Certain traffickers, having assembled from sundry countries, appointed one of them their chief and set out for the acquisition of wealth. Having come to a forest waterless and poor of food, they espied a large banyan-tree cool-shaded and beautiful. The merchants sat down in the shade of that tree and in their folly they thought : " This tree is wet and drips with water ; come, let us cut the eastern branch of this tree." The branch, being cut, produced clear and limpid water, and the merchants bathed and drank as much as they liked. A second time they considered in their folly : " Come, let us cut the southern branch of this tree." The branch, being cut, produced plenty of meat, and boiled rice, thick porridge, ginger and pea-soup. Having eaten and drunk as much as they liked, those merchants a third time considered in their folly : " Come, let us cut the western branch of this tree." That branch, being cut, produced women in wonderful garments and ornaments, adorned with jewelled ear-rings. Each of the merchants had five-and-twenty of them. From all sides they were ministered unto by them in the shade of that tree, and they dallied with them as much as they liked. A fourth time they considered in their folly : " Come let us cut the northern branch of this tree." That branch, being cut, produced

[1] *Mahāvānija-jātaka* (No. 493). *Jātaka*, vol. iv, pp. 350 ff. Cambridge transl., vol. iv, pp. 221 ff.

plenty of pearls and beryl-stones, silver and fine gold, embroideries (?), and woollen carpets, garments of Benares silk and blankets from the North. Having bound all this in bundles as much as they liked, a fifth time they considered in their folly : " Come, let us cut the root of this tree, so that we may get more."

Then the leader of the caravan rose and with hands joined he implored : " What offence hath the banyan-tree committed, O merchants ? So may ye be pleased. The eastern branch gave water, the southern one food and drink, the western one women, and the northern one all that a man can desire. What offence hath the banyan-tree committed, O merchants ? So may ye be pleased. One ought not to break a branch of the tree in whose shade one either sits or lies down. He who injureth his friend, is a bad man." But they, being many, did not mind the word of him who was alone and with whetted axes they attacked the root of the tree.

Now the Nāga king, incensed with wrath at their ingratitude and greed ordered his hosts to exterminate them. Then mail-clad Nāgas came forth, five-and-twenty in number, and three hundred bowmen and six thousand armed with shields. " Slay them and bind them," said the Nāga king, " let not one escape alive ; except the caravan-leader, reduce them all to ashes."

Having done so, the Nāgas loaded the rugs from the North and the other goods upon the five hundred wagons, and conveyed the waggons and chief of the caravan to Benares, and put up the goods in his house, and taking leave of him, returned to their own place of abode.

The Old Well [1]

Once upon a time there was at Benares a senior caravan-leader. He, taking merchandise and filling his waggons therewith, set out accompanied by many other traders. On their way, having come to a wood, they saw an old disused well. Therein was no water that they could see, and they were athirst ; so they resolved to dig deeper. As they dug, they came upon all kind of metals. But albeit they gat much treasure, they were discontented. They still dug on, saying : " There must be other more precious things." Now the senior caravan-leader spake : " O, merchants, greed is the root of destruction. We have won a great deal of wealth ; with this be ye content, and dig no more." But they listened not to him, and still dug on. Now that well was haunted by Nāgas. The Nāga king, who had his dwelling beneath grew angry at his palace being damaged by the falling of clods and earth. Save the caravan-leader, he slew them all with the breath of his nostrils and destroyed them. Then he came up from the Nāga world, and yoked the oxen to the carts,

[1] *Jarudapāna-jātaka* (No. 256). *Jātaka*, vol. ii, pp. 294 ff. Cambridge transl., vol. ii, pp. 205 f.

filled them with jewels, and seating the caravan-leader upon a fine waggon, he made certain young Nāgas drive the carts and brought him to Benares. There he led him into his house, set the treasure in order, and went back to his own Nāga abode. The caravan-leader distributed his wealth, so that there was a holiday throughout all Jambudvīpa, and, having vowed to perform the moral precepts and to keep the Sabbath, at the end of his life he went to Paradise.

The Nāga Pāṇḍura who let his Secret out [1]

Once upon a time five hundred merchants took ship and set sail, and on the seventh day, when they were out of sight of land, they were wrecked in mid-ocean and all save one man became food for fishes. This one by favour of the wind reached the port of Karambiya, and landing naked and destitute he went about the place, begging alms. The people thought: "Here is an ascetic, happy and contented with little," and they built him a hermitage for a dwelling-place, and he went by the name of the naked ascetic of Karamba. While he was living here, he met with great honour and gain, and both a Nāga king and a Garuḍa king came to pay their respects to him, and thename of the former was Pāṇḍura.[2] Now one day the Garuḍa king, being come to the ascetic, spake thus: "Sir, our people, when they seize Nāgas, many of them perish. We do not know the right way to seize Nāgas. There is said to be some mystery in the matter. Thou couldst, perhaps, wheedle the secret out of them." "All right," said the ascetic, and when the Garuḍa king had taken his leave, as soon as ever the Nāga king arrived, he questioned him, saying: "Nāga king, the Garuḍas say that in seizing you many of them perish. In attacking you, how can they seize you securely?" "Sir," he rejoined, "this is our secret; if I were to tell thee, I should bring about the destruction of all my kinsfolk." At last, however, the ascetic having promised to tell no one, the Nāga said: "Sir, we make ourselves heavy by swallowing very big stones and lie down, and when the Garuḍas come, we open our mouth wide, and show our teeth and fall upon them. They come on and seize us by the head, and while they strive to lift us up, heavy as we are, from the ground, the water covereth them, and in the midst of the water they die. In this manner a number of Garuḍas perish. When they attack us, why do they seize us by the head? If the foolish creatures should seize us by the tail and hold our head downwards, they could force us to disgorge the stones we have swallowed, and so, making us a light-weight, they could carry us off with them."

Then when the Nāga had gone away, up came the Garuḍa king and asked: "Well, Sir, hast thou learned the secret from the Nāga king?" "Yes, Sir," he said, and told him

[1] *Paṇḍara-jātaka* (No. 518). *Jātaka*, vol. v, pp. 75 ff. Cambridge transl., vol. v, pp. 42 ff.

[2] Pali *Paṇḍara* (' white ').

everything just as it had been told him. On hearing it, the Garuḍa king said: "The Nāga king hath made a great mistake. He ought not to have told another how to destroy, his kinsfolk. Well, to day I must first of all raise a Garuḍa wind and seize him." So, raising a Garuḍa wind, he seized Pāṇḍura the Nāga king by the tail and held him head downmost, and having thus made him disgorge the stones he had swallowed, he flew up into the air with him.

[The remainder of the story in which we hear how the Garuḍa, moved by compassion, released his victim, and the wicked ascetic received his due punishment, may be omitted.]

Of a possible representation of the *Paṇḍara-jātaka* on the Bharhut railing we shall have occasion to speak in the sequel when dealing with the *Maṇikaṇṭha-jātaka.*

How a Nāga and a Suparṇa were reconciled through the holy influence of a hermit [1]

At the time when Brahmadatta was king at Benares, a festival had been proclaimed and there was a large gathering. Not only many men, but also Devas, Nāgas, Suparṇas and so forth assembled. Now a Nāga and a Suparṇa who were looking at the crowd happened to stand side by side on the same spot. And the Nāga, not knowing the other to be a Suparṇa, laid his hand on the shoulder of his neighbour. The latter thought: "Who has put his hand on my shoulder?" looked round and recognized the Nāga. The Nāga, too looked and recognized the Suparṇa; frightened with the fear of death, out of the town he flew off over the surface of the river. The Suparṇa gave chase, and tried to catch him.

At that time there lived a recluse (it was the future Buddha) who abode in a leaf-hut on the bank of that river. To ward off the oppression of the sun's heat, he had taken off his garment of bark and put on a bathing cloth, and he had entered the river to bathe. Thought the Nāga: "I will save my life by means of that anchorite," and, quitting his natural shape and assuming the shape of a jewel, he hid in the bark garment. The Suparṇa pursuing him saw that he had hidden in the bark garment, but out of reverence he dared not touch it; so he bespake the ascetic in this wise: "With thy leave, Sir, I am hungry. Do thou take thy bark garment; I wish to eat that Nāga."

But the anchorite, after welcoming him in friendly terms, admonished him not to devour the Nāga, however hungry he might be. Then he came up from the river, put on his bark garment, and took both the Nāga and the Suparṇa to his hermitage where he rehearsed the blessings of loving kindness until they were both at one. Thenceforward they abode together happily in peace and harmony.

[1] *Uraga-jātaka* (No. 154). *Jātaka*, vol. ii, pp. 12 ff. Cambridge transl., vol. ii, pp. 9 ff. A similar story occurs in a Chinese Buddhist work; cf. Chavannes, *Cinq cents contes*, vol. ii, p. 287.

VIDHURA THE WISE[1]

[The *Jātaka* of Vidhura the Wise is a real romance covering more than seventy pages and consisting of no less than six chapters, each with its own title. In the hero of the story (who is the future Buddha) we recognize a personage from the *Mahābhārata*: Vidura, the half-brother of Pāṇḍu and Dhṛitarāshṭra, and consequently an uncle of the Pāṇḍavas and Dhārtarāshṭras. In the Great Epic he figures as the wise man whose prudent councils, too often disregarded, cannot prevent the fall of the Kaurava race. In the Jātaka he is the minister of the Kauravya king Dhanañjaya (a well-known epithet of Arjuna, the third Pāṇḍava) who resides at Indraprastha (Pali Indapatta). The story may be summarized as follows.]

It once befell that Śakra the ruler of the Devas, the Nāga king Varuṇa, a Suparṇa or Garuḍa king, and the Kauravya king Dhanañjaya met in a certain garden whither each of them had repaired in order to observe the duties of the Sabbath. Now among these four kings there arose a dispute as to which of them was greatest in virtue. They went for a decision to the wise Vidhura who declared the true ascetic to be the man endowed with their four virtues combined. Pleased with his answer, the kings presented him with rich gifts and departed, each to his own abode.

Now the Nāga king told his queen Vimalā of the marvellous eloquence and wisdom of Vidhura and this lady grew eager to hear him discourse on the Law. But, inasmuch as she feared that her husband would be unwilling to bring the Sage to her, she pretended to have a longing for Vidhura's heart. In order to comply with this strange wish the Nāga king instructed his daughter, Irandatī to seek for herself a husband who would bring him the heart of Vidhura.

The damsel went to the Himālaya and sang a pleasant song offering her love to any demon, man or sage, who would grant her wish. Now at that time a Yaksha general, named Pūrṇaka,[2] who was a nephew of the great king Vaiśravaṇa,[3] as he was riding on his magic horse three leagues in length, passed that spot. Struck by the sound of her voice, which he had heard in his previous life, he turned back and comforted her.

The fair Nāga maiden soon succeeded in winning his love. When as the Yaksha went to her father and sued for her to be his wife, he received the answer that his wish would be granted if he succeeded in procuring Vidhura's heart. Pūrṇaka first betook himself to his

[1] *Vidhura-jātaka* (No. 545). *Jātaka*, vol. vi, pp. 255 ff.; Cambridge transl., vol. vi, pp. 126 ff. The story in an abridged and somewhat different form occurs in the Chinese *Tripiṭaka*. Cf. Chavannes, *Cinq cents contes* vol. iii, p. 110.

[2] Vaiśravaṇa (Pali Vessavaṇa) is the patronymic of Kubera, the Indian god of wealth and sovereign of the Yakshas.

[3] Pali *Puṇṇaka*.

uncle Vaiśravaṇa, the lord of the Yakshas, to obtain his permission for the undertaking he had in view and described to him the beauties of the Nāga-world, the realm of king Varuṇa, with its wonderful palaces and gardens. As he knew king Dhanañjaya to be renowned for his skill in gambling, he resolved to conquer him in play and thus to seize the wise Vidhura. So he went to the city Indraprastha and challenged the king, offering as prize a marvellous jewel in the which the world of men and the world of the gods could be seen. The king, being defeated by the Yaksha, questioned him as to what prize he would have to give. Then Pūrṇaka made answer that he did not wish for any of the royal treasures: the prize he desired was Vidhura, the royal minister. King Dhanañjaya had to yield and the Yaksha general took Vidhura with him, not, however, without having allowed him to visit his home for three days and to exhort his sons. When Vidhura had discoursed at great length on the manner of conduct to be followed in a king's court, Pūrṇaka carried him off to the top of the Black Mountain, and there tried in vain to kill him, assuming various dreadful forms. The minister's wise words at last availed to impress the savage Yaksha, who confessed his true motives, and at the sage's own request took him to the abode of the Nāga king Varuṇa. Here, too, his firmness excited such great admiration in the Nāga-king and his wife that the former, while declaring that " the heart of sages is their wisdom ", not only granted his daughter to the Yaksha Pūrṇaka, but also enjoined the latter to carry Vidhura back to the court of the ruler of Indraprastha. The Yaksha, rejoiced at having at last obtained his bride, did as he was bidden, and soon the Kauravya king, forewarned by a dream, welcomed his wise minister at the door of the Hall of Truth.

One of the railing pillars of the Bharhut Stūpa is carved with a series of scenes which refer to the story of the wise Vidhura, as is clearly indicated by the inscription *Vitura-Punakiya-jātakam*, meaning ' the *jātaka* of Vitura and Punaka '. For further particulars we may refer the reader to the very full description by Sir Alexander Cunningham [1] who first identified the panels in question. For our present purpose it is of interest to note that the second scene shows Varuṇa, the king of the Nāgas, and his consort Vimalā seated side by side, while the Yaksha youth is shown standing in front of them with folded hands, evidently in the act of proffering his suit. The king is known by his five-headed snake-crest, while the queen has a single snake over her head. It is not clear whether the female figure in the first scene which, according to Cunningham must represent the daughter of the royal couple, the fair Irandatī, is also distinguished by the usual Nāga emblem, but on the published photograph there are traces of a snake issuing from behind her head.

M. Foucher has also recognized the *Vidhura-jātaka* among the frescoes decorating

[1] A. Cunningham, *Bharhut Stūpa*, pp. 79 ff., and pl. xviii.

PLATE XII.

Jātaka of Vidhura the Wise (Borobudur).

[To face p. 144

cave II of Ajaṇṭā.[1] Here, too, the story is rendered in a series of scenes. "It was the constant presence of the faithful charger already seen at Bharhut," M. Foucher remarks, "which suggested to me the identification and enabled me to follow the chief of the genii Pūrṇaka, first on his journey through the air, then to the beautiful Nāgī (it is she who is balancing on a swing in *Paintings*, fig. 66); then into the audience chamber and the gambling room of the king of Indraprastha; then to the wise minister (*Paintings*, pl. xxxiii; the last scene is also reproduced in *Frescoes*, pl. lx, 49); and finally in the company of the latter, once more to the palace of the King of the Nāgas. Therefore the panel equally represented on pl. xxxiii of the *Paintings* (to the left of the centre), where five persons are sitting together talking, can only represent the consultation, given by Vidhura, in the presence of his Master, to the kings of the Devas, the Nāgas, and the Garuḍas, which was the origin of the whole adventure."

Among the sculptures decorating the balustrade (upper row) along the first gallery of the Borobudur there are three square panels (Nos. 166–168) which evidently belong together.[2] The central panel (No. 167) is occupied by a figure wearing profuse ornaments who is seated cross-legged on a throne, and on account of his halo may be assumed to represent a Bodhisattva. Evidently he is shown in the act of delivering a discourse for the benefit of four personages sitting two to his right (No. 166) and two to his left (No. 168). As each of these four figures is distinguished by a royal standard placed at his side, they must be four kings. One of them is clearly a Garuḍa, the emblem on the top of his standard being a bird. The personage in front of him has a standard on which a conch is visible. It is very tempting to identify this triple bas-relief with the opening scene of the *Vidhura-jātaka*, in which the wise Vidhura decides the problem raised by the four kings. The next panel (No. 169) evidently shows Vidhura being brought into the presence of the Nāga king Varuṇa by the Yaksha general Pūrṇaka who is accompanied by his faithful steed.

Prince Padma sheltered by a Nāga[3]

[The *Mahāpaduma-jātaka* is a story of the well-known Phaedra type which it will be unnecessary here to render in detail.]

Prince Padma or 'the Lotus Prince', being falsely accused by his step-mother, is thrown down the Thieves' Cliff by order of the king, his father. But a deity that dwelt in

[1] Foucher, *Preliminary Report*, pp. 60 f., where references are given to Griffith, *Paintings*, and Lady Herringham, *Ajanta Frescoes*.

[2] Krom., op. cit., p. 351, plates: series 1 (B) a pl. xix.

[3] *Mahāpaduma-jātaka* (No. 472). *Jātaka*, vol. iv, pp. 187 ff.; Cambridge transl., vol. iv, pp. 116 ff. The Bodhisattva was Prince Padma, and his favourite disciple Ānanda was the Nāga king. *Jātaka Tales*, pp. 331 f.

the hill saves him and sets him " in the abode of the serpents of the Mountains ", within the hood of the king of the serpents ". The Nāga-king receives him into his abode and gives him the half of his own glory. After having tarried there during one year, he craves leave of his host to go back to the ' paths of men '. The serpent-king gives his consent, conveys him to the ' paths of men ', and provides him with the requisites of a recluse.

Prince Padma becomes a hermit in the Himālaya. When his father, having found out that he is still alive, comes to visit him in the solitude and inquires how he was saved, he answers in a verse : " A mighty Nāga, full of force, born on the mountain-top, caught me within his coils : therefore I did not die."

It deserves notice that in the *gāthās* which constitute the oldest part of the *jātaka*, no mention is made of the ' deity that dwelt in the hill ' saving the prince, but only of the Nāgarāja. Perhaps it was he who originally was conceived as the spirit of the mountain.

The story of Prince Padma is found on one of the Pagan terra-cottas now preserved in the Berlin Museum of Ethnography.[1] The panel shows two kneeling figures, apparently the prince and the mountain spirit, while the Nāga appears in the shape of a simple snake.

The Pious Layman and the Barber [2]

It happened in the days of the Buddha Kāśyapa, that a disciple who had attained the first grade of sanctification, took passage on board ship together with a barber. The barber's wife had entrusted her husband to the pious layman, saying : " Sir, let him be thy charge in better and in worse."

On the seventh day the ship was wrecked in mid-ocean. These two persons, clinging to one plank, were cast up on an island. There the barber killed some birds, cooked, and ate them, offering a share of his meal to the lay-brother. " No, I thank thee," said he, " I have had enough." He was thinking to himself : " In this place there is no aid for us save the Three Refuges," and so he pondered upon the blessings of the Three Gems.[3] Now, as he pondered and pondered, a Nāga king who had been born in that isle, changed his own body to the shape of a great ship. A Spirit of the Sea was the helmsman. The ship was filled with the seven precious things. The three masts were made of sapphire, the anchor(?) of gold, the ropes of silver, and the planks were golden.

The Sea-spirit stood on board, crying : " Any passengers for Jambudvīpa ? " Said the lay-brother : " Yes, that's where we want to go." " Come along, then, on board with

[1] Grünwedel, *Buddhistische Studien*, pp. 34 ff. ; fig. 38.

[2] *Sīlānisaṃsa-jātaka* (No. 190). *Jātaka*, vol. ii, pp. 111 ff. ; Cambridge transl., vol. ii, pp. 77 f.

[3] The Buddha, the Law, and the Community.

thee." He went aboard, and wanted to call the barber. But the Sea-spirit said: "Thou art allowed to come, but not he." "Why not?" "He is not a man of holy life, that's why I brought this ship for thee, not for him." "Very well," quoth the layman, "the gifts I have given, the commandments I have kept, the attainments I have developed—I give him a share of them." "I thank thee, master," said the barber. "Now," said the Sea-spirit, "I can take him aboard." So he conveyed them both oversea, and sailed upstream to Benares. There, by his power, he created a store of wealth for both of them, and bespake them thus: "Keep company with the wise. For if this barber had not been in company with this pious layman, he would have perished in the midst of the ocean."

Among the sculptures decorating the Western Gate of Sānchi there is one which has given rise to a good deal of speculation. It "represents a piece of water, with a barge floating on it whose prow is formed by a winged gryphon and its stern by a fish's tail. The barge contains a pavilion overshadowing a vacant throne, over which a male attendant holds a *chātta*, while another man has a *chaori*; a third man is steering or propelling the vessel with a large paddle. In the water are freshwater flowers and buds and a large shell; and there are five men floating about, holding on by spars and inflated skins, while a sixth appears to be asking the occupant of the stern of the vessel for help out of the water."[1]

Fergusson took this sculpture to represent "the triumphal conveyance of some relics across a lake or a river" and another author went a step further while explaining it as "the conveyance of relics from India to Ceylon which is intercepted by Nāgas." Professor Radhakumud Mookerji, on the other hand, believes it simply to represent a royal state barge. "The scene," he says, "is that of the king and some of his courtiers disporting themselves in an artificial piece of water; but it is also capable of a symbolical meaning, especially when we consider that the shape of the barge here shown is that of the sacred *Makara*."

Now the researches made by M. Foucher have established the general truth that the sculptured scenes of Bharhut and Sānchi refer as a rule either to incidents in the life of Buddha or to his previous existences. Such being the case, may we perhaps interpret the puzzling panel described above as an illustration of the *Sīlānisaṃsa-jātaka*? It is true that the water, on the surface of which the fantastic barge is floating, suggests a lotus-pond rather than a tempest-tossed ocean. But it should be remembered that the power of expression which the unknown artists of Central India possessed had its limitations. On the other hand, the five individuals half submerged by the waves, present more the

[1] Fergusson, *Tree and Serpent Worship*, p. 141, pl. xxxi, fig. 1. Radhakumud Mookerji, *Indian Shipping*, pp. 33 f.; plate facing p. 32.

appearance of shipwrecked seafarers, endeavouring to save their life as well as they may, than that of " courtiers disporting themselves in an artificial piece of water ". Especially the attitude of the man clinging to the boat is significant. It is tempting to recognize in him the barber of the story. Who, then, is the hero of the *Jātaka*, the pious layman who in reality was the Bodhisattva? We shall have to assume that his presence is indicated by the empty seat over which two attendants hold the emblems of royalty—the parasol and the fly-whisk. In this explanation, however, there is one serious difficulty: although it would be quite plausible if the personage in question were the Buddha in his ultimate existence, such a symbolical indication of the Great Being in one of his previous lives would not be in accordance with the usual practice of the early school. The sculptors of Bharhut and Sānchi, it is true, shrink from figuring the Buddha, but they never show any reluctance in representing the Bodhisattva. Another objection might be made on the strength of the appearance of the mysterious barge. Although it is true that its strange shape is well calculated to suggest a magical boat, it must be admitted that the winged gryphon forming the prow much more resembles a Garuḍa than a Nāga. On account of these considerations it will be safe to regard the proposed identification as merely conjectural.

The Hermit and the too tender Nāga [1]

In the days of king Brahmadatta there were two brothers who became anchorites and dwelt in leaf-huts on the bank of the Gaṅgā. A Nāga-king, Maṇikaṇṭha (' Jewel-throat ') by name, after assuming human shape, used to come and visit the younger brother who had his hermitage lower down the river. Such trusty friends they became that they could not live without each other. Whenever Maṇikaṇṭha had indulged in sweet conversation and the time of parting had come, he used to re-assume his serpent-shape, envelop the hermit with his snaky folds, and embrace him, spreading his large hood over his friend's head. For fear of him the hermit grew thin, he became qualid, lost his colour, grew paler and paler, and the veins stood out upon his skin.

The elder brother noticed the change which had come over him, and asked him how he had grown so thin and wan. The other told him all about it. " Well," said the first, " dost thou like him to come or not?" " No, I do not." " And what ornament does the Nāga-king wear when he visits you?" " A precious jewel." " Very well. When he comes again, before he has time to sit down, ask him to give thee the jewel. Then he will depart without embracing thee in his snaky folds. Next day stand at your door and ask him for it there;

[1] *Maṇikaṇṭha-jātaka* (No. 253). *Jātaka*, vol. ii, pp. 282 ff. Cambridge transl., vol. ii, pp. 197 ff. The *jātaka* is also told in the *Suttavibhaṅga, Saṅghādisesa*, vi, 1 (*Vinaya Piṭakam*, ed. Oldenberg, vol. iii, pp. 145 ff.).

on the third ask him on the bank of the Gaṅgā, just as he emerges from the water. He will never visit thee again."

The younger brother followed the advice and his request had, indeed, the desired result. When on the third day he had asked again for the jewel, the Nāga speaking from his place in the water, refused in the following words :—

> " Rich food and drink in plenty I can have
> by means of this fine jewel which you crave :
> You ask too much ; the gem I will not give
> nor visit you again while I shall live."

With these words the Nāga king plunged beneath the water and went to his own Nāga abode, never to return.

Then the ascetic, not seeing his beautiful Nāga king, became thinner still ; he grew more squalid, lost his colour worse than before, and grew paler, while the veins rose thicker on his skin.

Next time when his elder brother came to see him, and found him worse than ever, he had to confess that it was because he never saw the beautiful Nāga king again. Then his brother gave the moral of the story in the following verse :—

> " Importune not a man whose love you prize,
> for begging makes you hateful in his eyes.
> The Brahmin begged the serpent's gem so sore
> he disappeared and never came back more."

Among the *jātakas* illustrated on the railing of the Bharhut Stūpa there is one showing a hermit with matted hair seated in front of his hut, apparently in conversation with a huge five-headed cobra. (Plate IIc.) Mr. Rouse thinks that this sculpture refers to the story of the hermit and the Nāga Maṇikaṇṭha, whereas according to Dr. Hultzsch [1] it would represent the *Paṇḍara-jātaka*, which we have rendered above. Unfortunately there is no inscription to settle the case. The sculpture, as far as we can see, could be equally well associated with either of the two *jātakas*. In favour of Mr. Rouse's opinion we might point out that the Nāga seems to wear an oblong object round his neck, perhaps a jewel. If that were the case, it might be considered to be an indication that it is, indeed, the Nāga Maṇikaṇṭha.

Illustrations of the *Maṇikaṇṭha-jātaka* do occur among the terra-cotta plaques of Pagan.[2]

[1] *J.R.A.S.*, for 1912, pp. 406 f.

[2] On a plaque of the Petleik Pagoda, see *A.S.R.* for 1906–7, p. 131 ; pl. xliv. A fragmentary terra-cotta from Pagan, now in the Berlin Museum, is described and illustrated by Grünwedel, ***Buddhistische Studien,*** pp. 58 f. ; fig. 41.

The Virtuous Nāga Śaṅkhapāla [1]

A king of Magadha, Duryodhana, by name, in consequence of his good works and at his own special wish, was reborn in the Nāga world. But in course of time he grew weary of the splendours of the Nāgaloka, and desiring to be born as a man, resolved to keep the Sabbath. Now, finding that the observance of the Sabbath duties did not succeed in the Nāga-world, he used to go to a place not far from the Kaṇṇapeṇṇā river and, coiled round an ant-hill between the high road and a footpath, he kept the holy day.[2] While thus lying on the top of the ant-hill he made the vow: " Let those that want my skin or want my skin and flesh, let them take my flesh and the rest." Thus he vowed to give away his own body in charity and stopped there on the fourteenth and fifteenth of the half-month: on the first day of each half-month he returned to the Nāga-world.

Now one day when he lay there a party of sixteen villagers saw him lying on the ant-hill, and thinking: " To-day we have not caught so much as a young lizard, we will kill and eat this snake-king," they resolved to pierce his body with stakes just as he lay there coiled up. But Śaṅkhapāla rejoiced, as he saw his desire about to be fulfilled and he resolved not to open his eyes and not to look at them in anger, whatever mischief they might work upon him. After they had wounded him in eight different places and thrust bamboo sticks into his open wounds, they dragged him along. On their way they met a landowner, named Aḷāra, from Mithilā, who was on a trading expedition with a caravan of five hundred wagons. This man, moved by pity, released the captured snake by presenting each of the sixteen men with an ox, a handful of gold coins, besides garments and ornaments for their wives.

In this manner Śaṅkhapāla regained his liberty and went back to the Nāga-world, where Aḷāra, at his request followed him. The Nāga king bestowed great honour upon his guest together with three hundred Nāga maidens and satiated him with heavenly delights. But after having dwelt a whole year in the Nāga palace in the enjoyment of heavenly pleasures, Aḷāra said to his host: " My friend, I wish to become an ascetic," and taking with him everything requisite for the ascetic life, he left the abode of the Nāgas and went to the Himālaya. When afterwards in the course of his wanderings he came to Benares and was received and questioned by the king, he related the whole story of his friend Śaṅkhapāla.[3]

[1] *Śaṅkhapāla-jātaka* (No. 524). *Jātaka*, vol. v, pp. 161 ff.; Cambridge transl., vol. v, pp. 84 ff. The story also occurs in the *Chariyāpiṭaka* ii; 10 (*P.T.S.*, p. 91).

[2] According to the *Chariyā-p.* he kept the Sabbath " on the high-road at a cross-way, where sundry people used to pass ". The vow is expressed in somewhat different words.

[3] Aḷāra's account is in reality a repetition in verse of the *jātaka*, more detailed than the prose story which we have summarized above. The metrical version is mainly conceived in the form of a dialogue between the king of Benares and Aḷāra, between Aḷāra and the sixteen villagers and finally between Aḷāra and the Nāga.

PLATE XIII.

THE NĀGARĀJA ŚAṄKHAPĀLA CAUGHT BY THE VILLAGERS (AJAṆṬĀ FRESCO).

[To face p. [illegible]]

Among the *jātakas* identified by M. Foucher at Ajaṇṭā is also that of Śaṅkhapāla. (Plate XIII.) "This story," that author remarks,[1] "is fully represented on the wall to the left in Cave I. The key to this story was given me by the sight of a big serpent (*Paintings*, fig. 32), which several men are dragging along by means of a rope, running through his nose. All the other incidents enumerated below, viz. the intervention of the caravan-chief; the invitation of the Nāgarāja who points out to the latter with his hand the pond where he resides; and, to the right, the visit of the king of Benares to the ascetic (the latter figures in *Paintings*, pl. vi) could then be easily identified."

The Nāga Champaka who was caught by a Snake-charmer[2]

Between the realms of Aṅga and Magadha in the river Champā there was an abode of Nāgas and here a Nāgarāja, Champaka by name, held sway. One day the king of Magadha, having been defeated in battle by Aṅga, mounted his charger and took to flight. When he came to the Champā river, man and horse plunged into the stream. Now the Nāga king, Champaka, had built him under the water a jewelled pavilion, and there in the midst of his court he sat carousing deep. He gave the king of Magadha a friendly reception, made him sit down on his own throne, and asked why he came plunging into the water. The king told him the whole story and the Nāgarāja promised to make him master of both kingdoms. After having entertained his guest during a week, he assisted him in conquering Aṅga. From that time there was a firm friendship between the two. The king of Magadha caused a jewelled pavilion to be built on the bank of the river Champā and used to offer *bali* to the Serpent king, who would come forth with a large retinue from his palace to receive the tribute.

Now among the king's people there was a poor man (it was the future Buddha), who, seeing the Nāgarāja's glory, became covetous of it. In this desire he died and seven days after the death of the serpent king Champaka, that man, owing to his good works, was reborn as the ruler of the Nāgas. This, however, did not satisfy him, for he felt disgusted at his animal birth. A young Nāgī, Sumanā by name, comforted him. He put off his serpent shape and sat on the couch in magnificence of dress and adornment. Still he wished to be released of his serpent birth, so he resolved to keep the vows of the Sabbath day. But finding it difficult to fulfil the vow among the distractions of the Nāga-world, he repaired to the world of men. There, each Sabbath day, he lay on the top of an ant-hill by

[1] Foucher, *Preliminary Report*, p. 63.

[2] *Champeyya-jātaka* (No. 506). *Jātaka*, vol. iv, pp. 454 ff. Cambridge transl., vol. iv, pp. 281 ff. The same *jātaka* in a somewhat different form occurs under the title *Śrī-Champakanāgarājasya jātaka* in the *Mahāvastu*, vol. ii, pp. 177 ff., and in an abbreviated form in the *Chariyā-piṭaka*, ii, No. iii (*P.T.S.*, pp. 85 f.).

the high road, saying: " Those who desire my skin and so forth, let them take it, or if anyone would make me a dancing snake, let them make me so."

Those who went to and fro on the highway did him worship with scents and so forth, and the dwellers in the neighbouring village, thinking, " He is a Nāgarāja of great power," set up a pavilion over him, spread sand all around [1] and worshipped him with scents and so forth. And people began to crave sons by his aid, having faith in him and doing him worship. Thus he kept the Sabbath vows, on the fourteenth and fifteenth days of the half-moon, and on the first day of the lunar half following he would return to the abode of the Nāgas.

One day his chief queen, Sumanā, spake to him: " The world of men is full of dangers. Suppose some danger should come upon thee, tell me now by what sign I shall learn of it." Then the Nāga king led her to the bank of a lucky pond, saying: " If anyone strike me or do me harm, the water in this pond will become turbid. If the Suparṇas seize me, the water will disappear. If a snake-charmer seize me, the water will turn red as blood." Then he went forth again from the abode of the Nāgas and lay down on the ant-heap.

Now there was a young Brahmin of Benares come to Taxilā [2] to study at the feet of a teacher from whom he had learned a powerful charm. Going home along that road, he espied the Nāgarāja and thought: " I will catch this snake and I will travel through town and village, making him dance and amassing great profits." Then he procured magic herbs, and repeating the magic charm he approached the snake. The Nāga whose ears were pierced by that dreadful sound looked up and beheld the snake-charmer. Then he thought: " My poison is powerful, and if I send forth the breath of my nostrils, his body will be shattered like a handful of chaff. But then my Sabbath vow will be broken. I will not look upon him." The snake-charmer ate a herb, repeated his charm, spat upon him: by virtue of herb and charm, wherever the spittle touched him, blains arose. Then the man seized him by the tail, dragged him, laid him out at full length, squeezed him till he was weak, then catching tight hold of his head, crushed him hard. The snake opened his mouth wide; the man dropped spittle in it, and by the herb and charm broke his teeth, so that his mouth was full of blood. After thus ill-treating him most cruelly, the snake-charmer laid the snake in an osier basket, carried him to the village and made him perform to the crowd. So wonderfully did he dance [3] and so pleased were the people that they gave much money: in one day the snake-charmer would take a thousand *kārshāpaṇas* and things worth

[1] In an account of a very curious case of modern serpent-worship which occurred in Kāṭhiāvāṛ in the year 1874 we read of a cobra which had been mortally wounded. Then the villagers " spread sand for him and put a canopy over him to shield him from the sun ", *Ind. Ant.*, vol. iv, p. 83. Cf. below, p. 269.

[2] The famous town Takshaśilā (Pali Takkasilā) in Northern India which is mentioned by classical authors under the name Taxila.

[3] In the *Chariyā-piṭaka* it is said that the Nāga assumed any colour the snake-charmer thought of.

another thousand. So the man resolved to make him perform before King Ugrasena in Benares ; and then he would let him go.

Now when he had been absent for a full month, his wife Sumanā began to think : " My dear husband tarrieth long. It is now a month since he hath returned : what can the matter be ? " So she went and looked at the pond : lo, the water was red as blood. Then she knew that he must have been caught by a snake-charmer. So, leaving the snake world, she first came to the ant-hill where he had been caught, and making inquiries all along the way, at last she reached Benares where great preparations had just been made for the performance of the wonderful snake at the royal court. The Nāgarāja, looking up in the air, noticed his wife and, being ashamed, crept into his basket. " What is the matter now ? " King Ugrasena asked, and, looking this way and that way, he saw her poised in the air and questioned her as to who she was and what she desired. Then Sumanā made herself known to the king and told him all that had happened to her dear husband, how he used to keep the Sabbath and why such a powerful Nāga who could burn a whole town to cinders, had allowed himself to be caught by a mere mortal. She entreated the king to release her husband not by resorting to violence but by offering wealth as a ransom. The king did so, and the snake-charmer let him free on the royal word without even accepting the rich gifts offered him by the king.

Thus the Nāgarāja Champaka regained his liberty. He crept into a flower, where he put off his shape and re-appeared in the form of a young man magnificently arrayed. Reverently raising his joined hands, he stood before the King of Benares and invited him to come and visit his Nāga home. The king first hesitated to accept this invitation, but the Nāgarāja assured him under potent oaths that the king needed not fear his dangerous nature but would find him grateful for the great benefit received.

Then King Ugrasena in great pomp and accompanied by a splendid retinue travelled to the abode of Champaka the Nāgarāja, where he was right royally entertained. For seven days he with his retinue partook of the divine food and drink, and enjoyed all manner of pleasure. Sitting in his fair seat he praised the glory of the Nāgarāja Champaka. " O King of the Serpents," quoth he, " Why didst thou leave all this magnificence to lie on an ant-hill, in the world of men, and to keep the Sabbath vows ? " On this the Nāga king made answer : " Purity and self-control are found nowhere but in the world of men. When once I am reborn among men I shall reach the end of birth and death."

When King Ugrasena took his leave his host pointing to the treasures of gold and silver and jewels heaped up in his mansion, invited him to take whatsoever he wished. And he sent the treasure to the king loaded in several hundred carts. After this the king left the serpent-world with great pomp and returned to Benares.

[At first sight the *Champeyya-jātaka* gives the impression of being thoroughly Buddhistic Yet, on closer examination, it seems to be an old legend adopted by the Buddhists, like so many other ancient stories—a legend telling how a mighty Nāgarāja was caught by a snake-charmer and released by the intervention of the king of Benares, and how this monarch afterwards was entertained by the grateful Nāga. The metrical version is a real ballad in which the story is told in a charming manner. It is largely a dialogue without any indication to which personage the words spoken in each case are to be attributed The prose is merely a repetition of the metrical redaction. It is noteworthy that, whereas in the prose narrative the hero of the story is usually indicated as 'Bodhisattva' and 'Mahāsattva', these terms are nowhere used in the *gāthās* There he is either called Champeyya, or designated as *nāgarāja*, *nāga*, or *uraga*.]

The *jātaka* of the Nāgarāja Champaka has been recognized by M Foucher [1] among the frescoes of Ajantā "The decorators of Cave I," he says, "have a particular preference for the stories about Nāgas. Here we see first the king of Benares sitting in his palace (*Paintings*, pl xvii) then watching the dance of the cobra (ibid, pl. xviii); then talking to the Nāga king, who has resumed his human shape (ibid, pl xvi, 2, and *Frescoes*, pls. xxviii, 31, and xxix, 32), and finally loaded with presents in the aquatic palace of his new friend, to whom he is paying a visit."

Among the sculptures decorating the balustrade (upper row) along the first gallery of the Borobudur *stūpa* there is a panel which shows a Nāgarāja with his retinue receiving a human visitor who is standing opposite him with a servant and a horse. Professor Krom [2] suggests that possibly this scene refers to the introductory portion of the *Champeyya-jātaka*, where Champaka receives the king of Magadha after the latter's defeat.

The *jātaka* in question also occurs on a terra-cotta panel from Pagan now preserved in the Berlin Museum of Ethnography.[3]

The Story of the Wise and Virtuous Nāga Bhūridatta [4]

[This *jātaka* is a real romance covering more than sixty pages and consisting of no less than eight chapters, each with its own title. The story is continued through three generations: first we have the prince of Benares who marries a Nāga maiden, then their

[1] Foucher, *Preliminary Report*, pp. 55 f.

[2] Krom, *Barabudur*, vol. i, p. 351, plates, series 1 (B) a, pl. xix. This panel more probably refers to the story of Vidhura the Wise which we have rendered above, pp 143 ff.

[3] Grunwedel, *Buddhistische Studien*, pp. 83 ff., fig. 65 The three miniatures from the *Trai p'um*, reproduced p. 88, refer not to the *Champeyya*, but to the *Bhūridatta-jātaka*, as will be pointed out beneath.

[4] *Bhūridatta-jātaka* (No 543). *Jātaka*, vol. vi, pp 157 ff. Cambridge transl, vol vi, pp 80 ff. Cf. *Cariyā-piṭaka*, ii, No. 11 (*P.T.S.*, p 85).

two children, the boy Sāgara-Brahmadatta, and the girl Samudrajā, who in her turn is given in marriage to the serpent-king Dhṛitarāshṭra, and finally the four sons born from this union, of which the second, the real hero of the tale, is the future Buddha.]

I. A son of king Brahmadatta of Benares had been exiled by his father and lived as a hermit between the river Yamunā and the sea. There a young Nāga female from the Nāga world in the Ocean who had lost her husband saw his hut when she was wandering by the sea-shore. By a stratagem she found out that he was not an ascetic by faith, and that he was accessible to love. When she showed herself to him, he was charmed by her great beauty, and consented to be her husband. By her magic power she made a costly house and brought a costly couch and spread a bed. From that time he ate no roots or fruit but feasted on divine food and drink. After a while she conceived and brought forth a son whom they called Sāgara-Brahmadatta. Subsequently a daughter was born whom they called Samudrajā ('Sea-born').

Now the king of Benares died and the ministers came to the prince and asked him to assume the kingdom. He went to his wife and said: "Lady, my father is dead and his ministers have come to raise the royal umbrella over me; let us go and we will both reign in Benares and thou shalt be the chief among the sixteen thousand queens." "My lord, I cannot go." "Why?" "We possess deadly poison and we are easily displeased for a trifling matter, and the anger of a co-wife is a serious thing. If I see or hear anything and cast an angry look thereon, it will be instantly scattered like a handful of chaff; therefore I cannot go." When the prince asked her again the next day, she said: "I myself will on no account go. But these my sons are not young Nāgas: as they are your children, they are of the race of men; if thou lovest me, watch over them. But as they are of a watery nature (*udakabījaka*) and therefore delicate, they would die if they went by the road and bore the burden of the wind and sunshine. So I will hollow out a boat and fill it with water, and thou shalt let them play in the water and when thou hast brought them to the city thou shalt have a tank prepared in the precincts of the palace; in this way they will not suffer." With these words she took leave and with many tears she vanished and departed to the Nāga-world.

Now when the two children were grown up, the Nāga king Dhṛitarāshṭra sent a deputation to the court of Benares and asked the hand of the princess Samudrajā. But the king deemed this an unsuitable match, and dismissed the Nāga envoys who threatened him with the wrath of their monarch.[1] Albeit the Nāga youths wished to slay him on the spot by the blast of their nostrils, yet they reflected that as they had been sent to fix the

[1] There is a discrepancy here between the prose story and the metrical portion which mentions "Yamuna, the son of Varuṇa", and "a Kshattriya of Videha" (stanzas 4 and 6).

marriage day, it would not be right to go away and leave the man dead. So they returned to the Nāga king, who in his anger summoned Aśvataras and Kambalas and all other Nāgas to flock towards Benares, without however, doing any harm.[1] So the hosts of serpents invaded Kāśi and covered the roads and the buildings; they hung over the gateways and in the tops of the trees. So great a terror they wrought, that the king yielded to the clamour of the population and thrice exclaimed: "I will give unto Dhṛitarāshṭra my daughter Samudrajā."

The princess, however, was left ignorant of the real nature of her husband, who issued a proclamation that whosoever betrayed any signs of his snake-nature to Samudrajā should be punished. Therefore not one durst appear as a snake before her and she abode happily with him thinking that it was the world of men.

II. In the course of time Dhṛitarāshṭra's queen brought forth four sons whom they named Sudarśana, Datta (who was the future Buddha), Subhaga, and Arishṭa.[2] Even then she knew not that it was the world of the Nāgas. But one day they told Arishṭa that his mother was not a Nāgi, and he said to himself: "I will prove her." So one day, while she was giving him suck, he assumed a serpent's form, and hit her with his tail. She in her terror threw him on the ground and struck his eye with her nail so that the blood poured forth. In this manner she learned that it was the dwelling of the Nāgas. Arishṭa, having lost one eye, henceforth was always called Kāṇārishṭa ('One-eyed Arishṭa').

Now, when the four princes had grown up, their father gave them each a kingdom. They possessed great glory and each was attended by sixteen thousand Nāga maidens. The second son, Datta, used to go every fortnight to his parents and then he went with his father to visit the great king Virūpāksha[3] and to discuss questions which had arisen in the Nāga realm. Now one day when Virūpāksha had gone with his Nāga followers to the world of the gods, a question arose which none could answer but Datta. So, on account of his wisdom, Śakra, the king of the gods, gave him the name Bhūridatta.

At the sight of the Paradise of Śakra with its hosts of heavenly nymphs he conceived the wish to be reborn as a Deva.[4] "What have I to do with this frog-eating snake nature?" he thought, "let me observe the Sabbath duties so that I may obtain birth among the gods." His parents gave him an empty palace for keeping the Sabbath; but the Nāga maidens waiting on him with their musical instruments hindered him in his

[1] In the legend of Gūgā we hear of an army of snakes which, by order of Vāsuki, surrounded the walls and every house in the city of Bundi. They were ordered to hurt no one, but the people of the city were sore afraid. *Ind. Ant.*, xxiv, p. 54.

[2] Pali *Sudassana* and *Ariṭṭha*.

[3] Virūpāksha (Pali Virūpakkha), the guardian god of the Western quarter and chief of the Nāgas.

[4] This trait is also found in the version of the *Chariyā-piṭaka*.

purpose. So without telling anyone but his wife, he went to the haunts of men, and not far from a huge banyan-tree which stood on the bank of the Yamunā he lay coiled on the top of an ant-hill, and in this manner he kept the vow of the Sabbath. He said: "Whosoever desireth my skin or my muscles, or my bones, or my blood, let him take it."[1] When he had lain there all night, at daybreak ten Nāga girls used to come with musical instruments in their hands and conduct him back to the Nāga-world.

III. At that time a certain Brahmin who dwelt in a village near the gate of Benares was wont to go into the forest with his son Somadatta and kill wild animals; and by selling the flesh he made a livelihood. Once these two men were out hunting and, overtaken by the darkness, they passed the night among the branches of the banyan-tree which stood in the vicinity of the ant-hill on which the Nāga prince Bhūridatta was lying. The Brahmin woke at dawn and was listening to hear the sound of the deer, when the Nāga maidens came up and prepared the flowery couch for their master. The Nāga prince laid aside his snake's body and assuming a divine body adorned with all kinds of ornaments sat on his flower-bed with all the glory of a Śakra. The Nāga maidens honoured him with perfumes and garlands, and played their heavenly instruments and performed their dance and song. But when the Brahmin came down the tree and drew near, the Nāga maidens, seeing him, sank into the earth with all their instruments and departed to the abode of the Nāgas. Then he addressed Bhūridatta, and asked him: "Art thou a mighty Yaksha or a Nāga great in power?" Bhūridatta, remembering that it was a Sabbath day and therefore he must speak only the truth, answered "I am a Nāga great in magic power, invincible with fiery poison; in my anger I could bite with my fire a prosperous country. My mother is Samudrajā, my father Dhṛitarāshṭra. I am the youngest brother of Sudarśana, and Bhūridatta is my name." The Nāga prince, being afraid that the Brahmin might betray him to a snake-charmer, invited him to come to the pleasant home of the Nāgas. By his power he brought both the father and the son to the dwelling of the Nāgas where they obtained a divine condition. He gave to each of them four hundred Nāga maidens, and great was the prosperity they enjoyed.

The Brahmin, having dwelt a year in the Nāga realm, through his lack of previous merit began to grow discontented and longed to return to the world of men. The son wanted to stay, but at last consented to go. The serpent prince too gave his unwilling consent, and in parting presented his guest with 'the gem which granteth all desires.' But the Brahmin would not accept it, as he had resolved to embrace the ascetic life. When the Brahmin and his son had returned to the world of men, they saw a lake on the way. "Somadatta, let us bathe," the father exclaimed. So they both took off their divine

[1] This vow in somewhat different words occurs also in the *Chariyā-piṭaka.*

ornaments and garments, and wrapping them up in a bundle laid them on the bank and bathed; but at that very moment the ornaments vanished and returned to the Nāga world, and their former poor yellow clothes were wrapped round their bodies, and their bows, arrows, and spears came back as they were before. So the next day he went with his son into the forest and followed his old trade.

IV. At that time a Garuḍa which lived on a silk-cotton-tree near the Southern Ocean,[1] swept up the water of the sea with the wind of his wings and swooping down on the Nāga region, seized a Nāga king by the head (at that time the Garuḍas did not know how to seize Nāgas, they learned how to do so in the *Paṇḍara-jātaka*).[2] Although he seized him by the head, he carried him to the top of the Himālaya. There a Brahmin anchorite had built a hut of leaves and at the end of his walking-place there stood a great banyan-tree, at the foot of which he used to sit by day. The Garuḍa carried the Nāga to the top of the banyan and the Nāga in its efforts to escape twined its tail round a branch. The Garuḍa, being unaware of it, flew up in the sky and carried up the banyan-tree. He then bore the Nāga to the silk-cotton forest, with his beak split open its belly, and having eaten the fat dropped the body into the middle of the sea. The banyan-tree as it fell made a great noise, and the Garuḍa recognizing that it was the banyan at the end of the anchorite's walking-place, thought: "This tree was of great service to him—is retribution following me or not? I will ask him." So he went to him in the guise of a young pupil and questioned him. The anchorite answered that neither the Garuḍa nor the Nāga were guilty, as both had acted in ignorance. So pleased was the Garuḍa with this decision that as a fee for his lesson he gave the recluse a priceless spell and showed him the simples pertaining thereto.

The recluse in his turn imparted the precious spell to a poor Brahmin, named Ālambāyana,[3] and this man, having thus gained a means of livelihood, departed from the forest, and by successive stages reached the bank of the Yamunā. At that time a thousand Nāga youths who waited on Bhūridatta were carrying the all-wish-granting jewel. They had placed it on a hillock of sand, and there, after playing all night in the water by its radiance, they had put on all their ornaments at the approach of dawn, and sat down, guarding it. The Brahmin reached the spot while he was repeating his charm, and they, on hearing it, seized with terror lest it should be the Garuḍa king, plunged into the earth without staying to take the jewel and fled to the Nāga-world. The Brahmin, seeing the jewel, exclaimed: "My spell hath at once succeeded," and he joyfully seized the jewel and went his way.

[1] Above, p. 133. [2] Above, p. 141.

[3] In the *Chariyā-piṭaka* he is called Ālampāna.

Now at that very time the Brahmin hunter was entering the forest with his son Somadatta, and when he saw the jewel in the other's hand, he said to his son : " Is not this the jewel which Bhūridatta gave to us ? " The son, too, recognized the gem. The Brahmin hunter, eager to possess the jewel, addressed Ālambāyana and offered a hundred gold pieces for it. The latter, however, declared that he did not wish to sell the jewel, but he was ready to give it to the man who showed him the great Nāga. Then the wicked Brahmin resolved to show Ālambāyana the abode of Bhūridatta, notwithstanding the remonstrations of his son, who, disgusted at his father's treachery, plunged into the recesses of the Himālaya and became a recluse.

The outcast Brahmin now brought Ālambāyana to the spot where the Nāga prince was observing the Sabbath vows, and spake to him : " Do thou seize that great Nāga and take the red jewel which shineth on his head. His body is like unto a heap of white cotton. Seize him, O Brahmin."

Bhūridatta saw the traitor approaching with the snake-charmer, but he reflected that it was his duty not to break his Sabbath vow and not to yield to anger. " Let Ālambāyana cut me in pieces or cook me or fix me on a spit, I must at all events not be wroth with him." So closing his eyes, and following the highest ideal of determination, he placed his head between his coils and lay motionless.

V. Then the outcast Brahmin exclaimed : " O Ālambāyana, do thou seize this Nāga and give me the gem." Ālambāyana threw it into his hand, but the jewel slipped out of his hand, and, as soon as it fell, it went into the ground and was lost in the Nāga-world. The Brahmin finding himself bereft of the three things, the priceless gem, Bhūridatta's friendship, and his son, went off to his home, loudly lamenting.

Ālambāyana, having first anointed his body with divine drugs and chewed a little of them, so that it pervaded his body, uttered the divine spell, and, going up to Bhūridatta seized him by the tail, and, holding him fast, opened his mouth and having himself chewed a drug, spat into it. After he had made the snake full of the drug, and holding him by the tail with his head downwards had shaken him and made him vomit the food he had swallowed, he stretched him out at full length on the ground. Then pressing him like a pillow with his hands he crushed his bones, and then again seizing his tail, pounded him as if he were beating cloth.

Having thus made the serpent prince helpless, he prepared a basket of creepers and threw him into it. Then, going to a certain village, he set the basket down in the middle of it and made the snake dance. So wonderful was his dancing that the villagers were moved to tears and brought gold, garments, ornaments, and the like. Ālambāyana then resolved to proceed to Benares and on a Sabbath-day he announced to the king that he would exhibit the snake's dancing in his presence. So the king made a proclamation by beat of drum and collected a large crowd, and tiers of scaffolding were erected in the courtyard of the palace.

VI. On the day when Bhūridatta was seized by the snake-charmer, his mother Samudrajā had a terrible dream portending some misfortune. She fixed her thoughts especially on Bhūridatta, because she knew that he had gone to the world of men. When her eldest son Sudarśana came to pay a visit to his parents, she made him a partner of her fears. Great lamentation there was in Bhūridatta's house. The two younger brothers, too, heard the noise and tried to comfort their mother. As she could not be comforted, her three sons promised to make a search for him and within ten days to bring him back to her.

Then Sudarśana thought: " We must go to three different places—one to the world of the gods, one to the Himālaya, and one to the world of men. But if Kāṇārishṭa goes to the land of men, he will set that village or town on fire where he shall happen to see Bhūridatta, for he is fierce-natured and harsh—it will not do to send him." So he said to him: " Do thou go to the world of gods. If the gods have carried him to their world in order to hear the Law from him, then do thou bring him thence." But he said to Subhaga: " Do thou go to the Himālaya and search for Bhūridatta in the five great rivers and come back." He himself took the garb of an ascetic and set out for the world of men.

Now Bhūridatta had a sister, born of another mother, named Archimukhī,[1] who had a very great love for him. When she saw Sudarśana setting out, she bespake him: " Brother, I am greatly troubled, I will go with thee." " Sister," he replied, " thou canst not go with me, for I have assumed an ascetic's dress." Quoth she: " I will become a little frog and I will go inside thy matted hair."

Sudarśana first of all went to the place where Bhūridatta was wont to keep the Sabbath vow. When he saw the blood there he felt sure that Bhūridatta had been seized by a snake-charmer and overcome with grief he followed Ālambāyana's track. At last he came to the palace-gate of the king of Benares. Here a great crowd had collected. The snake-charmer had just placed the basket on a variegated rug, and gave the sign: " Come hither, great Nāgarāja." At that moment Sudarśana was standing at the edge of the crowd, while his captive brother put his head out of the basket and looked round surveying the people. Nāgas look at a crowd for two reasons: to see whether any Suparṇa is near or any kinsman; if they espy a Suparṇa, they do not dance for fear, if kinsman, they do not dance for shame.[2] The Nāga prince, as he looked, beheld his brother among the crowd,

[1] Pali *Achchimukhī*.

[2] The Cambridge translation has ' actors ' which is obviously due to an oversight: the text has *ñātake* (Skt. *jñātaka*) not *nāṭake*.

and repressing his tears he came out of the basket and went up to him. The crowd retreated in fear and Sudarśana was left alone; so his brother went up to him and laid his head on his foot and wept, and Sudarśana also wept.

Now Ālambāna thought: "The Nāga must have bitten yonder ascetic; I must comfort him." So he went up to him, but Sudarśana declared that the snake could do him no harm. Then the snake-charmer, hearing the power of his serpent belittled, waxed angry. But Sudarśana challenged him, saying that he would produce a frog more formidable than the great Nāga. Five thousand gold-pieces was to be the stake proposed by Sudarśana, and when his opponent ridiculed the idea of a mendicant possessing such a sum of money, the feigned ascetic called upon the king of Benares to be his surety and the king consented. After a long altercation with his adversary, Sudarśana called out to his sister: "O Archimukhī, come out of my matted locks and stand on my hand," and he put out his hand. Thrice she croaked like a frog, and then came out and sat on his shoulder, and, springing up dropped three drops of poison on his hand. Sudarśana stood with the poison on his hand, and exclaimed three times: "This country will be destroyed." Then the king exclaimed: "I am utterly at a loss—do thou tell us some way to prevent the land being destroyed." "O king, cause three holes to be dug here in succession." The king did so. Sudarśana filled the middle hole with sundry drugs, the second with cowdung, and the third with heavenly herbs; then he let fall the drops of poison into the middle hole. At the same moment a flame burst out, this spread and caught the hole with the cowdung, and then bursting out again it caught the hole filled with heavenly herbs, and consuming them all, it became extinguished. Ālambāyana was standing near the hole, and the heat of the poison smote him—the colour of his skin at once vanished, and he became a white leper. Filled with terror, he thrice exclaimed: "I will set the snake-king free." On hearing this, Bhūridatta came out of the basket, and assuming a form radiant with all kinds of ornaments, he stood with all the glory of Śakra, the chief of the gods. Sudarśana and Archimukhī joined him. Then Sudarśana told Brahmadatta, that Bhūridatta and he were the sons of Samudrajā and that the king was their maternal uncle. Then the king embraced them, led them into the palace and paid them great honour. Here Sudarśana told him their whole story and said: "O uncle, our mother is pining for want of seeing Bhūridatta, we cannot stay longer away from her." The king said that he was longing to see his sister, whereon Sudarśana said that his mother too was anxious to see both her brother, the reigning king, and her father, who had left his kingdom and become an ascetic. So they promised to take their mother to their grandfather's hermitage, and after fixing a day, they departed from the palace, and, sinking into the earth, returned to the Nāga-world.

VII. When Bhūridatta thus came among them, the city became filled with one universal lamentation He took to a sick-bed, and there was no limit to the number of Nāgas who came to visit him, and he tired himself out talking to them. In the meanwhile Kānārishta, who had gone to the world of gods, was the first to come back; so they made him the door-keeper of Bhūridatta's sick residence, for they said: "He is fierce and harsh and will be able to keep away the crowd of Nāgas."

Subhaga, after searching the whole Himālaya and after that the ocean and the rivers, came in the course of his wanderings to search the Yamunā. The outcast Brahmin, seeing that Ālambāna had become a leper, was afraid that he, too, would meet with the punishment due for his crime So he went on a pilgrimage to the Yamunā to wash away his guilt in the sacred bathing place of Prayāga [1] When he went down into the water, he said: "I have betrayed my friend Bhūridatta, I will wash away my sin." At that moment Subhaga came to the spot, and hearing these words, said to himself: "This is the wretch who hath betrayed my brother, I will not spare his life." So, twisting his tail round his feet and dragging him into the water, he held him down. Then Subhaga made himself known to the wicked Brahmin, reminded him of the crime he had committed in betraying his benefactor, and said that now the moment had come to take revenge. The other remonstrated that according to the well-known rule a Brahmin's life is not to be violated. This made Subhaga pause and in his uncertainty he thought best to carry the Brahmin to the Nāga-world and to ask his brothers for a decision. Then seizing him by the neck and shaking him, with loud abuse and revilings, he carried him to the gate of Bhūridatta's palace.

VIII. When Kānārishta saw that the other was being dragged along so roughly, he said: "Subhaga, do not hurt him. All Brahmins are the sons of the great Brahmā. The great Brahmā learned that if we were hurting his son, he in his wrath would destroy the whole Nāga world. In the world Brahmins rank as the highest, and possess great dignity. Thou doest not know what their dignity is, but I do." For Kānārishta in the birth immediately preceding this had been a sacrificing Brahmin, and therefore he spake so positively. Moreover, being skilled in sacrificial lore from his former experiences, he addressed Subhaga and the Nāga assembly in this wise: "Come, I will describe to you the character of sacrificial Brahmins" Then he extolled the greatness of the Brahmins who possess the sacred knowledge of the Veda and of the Vedic sacrifice, and gave sundry examples of the wonderful merit acquired by the worship of the sacred Fire.

Now Bhūridatta on his sick bed heard it all and he reflected: "Arishṭa has described

[1] Prayāga (now Allahābād) on the confluence of the Gaṅgā and Yamunā.

a false doctrine. I must break his speech and put true views into the assembly. So he rose and bathed, put on all his ornaments and sitting down in the pulpit, he gathered the whole Nāga community together. Then he summoned Arishṭa and said to him: "Arishṭa, falsely thou hast spoken in describing the Vedas and the sacrifices and the Brahmins, for the offering up of oblations by the priests according to the ritual of the Vedas is held to be undesirable nor does it lead to heaven." Then in a long and lucid sermon he forcibly set forth the futility of the Vedas and of the Vedic rites and the uselessness of fire-worship. He denounced the importance of the four castes and the claim to superiority maintained by the priestly caste. In particular he censured the sacrificing of animals, while pointing out how the priests in their greed uphold this cruel practice by means of ridiculous fabrications. Many of their traditions he showed to be idle stories too absurd to deserve the belief of any sensible man. Having thus confuted their arguments, he established his own doctrine, and the assembly of Nāgas hearing his exposition was filled with joy. The wicked Brahmin he caused to be dismissed from the Nāga world, and not even a word of censure he uttered to him.

Bhūridatta, having kept the precepts all his life and performed all the duties of the Sabbath, at the end of his life went with the host of Nāgas to fill the seats of heaven.

Let us now consider whether we can trace any plastic representations of the story of Bhūridatta which in the *Jātaka* book is narrated at such great length. In the art of India proper, as far as we know, no illustration of this *jātaka* is found. It occurs, however, we believe, on the great monument of Java, the Stūpa of Borobudur. Among the series of sculptural *tableaux* decorating the balustrade along the first gallery (upper row) there are four panels, numbered 187–90, which, as Professor Krom[1] has observed, obviously have reference to some Nāga legend. We are inclined to assume that the story in question is that of Bhūridatta. The first of these four panels (No. 187) shows a Nāga with his retinue in a river. One of his followers apparently makes a request. Possibly it is Bhūridatta informing his father, the Nāga king Dhṛitarashṭra of his wish to perform the Sabbath vow in the world of men. The second panel (No. 188) shows a Nāga seated under a tree in the attitude of *dhyāna*, or meditation. Two male persons, evidently meant for Brahmins, are standing by. On the assumption that the Nāga is again the hero of the story seated under the banyan-tree, we may recognize the wicked Brahmin and his son in the two other personages. It is true that according to the Pali text the Nāga prince was lying in his serpent shape on the top of an ant-hill. It must, however, be remembered that the sculptors

[1] Krom. *Barabudur*, vol. i, p. 353, plates, series 1 (B) *a*, pl. xxi.

of the Borobudur invariably represent their Nāgas as human beings, their serpent nature being only indicated by the snake-hood. Such being the case, the scene of Bhūridatta's penance could hardly be rendered in a more lucid manner than is done in the present sculpture. In the third relief (No. 189) we see a Nāga and a Nāgī seated on a throne, while a Brahmin is shown standing at their side in an attitude of supplication (*añjali*). We believe this person to be the Brahmin hunter who, after having been entertained by Bhūridatta in the Nāgaloka asks leave to return to the world of men. The fourth panel (No. 190), showing four Nāgas, one of which is seated on a throne could represent either the four Nāga princes reunited after their wanderings, or Bhūridatta preaching to a Nāga audience on the subject of the futility of Vedic rites.

There is yet a fifth panel which in all probability belongs to the same story but which is no longer *in situ*.[1] In 1896 when the late King of Siam visited Java, the Government at Batavia had the ill-advised courtesy to present their royal guest with a number of images and other sculptural remains taken from the Borobudur and other ancient sanctuaries of the Island. Among those art treasures which are now preserved at Bangkok, there is a Borobudur relief showing a procession of seven female figures, perhaps meant for Nāgīs, one of them carrying lotus-flowers and the others apparently beating time with their hands. There is good reason to assume that the sculpture in question is the missing No. 186 belonging to the balustrade of the first gallery. It, consequently, must supply us with the opening scene of the Nāga story illustrated in Nos. 187–90. On the assumption that this story is the *Bhūridatta-jātaka* there are two possible explanations. If the figures are provided with the usual Nāga head dress (which from the published photograph cannot be decided), they must be the Nāga damsels who distracted Bhūridatta from rigidly observing his Sabbath vow. In case the Nāga emblem is absent, they may be taken to represent the heavenly nymphs in Śakra's paradise, the sight of whose beauty caused Bhūridatta to conceive the wish that he should be reborn as a Deva.

If my explanation is right, the five Borobudur panels would thus supply us with a plastic rendering of five incidents of the Bhūridatta legend proper. At first sight it may seem strange that among the scenes selected for illustration we find neither the capture of Bhūridatta by the cruel snake-charmer nor his performance at the court of the Rāja of Benares. But, apart from the difficulty of representing an anthropomorphic Nāga in the

[1] Th. van Erp. *Hindu-javaansche beelden thans te Bangkok. Bijdr. tot de T. L. and Volkenk. van Ned. Indie*, vol. lxxix, pp. 504 ff., pl. iv. As the author has pointed out in the course of his paper, the stones of the two upper layers have been wrongly put together. It is difficult to account for panel No. 191, which presumably belongs to the same story. No. 185, on the contrary, could be well explained as the meeting of the prince of Benares and the Nāgī, related in the first chapter. The panel is unfortunately partly destroyed.

PLATE XIV.

Nâga image of Nālandā.

[To face p. 194

capacity of a dancing snake, it is quite in agreement with the spirit of the Borobudur artists to discard such scenes which, however dramatic and thrilling they may seem to the Western mind, would visualize the violent and ignominious treatment perpetrated by wicked men on that most holy and exalted being, the future Buddha.

Professor Grünwedel has published three miniatures from a Siamese book, *Trai-pum*, of the eighteenth century, which he believes to refer to the *Champeyya-jātaka*, but which in reality must be associated with the story of Bhūridatta.[1] Both these *jātakas*, it is true, are so very similar in the main trend of the narrative that a confusion between the two may easily occur. The first of the three miniatures in question shows a Nāga in animal shape wound round an ant-hill being assailed by a snake-charmer. On the second picture we see the latter on the shoulders of four men and attended by a parasol-bearer on his way to Benares with his captive in a basket carried by two servants. Finally the third miniature clearly presents us with the scene of the great performance at the court of Benares: the great Nāga seized by the snake-charmer who stands in the centre of the ring with the crowd of spectators all around, the king, sword in hand, occupying a prominent position on his throne.

These three scenes might refer equally well to the *Champeyya-* or to the *Bhūridatta-jātaka*. There is, however, one detail in the first picture which enables us to decide in favour of the last-mentioned *jātaka*. Right opposite the snake-charmer there is a princely figure standing on a kind of lotus-throne and holding a frog in his right hand, as has, indeed, been recognized by Professor Grünwedel. If we compare both stories, it must become perfectly clear, that this figure is not Sumanā, but Sudarśana with his frog-shaped sister Archimukhī, that consequently the king is not Ugrasena but Sāgara-Brahmadatta, and that the captured Nāga is not Champaka but Bhūridatta.

It is curious that the modern Siamese artist has rendered exactly those scenes which the ancient artists of Java (if at least our identification is correct) have preferred to omit from sculptural representation.

[1] Grünwedel, *Buddhistische Studien*, pp. 88 f. Cf. also K. Döhring, *Siam* (1923), vol. ii, p. 52, pl. lxxiv.

CHAPTER IV

The Nāgas in Fables and Fairy Tales

THE miscellaneous Nāga stories which are contained in the present chapter are derived partly from Brahmanical and partly from Buddhistic sources. The well-known Sanskrit work *Pañchatantra* has furnished the first two fables which, however, are only found in the *textus ornatior* of that work. From this circumstance it would be rash to conclude that the two fables in question are comparatively late productions. On the contrary, they contain elements which belong to a primitive sphere of thought. For this reason they have been included in the present work, although, strictly speaking, they do not refer to Nāgas. In each case the animal hero of the story is a serpent, but a fabulous serpent provided with truly Nāga-like properties. In the first of these two fables the story of the poor Brahmin and the gold-giving snake, we have, as it were, serpent-worship at its source. As soon as the Brahmin cultivator espies the animal (it is described as one of the hooded species) on the top of the ant-hill, he concludes that it must be the *devatā* and guardian of the field and he begins to worship it, hoping that it will yield him an abundant crop. So the snake figures here as a *genius loci,* but besides it is a guardian of gold and a giver of wealth—another familiar trait of snake-lore all over the world. Different versions of this fable are found in Western literature (e.g. Aesopus and *Gesta Romanorum*) ; yet, as Benfey justly remarked, it is truly Indian in spirit.[1]

The other fable from the *Pañchatantra* gives the story of the snake, himself the son of human parents, who is wedded to a maiden. He assumes human shape in the wedding night,[2] and his father promptly prevents him from returning to his animal state by burning the serpent hide which he had relinquished.

This is a familiar *motif* all over the world. In the *Vǫlsungasaga* (chap. viii) we read of Sigmundr and Sinfjǫtli who become werewolves, but are freed of their fate by burning the wolves' hides which they had imprudently donned. The swan-maidens of Norse mythology over whom power can be obtained by taking away their feathery garb while they have assumed human form may here be quoted. Likewise in the case of the *Bersekir* the potential ursinity is undoubtedly closely connected with the skin of the bear. Similar

[1] The moral of the story is, of course, the same as that of the well-known fable of the hen with the golden eggs. Cf. also the fable of the gold-spitting birds found in the *Mahābhārata* (*Sabhā-p.*, lxii).

[2] The Nāga, on the contrary, is said to revert to his serpent shape in sleep and during sexual intercourse. Cf. above, p. 111.

conceptions are very common in the folklore of the American Indians and the Eskimos: dog-children get rid of their animal state by the burning of the dog's skins, and the eagle-maiden becomes an ordinary human being, when robbed of her plumage.[1]

We now give some stories from the *Kathāsaritsāgara*, that marvellous collection of tales, which the Kashmirian poet Somadeva completed between the years A.D. 1063 and 1081.[2] It was a recast of a much earlier work (perhaps of the fifth century),[3] Guṇāḍhya's *Bṛihatkathā*, or 'Great Story-book', which unfortunately is lost, but which is said to have been composed in the vernacular. Guṇāḍhya, it will be seen, was himself reputed to be the son of a Nāga prince. Another Sanskrit version of this ancient book of stories is in existence, namely the *Bṛihatkathāmañjarī* by Kshemendra, who likewise was a native of Kashmir, but whose poetical skill was decidedly inferior to that of Somadeva. It was completed about A.D. 1037.

It cannot be said that in the stories of the *Kathāsaritsāgara* the Nāga appears always in a very typical character, although—it is true—he is usually represented as a denizen of a lake or pool. In some cases his character is so little pronounced that we have preferred to omit the story altogether. As an instance I may quote the fairy tale of King Kanakavarsha and Madanasundarī (*Kathās.*, lv, 26–238). The hero of the story is the son of Priyadarśana who in his turn is the son of the Serpent king Vāsuki. He is helped by his aunt, the Nāgī Ratnaprabhā, to win the favour of the god Kārttikeya, but, for the rest, there is nothing in the hero's character or adventures to bring out his lofty Nāga parentage.

In the short story of the jealous Nāga, a translation of which will be given below, neither the Nāga nor his faithless spouse, the Nāgī, show any specific Nāgan characteristics except that he inhabits a lake and finally destroys his wife and her lover by means of a fiery blast. In fact, there exist other versions of this tale in which the *rôle* of the deceived husband is assigned to some other demoniacal being: in a Pāli *jātaka* (No. 436) a similar story is told of an Asura, and in the *Arabian Nights* of a Jinn. The tale, after all, merely serves to illustrate that hackneyed theme: the wiles of women.[4]

'The Curse of a Nāga' reminds us of the incantation scene which occurs in another famous work of classical Sanskrit literature—Bāṇa's *Harshacharita*, or 'Life of Harsha'.

[1] For the above information I am indebted to Professor Uhlenbeck who refers me to Bolte-Polívka, *Anmerkungen zu den Kinder- und Hausmärchen der Brüder Grimm.*, vol. ii, pp. 234 ff., and Boas, *Indianische Sagen von der Nord-Pacifischen Küste Amerika's*, pp. 25 and 93, 115, and 264. For Indian and other parallels cf. Benfey, *Pantschatantra*, vol. i, pp. 260–9.

[2] C. H. Tawney's excellent English translation (two vols., Calcutta, 1880–4) is now being re-edited by N. M. Penzer, under the title *Ocean of Story* in ten volumes. We quote the original edition.

[3] J. S. Speyer, *Studies about the Kathāsaritsāgara*, p. 56.

[4] *Samugga-jātaka* (No. 436) in *Jātaka* (ed. Fausböll), vol. iii, pp. 527 ff.; Cambridge transl., vol. iii, pp. 313 ff. Cf. also *Kathās.*, lxiii, 6–66; Tawney's transl., vol. ii, pp. 79f.

It is a kind of historical romance dealing with the doings of Harsha-deva or Śrī-Harsha, the celebrated king-author of Kanauj and Thānesar (A.D. 606–47), and is composed in a highly artificial and rhetorical prose. In the third chapter of his work the author relates at great length how king Pushpabhūti, the progenitor of Harsha's house, at the request of a *Yogi*, named Bhairavāchārya, takes part in a magic rite, which has for object the laying of a Vetāla (*Vetāla-sādhana*).[1] The time selected for the gruesome rite is, as is usual in similar practices of black art, the fourteenth of the 'dark' fortnight (the period of the waning moon), in other words, a moonless night. The assistance of King Pushpabhūti is particularly required in that important phase of the rite which is indicated by the technical term of the closing of the Quarters (*dig-bandha*),[2] its object being to ward off the influence of evil spirits which haunt the regions of the sky. In the present instance each of the four assistants of the magician is entrusted with the care of one particular quarter. It is worthy of note that in this connexion the four quarters are enumerated in an order opposite to that followed in sacrificial ritual, namely: east, north, west, and south.

What happened next is related in the following words:[3] "The wardens of the regions having taken their stations, Bhairavāchārya confidently entered the cage composed of their arms, and proceeded with his awful work. The opposing fiends[4] having after fruitless resistance and much uproar been allayed, suddenly at the very instant of midnight the earth was rent open to the north and not far from the magic circle, displaying a fissure like that caused by the tusks of the mighty boar of doomsday. Forthwith, like an iron post torn up by the sky elephants, there ascended out of the chasm a spirit (*purusha*) dark as a blue lotus, with shoulders thick and square as the Great Boar's. The gleam of a *mālatī* wreath amid locks of crisp curled hair, sleek, dark, and growing thickly, produced the effect of a sapphire temple crowned with the blaze of a jewelled lamp. A throbbing voice and an eye naturally red suggested one drunk with the vapours of youth. A necklace tossed about his throat. Ever and anon he smeared shoulders comparable to the sky elephant's frontal globe with clay crushed in his clenched hand. Irregularly bespotted with moist sandal paste, he resembled a tract of autumn sky speckled with bits of very white cloud. Above a petticoat white as the *ketakī* petal his flank was drawn tight by a scarf, the long white cotton fringe of which, carelessly left loose, hung to the ground just as if it were the serpent Śesha supporting him from behind. His stout thick thighs planted slow paces as if he feared

[1] *The Harṣa-carita of Bāṇa*, transl. by E. B. Cowell and F. W. Thomas (London, 1897), pp. 90 ff.

[2] Cf. the 'Story of Prince Sudhana', below p. 185, and the legend of the Nāga king and the Magician, from the *Rājataraṅgiṇī*, below p. 245.

[3] We quote the passage with a few slight omissions and alterations from the excellent English translation by E. B. Cowell and F. W. Thomas (London, 1897), p. 93.

[4] The term used in the original is *kauṇapa*, which is a synonym of *rākshasa*.

to break through the earth: yet they could scarce support his mountain-like form with its burden of overmastering pride. Again and again he doubled his left arm athwart his breast, raised the right cross-wise, bent his leg, and furiously slapped his arms [1] with such a noise as though he would raise a storm to hinder the rite and maim the animate world of one sense."

We have quoted the passage in full, because the spirit described in it announces himself subsequently as 'the Nāga Śrīkaṇṭha, after whom this region, whereof I am lord, is named.' In the whole minute and, indeed, to our mind somewhat comical, description which we have cited there is practically nothing that would suggest a Serpent-demon. Not even the *phaṇa* or snake-hood, that most typical attribute of the Nāga is mentioned. It almost seems as if the author of this work of the seventh century had entirely lost sight of the true character of the spirit which he evokes. There is, however, in this passage one point of positive interest. The Nāga in question calls himself the guardian of the country Śrikaṇṭha which, as he says, was named after him. In that capacity he claims an oblation (*bali*) from the magician. Now the country Śrikaṇṭha is that tract of Northern India to which the district of Sthāṇvīśvara (modern Thānesar), the domain of King Pushpabhūti, belonged. In the same third chapter of Bāṇa's work the land of Śrīkaṇṭha is eulogized in a long passage which, however conforming to the *Kāvya* style, is not purely conventional. The mention of the wheat fields, the cumin beds watered by the pots of the Persian wheel, the troops of camels, the vine-arbours, and pomegranate orchards, the date palms and *pīlu* trees, will evoke vivid memories in anyone who has had the good fortune to visit the Land of the Five Rivers.[2] For our present purpose, however, it is of greater importance that the Nāga figures here as a guardian spirit of that country. He might be called a *genius loci* in a somewhat extended sense.[3]

The ancient theme of the hereditary feud between Garuḍa and the Nāgas, so often referred to in the Great Epic and in the Jātaka Book, has nowhere found more eloquent expression than in the pathetic tale of Jīmūtavāhana, the fairy prince, who sacrifices himself to save an unfortunate Nāga from being devoured by the Giant-bird. The numerous versions of this legend in Sanskrit literature [4] testify to its great popularity. In the

[1] An Indian challenge to combat.

[2] Geographically the country round Thānesar does not really belong to the Land of the Five Rivers, although for administrative purposes it is included in the present province of the Punjab.

[3] The term *kshetrādhipati* (lit. 'lord of the field') used by Bāṇa is practically identical with the words *kshetrapāla* and *kshetradevatā*, which occur in the fable of the Brahmin and the gold-granting snake from the *Pañchatantra*.

[4] For an exhaustive treatment of the legend, the various redactions, and their mutual relationship we refer the reader to F. D. K. Bosch, *De Legende van Jīmūtavāhana in de Sanskrit-litteratuur* (Doctor's thesis), Leiden, 1914.

Kathāsaritsāgara the story is twice narrated in great detail, and from the circumstance that in Kshemendra's *Bṛihatkathāmañjarī*, too, it occurs in two different chapters it may be safely concluded that the early *Bṛihatkathā* from which both those works are derived must have contained a double version of the Jīmūtavāhana legend. The reason of this two-fold treatment is the following: the legend in question has been embodied in the well-known collection of stories, entitled *Vetāla-pañchaviṃśatī*, or 'the Twenty-five Tales of the Vetāla'. Now this collection must have been included in the 'Great Story-book', and hence it is found in both the recasts of that ancient work which we owe to the two Kashmirian poets Somadeva and Kshemendra respectively. Besides this, two prose redactions of the Vetāla stories, the one by Śivadāsa, and the other by Jambhaladatta, are known to exist, and in both the legend of Jīmūtavāhana is one of the five-and-twenty tales. In another metrical production of the poetaster Kshemendra, the *Avadāna-kalpalatā*, we meet with the legend in a highly artificial and flowery garb. The work in question is a collection of a hundred-and-eight *avadānas* or edifying stories. The Jīmūtavāhana legend [1] which forms the concluding *avadāna* of the collection, is due not to Kshemendra himself but to his son Somendra (hardly a better poet than his parent!), who finished his father's work by completing the auspicious number of a hundred-and-eight. Finally we have to mention the Sanskrit play *Nāgānanda* or 'Joy of the Nāgas', in which the legend was dramatized by the same royal author, Śrī-Harsha, whom we have had occasion to refer to above.[2] The question whether the play is really due to the famous ruler of Thanesar or to one of his court-poets we may leave undecided. The title assigned to it was evidently chosen in connexion with the joyful conclusion, the Nāgas being freed from the danger of Garuḍa owing to the hero's noble self-sacrifice.

The version of the legend which we reproduce below follows the first redaction of the *Kathāsaritsāgara* (ch. xxii). The other redaction (ch. xc) found in the same work, which presents the legend as a Vetāla story, has this peculiarity that here Jīmūtavāhana is called 'a portion of the Bodhisattva'.[3] As, however, the story of Jīmūtavāhana is not found in any Indian collection of *jātakas*, there is good reason to assume that the identification of the hero with the future Buddha was an afterthought and that originally the legend had no connexion with Buddhism at all, however much it may conform in spirit to the lofty ethical ideals of that religion.

[1] It was edited in Dr. Bosch's work, pp. 118 ff., from the Cambridge MS. A summary of the contents of Kshemendra's *Avadāna-kalpalatā* (also called *Bodhisattvāvadāna-kalpalatā*) will be found in Rajendralal Mitra's *Sanskrit Buddhist Literature of Nepal* (Calcutta, 1882), pp. 57 ff.

[2] There exist two English translations of the *Nāgānanda*, the one by Palmer Boyd (London, 1872), and the other by B. Hale Northam (London, without date), and a French version by Abel Bergaigne (Paris, 1879).

[3] The expression used *Kathās.*, xc, 8, 127, and 177, is *Bodhisattvāṃśa*, "a portion of the B." In the *Nāgānanda* (transl. Palmer Boyd, p. 85), Garuḍa says: "This is a Bodhisattva whom I have slain".

This much is certain, that the legend of Jīmūtavāhana clearly presupposes an anthropomorphic Nāga ; otherwise it would be unaccountable how Garuḍa can mistake the Vidyādhara prince for Śaṅkhachūḍa, the Nāga victim destined to serve for his food. Even if we assume a Nāga of human shape but provided with the usual snakehood, it seems somewhat strange that Garuḍa should not have noticed his mistake until Śaṅkhachūḍa himself calls his attention to this and other peculiarities which characterize him as a Nāga, but are naturally absent in Jīmūtavāhana. In the second version of the *Kathāsaritsāgara* (xc, 173), Śaṅkhachūḍa says to Garuḍa : " Seest thou not my hoods and my double tongue ? " In the *Nāgānanda* (Act iv, verse 98) he mentions these and besides some other characteristic signs of the Nāga ; the *svastika* on his breast, the scaled skin (*kañchuka*), the double tongue, and the three-fold snakehood with its jewels. We quote Palmer Boyd's translation.[1] " Not to mention the mark of the Swastika on the breast, are there not the scales on my body ? Do you not count my two tongues as I speak ? Nor see these three hoods of mine, the compressed wind hissing through them in my insupportable anguish ? While the brightness of my gems is distorted by the thick smoke from the fire of my direful poison ? "

It is only in the *Nāgānanda* that such prominence is given to these peculiar features of the Nāga. The other authors in rendering the legend have wisely omitted them.

The circumstance that the Jīmūtavāhana story evidently conceives the Nāga as a being human or almost human in appearance seems to indicate that it is not an ancient myth like the ' Serpent sacrifice ' of the *Ādi-parvan* (in which the Nāgas are clearly conceived in serpent shape), but a legend of a comparatively late date.

It is also significant that we do not know of any representation of the Jīmūtavāhana legend in the plastic art of India. If the story had been known as an edifying legend among the early Buddhists, they would surely have figured it on their sacred monuments. But it is found neither at Bharhut, Sanchi, or Ajāṇṭa nor on the Borobudur with its wealth of *jātakas* and *avadānas*. A sculptural or pictorial rendering of the self-sacrifice of Jīmūtavāhana would, of course, be readily identifiable.

This is the more remarkable as the *motif* of Garuḍa seizing a Nāga is a decorative device not at all uncommon in Indian art. First of all we meet it in the Græco-Buddhist school of Gandhāra in many replicas, the serpent deity being invariably shown in a human form, but distinguished by the usual snake issuing from his or her back. Now in nearly all the specimens known to us the victim is a female, so that a connexion with the Jīmūtavāhana

[1] *Nāgānanda* (transl. Palmer Boyd), p. 84. The translator observes that the passage might serve as a *locus classicus* for the Hindu conception of a Nāga.

legend is at once precluded. The best-known example is the sculpture from Sanghao, in the north-east corner of the Peshawar district, which has often been reproduced and described.[1] It shows a Nāgī being carried off by Garuḍa who with his talons has seized her by the waist, while in his beak he holds the snake issuing from her neck. Subsequently several more specimens have come to light: some like the Sanghao sculpture, but in others we have quite a group of figures: Garuḍa having seized two unfortunate victims, usually a male and a female, at the same time, while a third one has been thrown down by the wind of his wings and others, again, are making a vain attempt to come to the rescue. By comparing these various sculptures it has become evident that they originally must have belonged to the head-dress of those figures in princely attire which represent Bodhisattvas. They obviously imitate ornaments made of silver or gold. (Plate XV, *a* and *b*.)

Whereas in these Gandhāra sculptures the victim of Garuḍa—to make the subject, as it were, more pathetic—is invariably anthropomorphic, we find that sculptural art in its purely Indian expression of the same subject prefers to render the Nāga in his animal shape. On a coping stone from Amarāvatī decorated in the usual fashion with the well-known *motif* of the garland-carriers we note among the various emblems employed to fill the open spaces, such as the sacred tree, the wheel, and the *stūpa*, also a Garuḍa holding a five-headed Nāga in his beak. The bird, shown *en face*, is treated in a conventional manner; but the main point of interest is that both the Garuḍa and the Nāga are here theriomorphic.[2]

The same is the case with a piece of sculpture excavated from the Kaṅkālī Ṭīlā at Mathurā and now preserved in the Provincial Museum of Lucknow.[3] This fragment which must have formed the end of a *toraṇa* architrave, is carved on one side with the figure of a Garuḍa in conflict with a Nāga. The former, here *en profil*, is likewise conventionally treated but has distinctly the type of a bird of prey. Only his ear looks remarkably human, and is provided with an ear-ring. The most fantastic part of his body, however, is his tail, which has, moreover, received a curious twist so as to make it fit into the rather narrow space available. The serpent which is shown here in a less helpless state than in the Amarāvatī sculpture is three-headed, the double-tongue being plainly visible. Its body is wound twice round its enemy's neck, while with its tail it holds on to a tree. (Plate XV, *c*.)

[1] Grünwedel, *Buddhist Art*, pp. 108 ff., fig. 61. V. A. Smith, *Hist. of Fine Art*, pp. 117 ff., figs. 70 and 70*a*. Foucher, *Art gréco-bouddhique*, vol. ii, pp. 32 ff., figs. 318–21. Spooner, *Handbook*, p. 59. The Sanghao sculpture has been recognized as an Indian adaptation of the group of Ganymede carried off by the eagle of Zeus, a famous work of the sculptor Leochares.

[2] Fergusson, *Tree and Serpent Worship*, pl. lvi, fig. 1. Grünwedel, *Buddhist Art*, fig. 101. Foucher, *Art gréco-bouddhique*, vol. ii, fig. 466.

[3] V. A. Smith, *Jain Stūpa*, p. 28, pl. xxv, fig. 1.

(*a*) Garuḍa seizing Nāgī (Gandhāra).

(*b*) Garuḍa attacking Nāgas (Gandhāra).

(*c*) Garuḍa and Nāga (Mathurā).

[*To face p.* 172

The Gold-granting Snake and the poor Brahmin.[1]

In a certain place there lived a Brahmin, named Haridatta, who used to till the ground. But as time went by he never reaped any crop. Now one day towards the end of the hot season the Brahmin, overcome by the heat, had lain down to sleep in the shade of a tree in the middle of his field. Seeing not very far off on the top of an ant-hill a huge snake with his large hood expanded, he thought: "Surely this must be the genius of the field (*kshetra-devatā*), who hath never yet been worshipped by me. That is why my tillage hath borne no fruit. Let me, therefore, pay him worship." Having thus resolved, he begged milk from somewhere, put it into a dish, and, approaching the ant-hill, said: "O guardian of the field (*kshetrapāla*), all this time I knew not that thou wast dwelling here. Therefore have I paid thee no reverence. So do thou now pardon me." Having thus spoken and offered the milk, he went home. But on the morrow when he came back and looked, he saw a gold *dinār* in the dish. In this manner day after day he went by himself to offer milk to the snake, and every time he obtained a gold *dinār*.

Now one day as he had to go to a certain village, the Brahmin appointed his son to bring milk to the ant-hill. His son, too, having brought the milk and put it down, went home and the next day when he went again, he found one gold *dinār*. "In sooth," he thought, "that ant-hill must be full of gold *dinārs*. Therefore let me slay him and take it all." Thus he resolved, and next day when he brought the milk the Brahmin's son seized a cudgel and hit the snake on the head. Somehow, by the power of fate, the snake did not lose his life, but in his wrath he bit the boy with his sharp, poisonous fangs, so that he died instantly. His kinsmen, not far from the field, performed the last honours by cremating his remains. Now on the second day the father come home. On learning from his people by what cause his son had been lost, he was reminded of the story of the golden geese whom a king out of greed ordered to be killed. But again early the next morrow the Brahmin, taking milk, went thither and praised the snake. Thereupon the snake, still hiding within the gates of the ant-hill, made answer to the Brahmin: "Out of greed art thou come, casting off even the sorrow for thy son. Henceforward it is not meet that there should be friendship between thee and me. Thy son in the infatuation of youth hath hit me. I have bitten him. How am I to forget the cudgel stroke? And how art thou to forget the pain of the grief for thy son?" After these words the snake gave him a costly

[1] *Pañchatantra* (ed. Kosegarten), lib. iii, fab. 5. *Pūrṇabhadra's recension* (ed. Hertel), lib. iii, fab. 6. Richard Schmidt, *Das Pañcatantram* (*textus ornatior*), pp. 219 ff. Cf. Benfey, *Pantschatantra*, vol. ii, pp. 244, ff. (vol. i, pp. 359 ff.), and H. H. Wilson, *Trans. R.A.S.*, i, 1827, pp. 176 ff. A modern version of this fable will be found in Tod's *Annals*, vol. i, pp. 777 ff.

jewel and said again: "Do thou not come again." Then the Brahmin took the jewel and went home, blaming his son's judgment.

Therefore it is said:—

> Behold that flaming pyre, my broken crest behold,
> Friendship once being cracked ne'er waxeth as of old.

The Maiden that Wedded a Snake[1]

In the town of Rājagṛiha there once lived a Brahmin, Devaśarman by name. When his Brāhmaṇī wife saw the boys of the neighbours, she wept exceedingly, because she had no children. Now on a certain day the Brahmin spake to her: "My dear, cease grieving. Lo, while performing a sacrifice for the attainment of sons, I was addressed in clear accents by an invisible being in this wise: 'O Brahmin, thou shalt have a son surpassing all human creatures in beauty, character, and good fortune.'" At these words the Brāhmaṇī's heart was filled with extreme gladness and she said: "May that presage become true." In the course of time she conceived, and when her days were accomplished she brought forth a snake. When her attendants saw it they all cried out: "Throw him away!" But she, not heeding their words, took him, bathed him, and with the affection due to a son placed him in a spacious and clean vessel. As his body was strengthened by means of milk, fresh butter and other food, he, after some days, became full-grown. Once the Brāhmaṇī, beholding the marriage festival of a neighbour's son, spake to her husband with a voice, choked with tears: "In every respect thou showest me contempt, for thou takest no care about the marriage festival of my boy." At these words of her the Brahmin said: "Lady, am I to penetrate into the Nether World and beseech Vāsuki? Foolish one, who else will grant his daughter to a snake?" But when he observed the exceeding distressed countenance of his wife, out of consideration for her, he took ample provender and, sith he loved her dearly, he wandered abroad so that after several months he reached a town, Kukkuṭanagara by name, the which was situated in a remote country.

There he was hospitably received in the house of a kinsman upon whom he could well rely, as they fully knew each other's affection. After having been entertained with a bath, food, and so forth, the Brahmin passed the night with that relative, and early on the morrow when he departed and took his leave, his host bespake him in this wise: "For what reason art thou come hither? And where art thou going?" At these words he made answer: "I am come to seek a seemly girl for my son." "If such be the case" quoth

[1] *Pūrṇabhadra's Pañchatantra*, lib. i, fab. 24. Richard Schmidt, *Das Pañcatantram (textus ornatior)*, pp. 115 ff. Cf. Benfey, *Pantschatantra*, vol. ii, pp. 144 ff. A modern version of this fable as current in Kumaon has been communicated by the Rev. E. S. Oakley, *Jl.U.P. Hist. Society*, vol. i, pp. 37 f.

the other, "let me tell thee that I have a very beautiful daughter. And thou mayest freely dispose of my person. Do thou take her then for thy son." The Brahmin guest gladly consented, and, taking the girl and her retinue withal, he returned to his own place. Now, when the country people with eyes agape with delight beheld her uncommon beauty distinguished by such wonderful charms, they spake to her attendants: "How can it be that respectable people have bestowed such a jewel of a girl upon a snake?" On hearing this all her chamberlains were alarmed: "Snatch her away," they said, "from that wretched Brahmin who is prompted by an evil demon." But the girl quoth: "Cease your abuse. For it hath been said:—

The order of a king is spoken only once,
the word the virtuous speak is spoken only once,
A girl is wedded by her father only once,
in these three cases it is once and only once."

And she told a fable to show that whatsoever hath been ordained by Fate, can not be changed. "Besides," she added, "let my father not be open to censure by having spoken an untruth with regard to his daughter." After these words her companions gave way and she was married to the snake. Then, prompted by devotion, she began to minister to her husband by drenching him with milk and so forth. Now on a certain night the snake came out of the spacious basket which had been placed in the bedroom and assuming human shape he mounted her couch. She, believing him to be a stranger, trembled over all her limbs, and, opening the door, she wished to fly away. But he said to her: "My dear, please stay. I am thy husband." And in order to give her confidence he entered the snake body which had remained inside the basket and then came out again. When she beheld him adorned with a lofty diadem, ear-rings and sundry kinds of bracelets, she threw herself at his feet. Next they both enjoyed the joys of love. When his father, the Brahmin, having arisen before them, saw it, he seized the cast-off snake-hide which was still in the basket, and, in order to prevent his son from entering it again, he cremated it in the sacred fire. Next morning he and his wife out of supreme gladness showed all people their own son who was so full of affection and looked, indeed, like the son of a prime minister.

The Poet Guṇāḍhya, the Son of a Nāga [1]

[Guṇāḍhya, at the request of Kāṇabhūti, tells him the story of his life from his birth onwards.]

In the land of Pratishṭhāna there is a town, Supratishṭhita by name; in that place there once lived a certain excellent Brahmin, called Somaśarman. To him two sons were

[1] *Kathās.*, vi, 8–20; Tawney's transl., vol. i, pp. 32 f.

born, my friend, Vatsa and Gulma, and a third child, namely, a daughter called Śrutārthā. In the course of time that Brahmin, together with his wife, went the way of all flesh; then his two sons took constant care of their sister. Suddenly she became pregnant; then Vatsa and Gulma, as no other man came in their sister's way, began to suspect one another. But Śrutārthā, knowing their minds spake to her two brothers thus: "Do not conceive an evil suspicion, listen, I will tell you the truth. There is a prince, named Kīrtisena, who is the brother's son of Vāsuki, the Nāga king. By him I was seen when I had gone to bathe. Then, being overpowered with love, he told me his name and parentage, and made me his wife according to the marriage of the Gandharvas.[1] He belongs to the priestly caste, and it is by him that I have become pregnant." On hearing this Vatsa and Gulma said: "What confidence can we place in all this?" Thereupon she silently invoked the Nāga prince, and as soon as he was invoked he appeared and spake to Vatsa and Gulma: "Your sister, whom I have made my wife, is a glorious Apsaras[2] fallen down to earth in consequence of a curse; and ye, too, have dropped to earth in consequence of a curse. A son shall without fail be born to your sister here: then she and you shall be freed from your curse." After these words he disappeared, and in a few days a son was born to Śrutārthā; know, my friend, that I am that son.

King Udayana of Vatsa and the Wonderful Lute[3]

[Mṛigāvatī, the queen of king Sahasrānīka of Vatsa, was carried off by 'a bird of the race of Garuḍa'. In the hermitage of the warlike seer Jamadagni her son Udayana was born. The boy grew up to size and strength in that grove of penance. Jamadagni performed for him the sacraments appropriate to a member of the warrior-caste and instructed him in the Veda and in the practice of archery.]

Once upon a time Udayana, roaming about in pursuit of deer, saw a snake which had been forcibly captured by a Śabara.[4] Moved by pity for the beautiful animal, he said to the Śabara: "Do thou release that snake at my word." Quoth the Śabara: "My lord, this is my livelihood; for in my property I ever maintain myself by exhibiting a dancing snake. My snake previously having died, I searched the great wood and finding this one, I captured it by means of spells and potent herbs." On hearing this, the generous Udayana gave the Śabara a bracelet which his mother had bestowed upon him and thus caused him to release the snake. Whenas the Śabara had departed with the bracelet, the serpent,

[1] A marriage without ceremonies and only dependent on the consent of the two parties concerned.

[2] A heavenly nymph.

[3] *Kathās.*, ix, 74–82; Tawney's transl., vol. i, pp. 55 f.

[4] A wild mountaineer.

greatly pleased, made a bow and then bespake Udayana in this wise: "I am the eldest brother of Vāsuki and my name is Vasunemi. Do thou take from me, whom thou hast saved, this lute sweet in the sounding of its strings and divided according to the division of the quarter-tones, and betel leaf together with the art of making unfading garlands and forehead-marks." Then Udayana, furnished with all these gifts and dismissed by the serpent, returned to the hermitage of Jamadagni, raining nectar, so to speak, upon his mother's eyes.

[The Śabara, found in possession of a bracelet marked with Sahasrānīka's name, is taken to the king; and this leads to the reunion of the two consorts who had been separated for fourteen years. In the sequel it is related that Udayana used the lute to capture wild elephants.[1]]

The Story of the Jealous Nāga [2]

[Three travellers who chanced to meet one another on the way, had all suffered the same sad experience: each of them, while abroad, had been deceived by his wife in a most repulsive manner. So, weary of the troublous life of a house-holder, they resolved to repair to the wilderness and to become anchorites.]

Now, while these three companions were on their way to the forest, towards the close of the day they arrived at a tree which stood on the bank of a lake. Having eaten and drunk, they had climbed that tree to stay there for the night, when they saw a traveller arrive and lay himself down to sleep under that tree. After a while they beheld another person come forth from the middle of the lake and spit out of his mouth a woman together with a couch. After he had embraced the woman he fell asleep on the couch. Now, as soon as she saw her companion sleeping, the woman stood up and approached the traveller. After she had finished dallying with him he asked her who they both were. "He is a Nāga," she replied, "and I, a Nāga-daughter, am his wife. Be not afraid of him; for I have made love with ninety-nine wayfarers, and now through thee the number of hundred hath been made full." But while she was still thus speaking the Nāga happened to awake and, seeing her in company with the traveller, he sent forth a blaze from his mouth and reduced both of them to ashes. The Nāga having vanished in the lake, the three friends communed: "If women, albeit they be guarded inside one's body, cannot be kept safely, what can one expect of them at home? Fie, o fie upon them!"

Having thus passed the night, they, with a tranquil mind, proceeded to the wood.

[1] *Kathās.*, xi, 3–4; Tawney's transl., vol. i, p. 67.
[2] *Kathās.*, lxiv, 152–60; Tawney's transl., vol. ii, pp. 98 f.

The Nāga who let His Secret Out [1]

A certain Nāga, fleeing in fear of Garuḍa, assumed human form, and found a refuge somewhere in the house of a courtesan. Now this woman was wont to receive five hundred elephants for her wages, and owing to his supernatural power, the Nāga availed to pay her this amount every day. The wench, however, persisted in asking him: "Whence dost thou daily get so many elephants? Tell me, who art thou?" At last, deluded by love, he answered her: "Do not tell any one! Out of fear of Garuḍa I am tarrying here. I am a Nāga." Then the courtesan mentioned it in secret to a bawd.

Now Garuḍa, while searching the world, came to that place in human shape and approaching that bawd, he spake to her: "I wish to stay to-night in the house of thy daughter, Madam. Please take the wages from me." "There is a Nāga staying here," the bawd rejoined, "who constantly pays us five hundred elephants. Then what need have we of thy wages of one day?" Sith Garuḍa had now learnt that a Nāga was staying there, he in the semblance of a guest entered that harlot's house. And when he beheld that Nāga on the top of the upper terrace, Garuḍa revealed himself in his true form, and flying up, slew and devoured him.

Therefore let a wise man never recklessly disclose a secret to women.

The Curse of a Nāga [2]

When Prince Mṛigāṅkadatta with his eleven companions had set out for Ujjayinī in quest of his beloved Śaśāṅkavatī, they reached a desolate wilderness in the Vindhya mountains, and there he saw standing at the foot of a tree an ascetic besmeared with ashes and wearing a deer-skin and a tuft of matted hair. The prince with his followers approached and asked him: "Why standest thou here alone, reverend sir, in this forest which is devoid of hermitages?" Quoth the anchorite: "I am the disciple of a great *guru*, named Śuddhakīrti, and I know the potency of innumerable spells. Once on a time, having chanced upon a boy of noble birth who was provided with auspicious marks, I, by dint of great exertion, caused him while still alive to be possessed by a spirit. When that boy was possessed, I questioned him and he told me of many a place for potent herbs and draughts, and thus spake: 'There is here in the Vindhya forest northward from this place a solitary *sissoo*-tree and beneath it there is the great dwelling of a Nāga king. The water of it is covered with moist dust, but at noon-time it is disclosed by the couples of geese disporting themselves among the lotus-flowers. There dwelleth a mighty lord of the Nāgas,

[1] *Kathās.*, lxi, 170–9; Tawney's transl., vol. ii, pp. 54 f. Benfey, op. cit., vol. i, pp. 364 f.

[2] *Kathās.*, lxx, 53–77; Tawney's transl., vol. ii, pp. 149 f.

Pāṛāvatākhya [1] by name, who from the war between the gods and the titans hath obtained a matchless sword, named 'Beryl-beauty'. The man who winneth that sword will become the monarch of the fairies, and unconquerable will he be. But it can only be obtained with the help of heroes.' When that possessed boy had thus spoken I dismissed him. From that time onward I have wandered about over the earth desirous to obtain that sword and caring for nothing else; but failing to find helpers, I am weary and have come here to die."

When Mṛigāṅkadatta had heard this from the ascetic, he said to him: "I and my companions shall be thy helpers." The ascetic gladly accepted his offer, and went with him and his followers, by the help of an ointment rubbed on the feet, to the dwelling-place of that Nāga. When at the appointed sign the ascetic had closed the quarters [2] and stationed Mṛigāṅkadatta and his companions, he cleared the water from dust by scattering enchanted mustard-seeds and began to offer an oblation with Nāga-subduing spells. And by the power of his incantations he conquered portentous clouds and all similar impediments. Then from that *sissoo*-tree there issued forth a heavenly nymph, murmuring, as it were, bewildering charms with the tinkling of her jewelled ornaments and approaching the magician, she in a moment with her sidelong glances pierced his heart. He lost his self-command and forgot his spells, while she firmly embracing him, flung from his hand the sacrificial vessel. Now the Nāga Pārāvatākhya had gained his opportunity, and he came forth from his dwelling-place like a dense cloud on the day of doom. The heavenly nymph vanished and the ascetic, beholding that Nāga, terrible with flaming eyes and roaring horribly, died of a broken heart.

When he was destroyed, the Nāga, laying aside that awful form, cursed Mṛigāṅkadatta and his friends who had rendered him assistance, saying: "Sith by associating yourselves with that man, ye acted to no good purpose, ye shall for a certain time be separated from one another." After these words the Nāga vanished out of sight and instantly Mṛigāṅkadatta and his friends had their eyes dimmed with darkness, and were deprived of the faculty of hearing sounds. Separated by the power of the Nāga's curse, they went hither and thither—shouting and searching for one another.

The Legend of Jīmūtavāhana [3]

In the Himālaya mountains there once reigned a monarch of the Vidyādharas named Jīmūtaketu who possessed a wonderful tree which granted all wishes. Through

[1] Tawney has 'Pārāvatāksha'. A Nāga Pārāvata of the race of Airāvata is mentioned *M. Bh., Ādi. p.*, lvii, 11.

[2] Cf. above, p. 168.

[3] *Kathās.*, xxii, 16–53, 168–256; Tawney's transl., vol. i, pp. 174–86. For other redactions of the legend see above, p. 170.

the favour of this tree he obtained a son whom he named Jīmūtavāhana. This prince was so filled with compassion for all creatures that, when grown up, he persuaded his father to forego the selfish possession of the wishing-tree and to let it serve instead for the benefit of the whole world. This generous act excited the hostility of his kinsmen who were determined to seize the kingdom by force. But Jīmūtavāhana, convinced of the futility of all worldly greatness, prompted his father to abandon his royal state rather than fight his own relations and attain prosperity by the slaughter of others. So the prince, accompanied by his parents, retired to the Malaya mountains where they abode in a hermitage shaded by sandal trees.

Here Jīmūtavāhana formed a firm friendship with Mitrāvasu who was the son of Viśvāvasu, the overlord of the Siddhas. Now this Mitrāvasu had a younger sister of great beauty, called Malayavatī, whom he offered in marriage to his friend. "O Prince," Jīmūtavāhana replied, "thy sister hath been my wife in a previous birth and thou wert my friend like unto a second heart. For I am one who can remember his former states of existence. Therefore is it seemly that I should marry her." Then with the consent of their parents Jīmūtavāhana married the Siddha princess and they abode in the Malaya mountains in great felicity.

Now once upon a time, accompanied by his friend, Mitrāvasu, he went to view the shore of the ocean. There he beheld a young man [1] who, greatly perturbed, was trying to keep back his lamenting mother while he was led by another person, apparently a soldier, to the flat top of a high cliff. "Who art thou? What wilt thou? And why does thy mother lament?" Thuswise the prince questioned him, whereupon he related him his story.[2]

"In bygone times Kaśyapa's two wives, Kadrū and Vinatā, had a dispute. The former said that the Sun's horses were black, the other that they were white. And they decided that bondage was to be the forfeit of her that lost the wager. Then Kadrū bent on winning, induced her sons the Nāgas, to defile the Solar steeds by means of blasts of venom; and showing them to Vinatā in that condition, she conquered her by fraud and made her a slave. (Fie upon the mutual spite of womenfolk!) Came Garuḍa, the son of Vinatā, and with winning words besought Kadrū to liberate his mother from her bondage. Then Kadrū's sons, the Nāgas, reflecting for a while, spake to him: "O son of Vinatā, the gods have just begun to churn the sea of milk; fetch thou the nectar and give it to us as an equivalent. Then do thou take thy mother unto thee; for thou art the best of mighty

[1] In the other redaction found in the *Kathās.* (xc, 94–105), Jīmūtavāhana's attention is first drawn by the heaped-up bones of former victims of Garuḍa, and by way of explanation Mitrāvasu tells him the origin of the feud between the Nāgas and Garuḍa. The same presentment is found in the *Nāgānanda*, act iv.

[2] Cf. supra, pp. 50 f.

warriors." Hearing these words, Garuḍa went his way to the Milk-ocean, and for the sake of winning the nectar, he showed exceeding valour. Pleased with his prowess, the god Vishṇu deigned to speak to him : " I am satisfied with thee ; choose some boon." "May the Nāgas become my food"—thuswise the son of Vinatā, wroth at the bondage of his mother, chose a boon from Vishṇu. When the god had consented and Garuḍa by his own heroism had won the nectar, Indra, having heard the whole story, addressed him in this manner : " O King of birds, so must thou act that the nectar be not eaten by those foolish snakes and that I may avail to reconquer it from them." Upon these words Garuḍa consented, and, elated by the boon of Vishṇu, went to the Nāgas, carrying a vessel of nectar. From afar he spake to those foolish ones who were afraid of the power which he had attained through the boon : " Here is the nectar brought by me. Release my mother and take it. If ye be afraid I will put it for you on a bed of *darbha* grass. Having procured my mother's release, I will go away and ye may make the nectar your own." The Nāgas consenting, he placed the vessel on a pure bed of *kuśa* grass, and they let his mother go. Now when Garuḍa—having thus freed his mother from bondage—had departed, and while the Nāgas were confidently about to take the nectar, Indra suddenly swooped down, and bewildering them by his power, bore away the bowl of nectar from the bed of *kuśa* grass. Then in their perplexity the Nāgas licked the bed of *darbha* grass, if peradventure some drops of nectar might be spilled on it. Thereby their tongues were split and they became double-tongued for nothing. (What but ridicule can ever be the portion of the over-greedy !)

" Now, since the Nāgas had failed to seize the nectar, their foe Garuḍa through Vishṇu's boon, began to devour them—swooping down upon them ever and again. At his attacks the snakes were dead with fear, their wives miscarried, and the whole serpent race was waning rapidly. Then Vāsuki, the Serpent-king, deemed the entire Nāga world ruined at one stroke, and as a suppliant he proposed this pact to Garuḍa, their irresistible foe : ' Every day I shall send one Nāga for thy food, O King of birds, on a rock which riseth from the sandy shore of the ocean. But do thou no longer invade Pātāla so destructively ; for, were the Nāga world to perish it would be thine own loss.' Garuḍa, having agreed to the proposal made by Vāsuki, proceeded daily to eat one single Nāga sent to him. In this wise innumerable serpents have met destruction on this spot. I, too, am a Nāga named Śaṅkhachūḍa and to-day my turn hath come. Therefore by the command of the Serpent-king I am come hither to this rock of slaughter to supply food to Garuḍa, my mother lamenting my fate."

Jimūtavāhana, deeply grieved at these words of Śaṅkhachūḍa, spake to him : "Alas, how dastardly does Vāsuki bear his royal state that by his own hand his subjects are led unto the carnage of their foe ! Why hath not that coward first of all delivered up himself to Garuḍa? Why chooseth he to be a witness of the ruin of his own race? And Tārkshya,[1] too, albeit he be born from Kaśyapa, how dire an evil doeth he commit for the sake of nothing but his body. How great the folly even of the great! So let me then to-day deliver at least thee alone from Garuḍa by giving up my own body: do thou not despair, my friend."

Hearing this speech, Śaṅkhachūḍa firmly spake to him: "This be far from me! O noble heart, do not speak so again. It is not meet that a string of pearls be destroyed for the sake of common glass. Nor will I incur the blame of having brought dishonour upon my house."[2] Thus saying, the good Nāga tried to dissuade Jīmūtavāhana. Then deeming that the hour of Garuḍa was near at hand, Śaṅkhachūḍa went to pay homage at the time of his approaching death to Śiva, surnamed Gokarṇa, whose shrine stood on the shore of the ocean. When he was gone, Jīmūtavāhana—that very treasure-house of compassion—deemed that he had gained an opportunity to save the Nāga's life by giving up his own. Thereupon he sent away his friend Mitrāvasu to his own house on the pretext of some task, artfully pretending that he himself had forgotten it.

At the very moment the Earth stricken by the tempest of Tārkshya's wings, on his approach shook, as if trembling with marvel at the valour of the noble prince. By that sign Jīmūtavāhana weened that the great Serpent-foe was near, and moved by mercy he hastily ascended the rock of slaughter. At that moment Garuḍa swooped down, and, with his own shadow darkening the sky, bore off that noble soul, striking him with his cruel beak. While shedding a shower of blood and dropping his crest-jewel torn out by Garuḍa, he was carried off to a high mountain peak where the giant bird began to eat him. At that time a rain of flowers fell from heaven, and at the sight thereof Tārkshya greatly marvelled, wondering what it meant.

Meanwhile, the Nāga, Śaṅkhachūḍa, having bowed low before Gokarṇa, came back and beheld the rock of slaughter sprinkled over with a shower of blood. "Alas," he cried out, "for my sake that noble heart hath surely offered up his life. Then whither in this moment hath he been borne away by Tārkshya? I will quickly seek him, if peradventure I may find him." With these words the good Nāga went, following the track of blood. Garuḍa, in the meanwhile, seeing his victim jubilant, paused with amazement, and bethought himself: "How, this is some one else: albeit he be devoured by me, he never falters, yea, showeth the utmost joy." While Tārkshya thus considered, Jīmūtavāhana, even in that plight intent on the fulfilment of his aim, spake to him in this wise: "O King

[1] Another name for Garuḍa.

[2] In the corresponding passage, *Kathās.* xc, 141, Śaṅkhachūḍa is said to be a scion of the noble house of Śaṅkhapāla. This name is familiar from the Pali *jātaka*, No. 524. Cf. above, p. 150.

of birds, in this frame of mine there still remaineth flesh and blood : then why hast thou, although not yet satisfied, of a sudden ceased thy meal ? " At these words the lord of birds overcome with wonder, thus questioned him : " Thou art no Nāga, my good friend. Speak, who art thou ? ' " I am a Nāga ; eat me and complete what thou hast begun. The firm in mind never leave unfinished the task once undertaken." While Jīmūtavāhana thuswise made answer, Śaṅkhachūḍa, having meanwhile arrived, cried from afar : " Hold, hold, O Garuḍa ; he is no Nāga, I am the Nāga meant for thee. Then let him go. Alas, what great mistake hast thou made thus recklessly ! " Upon these words the monarch of the feathered tribe was sore confounded, but Jīmūtavāhana felt pain, seeing his wish thus foiled. Then, understanding from their discourse that his victim was the prince of the Vidyādharas, Garuḍa felt deep remorse. " Alas," quoth he, " in my cruelty I have incurred great sin. How easily do they contract guilt, who follow evil courses. Praiseworthy above all is this noble soul who, offering up his life for another's good, puts this whole world to shame, overpowered as it is by the delusion of selfishness." At this thought Garuḍa, to cleanse himself of sin, wished to enter the fire. But Jīmūtavāhana spake to him : " Lord of the winged tribe, why art thou thus perplexed ? If in good sooth thou dreadest sin, then henceforward let these serpents no longer serve for thy food. Besides, repent of those which thou didst slay before. This, indeed, is here the remedy for guilt ; none other will avail."

Whenas, moved by compassion with all sentient beings, he spake to him thuswise, Tārkshya gladly accepted his word, as though it had been uttered by a ghostly father. And he went hastily to fetch nectar from heaven to heal his bruised limbs and to quicken those other serpents whereof nothing remained but the bones. But then the goddess Gaurī herself appeared in visible form and sprinkled Jīmūtavāhana over with nectar, as she was pleased with the devotion of his spouse ; and thereby his limbs were renewed to greater beauty, while in the sky the gods joyfully beat the celestial drums. When he had arisen safe and sound, Garuḍa, too, brought nectar, and along the whole sea-shore he showered nectar from the sky. By the which all serpents slain before by Garuḍa rose up alive and the forest along the coast was suddenly filled with serpents so numerous that it seemed as if the whole snake-world had come forth from Pātāla to behold Jīmūtavāhana by whose heroism they were now released from the dread of Garuḍa. Then his relatives, seeing him with restored body and with undying fame, rejoiced in him ; his wife rejoiced, so did her kinsfolk and his parents, too. Who would not exult at sorrow being turned to joy ? Śaṅkhachūḍa, being dismissed by Jīmūtavāhana, went back to the Nether World (*Rasātala*), but the latter's fame spread of its own accord through the three worlds. Then, through the favour of Gaurī, all his kinsmen who for long had been estranged from him, timidly approached that Ornament of the Fairy race, prostrating themselves before him. And at their entreaties the beneficent Jīmūtavāhana returned from the Malaya mountains to his own home, the slope of snowy Himavant. There, united with his parents and with Mitrāvasu and Malayavatī, that resolute prince enjoyed for long the rank of sovereign liege of the Vidyādharas

The Story of Prince Sudhana [1]

Once upon a time there were in the land of Pañchāla two kings: one was king of Northern Pañchāla and the other of Southern Pañchāla. The king of Northern Pañchāla, Mahadhana by name, who resided at Hastināpura, was a righteous ruler and his kingdom was wealthy and prosperous and free from scarcity and pestilence. At his capital there was a beautiful great pool covered with all kind of lotus-flowers and enlivened by sundry water-fowl. In that pool there dwelled a young Nāga, Janmachitraka by name, who from time to time caused a copious outpour of rain to fall. So the crops were abundant, the land produced plenty of food, and the people honoured and fed Shamans, Brahmins, and mendicants. But the king who ruled in Southern Pañchāla was cruel and violent, and used to terrorize his subjects by harsh punishments. Owing to his unrighteousness the rain-god did not in due time grant a plentiful outpour of rain. Therefore a great multitude of people, fearing for their lives, quitted his realm and went to dwell in the domains of the king of Northern Pañchāla.

Now once upon a time the king of Southern Pañchāla, under pretext of a hunting party, went forth to inspect the country. He saw the towns and villages desolate, and the gardens and temples ruined and decayed. Then he asked why a large part of the population had left the country and whither they had gone. After some hesitation the ministers told him the truth. The king then promised that henceforward he would rule righteously like his neighbour, the king of Northern Pañchāla. But the ministers said: "Majesty, that country possesseth yet another blessing: at the capital there is a great pool covered with all kind of lotus-flowers and enlivened by sundry waterfowl. There dwelleth a young Nāga, Janmachitraka by name, who from time to time granteth a copious downpour of rain, so that the crops are very abundant." "Is there a means," the king asked, "whereby that young Nāga could be brought hither?" "Majesty," the ministers replied, "sorcerers in possession of magical spells could bring him hither."

Then the king ordered a golden casket to be bound to the top of a banner and by sound of bell he caused a proclamation to be made in his domains: "Whosoever will bring the young Nāga, named Janmachitraka, from Northern Pañchāla, I will give this golden

[1] *Divyāvadana*, xxx, pp. 435 ff. Another version of the story is found in Kshemendra's *Avadāna-kalpalatā*, xiv, under the title *Kinnarī Avadāna*.

PLATE XVI.

JANMACHITRAKA AND THE SORCERER (BOROBUDUR).

[To face p. 184

casket unto him, and I will honour him with great honour." Then a certain snake-charmer, being gone to the ministers, said: "Grant ye me that golden casket: I shall bring the young Nāga named Janmachitraka." "Take it," the ministers said. But he rejoined: "Let it remain in the hand of him among you who is trustworthy and reliable. I will take it when I have brought you Janmachitraka, the young Nāga." They agreed and he, after entrusting the golden casket to a reliable person, went his way to Hastināpura. When he had observed the pool on all sides, he thought: "On this spot the young Nāga Janmachitraka dwelleth; now I must go home to fetch an offering." And he told the ministers that he would bring them the young Nāga on the seventh day.

Now Janmachitraka had noticed the snake-charmer and thought: "That man hath surely come hither to abduct me; on the seventh day he will abduct me, and being separated from my parents, I shall be sorely grieved. What am I to do? Whither am I to turn for protection?" Now not far from that pool there lived two hunters, Sāraka and Halaka, who were wont to resort to that pool for their living. They killed deer, hogs, and other land animals, which came to the pool, and also aquatic animals such as fishes, tortoises and frogs. Now Sāraka had died, but Halaka was still living. Janmachitraka, the young Nāga, reflected: "Who else can protect me but Halaka, the hunter?" Then, assuming human shape, he repaired to Halaka, the hunter and spake to him: "Well, my man, doest thou know by whose power the country of king Dhana is so wealthy and prosperous and free from scarcity and pestilence?" "Yes, I know," he rejoined, "it is because the king is just and ruleth his kingdom according to righteousness." "Is there not something besides?" The hunter answered: "There is yet another blessing. In this country there dwelleth a young Nāga, Janmachitraka by name, who from time to time causeth a copious downpour of rain to fall. So the crops are abundant and the land produceth plenty of food." "Now, how would it be if they abducted that young Nāga from the country?" "Bad, indeed, not only for himself—being separated from his parents—but also for the king and the kingdom." "And what wouldst thou do to the man who wished to abduct him?" "I would take his life." "Doest thou know that young Nāga?" "No, I don't." "I am that Nāga. There is a snake-charmer from Southern Pañchāla who wisheth to abduct me and take me to his country. He hath gone to fetch an offering, and on the seventh day he will come back. Then after fixing pegs of acacia wood in the ground to the east, south, west, and north of the pool and winding them round with many-coloured threads,[1] he will repeat his spells. Now thou must keep thyself hidden in the vicinity and when he hath proceeded so far that the water cometh up boiling from the pool and I rise too from it, then thou

[1] A similar magical rite practised by the Maraṭha women is described by Fergusson, *Tree- and Serpent-worship*, p. 236.

must hit that snake-charmer with an arrow in a vital spot. Then do thou quickly advance and tell him to withdraw his spells, as otherwise thou wilt cut off his head. For, if he were to lose his life without having withdrawn his spells, I should have to remain spell-bound as long as I live."

The hunter promised him his assistance, and on the appointed day did exactly as the Nāga had bidden him. When he saw the snake-charmer killed, the Nāga, being freed from his spells, rose from the pool, and embracing the hunter, he said : " Thou art my mother, thou art my father. It is through thy help that I have not been separated from my parents. Come, let us go to their abode." Then, taking him to his abode, he satiated him with food and drink, showed him his jewels, and introduced him to his parents. They offered him a boon and gave him sundry jewels. He took them and came up from the pool. Now, not far from that pool there was the hermitage of a seer. When the hunter had told him the whole story of the young Nāga, that seer said : " Of what avail are jewels and gold ? In his abode there is the lasso named ' infallible ' ; do thou ask for that." Then the hunter grew eager to possess the infallible lasso and, as the seer had told him, he went back to the dwelling of the Nāgas and there at the gate he saw the infallible lasso. Then he thought : " Here is the lasso for which I must ask," and thus he entered the abode of the Nāgas. The young Nāga Janmachitraka and the other Nāgas gave him friendly greeting, and presented him with jewels. But he said : " Enough of these jewels ; grant me the infallible lasso." Quoth the Nāga : " Of what avail is it unto thee ? When we are assailed by Garuḍa, then we protect ourselves there withal." " By you," the hunter rejoined, " it is only employed on rare occasions, when you are assailed by Garuḍa ; but I could employ it constantly." Then Janmachitraka, the young Nāga, thought : " He hath rendered me a great service, so with the leave of my parents, I will give it unto him." Then he gave the lasso unto him, and the hunter, being greatly pleased and rejoiced, took the infallible lasso, left the abode of the Nāgas, and went home.

The *avadāna* of Prince Sudhana, the introductory portion of which has been rendered above, is illustrated on the Borobudur in a succession of twenty bas-reliefs.[1] These twenty reliefs open the series of a hundred-and-twenty large panels (2 m. 40 wide) which decorate the main wall along the first or lowermost gallery and which run parallel with the same number of *tableaux* relating to the legend of Buddha immediately above. The story of Sudhana, as illustrated here, was first identified by the Russian scholar S. d'Oldenburg

[1] Wiener, *J.A.O.S.*, vol. xviii (1897), pp. 196 ff. Foucher, *B.E.F.E.O.*, vol. ix (1909), pp. 12 ff. N. J. Krom, *Barabudur*, vol. i (1920), pp. 125 ff. ; plates series 1*b*, i–ii (Nos. 1–4).

and subsequently has been described in detail by M. Foucher. In Dr. Krom's great work they are fully discussed and illustrated.

The introduction, in which the young Nāga Janmachitraka plays a leading part, is represented by four panels, the first of which shows the king of Northern Pañchāla and the next one his southern neighbour, each of them attended by a numerous suite. More important for our present purpose is the third *tableau*, particularly the middle portion, which renders the incantation scene (Plate XVI). In the centre we see the pond surrounded by trees and enlivened by birds. The Nāga is seen rising from his pool unwillingly, as the position of his hands seems to indicate. To his right the sorcerer, in the semblance of a Brahmanic ascetic with a long beard and matted hair, is seated behind a blazing fire, the fuel being placed on a kind of altar. On the other side the hunter Halaka hidden by the foliage keeps his bow and arrow in readiness. The only detail which is wanting is the four acacia (*khadira*) pegs wound with many-coloured threads, which in the story the snake-charmer uses to close the quarters. On the same panel two subsidiary scenes are depicted : to the right the Nāga imploring the hunter's assistance and to the left the snake-charmer conversing with a person of rank, presumably a minister of the king of Southern Pañchāla. The fourth panel of the series portrays Halaka's joyful reception in the abode of the Nāgas. At first sight it is somewhat surprising that the hunter, necessarily a low-caste man, appears here in princely attire, but we may perhaps assume that he has donned a robe of honour presented by his Nāga hosts. To the right the two parents of Janmachitraka are seated on a throne.

The Legend of the Young Nāga [1]

A certain young Nāga was seized by Suparṇa, the king of birds, and carried aloft to the wooded slope of Mount Sumeru to be devoured. Beholding there the Bhikshus deeply engaged in meditation, his heart became believing, and while dying he thought within himself : " These holy men are freed from such-like tribulation." Having died, he was reborn at Benares in a household of Brahmins devoted to the six priestly works,[2] and there he grew up to manhood. Thereupon under the spiritual rule of the Buddha Kāśyapa having renounced the world, he relinquished all sinful lust and by strenuous striving attained to the rank of an Arhat. Now he remembered his previous birth : " Where have I been in my last existence ? Among animals. Where am I now reborn ? Among men. Where are those who were my parents ? " And looking round, he saw how they stood

[1] *Divyāvadāna*, xxiv, pp. 344 ff. For the introductory passage, cf. *Avadānaśataka*, vol. ii, p. 127.

[2] The six works of the Brahmin, according to *Manu*, i, 88, are the teaching and the study of the Veda, the performing of sacrifices for himself and for others, and the giving and receiving of gifts.

weeping in the Nāga world. Thither he went and questioned them : " Mother, father, why do ye weep ? " They answered : " Sir, our young son, born to us in our old age, hath been borne away by Suparṇa, the king of birds." Quoth he : " I am that very son." " Sir," they said, " so wretched is the state of a Nāga that we deem it impossible to attain to a good birth, much less can he reap the benefit of such good works." And, falling down at his feet, they spake : " Sir, thou art in need of alms and we stand in need of religious merit. Do thou come hither day after day, and having taken thy food, go thy way whither thou wilt."

Thus he enjoyed heavenly ambrosia in the Nāga world, after the which he returned to the world of men. Now he had a novice for his disciple. To him the Friars once said : " Novice, where is thy master wont to take his food ? " Quoth he : " I wot not." Said they : " He constantly enjoyeth heavenly ambrosia in the Nāga world. Why doest not thou go too ? " " My master," he rejoined, " is great in magic and miracle. How can I go whither he goeth ? " " If he goeth thither by magic, then do thou seize the lappet of his robe." Said he : " But if I were to fall ? " " My dear boy," they answered, " if Sumeru, the chief among all mountains, were attached to the lappet of his robe it would not fall, much less wilt thou fall. Mark thou the spot where thy master will vanish." On that spot he took his stand even before his master's arrival, and at the moment the latter was going to vanish, he seized the lappet of his robe. Thus they both flew through the air, and the Nāgas, having espied them, prepared two seats and swept two circles. Then the master reflected : " For what reason have they prepared a second seat ? " and looking round he saw the novice. " My dear boy," quoth he, " thou, too, art come ? " " Yea, Master, I am come." " Very good."

Now the Nāgas reflected : " This holy man who is great in magic and miracles can be made to take divine ambrosia. But the other cannot." And to the master they gave divine ambrosia, but to the novice they gave common food. Now the novice was wont to hold his master's bowl. When after the meal he had taken the bowl, there remained in it just one grain of boiled rice. The novice put it in his mouth and thereby he enjoyed the divine taste. Then the novice thought : " How jealous these Nāgas are. Albeit we be seated together, to him they have given divine ambrosia and to me common food." And he began to conceive an aspiration for his future life,[1] saying within himself : " Sith under the Lord Kāśyapa, the perfect and unequalled Buddha, the worshipful one, I have practised the ascetic life, I pray that through that root of merit I may cause this Nāga to be removed from the Nāga world and that I may be reborn here instead." At the very moment water

[1] This *praṇidhāna* has the character of an Act of Truth.

Bronze Buddha sheltered by Muchilinda (Cambodia).

[To face p. 188.

began to flow from his hands. And the Nāga began to be oppressed by a headache. Said the Nāga : " Sir, this novice hath conceived an evil thought, the which do thou cause him to suppress." "My dear boy," quoth his master, "this is pernicious ; suppress that thought." But the novice uttered the following stanza :—

Free course hath been allowed this thought of mine ;
How were I able to suppress it now ?
Lo, Rev'rend Sir, e'en in my present state
From both my hands freely the waters flow.

Thus he caused the Nāga to be removed from that world and even there was he himself reborn.

CHAPTER V

THE PRINCIPAL NĀGA-RĀJAS

IN the Great Epic, as well as in Puranic literature, we meet with extensive lists of Nāgas. After the account of the rape of the nectar by Garuḍa, told in the *Ādi-parvan*, Śaunaka wishes to hear the names of the sons of Kadrū. Sauti then enumerates no less than seventy, eight Serpents,[1] and declares at the end that these are only the principal Nāgas, as owing to their enormous number it would clearly be impossible to name them all. Again, after the conclusion of the Serpent Sacrifice, Sauti, at the request of Śaunaka, sums up the chief Nāgas who have perished in the sacrificial fire of king Janamejaya, and adds the same remark regarding the impossibility of giving a complete list of their names. Here the victims are divided into five groups as descendants of Vāsuki, Takshaka, Airāvata Kauravya, and Dhṛitarāshṭra.[2] Another long catalogue of Nāgas, comprising sixty-eight names, is inserted in the episode of Mātali's visit to Bhogavatī.[3] It differs materially from the lists of the *Ādi-parvan*, although both have a certain number of names in common. Shorter rolls, containing twenty and nineteen names respectively, occur in the description of the court of Varuṇa in the *Sabhāparvan* and in the account of Baladeva's apotheosis in the *Mausala-parvan*.[4]

The *Harivaṃśa* gives two different catalogues of divine serpents, one of twenty-six and the other of eighteen names.[5] In the *Purāṇas*, too, such lists occur, e.g. in the *Bhāgavata* one of fifteen names, and in the *Vāyu* one of forty-one, which partly agrees with the first list of the *Harivaṃśa*.[6]

The most extensive catalogue is undoubtedly that of the *Nīlamata*, which contains more than five hundred names of Nāgas. We shall have occasion to deal with it in the next chapter.

Let us now turn to Buddhist literature. In the introductory portion of the *Saddharma-puṇḍarīka*[7] Buddha is described seated in all his glory on the top of the Vulture Peak in the midst of an incredible multitude of divine beings. These include also myriads of

1 *M.Bh.*, *Ādi-p.*, xxxv, 5–16.
2 *M.Bh.*, *Ādi-p.*, lvii.
3 *M.Bh.*, *Udyoga-p.*, ciii, 9–16.
4 *M.Bh.*, *Sabhā-p.*, ix, 8–10; *Mausala-p.*, iv, 15–16.
5 *Hariv.*, 227–30 and 9,501–04 (cf. also 12,821).
6 *Bhāgavata-p.*, v, xxiv, 29–31; *Vāyu-p.*, ii, viii, 66–71.
7 *Saddharmapuṇḍarika* (ed. Kern and Bunyiu Nanjio), p. 4. Burnouf, *Lotus de la bonne Loi* p. 3.

PLATE XVIII.

ROCK-SCULPTURE AT MĀMALLAPURAM.

[To face p. 130

Nāgas, headed by the eight great Nāga chiefs: Nanda, Upananda, Sāgara, Vāsuki, Takshaka, Manasvin, Anavatapta, and Utpala.

The *Mahāvyutpatti*,[1] a Buddhist Vocabulary in Sanskrit, supplies a list of eighty Nāga-rājas and another of fifty-five common Nāgas. The names, with a few exceptions, differ from those of the Brahmanical catalogues. Here we may expect, in the first place, to find those Nāgas who play a prominent part in the Buddha legend and in the Jātakas. The roll is, indeed, headed by Śaṅkhapāla, and contains the glorious names of Anavatapta, Elāpatra, Nandopananda (taken as one name !), Kāla and Kālika, Girika, Vidyujjvala, Apalāla, Āmratīrtha, Chāmpeya, Paṇḍara, and Maṇikaṇṭha. Varuṇa and Sāgara, who in Brahmanical mythology are gods of the sea, we find here included among the Nāga-rājas.

In surveying the numerous names of Nāgas mentioned in the Brahmanical epics, it will be noticed that a great number of them indicate colours, such as: Piñjaraka (reddish-yellow, gold-coloured), Piṅgala (tawny), Lohita (red), Aruṇa (ruddy), Kapila (brown, reddish), Kalmāsha (black spotted), Śabala (brindled), Chitra (variegated), Nīla (dark blue), Kṛishṇa (black), and Śveta (white). Other names are adjectives indicative of various qualities, such as: Ugraka (terrible), Āpta (apt), Sumana (kind), Karkara (hard), Nishṭhurika (hard), Vṛitta (round), Kṛiśaka (thin), Badhira (deaf), and Andha (blind).

A few are names of animals, e.g. Kuñjara (elephant), Aśvatara (mule), Tittiri (partridge), Khaga (bird), and Kukura (dog). But a considerable number are names of plants. Foremost are those indicating the lotus, which may have been selected on account of its connexion with the water, namely Padma and Mahāpadma, Kumuda, Puṇḍarīka, and Utpalaka (*Mahāvyutp.*). Other names indicative of vegetables are Karavīra (oleander, poisonous !), Kushmāṇḍa (kind of pumpkin), Piṇḍāraka, Vilvaka (*bilva* = ægle marmelos) and Bilvapatha, Haridraka (*haridra* = yellow sandal-tree or curcuma longa), Śirīshaka (*sirīsha* = acacia sirissa), Kardama (a poisonous turnip), and Bahumūlaka. The names of Karkoṭaka and Kulika are, perhaps, also to be reckoned as in this category.

It is remarkable that several Nāga-rājas bear royal or *kshatriya* names, some of them being actually borne by personages of the epics. Examples are: Dhṛitarāshṭra, Dhanañjaya, Āryaka, Kauravya, Janamejaya, Dilīpa, Pṛithuśravas, and Ambarīsha. The *Mahāvyutpatti* also mentions Udayana, Rāghava, and Baladeva.

Another point of interest is the frequent occurrence of pairs of names, which in the lists are regularly coupled together into one compound. In some cases the names by their very form indicate a close connexion. Instances are: Karkoṭaka-Dhanañjaya, Kambala-Aśvatara, Nanda-Upananda, Kuṇḍodara-Mahodara (cf. Mahodara and Chūḷodara in the

[1] *Mahāvyutpatti* (ed. Minayeff), pp. 48 f.

Pali chronicles of Ceylon), Badhira-Andha, Virasa-Surasa, Durmukha-Sumukha, Kāla-Upakāla (*Mahāvyutpatti*). In the legends, too, as we have seen, we meet with such pairs of Nāgas who always act in common. A typical instance is the pair Nanda and Upananda, who in the Buddha legend are so intimately combined that finally they are considered to be only one. Another such pair bearing the curious names of Kambala (" Blanket ") and Aśvatara (" Mule ") are mentioned both in Brahmanical and Buddhist lore. In a Buddhist text they are designated as ' Nāgas of the Ganges '.[1]

Śesha the World-Serpent

In the lists of divine serpents found in epic literature Śesha (or Ananta) usually figures first. He is often extolled as the sovereign of all Nāgas, but there are other prominent Nāga-rājas, especially Vāsuki, for whom the supreme rank is claimed.[2] In the *Bhagavadgītā* (x, 28–9) both are mentioned side by side, Vāsuki evidently being considered as the first among the snakes (*sarpa*), and Ananta as the chief of the Nāgas. It is, however, questionable whether it is the poet's intention to make a clear distinction between those two classes of beings. In other passages of the Epic it is Vāsuki who is called the head of the Nāgas. In the *Harivaṃśa*, where Brahmā appoints kings to rule over the different classes of creatures, it is said : " He annointed Vāsuki king of the Nāgas, Takshaka of the snakes, and Śesha of all fanged beings (*daṃshṭriṇām*).[3] This passage seems to imply a superior rank claimed for Śesha. Elsewhere again in the Great Epic it is Dhṛitarāshṭra to whom the first place among the Nāgas is assigned.[4]

We have seen that Śesha or Ananta, ' the Endless One ', as he is also called, is specially known as the bearer of the earth. Although he is not mentioned as such in Vedic literature, the idea of the world-serpent is a conception which undoubtedly belongs to a primitive sphere of thought. It has its parallel in the ' Midgardsormr ' of Norse mythology, the great world-snake which lies in the sea, engirding the whole earth. It is obvious that in the *Mahābhārata* version of the myth the old world-snake has been strangely brahmanized : he has been made into a pious ascetic after the heart of the priestly compilators of the Great Epic.[5]

The pre-eminence of Śesha among the Nāga race is evidenced by many another tale of Hindu mythology. When the *devas* have decided to churn the Ocean in order to obtain the drink of immortality and find themselves unable to move Mount Mandara, which is

[1] *Harivaṃśa*, 228, 4,443, 9,501, 14,341. *Mahāvastu*, vol. i, p. 263, ll. 1 and 12. *Jāt*, vi, p. 165, l. 4.

[2] The *Amarakośa* gives both Śesha-Ananta and Vāsuki as the name of the *Sarparāja*.

[3] *Hariv.*, 267 ; cf. also 12,496.

[4] *Virāṭa, p.*, ch. ii, 17.

[5] Cf. above, p. 57.

to be used as their churning-stick, they resort to Vishṇu and Brahmā for help. At the command of these two gods the Serpent King Ananta lifts the mountain 'together with the forests and beasts'.[1]

Besides carrying the earth, Śesha has yet another important function, due perhaps to a later development of the ancient myth of the world-serpent. It is a well known Indian conception that the Universe is periodically created and re-absorbed by the deity. So a period of divine creative action is followed by a period of divine rest. Now during his inactivity Vishṇu conceived as the supreme deity is supposed to sleep in the midst of the waters of the ocean and to repose upon the coils of Śesha. At last Brahmā, the Creator, is born from a lotus-flower rising from Vishṇu's navel, and the supreme deity awakes from his sleep to renewed action. His first deed is the destruction of the two demons, Madhu and Kaiṭabha, who threaten the new-born Brahmā. In different forms this cosmogonic myth is related in the *Mahābhārata* [2] and in the *Purāṇas*.

Vishṇu 'resting on Śesha' (*Śesha-śāyin* or *Ananta-śāyin*) is a favourite theme of plastic art. He is shown reclining on the couch formed by the windings of the Nāga whose polycephalous hood forms a canopy over the god's head. Usually the goddess Śrī is seen kneeling at the feet of her lord. The presence of Brahmā on the lotus and of the two demons seems to indicate that the subject which the Indian artists intended to portray in these sculptures is not so much Vishṇu's sleep as Vishṇu's awakening signalized by the birth of the creative force embodied in Brahmā, in other words, the Creation of the Universe.

An early example is found in one of the cave-temples of Māmallapuram on the coast of Coromandel, which are due to the Pallava dynasty and must belong to the seventh century.[3] In this grand rock-cut sculpture the majestic figure of the god asleep on his serpent-bed is two-armed and unadorned. His head covered with a high conical mitre, which is peculiar to Pallava art, is surrounded by Ananta's hood, consisting of five snake-heads. The figure of Brahmā on his lotus is absent, but at the lower end of the couch stand the two warlike demons in an attitude of defiance.

Another remarkable instance is the beautiful relief in the Gupta temple of Deogaṛh in Bundelkhaṇḍ.[4] This panel, which may be ascribed to the seventh century, lacks the grand and simple style of the rock-sculpture of Coromandel, but the numerous figures of which it is composed show that easy and varied grace which is peculiar to the best works of Gupta art. Here the sleeping Vishṇu has his usual four arms, a somewhat awkward

[1] *M.Bh.*, *Ādi-p.*, xviii, 4–8.

[2] *M.Bh.*, *Vana-p.*, cciii. Cf. *Bhīshma-p.*, lxvii, and *Śānti-p.*, cccxlvii.

[3] *A.S.R.* for 1910–11, p. 56, pl. xxix, b. Krishna Sastri, *South Indian Images*, pp. 50 f.; fig. 32.

[4] Cunningham, *A.S.R.*, vol. x, p. 107. Burgess, *Ancient Monuments*, pl. 111. V. A. Smith, *Fine Art*, pp. 162 f.; pl. xxxv, and *Ostasiatische Zeitschr.*, iii (1914), fig. 17. V. C. Bhattacharya, *Indian Images*, pp. 6 ff., pl. iii.

feature in a reclining figure. The hood of the serpent Śesha is composed of no less than seven snake-heads, each provided with the legendary jewel. Lakshmī is shown in the act of caressing her husband's right foot. The centre of the upper part of the panel is occupied by the four-faced Brahmā seated on his lotus and carrying a water-pot (*kamaṇḍalu*) in his left hand and an antelope's hide (*ajina*) over his left shoulder. He is accompanied by several other deities: Skanda on his peacock, Indra on his elephant, Śiva and Pārvatī on the bull Nandin, and a fifth flying figure of uncertain meaning. The row of six figures beneath has been explained as the five Pāṇḍavas and their common spouse Draupadī, but this identification seems doubtful.

Among the numerous examples of later date we wish only to quote the inscribed fountain-slab of Sālhi (Chamba State) in the Western Himālaya.[1] As appears from the inscription, this huge carved stone must have been erected in the year A.D. 1170. It is curious that here Śesha is portrayed as a human figure; he is not provided with the usual hood, but the lower half of his body is that of a serpent.

The examples quoted will suffice to show that Vishṇu resting on Ananta is a subject often met with in Brahmanical art. Outside India proper it seems to be unknown with one notable exception, namely, the first of the wonderful series of sculptured panels illustrating the story of the Rāmāyaṇa, which decorate the Śiva temple of Prambanan on the island of Java.[2] The centre of the *tableau* is occupied by the four-armed god seated in easy posture on the Nāga in the midst of the ocean which is enlivened by numerous aquatic animals. On the right side of Vishṇu we notice the quaint figure of Garuḍa while the group of diademed figures on his left, headed by a bearded personage, evidently represent the gods entreating him to protect the world against the demon-king Rāvaṇa. The whole scene as pictured on this Javanese temple recalls the famous passage in Kālidāsa's *Raghuvaṃśa* (xiii, 6), describing how Vishṇu, just awakened from his cosmic sleep, is approached by the gods.

It will be observed that in the Prambanan sculpture Vishṇu is not shown in his usual recumbent position, but is seated on the world-serpent. In India proper, too, we find in a few rare cases the god sitting in *lalitāsana* posture on the top of the coiled-up snake, its hood forming, as it were, a canopy over his head.[3] An early example is the colossal rock-cut image in the veranda of Cave III at Bādāmī.[4]

[1] J. Ph. Vogel, *Antiquities of Chambā State*. Part i (1911), p. 219; pl. xxxi.

[2] I. Groneman, *Tjandi Parambanan*, pp. 9 f., pl. xi. W. Stutterheim, *Rāma-legenden*, pp. 138 ff.; pl. 3.

[3] Krishna Sastri, *South Indian Images*, p. 52, calls this iconographical type 'Vaikuṇṭha-Nārāyaṇa'. Cf. his plates, figs. 33 and 38.

[4] J. Burgess, *A.S.R., Western India* (London, 1874), p. 22; plate. The cave contains an inscription dated Śaka 500 (A.D. 578).

PLATE XIX.

VISHṆU RECLINING ON ŚESHA (MĀMALLAPURAM).

[To face p. 194

VISHṆU SEATED ON ŚESHA (BĀDĀMI).

The world-serpent Śesha is also associated with the third incarnation of Vishṇu. At the beginning of the *kalpa* the supreme deity, assuming the semblance of a gigantic boar, dived into the depth of the primeval waters and brought the earth up from the abyss. In its original form this *avatāra* was a cosmogonic myth of a primitive type, as is evident from certain passages in the *Brāhmaṇas*, where it is briefly referred to.[1] In the second canto of the *Rāmāyaṇa* it is Brahmā who assumes the shape of a boar, but according to the versions found in the *Mahābhārata* and the *Purāṇas* the primeval boar is identified with Vishṇu.[2] Thus the gradual development of the myth can be clearly traced in Sanskrit literature.

The introduction of Śesha must be ascribed to a comparatively late date, as no mention of him is made in any of the versions of the myth referred to above. In technical works, however, dealing with iconography we find it stated that in plastic representations of the third *avatāra* it is the serpent-king Śesha who supports one of the feet of the boar while rising from the waters.[3] In this manner the primeval boar, Ādi-varāha, is connected with the primeval snake, Ādi-śesha.

The earliest known rendering of the Varāha *avatāra* in plastic art is the large rock-sculpture of Udayagiri (Gwalior State) which must belong to the Gupta period (*c.* A.D. 400).[4] The colossal figure of the boar-headed god, carrying the earth-goddess on his left shoulder, is shown treading with his left foot on the coils of the world-serpent. The upper portion of the Nāga consists of a human figure, with both hands joined in the attitude of reverence. It is surrounded by a large canopy-like hood of no less than thirteen snake-heads, seven in front and six in the intervals behind.

Two other early representations of this scene occur among the rock-carvings of Bādāmī (sixth century A.D.) and of Māmallapuram (seventh century A.D.).[5] Here we find Śesha in the same position. At Māmallapuram he wears a five-fold snake hood, but the lower part of his body is invisible, as he is shown rising from the waves of the ocean. At Bādāmi the serpent Śesha is accompanied by a Nāgī, presumably his consort. This is also the case with the Varāha from Baragaon, now in the Calcutta Museum.[6] (Plates XIX–XXI.)

Whereas the usual way of representing Vishṇu's third incarnation is that of a boar-headed human figure (mostly four-armed and provided with the emblems of this deity),

[1] *Taitt. br.*, i, 1, 3, 5, and *Śatap. br.*, xiv, 1, 2, 11 (*S.B.E.*, xliv, p. 451).

[2] *Rām.* (Bombay), *Ayodhyā-kāṇḍa*, cx, 4. *M.Bh.*, *Vana-p.*, cxlii, 28–62, and cclxxii, 49–55. ***Vishṇu-puārṇa***, iv (transl. Wilson, pp. 27 ff.). *Bhāgavata-purāṇa*, iii, ch. xiii.

[3] Gopinatha Rao, *Elements of Hindu Iconography*, vol. i, pp. 128 ff.

[4] Cunningham, *A.S.R.*, vol. x, pp. 48 f., pl. xviii. Burgess, *Ancient Monuments*, pl. 216–17.

[5] *A.S.R.* for 1910–11, p. 57, p. xxix, c. The proposed identification of the Nāga figure with the demon Hiraṇyāksha should be abandoned.

[6] Burgess, *Ancient Monuments*, pl. 234.

there are a few instances in which he is portrayed entirely in animal shape. The best known example is the colossal stone boar of Eraṇ (Sāgar district, C.P.), which, as recorded in an inscription, was fashioned in the first regnal year of the Hun king Toramāṇa. A similar figure, but much smaller in size, from Dudhai (Jhansi district, U.P.), is now preserved in the Lucknow Museum. In this sculpture the serpent Śesha, his hands joined in adoration, is visible between the feet of the divine boar.[1]

From our brief survey it will be seen that in sculptures portraying the Boar incarnation the serpent Śesha is rarely missing. His usual appearance is that of a snake combined with the upper half of a human figure, which is provided with the familiar Nāga hood. In most cases his two hands are raised in the gesture of *namaskāra*. Now it is curious that according to the *Vishṇudharmottara*[2] the figure, of Ādi-śesha should have four hands, two of which are to be in the *añjali* pose, while the remaining two should carry a plough (*hala*) and a mace (*musala*). Although in the sculptures known to us Śesha is always two-handed, the passage in question is of some interest. It should be remembered that the plough is the typical emblem of Baladeva (Balarāma, Balabhadra) who on that account is often designated by such names as Halāyudha or Haladhara ('Plough-bearer'). According to Amara he is also called Musalin or 'the Mace-bearer'. In describing his image, it is said by Varāhamihira[3]: "Baladeva must be made holding a plough in his hand, with eyes unsteady with drink, and wearing a single ear-ring. His complexion is fair like the conch-shell, the moon, or lotus-fibre."

The image of Baladeva is distinguished by yet another peculiarity: it is furnished with a snake-hood said to indicate his connexion with the world-serpent Śesha. Ancient Nāga images found in the neighbourhood of Mathurā are nowadays regularly worshipped under the name of Baldeo or Dauji ('the elder Brother'). Modern idols of this deity which are manufactured in such large numbers at Mathurā (vulgi Muttra) and Bindrāban, are nothing but imitations of ancient Nāga figures.[4]

Now it is well known that Baladeva, the elder brother of Kṛishṇa, is believed to be an incarnation of Śesha. In the *Ādi-parvan* of the Great Epic this divine origin is only briefly stated in the course of a passage relating to the birth of a great number of heroes from various deities.[5] In a more ample and picturesque manner we find Baladeva's identity

[1] *Memoirs, A.S.I.*, No. 11, pp. 12 f., pl. iii.

[2] Quoted by Gopinatha Rao, op. cit., vol. i, p. 134.

[3] *Brihat saṃhitā*, lviii, 36. Kern, *Verspr. Geschr.*, vol. ii, p. 48. An ancient image of Baladeva found at Tumain (Gwalior State) is reproduced *A.S.R.* for 1918–19, part i, pl. xiiia.

[4] *A.S.R.* for 1908–09, pp. 161 ff., pl. lvb.

[5] *M.Bh.*, *Ādi-p.*, lxv, 41. Cf. *Vishṇu-purāṇa* (transl. Wilson), p. 546.

PLATE XXI.

BOAR INCARNATION OF VISHṆU (BARAGAON).

[To face p. 196

with the world-serpent put forward when his death is described subsequent to the destruction of the Yādava race. "Kṛishṇa," so the text says,[1] "found his elder brother Balarāma seated alone in solitude and engaged in *yoga*. Then from his mouth there issued forth a large white Nāga—thousand-headed, red-mouthed, in size like unto the girth of a mountain, who, leaving his body, sped towards the great ocean. There Sāgara received him and so did the divine Nāgas and the pure and holy Rivers. Karkoṭaka, Vāsuki, and Takshaka, Pṛithuśravas, Aruṇa, and Kuñjara, Miśrin, Śaṅkha, Kumuda, Puṇḍarīka, and also the great Nāga Dhṛitarāshṭra, Hrāda, Krātha, Śihikaṇṭha, Ugratejas, and the two Nāgas Chakramanda and Atishaṇḍa, the excellent Nāga Durmukha and Ambarīsha and King Varuṇa himself, they all, while going to meet and welcome him, rejoiced and reverenced him with gifts of honour, water, and offerings."

There is a curious passage in the *Anuśāsana-parvan* [2] in which a certain 'Nāga' (the term 'Nāga' the commentator explains in the sense of 'elephant') Reṇuka is deputed by the gods to the elephants that carry the earth in order to consult them on the secrets of the Dharma. Now the world-elephants, instead of enlightening Reṇuka on the Dharma, tell him a *mantra* to be used in the worship of the Nāgas headed by Baladeva and of 'whatsoever mighty serpents be born from their race'. This *bali* or offering to the snakes must be brought on the eighth day of the waning moon of the month Kārtika and should be deposited after sunset on an ant-hill together with certain flowers,[3] and dark-coloured (*nīla*) garments and ointments. The object of this rite is to acquire such strength as Vishṇu showed himself to possess when he raised the earth, which will enable the world-elephants to fulfil their task without being troubled by fatigue. Besides which every man, to whatever caste he may belong, will reap great benefit by offering the *bali* for one year: all the powerful Nāgas in the three worlds will be his 'honoured guests' during a hundred years.

The passage in question is not only interesting in associating the world-elephants (*diṅ-nāga*) with the worship of the Nāgas, but also on account of the prominent place it assigns to Baladeva among the latter. Evidently his name has something to do with the special virtue attached to the rite, namely the imparting of strength (*bala*).

The chapter from the *Harivaṃsa* called 'Akrūra's vision of the Serpent-world' which we have rendered above,[4] gives an extensive description of Baladeva-Śesha, in which the superman and the supersnake are curiously blended. On the one hand, he is said to be

[1] *M.Bh., Mausala-p.*, iv, 13–17. *Vishṇu-p.* (transl. Wilson), p. 611.
[2] *M.Bh., Anuśāsana-p.*, cxxxii.
[3] The flowers are called *gajendra-kusuma*; can this be a synonym of *nāga-pushpa*?
[4] *Harivaṃśa*, lxxxiii (4388–4460). Cf. above, pp. 91 f.

thousand-headed ; on the other hand he is long-armed, holds a plough and a mace, and wears a dark-coloured garment, a single ear-ring and a gold-crested diadem.

In the *Rāmāyaṇa* [1] the serpent Śesha is said to have his seat in the East. When Sugrīva deputes the hosts of his monkeys to the four quarters in order to search for Sītā, he describes the wonderful seas and mountains which they will encounter in those far-off regions. In the East they will see such wonders as the Milk Ocean, the white mountain Ṛishabha, which stands in the midst of it, the terrible 'Mouth of the Mare', and on the north of it the Golden Mountain. " There, O monkeys, ye will behold the earth-carrying Serpent, white like the moon and having eyes wide as lotus-leaves, seated on the top of the mountain and worshipped by all gods—the thousand-headed god Ananta, clad in a dark blue garment. A three-headed golden palm-tree, the banner of that great being, placed on the top of the mountain, shineth together with its pedestal."

The poets of the classical period are never tired of bringing in Śesha ; they refer in particular to the white colour of his body and to the amazing splendour of the jewels shining in his thousand heads. In gnomic stanzas the world-carrying snake is quoted as the paragon of endurance.[2]

We shall see beneath that Anatnāg or Anantanāga, in Kashmir, as the name indicates (the modern name of the place is Islāmābād), is connected with the worship of the world-serpent Śesha.

Vāsuki, the King of Serpents

In one of the Books of Domestic Ritual [3] there is a description of rites to be performed in connexion with the building of a house (*vāstu-śamana*). It ends with the ten offerings (*bali*) to be given to the regents of the ten regions (*diśas*)—namely to Indra (East), Vāyu (S.E.), Yama (S.), Pitaras (S.W.), Varuṇa (W.), Mahārāja (N.W.), Soma (N.), Mahendra (N.E.), Vāsuki (downwards), and Brahmā (upwards in the sky, i.e. throwing the *bali* into the air).

A *Brāhmaṇa* text [4] also describes a *vāstu-praśamana,* i.e. a ceremony performed on laying the foundation or setting out the ground for a new house, a sacrifice performed on preparing a foundation or on entering a new mansion. Here, too, the deities of the quarters are mentioned in the same order, Vāsuki evidently being regarded as the genius presiding over the Nether World.

[1] *Rām., Kishkindhā-k.*, xl, 51–53. This and the following chapters (xl–xlvii) are considered by Jacobi (*Das Rāmāyaṇa*, p. 37) to be a later addition to the ancient epic. The *Mahābhārata* is certainly more original in locating Śesha in the Nether World (*Rasātala*).

[2] Böhtlingk, *Indische Sprüche*, Nos. 4,569 (= *Śāk.*, 101), 6,012 and 6,750.

[3] *Gobhila-gṛihyasūtra*, iv, 7, 27–41 : *S.B.E.*, vol. xxx, p. 123.

[4] *Sāmavidhāna-brāhmaṇa*, iii, 3, 5.

In the *Kauśika-sūtra*,[1] which is closely connected with the *Atharvaveda*, we find a *bali* prescribed for the protection of the house. It is to be offered in the different parts of the dwelling to various deities: as in the corners (*sraktishu*) to Vāsuki, Chitrasena, Chitraratha, Takshaka, and Upatakshaka.

We have little doubt that the Vāsuki mentioned in these rites as the presiding deity of the lower regions and as a guardian spirit of the house is identical with the serpent-king of epic literature.

The name Vāsuki has the appearance of a patronymic derived from Vasuka (cf. such names as Sātyaki and Māruti); the word *vasuka* as an appellative indicates various plants, but it could also be abbreviated from some royal name (e.g. Vasudeva). The serpent-king Vāsuki, as far as we know, is never designated by any other name.

In the catalogues of the principal Nāgas found in the *Mahābhārata* and in the *Purāṇas* Vāsuki usually figures second, immediately after Śesha. But as Śesha, the first-born among snakes, is absorbed by his ponderous duty of carrying either the earth or the supreme deity, it is Vāsuki who acts as the real sovereign ruler of the serpent tribe whenever an active leadership is required. It is Vāsuki who, in the *Ādi-parvan*, presides over the communings of the Nāgas when they are assembled to discuss means of escape from the cruel fate awaiting them. Vāsuki also bestows his sister Jaratkāru in marriage upon the like-named anchorite, so that a saviour of his people may be born from their union.

When the final struggle between Arjuna and Karṇa is about to take place, it is said that all divine beings take the side of one or other of the two heroes.[2] "Vāsuki," the poet, says, "and Chitrasena, Takshaka as well as Maṇika and all serpents that are the sons of Kadrū with their offspring and the poisonous Nāgas, the Airāvatas, the Sauraseyas and the Vaiśāleyas, all these snakes were on the side of Arjuna, and the inferior snakes on that of Karṇa." It is somewhat surprising to find Vāsuki and Takshaka mentioned here as allies of Arjuna, as the Pāṇḍava had a feud with the latter and had carried off the former's sister.[3]

We have seen above that in the ancient myth of the Churning of the Nectar (*amṛita-manthana*) Śesha is introduced at the request of the gods and uproots Mount Mandara which they wish to use as their churning-stick. The snake Vāsuki they made their churning-rope, and in this wise they churned the Ocean. Now after a thousand years the poison-spitting heads of the serpent bit the rocks with their fangs. A terrible fire-like poison called *hālāhala*, came forth, and threatened to burn up the whole world with gods, demons, and

[1] *Kauśika-sūtra*, 74, 8.

[2] *M.Bh.*, *Karṇa-p.*, lxxxvii, 43–45. The text has Saurabheyā.

[3] *M.Bh.*, *Virāta-p.*, ii, 14; the commentary identifies this sister of Vāsuki with Ulūpī.

men. Then the gods eager for protection repaired to Śiva and lauded him, saying: "Save us, save us." Whereupon Śiva swallowed that terrible poison *hālāhala* as if it had been nectar.[1]

This quaint and curious myth lent itself admirably to plastic representation, one of the earliest renderings being that found on one of the caves of Udayagiri (Gwalior State).[2] As later instances may be quoted a sculpture from Gaṛhwā (Allahābād district) perhaps of the tenth century,[3] and a wood-carved panel decorating the window of the temple of Mirkulā Devī in Chambā State. Up to the present day it occurs in minor decorative art.[4]

"The subject," Mr. Havell says, "is a favourite one in Indian art, but it was never treated on so magnificent a scale or with so splendid an effect as in the bas-reliefs which adorn the colonnades of the great temple of Angkor Vat, in Cambodia, built about the twelfth century by Sūrya-varman II, one of the last of the Hindu kings who ruled over the Indian colony in the Further East." [5]

The *motif* of the great Nāga carried by gods and demons has, moreover, found a remarkable and highly effective employment in the Khmer art of Cambodia. At Angkor Thom the approach of the Gate of Victory is guarded outside by two gigantic snakes placed on both sides of the road leading up to the gate. Each of these two monsters is held by a long row of fifty-four figures, measuring more than 8 feet in height (2 m. 50). It will be noticed that the total number of these stone giants, meant no doubt for the gods and the demons, represents the auspicious figure a hundred-and-eight. On the far end of the gate the enormous serpent raises aloft its seven-fold head, threatening, as it were, all who approach the precincts of the royal enclosure.[6] (Plate XXII.)

In the *Nāgarakṛitāgama* (65, 4),[7] the eulogy in old Javanese composed in honour of King Hayam Wuruk of Majapahit by his court-poet Prapañcha in the year A.D. 1365, we read that the king on the occasion of a *Śrāddha* presented a wonderful offering, namely 'the Mount Mandara being turned round by the gods and the demons'. A piece of sculpture has been recovered which not only represents the subject in question, but has been identified with the festive offering of the Javanese king. From an artistic point of view it does not perhaps deserve the praise bestowed upon it by the royal poet, but it clearly shows every

[1] *Rām.* (Bombay), *Bāla-k.*, xlv, 18–26.
[2] Burgess, *Ancient Monts.*, pl. 215.
[3] Burgess, op. cit., pl. 245.
[4] H. H. Juynboll, *Schnitzarbeit in Sandelholz aus Britisch-Indien. Ostasiatische Zeitschrift*, vol. ii, pp. 445 ff.
[5] E. B. Havell, *The Ideals of Indian Art*, pp. 64 f., pl. iv.
[6] H. Marchal and Oscar Miestchaninoff, *Sculptures khmères*, pls. ix and x.
[7] *Nāgarakṛitāgama*, ed. Kern, p. 155. *Cf. Not. Bat. Gen.*, vol. xxxi, pp. 112 f., and *Tschr. Bat. Gen.*, vol. lviii, p. 441.

Great Nāga of Angkor Thom (Cambodia)

[To face p. 200

detail: the divine tortoise supporting the mountain and the serpent Vāsuki wound round it.

Vāsuki, as we noticed above, is regarded as the sovereign liege of the Nāgas, and, consequently he is often extolled as the lord and ruler of their city, Bhogavatī. Although the Nāga-loka or 'World of Snakes' is usually located in the subterranean regions, the serpent city is sometimes said to be situated in the South. In the *Rāmāyaṇa*,[1] when Sugrīva deputes an army of monkeys under Hanumant to the South, he says: "There is the mountain, named Kuñjara, lovely to the eyes and to the heart, where the dwelling of Agastya has been fashioned by Viśvakarman. There is his divine house (*śaraṇa*) of gold adorned with various gems, a *yojana* wide and ten *yojanas* high. There is the town, named Bhogavatī, the abode of snakes, with large roads, invincible, guarded on all sides by terrible serpents, sharp-fanged and great of poison, wherein dwelleth Vāsuki the very dreadful king of snakes."

In the *Mahābhārata* [2] also there is a description of the southern region: it is the abode of the deceased ancestors (*pitaras*), the place where Rāvaṇa performed asceticism to obtain immortality, and where Garuḍa ate the gigantic elephant and tortoise. "Here also is the town named Bhogavatī, ruled by Vāsuki, by the Nāga Takshaka and by Airāvata."

The two passages quoted clearly bear a mythological character, although it is worthy of note that in the *Rāmāyaṇa* Bhogavatī seems to be associated with the dwelling of Agastya. It may be remembered that up to the present day that saint is believed to dwell on the mountain-peak in the southern portion of the Western Ghāṭs named after him, Agastya-malai.[3]

There are, however, other passages in the Great Epic, where Bhogavatī is not relegated to a remote region in the South, but is mentioned as a place of pilgrimage within reach of the faithful. Where Baladeva's visit to a great number of *tīrthas* is narrated, it is said that he also came to a sacred place, named Nāga-dhanvan, which must have been somewhere in the vicinity of the river Sarasvatī.[4] "Where is the abode of Vāsuki, the serpent-king of great splendour, which is beset by many serpents. Here the gods gathered, and according to the rule, annointed Vāsuki, the best of snakes, as king of all serpents. At that place there is no danger from snakes."

It is very curious that elsewhere [5] the Bhogavatī is the name of a river which, if we are to believe the commentator, is identical with the Sarasvatī, the sacred river of Kurukshetra. This would take us to the same tract, the country near the Dvaita-vana,

[1] *Rām.*, *Kishkindhā-kāṇḍa*, xli, 34–8.
[2] *M.Bh.*, *Udyoga-p.*, cix, 19.
[3] *Imperial Gazetteer*, vol. v, p. 71.
[4] *M.Bh.*, *Śalya-p.*, xxxvii, 29–33.
[5] *M.Bh.*, *Vana-p.*, xxiv, 20.

where evidently Nāga-dhanvan is to be sought. Are we, then, to assume that Bhogavatī, 'the Winding One' was originally the appellation of a real river ? If such were the case, it would not be difficult to explain how the name came to be transferred to the mythical realm of the winding ones, i.e. the snakes.

In the course of that lengthy enumeration of places of pilgrimage (*Tīrthayātrā-parvan*)[1] which is inserted in the third canto of the Great Epic, we find Bhogavatī again mentioned as a definite *tīrtha* consecrated to Vāsuki. But here it is located at Prayāga, the very sacred place where the holy rivers Gangā and Yamunā meet. It is of interest to note that down to modern times the spot has remained associated with the worship of the great serpent-king.

Whereas Śesha is closely connected with Vishṇu, we find Vāsuki associated with Śiva : the serpent-king is supposed to be slung round that god's neck. " Although one attain to the rank of the great," a proverb says,[2] " one will reap the fruit of one's work (*karman*) : Vāsuki, though attached to the neck of Śiva, enjoys nothing but air."

In the fairy tales Vāsuki generally figures as the thousand-headed monarch of the serpents. In the legend of Jīmūtavāhana it is Vāsuki who makes a pact with Garuḍa and promises to send him daily one Nāga for his food. The high-minded hero of the tale, hearing this, exclaims : " Why could not Vāsuki, having a thousand mouths, speak with only one mouth ? 'Eat me first, O Tārksha !' "[3]

In the *Kathāsaritsāgara*[4] we hear of a festival (*yātrotsava*) in honour of Vāsuki which was celebrated in the country of Lāṭa. The poet speaks of the great crowds that had assembled on the occasion, the temple with the idol covered with wreaths, and the lotus-studded lake sacred to the serpent-king, which was at some distance from the temple and was overhung with trees. It is impossible to determine whether such a snake temple really existed in Lāṭa, or Lāṛ (Khandesh-Gujarāt), but up to the present time Vāsuki is worshipped in this part of India.

Vāsuki has retained an important place in Indian folk-lore, as is proved by the well known legend of the Iron Pillar of Delhi. The foot of the pillar was believed to rest on the head of the serpent-king and thereby to secure the stability of the kingdom. Now, when the incredulous king had the pillar dug up, its base was found wet with the blood of the serpent Vāsuki, and it could never again be firmly fixed, and shortly afterwards the Hindu kingdom of Delhi was conquered by the Muslims.[5]

[1] *M.Bh.*, *Vana-p.*, lxxxv, 86.
[2] *Hitopadeśa*, ed. Schlegel, i, 142.
[3] *Kathās.*, xc, 108. Likewise in the *Nāgānanda*, act iv. Cf. above, pp. 181 f.
[4] *Kathās.*, lxxiv, 208–12 ; Tawney's transl. vol. ii, p. 225.
[5] Cunningham, *A.S.R.*, vol. i, pp. 171 ff., and vol. xx, pp. 139 ff. W. Crooke, *Popular Religion*, vol. ii, p. 132. *Jl. Panjāb Hist. Society*, vol. ix, pp. 75 f.

In the valleys of the Western Himālaya, as we shall see in our last chapter, Vāsuki, under the name of Bāsak Nāg, not only lives up to the present day in many a popular legend, but is also extensively worshipped. The same is the case in Nepal.

The cult of Vāsuki has spread far beyond the borders of India proper. In the island of Bali he is known as Basúki or Nága Basáki, and is reckoned among the attendants of the sea-god Baruna (Sanskrit Varuṇa). The Balinese represent Basúki as a crowned giant-snake resting on the waves. He may be observed also in the nocturnal sky, while travelling from the mountain-lakes of Bali to those of the neighbouring island of Lombok or vice versa. The temple of Besaki, which is regarded as the most sacred shrine of Bali, is the centre of his worship.

The inhabitants of Java, too, who still know the serpent-king Bĕsuki by literary tradition, must once have taken part in his worship before being converted to Islām. The town of Bĕsuki situated on the northern coast of eastern Java seems still to retain the memory of his cult.

Takshaka

We have seen that in the cycle of sagas grouped round the Serpent Sacrifice of king Janamejaya it is Takshaka who is the chief Nāga hero. He is the most typical snake-demon of the epic—poisonous, fierce, and relentless. The name Takshaka, which as an appellative means 'a wood-cutter or a carpenter', is difficult to account for. As far as I know, no explanation of it is offered. At any rate, it seems to point to its bearer being a godling produced by and living in the popular mind. "His name," Professor Washburn Hopkins says,[1] "and his especial glory show or indicate a historical character." So positive an assertion seems somewhat bold. If Hopkins is right in claiming a historical origin for the multiform dragon of the *Ādi-parvan*, that origin surely must be relegated to a very remote antiquity. Takshaka is one of the few Nāgas whose name is mentioned in Vedic literature. Both in the *Atharva-veda* and in various *Sūtras* he is called 'Takshaka Vaiśāleya'. This second appellative, which appears to be forgotten in post-Vedic times,[2] may be either a patronymic meaning 'the son of Viśāla' or a metronymic meaning 'the son of Viśālā'. A river Viśālā is mentioned in the epics.

Three hymns of the *Atharva-veda* (iv, 6; v, 3; x, 4), according to the *Kauśika-sūtra*, are intended to be addressed to Takshaka. In one hymn (viii, 10) he is mentioned by name. In this hymn the cosmic principle Virāj is successively associated with various classes of

[1] *Epic Mythology*, p. 29.

[2] In *Harivaṃśa*, verse 9,501, Takshaka receives the epithet *viśālāksha* 'wide-eyed', perhaps a reminiscence of the ancient patronymic (or metronymic) *Vaiśāleya*. The term Vaiśāleya in the plural occurs in the *Karṇa-p.*, ch. lxxxvii, 44, to indicate a tribe of Nāgas.

beings: gods, *asuras*, men, Manes (*pitaras*), tree-sprites (*vanaspati*), the seven seers, Gandharvas and Apsarases, Yakshas (called 'other folks') and Snakes (*sarpa*). In each case the two chief representatives of the group are mentioned as the calf (*vatsa*) and the milker of Virāj, which evidently is conceived as a cow. The process of milking is performed with a vessel varying in material according to the peculiar class of beings which are supposed to use it. The substance produced in each case by the milking operation varies likewise. Now in the case of the Snakes (*sarpa*) the 'calf' is Takshaka Vaiśāleya, the 'milker' is Dhṛitarāshṭra Airāvata, the vessel used is the 'gourd-vessel' (*alābu-pātra*), and the substance produced is poison.[1]

The ancient myth which in the *Atharva* is presented in such a schematic and abstruse form is narrated at great length in the *Harivaṃśa* and in some *Purāṇas*.[2] Here it is the story of the culture hero and first king, Pṛithu the son of Vena (after whom the Earth was named Pṛithivī !) who, after making the earth even and habitable, forced her to yield nourishment to all kinds of creatures. In this passage too Takshaka and Dhṛitarāshṭra Airāvata figure as the chief representatives of the Nāgas, as the divine Snakes are called here.

We have seen that in the *Kauśika-sūtra* (lxxiv, 8) a *bali* is described for the protection of the house and to be offered to various deities, including not only Takshaka but also his double, named Upatakshaka. In the 'Institutes of Vishṇu' (lxvii, 5), too, Takshaka and Upataksha are mentioned as recipients of a food-offering which the Aryan householder is to present to a great number of deities.[3] This second Takshaka (recalling the Nāga pair Nanda and Upananda) does not, as far as we know, make his appearance in any myth or legend.

In one of the 'Books of Domestic Ritual'[4] Takshaka Vaiśāleya together with another demon, named Śveta ('the White One') Vaidarvya, is invoked in connexion with the ritual to be observed at the *Pratyavarohaṇa*, i.e. the concluding ceremony of the rites devoted to the Serpents.

In the *Rāmāyaṇa*[5] it is repeatedly stated that Rāvaṇa has vanquished Vāsuki, conquered his town Bhogavatī, and carried off the wife of Takshaka. But no particulars are given and not even the name of Takshaka's consort is mentioned. The incident is only brought in as one of the many exploits of the great ruler of Laṅkā. It shows at any rate the

[1] *A.V.*, viii, 10, 29, Whitney's transl., vol. ii, p. 515.

[2] *Hariv.*, 375–7. The same myth occurs in *M.Bh.*, *Droṇa-p.*, lxix, 10–27, and *Bhāg-p.*, iv 18. It is briefly referred to in the *Vishṇu-p.* (transl. Wilson, 1840, p. 104). According to Wilson it is found also in the *Matsya-*, *Brahma-*, and *Padma-purāṇa*.

[3] *S.B.E.*, vol. vii, p. 212.

[4] *Śānkh. Gṛihya-s*, iv, 18, 1 ; *S.B.E.*, vol. xxix, p. 131.

[5] *Rām.*, *Āraṇya-k.*, xxxii, 13–14 ; *Yuddha-k.*, vii, 3, 9 ; *Uttara-k.*, xxiii, 4–5.

PLATE XXIII.

SHRINE AT PANATARAN (JAVA).

[To face p. 234

important place held by Takshaka among the Nāga kings. In one passage where Rāvaṇa's victory over the Nāgas is related, four chiefs of the Serpent tribe are enumerated, namely Vāsuki, Takshaka, Śaṅkha, and Jaṭin. The town Bhogavatī is here clearly located in the Nether World (*Rasātala*) in the womb of the Ocean.

Takshaka's name also occurs in the ancient hymn to the Nāgas, which, as we have seen,[1] is preserved in the *Paushya-parvan.* There it is said that his dwelling-place was formerly in Kurukshetra and in the Khāṇḍava Forest, and that he and his son Aśvasena lived in Kurukshetra along the river Ikshumatī. This is in close agreement with what we read in the narrative of the conflagration of the Khāṇḍava-vana. It was the abode of Takshaka, 'the friend of Indra', and on that account the latter guarded the forest and prevented Agni from burning it down. But during the absence of Takshaka, who had gone to Kurukshetra, the Fire-god at last succeeded with the assistance of Arjuna and Kṛishṇa. It was with the greatest difficulty that Takshaka's son, Aśvasena, escaped.

From these data we may perhaps conclude that the original home of the cult of Takshaka was Indraprastha, from where it was carried northward to Kurukshetra. It is, on the other hand, tempting to connect the name of the famous city of Takshaśilā—the Taxila of the Greeks—with the serpent-demon and to explain it as 'the Rock of Taksha(ka)'.[2] Here the serpent sacrifice of King Janameya is supposed to have taken place. But in the course of excavations carried out by Sir John Marshall on the site of Taxila no evidence of local snake worship has come to light.

Of the worship of Takshaka in Kashmīr we shall speak in the next chapter; it is vouched for by the Mahābhārata and by the local poets Bilhaṇa and Kalhaṇa.

The last-mentioned author, in his famous chronicle,[3] gives yet another reference, which, however brief, is of some interest. He relates that the physician Īśānachandra, the brother-in-law of Chaṅkuṇa (the Tuḫkhāra minister of king Lalitāditya), built a *vihāra*, 'after having obtained wealth through the favour of Takshaka.' The popular belief that serpents are guardians and givers of wealth is common enough not only in India but all over the world. We have repeatedly had occasion to refer to it in these pages. But the circumstance that in the present instance the recipient was a physician is significant; it reminds us of a modern folk-tale in which a certain witch through the favour of Takshaka obtains the power to cure diseases and especially snake-bite.[4]

[1] Cf. above, p. 62.

[2] S. Lefmann, *Geschichte des alten Indiens*, p. 176, footnote. According to *Rām.*, *Uttara-k.*, ch. ci, ii, the city of Takshaśilā was named after its founder, Taksha the son of Rāma's half-brother Bharata.

[3] *Rājat.*, iv, 216; Stein's transl. vol. i, p. 144.

[4] W. Crooke, *The Tribes and Castes of the N.W. Prov. and Oudh*, vol. ii, pp. 170 f. Cf. also the same author's *Popular Religion*, vol. ii, p. 285.

May we infer from these data that Takshaka was supposed to procure antidotes against snake-bite and thus came to be looked upon as a patron of the medical profession? The same Takshaka is regarded as the most poisonous of all Nāgas, as is evident from the legends which we have reproduced from the *Mahābhārata*. In the same epic the following is said of Bhīshma, the grim old warrior of the Kauravas: "Like the terrible great Nāga, Takshaka, swelling with poison, even so is the powerful Bhīshma in battle, wrathful and sharp of weapons." [1]

In later literature Takshaka retains his evil reputation. The great physician Suśruta,[2] in speaking of a certain drug called Tārkshya, says that it will kill the poison even of Takshaka. And in the *Hitopadeśa* [3] we meet with a stanza which says: 'If one were submerged in the ocean, or fallen from a mountain, or bitten even by Takshaka, the duration of one's life being fixed, the vital spots are protected.'

Our account of Takshaka would be incomplete without noting the curious fact that down to the present day the serpent-king of the *Paushya-parvan* possesses a shrine in Central India where he is worshipped under the name of Takshakeśvara or Tākhā-jī; and curiously enough he shares the worship of the country folk with Dhanvantari, the Indian Aesculapius. The shrine in question stands on a most romantic spot not far from the village of Navali or Naoli, which is situated on the table-land at the foot of which Bhanpura lies. It now forms part of the territory of Indore and in ancient times must have belonged to the Mālava country.

The following description we quote from Colonel Tod,[4] who visited the place in December, 1821: "In the evening I went to visit *Tākāji-ca-coond*, or 'fountain of the snake-king'. It is about two miles east of Nāoli; the road through a jungle over the flat highland or Pathar presents no indication of the object of research, until you suddenly find yourselves on the brink of a precipice nearly two hundred feet in depth, crowded with noble trees, on which the knotted *koroo* was again conspicuous. The descent to this glen was over masses of rock; and about half-way down, on a small platform, are two shrines; one containing the statue of *Takshac*, the snake-king; the other of *Dhunantra* [i.e. Dhanvantari], the physician, who was produced at the 'churning of the ocean'. The *coond*, or fountain, at the southern extremity of the abyss, is about two hundred yards in circumference, and termed *athāg*, or 'unfathomable', according to my guide; and if

[1] *M.Bh.*, *Bhīshma-p.*, cvii, 15.

[2] Suśruta, vol. ii, p. 275, l. 21.

[3] *Hitop.* (ed. Schlegel and Lassen), p. 47 verse 14.

[4] James Tod, *Annals and Antiquities of Rajasthan* (1829–32), vol. ii, p. 718. For a more recent description we refer to the *Progress Report Archl. Survey, W.C.*, for 1919–20, p. 88, pl. xiii.

we may judge from its dark sea-green lustre, it must be of considerable depth. It is filled by a cascade of full one hundred feet perpendicular height, under which is a stone seat, sacred to the genius of the spot. At the west side issues a rivulet, called the *Takhaili*, or serpentine, which, after pursuing a winding course for many miles, some hundred feet below the surface of the Pathar, washes the eastern face of Hinglazgurh, and ultimately joins the Amjār."

Tod's account is accompanied by a plate reproduced from a drawing by his native artist, Ghassi, which shows the stone image of Takshaka standing with his seven-fold snake-hood and the coils of the snake's body being visible on both sides. He has two arms, but the objects held in his hands are not clear : they are perhaps a cup and a fruit. He is accompanied by two attendants of much smaller size, apparently male and female, the former holding a snake in his right hand.

Dhṛitarāshṭra Airāvata (Elāpattra)

Among the great Nāga-rājas none has had a more curious career than Dhṛitarāshṭra Airāvata. As in the case of Takshaka Vaiśāleya, it is impossible to decide whether the second appellation is to be regarded as a patronymic or a metronymic, in other words, whether he is the son of Irāvant or the son of Irāvatī. If we compare it with a serpent name like Arbuda Kādraveya,[1] we feel inclined to decide in favour of the metronymic, and to associate Dhṛitarāshṭra with the river Irāvatī, the modern Rāvī. But apart from this uncertain linguistic evidence, there is nothing in literary tradition to justify such an assumption.

We have seen that in a hymn of the *Atharva-veda* (viii, 10) Takshaka Vaiśāleya and Dhṛitarāshṭra Airāvata are mentioned side by side as the chief representatives of the Serpent race.[2] In the remarkable ' Hymn to the Nāgas ' which occurs in the *Paushya-parvan* we also find the names of both these Nāga kings ; but in this ancient *stotra* it is evidently Dhṛitarāshṭra who is considered to be the sovereign lord of all Nāgas. In another undoubtedly early passage in the Great Epic [3] the hero Arjuna is lauded by his eldest brother Yudhishṭhira : it is said that he is the foremost among all archers and, in order to emphasize his pre-eminence, a number of beings are enumerated who are first of their kind. Thus Dhṛitarāshṭra is stated to be the best of the Nāgas, and Airāvaṇa the best among elephants.

Now it is worthy of note that, notwithstanding this lofty rank assigned to Dhṛitarāshṭra Airāvata, he takes no leading nor even an active part in any of the numerous

[1] *Aitareya-Brāhmaṇa*, vi, 1. *Kaushītaki-Brahmaṇa*, xxix, 1.
[2] Above, pp. 203 f.
[3] *M.Bh.*, *Virāṭa-p.*, ch. ii, 17.

Nāga stories collected in the *Mahābhārata*. His name occurs in lists of Nāgas, but whenever it is mentioned elsewhere in the Great Epic he seems to be regarded as a remote ancestor of the Nāga race. The Nāgī Ulūpī announces herself to Arjuna as a daughter of the Serpent Kauravya who is ' born from the race of Airāvata '. The same expression is applied to the young Nāga prince Sumukha, whom Mātali chooses for a son-in-law. In the metrical version of the story of Uttaṅka (*Āśvamedhika-parvan*) it is not Takshaka who steals the queen's ear-rings, but a certain snake ' born from the race of Airāvata '. It will be noticed that preferably the second name, Airāvata, is used. The result was that the connexion between the names Dhṛitarāshṭra and Airāvata is lost sight of, and in the lists of Nāgas we find them both separately as if they indicated two different beings of the Nāga race.[1] Indeed, the ancient Serpent monarch is entered not twice, but three times in the catalogues of Nāgas which are found in the Great Epic. They contain not only the name Dhṛitarāshṭra and the patronymic (or metronymic) Airāvata, but also the name Elāpattra which has been recognized as a Prākrit form of the Sanskrit Airāvata. The compilers of the *Mahābhārata* obviously were not aware of the identity of both names. Not only do we find Elāpattra mentioned as a separate Nāga in the lists, but he is also introduced in the episode of the assemblage held by the Nāgas, after the Serpent mother Kadrū had pronounced her curse. It is very curious that Elāpattra figures here as the wise (and, no doubt, old) Nāga who gives the good and decisive advice and who, moreover, knows what will happen in the future. For the rest, the Nāga Elāpattra does not play a prominent part in Brahmanical tradition ; in Buddhist tradition, on the contrary, he enters upon a new and remarkable career.

It is clear that the form Elāpatra or Elāpattra cannot be a regular Prākrit derivate from the Sanskrit Airāvata, but must be an example of popular etymology. The word *elā-pattra* as an appellative means ' cardamum leaf ' ; in a Buddhist legend which we have rendered above an attempt is made to account for that name. There it is said that Elāpattra had been born as a Nāga because in a former birth he had destroyed an *elā* tree ! The legend in question further relates that the Nāga Elāpattra came from Taxila to the Deerpark of Benares to pay reverence to the Buddha. In connexion with this legend we have drawn attention to a Bharhut sculpture provided with an inscription in which the Nāgarāja is called ' Erapata ', an intermediate form between ' Airāvata ' and ' Elāpattra '.[2]

The Chinese pilgrim Hiuen Tsiang mentions Elāpattra among the three great Nāga kings who obtained a share of the Buddha's relics. Moreover, on his way to Taxila he saw

[1] In the *Harivaṃśa* we have two lists of Nāgas, the one (227–30) headed by Śesha, Vāsuki, Takshaka and Airāvata, the other by Śesha, Vāsuki, Takshaka and Elāpatra.

[2] The name Elāpattra (with *l* !) must be a Māgadhī form.

the very place which was supposed to be the abode of that Nāga. "North-west of the capital (Taxila) about 70 *li*," he says,[1] "is the tank of the Nāgarāja Elāpattra; it is about 100 paces round, the waters are pure and sweet. Lotus-flowers of various colours, which reflect different tints in their common beauty, garnish the surface. This Nāga was a Bhikshu who, anciently, in the time of Kāśyapa Buddha, destroyed an *elāpattra* tree. Hence, at the present time, when the people of that country ask for rain or fine weather, they must go with the Shamans to the side of the tank, and then cracking their fingers, after praying for the desired object, they obtain it."

Sir Alexander Cunningham[2] has recognized the sacred tank of Elāpattra in a small square reservoir of clear water not far from Hasan Abdāl, about 10 miles to the north-west of Shāh Dheri, the site of the ancient city of Takshaśilā. Although no longer associated with the Nāga king, the tank is still held in reverence both by the Muslims and the Sikhs, who have each their own legend to account for the sanctity of the place. The shrine of the Muhammadan saint is described as being situated on the peak of a lofty and precipitous hill, about one mile east of the town. "At the north-west foot of this hill numerous springs of pure limpid water gush out of the ground, and form a clear and rapid rill which falls into the Wah rivulet, about half a mile to the west of the town."

When Hiuen Tsiang after his visit to the Nāga tank pursued his way towards Taxila, he passed through a gorge between two mountains, where he noticed a *stūpa* which was ascribed to the emperor Aśoka. It marked the spot where Śākyamuni had delivered a prophecy that at the time of the future Saviour, Maitreya, there would appear four great treasures, and that one would come to light in the territory of Taxila. "According to tradition," the pilgrim adds, "we find that whenever there is an earthquake, and the mountains on every side are shaken, all round this sacred spot to the distance of 100 paces there is perfect stillness. If men are so foolish as to attempt to dig into the place, the earth shakes, and the men are thrown down headlong."

The passage which we have quoted from Hiuen Tsiang is of very great interest. We see from it, in the first place, that Elāpattra was worshipped as a regent of the weather and a giver of rain. We know from other sources that this was and still is considered the most important function of the Nāgas in general; but it is a curious circumstance testified by the Chinese pilgrim that in the present case Buddhist monks (*śramaṇas*) acted as agents to obtain the good offices of the serpent-demon.

Another point of decided importance is that Hiuen Tsiang's account enlightens us regarding the locality where Elāpattra was believed to abide. The tank of the Nāga was

[1] *Si-yu-ki* (transl. Beal), vol. i, p. 137. Watters, *Travels*, vol. viii, pp. 241 ff.
[2] *A.S.R.*, vol. ii, pp. 135 ff.

situated some distance to the north-west of Takshaśilā, apparently not far from the high road leading from that town to Udakabhāṇḍa, the place where the Indus was crossed. In this connexion we wish to call attention to a stanza found in the *Divyāvadāna*.[1] In the course of a prophecy regarding the state of the world in the days of the future Buddha Maitreya, it is said that there will be four Mahārājas connected with four great treasures (*chatur-mahānidhi-sthāḥ*) and then a verse is quoted as containing the names of those four future monarchs, namely Piṅgala in Kaliṅga, Pāṇḍuka at Mithilā, Elāpattra in Gandhāra, and Śaṅkha at Benares. Now there is good reason to assume that the stanza introduced here by the Buddhist author was not originally meant to give the names of future kings, but enumerated four prominent Nāga-rājas and the places where they were worshipped. On the strength of the testimony of Hiuen Tsiang we can say this with certainty as far as Elāpattra is concerned. In the sequel we shall be able to prove the same with regard to Śaṅkha, the Nāga of Benares. The name Piṅgala occurs in the list of Nāgas contained in the *Mahābhārata*, Ādi-parvan, xxxv.

It reminds us of the ancient conception of four Nāga kings presiding over the four quarters to which we have called attention in our 'Introduction'. In that connexion we have quoted a snake-charm preserved in the Pali Canon which speaks of four tribes of serpent-kings (*ahirāja-kulāni*).[2] The first two are called Virūpakkha and Erāpatha ; this can be nothing but another Prākrit form of the Sanskrit Airāvata, likewise due to popular etymology.

There exists yet another popular idea which likewise must belong to a primitive sphere of thought, and is very often referred to in epic and classical literature. It is that of four (later, eight) gigantic elephants supporting the world and guarding the quarters.[3] Their names vary a good deal, but are partly Nāga names (Vāmana, Virūpāksha, Kumuda, Mahāpadma, Puṇḍarīka, Pushpadanta, Śaṅkha. Usually the chief of these 'world-elephants' (*dig-gaja, diṅ-nāga*) is said to be Airāvata, the guardian of the eastern region and at the same time the riding animal of Indra. Thus we see the ancient serpent-demon re-appear in a new dignity.

According to Indian mythology Airāvata (or Airāvaṇa), the four-tusked riding-elephant of Indra, was one of the wonderful objects produced at the Churning of the Ocean. This much is certain that the warlike god of the Ṛigvedic hymns is represented as using a chariot, not an elephant. Whether the idea of the four elephants who carry the earth and

[1] *Divyāvadāna*, p. 61. The MSS. have the form 'Elapatras'.

[2] See above, p. 10.

[3] Cf. E. W. Hopkins, *Epic mythology*, pp. 17 f. In the *Rām.*, *Bāla-k.*, ch. xl, 12–43, the four "space-elephants" are described as carrying the earth. They are here located in the Nether World (*rasātala*).

guard the quarters is later than that of the four dragons discharging the last-mentioned office, it is impossible to decide with certainty. Both these notions seem primitive. But we know at least that the four sky-dragons appear in Indian literature at a considerably earlier date than the four sky-elephants. There is, therefore, some reason to assume that the former are the original, and that the elephants represent a later development. If this assumption were correct, it would explain at the same time how the Sanskrit word *nāga* has come to be used in the sense of ' an elephant '. It can be imagined that from the sky-dragons it was in the first instance transferred to the sky-elephants, and subsequently applied to the elephant in general.

In this connexion it is of interest that in Hiuen Tsiang's account the tank of Elāpattra near Taxila appears to be associated with the popular belief regarding ' the four Treasures '. The Chinese pilgrim, it is true, does not clearly state that Elāpattra was the guardian spirit of the treasure of Taxila. But we have seen that in the *Divyāvadana* the four supposed *mahārājas* of the future (in reality four Nāgas), Piṅgala, Pāṇḍuka, Elāpattra, and Śaṅkha, are definitely connected with the four great treasures. These treasures, which have much haunted the imagination of ancient India, are mentioned elsewhere in Buddhist literature. In the *Nidānakathā* [1] it is said that they came into existence at the time when Śākyamuni was born: in other words, they belonged to 'the Seven Connatal Ones'. The *Mahāvastu*,[2] in the course of a passage which in the sequel we shall have occasion to discuss more fully, mentions not only their names but also the places where they were believed to lie hidden. " The four great Treasures," that text says, " are Saṅkha at Benares, Paduma at Mithila, Piṅgala in Kaliṅga, and Elāpatra at Taxila." It will be observed that the names of the treasures are identical with those of the Nāgas mentioned in the stanza of the *Divyāvadāna*, and we may safely conclude that these Nāgas were the guardians of the treasures. The only discrepancy between the *Divyāvadāna* and the *Mahāvastu* is that, instead of Pāṇḍuka, the latter text has Paduma (Sanskrit Padma). This we may suppose to be correct, for in Brahmanical tradition, too, we find Padma and Śaṅkha as the names of the chief treasures and of their guardians.[3] For our present subject the main point of interest is that we find the ancient Nāgarāja Airāvata, disguised under his name of Elāpattra, in the function of guardian spirit of one of the four great Treasures, which, moreover, has been designated after him.

[1] *Nidānakathā*, p. 54, ll. 7–9; *Birth Stories*, p. 68 (footnote). The *Lalita-vistara* and *Mahāvastu* speak of five thousand treasures.

[2] *Mahāvastu*, vol. iii, p. 383, ll. 18–20.

[3] In the description of the court of Kubera (*M.Bh.*, *Sabhā-p.*, ch. x, 39). The *Amara-kośa* also mentions Padma and Śaṅkha as the chief treasures. Cf. also *Rājat.*, i, 30. *Hariv.*, 2,467.

In Buddhist literature the Nāgarāja Airāvata also survives under his original name of Dhṛitarāshṭra in its Pali form Dhataraṭṭha. We meet him in the great Jātaka Book. In the story of Bhūridatta which we have reproduced above,[1] Dhataraṭṭha figures as the monarch ot the Nāgas who deputes an ambassador to the king of Benares and woos that king's daughter. He is called 'the lord of many Nāgas'; his residence is in the river Yamunā. When the proud king of Benares refuses to grant his daughter to a snake, however powerful he may be, the angry Nāga ruler sends his serpent army to invade the country of Benares and the king has to submit to his wishes.

Dhṛitarāshṭra, however, appears in Buddhist literature also in another dignity. In the course of our survey we have had occasion to refer to the ancient notion of four dragons or elephants guarding the cardinal points. Now it is well known that Indian mythology recognizes also a group of four divinities who are the regents of the quarters. In Brahmanical books they are usually indicated as the four World-protectors (*lokapāla*).[2] Their names vary to a certain extent, but the usual presentation is that Indra rules the East, Yama the South, Varuṇa the West, and Kubera the North. Sometimes these four World-protectors are associated with the four elephants of the quarters in a very simple manner: the *lokapālas* mount the respective elephants and in this manner, as we have seen, Airāvaṇa becomes the riding animal and war-elephant of the great Indra.

In Buddhist mythology, too, there is a group of four gods who are connected with the four cardinal points. Usually they are designated as 'the four Kings' (*chatvāro mahārājās*), and under this name they play a prominent part in the legend of Buddha's life. In an ancient Pali text[3] they are said to wait upon the Buddha "standing in the four directions like great firebrands". At several important moments of the Master's career they make their appearance—ever ready to assist him. Their association with the four cardinal points is often lost sight of and it is even a very common presentation that the four Mahārājas rule one of the seven superimposed heavens. The Deva-loka of the four Kings is then the one nearest the earth.

The names of these Buddhist gods of the quarters do not, as far as we know, occur in the earlier Pali books. The Jātaka Book mentions them only once.[4] In the Sanskrit scriptures of the Buddhists they are regularly found in a very stereotyped form.[5] Each of

[1] See above, pp. 154 ff.

[2] E. W. Hopkins, *Epic Mythology*, pp. 149 ff.

[3] *Mahāvagga*, i, 16; *S.B.E.*, vol. xiii, p. 122.

[4] *Jāt.*, vol. iii, pp. 257 f.; Cambridge transl., vol. iii. p. 166,

[5] In the *Lalitavistara* at the end of the 24th chapter is found a benedictory hymn in which the protection of the deities of the quarters is invoked upon travelling merchants. Cf. above, p. 10.

them is the overlord of a certain class of demons or demigods, is provided with fixed emblems, and is, moreover, distinguished by a distinct colour. The regent of the East is Dhṛitarāshṭra, the king of the Gandharvas or heavenly musicians, who is white of complexion and holds a mandoline as his emblem. The southern region is presided over by Virūḍhaka, the lord of the Kumbhāṇḍas, who is green and carries a sword and a helmet made of the skin of an elephant's head. Virūpāksha, the red ruler of the West, whose attributes are a jewel and a snake, is the monarch of the Nāgas. The ruler of the North is Vaiśravaṇa the Yaksha king, whose colour is yellow and who holds in one hand a short pike with a flag attached to it and in the other a jewel-spitting mongoose.[1]

Now it will be noticed in the first place that these Buddhist regents of the quarters are different from the four *lokapālas* of Brahmanical tradition, except the ruler of the North, who in both groups is the god of riches, Kubera, whose patronymic is Vaiśravaṇa. As regards the remaining names of the Buddhist group, it may be pointed out that two of them are also found in the ancient snake charm which has been preserved in the Buddhist Canon. The Pali name 'Virūpakkha' is of course identical with Sanskrit 'Virūpāksha', and we have seen above that 'Erāpatha' is a Prākrit form of Sanskrit 'Airāvata', which in its turn is a patronymic (or metronymic) of Dhṛitarāshṭra. It is therefore very probable that the Buddhist group of the four kings was originally derived from the primitive idea of the four Nāgarājas of the quarters.

In the stereotyped group Virūpāksha has become the lord of the Nāgas and in that capacity he holds a snake and a jewel. Although originally he must have been a Nāgarāja he figures in the *Rāmāyaṇa* as the world-elephant of the East.[2] Dhṛitarāshṭra, who likewise was a king of the Nāgas, now appears in a new office. He has received the rank of king of the Gandharvas. It is significant that a Gandharva of that name is unknown to either Brahmanical or early Buddhist tradition. The different groups of gods and deified animals protecting the quarters show so many variations and are mutually mixed to such an extent that it is an extremely difficult task to trace their historical development. This much is certain that there must have existed a close connexion between those different groups, that the names must often have been interchanged, and that the similarity in conception must have led to manifold confusion. We do not pretend to have succeeded in solving the many difficulties connected with the problem.

Let us sum up the conclusions we have arrived at in the course of our survey. From Vedic times Dhṛitarāshṭra Airāvata must have held a high rank among Nāgas, being

[1] A. Grünwedel, *Buddhist Art in India*, p. 136. 'The four Kings' are a favourite subject in the art of Central Asia and the Far East.

[2] *Rām.*, *Bāla-k.*, ch. xl, 13.

apparently considered as their sovereign before Vāsuki usurped that dignity. This position he still holds in the earlier parts of the Great Epic, whereas in the younger portions Dhṛitarāshṭra and Airāvata are mentioned side by side : they have become two separate serpent-demons and their original identity is forgotten. Dhṛitarāshṭra (Pali Dhataraṭṭha) still figures as the king of Serpents in the *Jātaka* Book ; besides he is reckoned among 'the four Great Kings' of Buddhist mythology. As such he is the regent of the East and lord of the Gandharvas. Airāvata, who in the *Mahābhārata* is still remembered as a Nāga patriarch, becomes one of the *diṅ-nāgas* or 'elephants of the quarters' ; he is placed in the East and associated with Indra, the *Lokapāla* of that region, who uses him as his riding animal. Under the Prākrit name 'Elāpattra' too he appears as a separate snake deity in the later portions of the *Mahābhārata*, but especially in Buddhist literature, where he is esteemed as a great Serpent king worshipped in the North and as the guardian spirit of one of 'the four Great Treasures'. Thus the ancient Snake of the Vedic period has developed into three different beings, each of which has followed his own remarkable career in Indian mythology.

Karkoṭa(ka)

The word *karkoṭa* as an appellative indicates different plants ; it also occurs as the name of a presumably un-Aryan tribe.[1] There is probably some connexion between the Nāga name 'Karkoṭa' and the word *śarkoṭa*, which in the *Atharva-veda*[2] is used to indicate some kind of poisonous snake. M. Przyluski informs me that in his opinion the word was borrowed from some Austro-Asiatic language and that the meaning of it must have been 'provided with a crest or hair-tuft'.

In the lists of principal Nāgas found in epic literature the Nāga-rāja Karkoṭa(ka) takes an honourable place ; usually he comes immediately or very soon after the great Serpent deities Śesha, Vāsuki, Takshaka, and Airāvata. In the *Mausala-parvan* he even heads the band of great Nāgas who come to meet Baladeva-Śesha on his re-assuming his divine state. In the *Harivaṃśa* too he is specially mentioned among the Serpents who wait upon the deified Baladeva.[3]

Karkoṭa does not figure in the legends of the Great Epic[4] with one notable exception, the far-famed tale of King Nala, in which he shows his gratitude to the hero of the story who had saved him from the fire. It will suffice to refer to the episode which we have rendered above.

[1] *M.Bh.*, *Karṇa-p.*, xliv, 43.

[2] *A.V.*, vii, 56, 5 and 7.

[3] Cf. above, pp. 92 and 197.

[4] In the Grantha redaction of *M.Bh.*, the Karkoṭaka is the spokesman of the obedient Nāgas and promises to assist his mother Kadrū in deceiving her sister Vinatā. Cf. Charpentier, *Die Suparṇasage*, pp. 170 and 303.

His eminence among the Serpent tribe appears from the fact that the most illustrious royal house which ruled over Kashmir and included the great Lalitāditya, the founder of the Mārtaṇḍ temple, among its scions, boasted the Nāga Karkoṭaka as the procreator of its race.

Karkoṭa also has a place in the serpent worship of the present time. He is stated to have a shrine at Baṛhā Kuṭrā in the Banda district of the United Provinces.

It is especially in the kingdom of Nepal that Karkoṭa takes a prominent position in popular worship and legend. He is considered to be foremost among the Nāgas of Nepal, and it is said that, when Mañjuśrī (or Vishṇu) pierced the mountain barrier and drained the country, so that all Nāgas were carried away by the rush of the waters, Karkoṭa alone remained. From that time he resides in the great lake called Tau-dahan, or Tau-dah, which occupies the south-eastern extremity of the valley.

Once upon a time, during the reign of king Harisiṃha, so the story says, Karkoṭaka assumed the appearance of a Brahmin and approached a certain physician with the request that he would visit his wife who was ill. When the physician agreed, the supposed Brahmin took him to the lake and invited him to close his eyes and throw himself into the water. He did so, and within a moment he found himself in the subterraneous palace of the Serpent-king. 'The walls were of gold, the windows of diamonds, the beams of sapphires, the pillars of topazes enriched with rubies. The jewels incrusted in the heads of the Nāgas spread a brilliant light. The consort of Karkoṭaka was seated upon a jewelled throne under a triple parasol of diamonds. The physician fortunately had taken his drugs with him. He examined the eyes of the Nāga queen and applied an unguent which had the desired effect. Then Karkoṭaka granted him the boon that his descendants should excel as oculists. On his return the successful physician was greatly honoured by the king.[1]

Śaṅkha

The word *śaṅkha* as an appellative means a conch-shell ; its close connexion with the water renders it particularly suitable to designate a serpent-demon. This, besides its being a word of good augury, accounts for its frequent occurrence in Nāga names. In the lists of Nāgas which are found in the *Mahābhārata*, the *Harivaṃśa* and the *Bhāgavata*, we find the following examples : Śaṅkha, Mahāśankha, Śaṅkhamukha, Śaṅkhapiṇḍa, Śaṅkhaśiras, Śaṅkhaśīrsha, Śaṅkharoman, Śaṅkhapāla, and Śaṅkhachūḍa. The two last-mentioned names have acquired a special renown in Buddhist tradition. The Nāga Śaṅkhapāla is the hero of a Jātaka who realizes in an extraordinary manner the virtue of forbearance.

[1] Sylvain Lévi, *Le Népal*, vol. i, pp. 246, footnote, and 320 ff. The story is related in the *Vaṃśāvalī*, or local chronicle, 178.

Śaṅkhachūḍa is the unfortunate Nāga victim in the touching tale of Jīmūtavāhana, which has gained such wide celebrity.[1] In one version of this popular story, found in the *Kathāsaritsāgara* (xc, 141), Śaṅkhachūḍa is said to belong to the glorious race of Śaṅkhapāla.

In the same book[2] mention is made of a town Śankhapura and of a "great purifying lake of clear water, sacred to Śaṅkhapāla, king of the Nāgas, and called Śaṅkhahrada." To the south of it there was a grove of *tapichchha*, *kiṃśuka*, and *aśoka* trees. The poet describes the "holy bathing festival (*snānayātrotsava*) which was held at that lake. Its banks were crowded and its waters troubled on every side by people who had come from all countries, like the sea when the gods and Asuras churned it." It is, of course, quite possible that the town of Śaṅkhapura and the lake of Śaṅkhapāla existed only in the imagination of the poet, but his description of the festival in honour of the Nāga king was probably based on what he had witnessed himself in his native country, Kashmir.

Regarding the Nāga Śaṅkha no myths or legends are known to exist, but the place where he was worshipped can be fixed with a considerable degree of certainty.[3] In the *Divyāvadāna* [4] Śaṅkha is said to be the name of the future king whose family priest, Brahmāyu, will become the father of Maitreya, the Buddha to come. In this connexion the author quotes a stanza containing the names of four future kings, including the said Śaṅkha of Benares, but we have seen that the verse quoted gives in reality the names of four Nāgarājas and the places where they were worshipped.

This is proved by a passage in the *Mahāvastu*,[5] which, however brief, throws light on the cult of the Nāgas in ancient India. The passage is contained in the chapter called 'the Questions of Nālaka'. Nālaka Kātyāyana, the nephew of the famous *ṛishi* Asitadevala, came to Benares in order to consult the Buddha and to be ordained as a member of his community. In this connexion the text says: "There are four great Treasures: Śaṅkha at Benares, Paduma at Mithilā, Piṅgala in Kaliṅga, and Elāpatra at Taxila. At Benares there is a monthly assembly in honour of Śaṅkha. The Nāgarājas, who are the guardians of the treasures (*nidhānādhipatayo*), being invited, repair thither." Then we are told that Elāpattra, the Nāga of Taxila, also came to the festival of his fellow-

[1] Both legends we have rendered above, pp. 150 f. and 179 ff.

[2] *Kathās.*, civ, 85–92; Tawney's transl., vol. ii, p. 416.

[3] Among the places visited by Baladeva in the course of his pilgrimage, the *Mahābhārata* (*Śalya-p.*, xxxvii, 19–25) mentions a Śaṅkha-tīrtha which must have been somewhere in the vicinity of the Sarasvatī. But the object of worship was a sacred tree (*naga*), called Mahāśaṅkha, and there is no evidence that the locality had any connexion with the Nāga Śaṅkha. The *Bhāg.-p.*, lv, 24, 31, mentions a Nāga, of the name of Mahāśankha.

[4] *Divyāvadāna*, p. 61, ll. 1–3. Cf. above, p. 210.

[5] *Mahāvastu*, vol. iii, p. 383, ll. 18–20. The text has *Saṅkha*.

serpent Śaṅkha. We shall see in the sequel that not only the periodical festival mentioned here, but also the presence of other Nāgas on such a joyful occasion, however fantastic it may appear at first sight, is in perfect agreement with the practices of the present day observed in connexion with Nāga worship in the Western Himālaya.

Another point of decided interest is that the passage quoted above acquaints us with the existence of the cult of the Nāga Śaṅkha at Benares at an early date. It was even believed to have existed in the days of Buddha.

Now it is very curious that according to the *Buddha-charita*, the Buddha, after having arrived at Benares from Uruvilvā, first stayed at a locality designated by the name of *Śankhamedhīya Udyāna*, i.e., 'the Garden or Grove of the Sacrifice of Śaṅkha.'[1] It is tempting to connect this name with the passage from the *Mahāvastu* which we have quoted above and to explain the name as the grove where the festival in honour of the Nāga Śaṅkha used to be held. Again, we venture to refer the reader to the modern Nāga worship of the Western Himālaya, which we shall discuss more fully in our last chapter. Here it will suffice to say that in those parts the annual *melā* in honour of the Nāga is usually held in a grove surrounding the temple and that the festivities culminate in the sacrifice of a goat or a ram.

It would be highly interesting to know whether at present any trace of the worship of Śaṅkha is still preserved at Benares. It is remarkable that Hiuen Tsiang,[2] in his account of that place, before entering upon his detailed description of the great convent of the Deer-park, speaks of a *stūpa* ascribed to Aśoka and standing to the north-east of the town and on the western side of the River Varana (the modern Barna). In front of the *stūpa* there was a stone pillar " bright and shining as a mirror ", on which one could see " the figure of Buddha as a shadow ". Unfortunately the pilgrim leaves us in the dark as to the special reason which had induced Aśoka to raise a *stūpa* and a column on that particular spot. If we may conclude that it had some connexion with the career of the Buddha, as, indeed, Hiuen Tsiang's words seem to imply, it might be conjectured that those memorials marked the place which the Master had hallowed by his presence before proceeding to the Deer-park in order to set the Wheel of the Good Law in motion. The circumstance, mentioned by the pilgrim, that they stood near the right bank of the Barna, the charming little river which flows into the Ganges beneath the city of Benares, would well suit a site sacred to a Nāga.[3]

[1] *Buddha-charita*, xv, 102 ; *S.B.E.*, vol. xlix, p. 171. The *Mahāvastu*, vol. iii, p. 328, l. 14, also mentions the locality under the name of *Saṅkhamedhī*.

[2] *Si-yu-ki* (transl. Beal), vol. ii, p. 45. T. Watters, op. cit., vol. ii, p. 48.

[3] Since writing the above I have received a communication from the Principal of Queen's College at Benares informing me that there exists at or near that town no shrine dedicated to the Nāga Śaṅkha.

MAṆI

It is not surprising that the word *maṇi*, meaning 'a pearl, a gem, a jewel', is often found in Nāga names. As examples we may quote Maṇi or Maṇi-nāga and Maṇimant, which regularly occur in the lists of divine serpents found in the Great Epic and the *Purāṇas*. Buddhist tradition has preserved names like Maṇikaṇṭha, Maṇichūḍa, Maṇibhadraka, and Maṇiakkhika. The last-mentioned Nāga figures in the *Mahāvaṃsa*, the chronicle of Ceylon.[1]

To account for these names it might be adduced that the pearl, like the conch-shell, suggests a close connexion with the sea, which frequently is described as an abode of the Nāgas. But, as we find that other demoniacal beings like Yakshas, not usually associated with the water, bear also personal names compounded with the word *maṇi* (a well-known instance is the Yaksha chief Maṇibhadra), it is preferable to take the word in the more general sense of a jewel. We know that both Nāgas and Yakshas are believed to be guardian spirits of precious jewels, which occasionally they bestow on their devotees. It is not at all surprising that this characteristic, which must have contributed in no small degree to their popularity, should be found expressed in their names.

The Nāga Maṇi is not only mentioned in the lists of Nāgas, but in two passages of the *Mahābhārata*, which enlighten us regarding the locality of his cult. In the *Sabhā-parvan*[2] there is a famous episode called 'the Death of Jarāsandha', in which it is related how Kṛishṇa accompanied by Arjuna and Bhīma travels to Magadha and how Jarāsandha, the wicked king of that country, is finally killed by Bhīma. When the three heroes approach Rājagṛiha, the capital of Magadha, Kṛishṇa describes the town with its fragrant *lodhra* groves, which is engirded and sheltered by five mountains (whence its name Girivraja). In the course of his description, Kṛishṇa says: "Here are Arbuda and Śakravāpin, the two Serpents who are tormenters of their foes, and here is the excellent abode of Svastika and of Maṇi-nāga. Manu (Maṇi ?) hath made Magadha such that the clouds cannot keep aloof from it; Kauśika and Maṇimant, too, have shown it their favour."

The other reference to Maṇi is found in the extensive account of places of pilgrimage which belongs to the *Vana-parvan*.[3] Immediately after the mention of Rājagṛiha we read the following: "Going thence to Maṇi-nāga, one will reap a benefit equal to a gift of a thousand kine. Whosoever partakes of the water of the *tīrtha* of Maṇi-nāga, had he been bitten even by a venomous snake, the poison will have no effect on him. By sojourning there during one night, he will reap a benefit equal to a gift of a thousand kine." It will be

[1] Cf. above, pp. 119 f.

[2] *M.Bh.*, *Sabhā-p.*, xxi, 9–10.

[3] *M.Bh.*, *Vana-p.*, lxxxiv, 106–7.

MAṆIYĀR MAṬH (OLD RĀJGIR).

[To face p. 218

noticed that both the passages quoted agree in locating the abode of the Nāga Maṇi at Rājagṛiha, the ancient capital of Magadha. The water of the *tīrtha* was believed to be an antidote against snake-bite, a circumstance which accounts for its popularity.

When in the cold season of 1905–06 Sir John Marshall and Dr. Bloch undertook excavations on the site of Rājagṛiha [1], they noticed in the centre of the site of the ancient capital a modern dilapidated shrine which had been raised upon a mound of *débris*. This mound proved to contain the remains of a curious circular structure built of brick and decorated with ten well preserved stucco figures. Out of these ten figures, which measured about 2 feet in height, five represented Nāgas and one a Nāgī, all shown standing and provided with the usual snake-hood. From their style these images could be attributed to the Gupta epoch (Plate XXIV). According to Dr. Bloch's conjecture, the building "was some kind of Pantheon of Rājagṛiha, and the various figures of Nāgas and Nāgīs represent certain serpent-deities whom popular religion worshipped at distinct places on the surrounding hills." Dr. Bloch informs us that the name 'Maṇiār Maṭh', by which the shrine was known, is associated by popular tradition with a certain Nāga Maṇikāra ('Jeweller'). This may be so, but a Nāga of this name is unknown to ancient literature. Is it not far more probable that the mysterious Nāga sanctuary and the name of the locality have something to do with the serpent demon Maṇi whose cult at the ancient town of Rājagṛiha is vouched for by the two passages quoted from the *Mahābhārata* ?

In demolishing the modern structure which occupied the top of the mound, Dr. Bloch found concealed inside the masonry of its roof, a small image of a seated Nāga with an inscription dated *Saṃvat* 1547, along with a basalt slab carved with two human feet. This slab had an inscription recording that it was put up in *Saṃvat* 1837 (A.D. 1781) by a lady, Sītābai, the wife of Moṭi Lāl, the son of Keso Dās, and that it represented the footprints of the Nāga Śālibhadra.

[1] *A.S.R.*, 1905–6, pp. 103 ff. ; pl. xxxix–xl.

CHAPTER VI

The Water-Spirits of the Happy Valley

Among the later works of Sanskrit literature there is one possessing a special interest in connexion with the present subject. It is the famous chronicle of Kashmir, the *Rājataraṅgiṇī*, completed by the Brahmin Kalhaṇa in the year A.D. 1150.[1] It is the last great work produced by Sanskrit literature during the Hindu period. The author has set himself the task of describing the history of the kings who had succeeded each other on the throne of Kashmir. Although Kalhaṇa's work was meant in the first place to be a *kāvya* or poetic composition, the writer shows in it a remarkable historical sense. This is particularly manifest in the eighth or last book of his great work, in which Kalhaṇa describes the history of his own time. His account of the earlier history of Kashmir which is contained in the previous books is largely mixed with legendary lore. This circumstance we have little reason to deplore, for in this manner Kalhaṇa's work has preserved many a local legend of great charm and interest.

From more than one passage in Kalhaṇa's chronicle it is obvious that in the Happy Valley the Nāgas were eminently popular deities. The people of Kashmir had, indeed, good reason to hold them in veneration. For here, too, they were the water-spirits inhabiting lakes and springs, who, when duly propitiated, granted timely rain for the crops. But, when roused to anger, they caused hail-storms, heavy snow-fall, and disastrous floods. Down to the present day the word *nāg* is used in Kashmir to indicate the source of a river or rivulet.

" From early times," Sir Aurel Stein says,[2] " considerable importance must have been attached to their worship, as is proved by the long account given of them in the *Nīlamata*, by the numerous temples erected near the more famous springs, and the popularity and undoubtedly ancient origin of the pilgrimages directed to the latter. The belief in Nāgas is fully alive also in the Muhammadan population of the Valley, which in many places has not ceased to pay a kind of superstitious respect and ill-disguised worship to these deities. The popular conception of the Nāgas, as now current, represents them under the form of snakes, living in the water of the springs or lakes protected by them."

[1] Kalhaṇa's *Rājataraṅgiṇi* or *Chronicle of the Kings of Kashmir*, edited by M. A. Stein, Bombay, 1892. In dealing with the legends relating to the Nāgas which are contained in Kalhaṇa's work, I am greatly indebted to Sir Aurel Stein's excellent English translation (two vols., Westminster, 1900).

[2] Footnote at *Rājat*, ii, 30.

At the outset of his Chronicle [1] Kalhaṇa relates that the land of Kashmir within its mountain-walls had offered shelter to the Nāgas, who found a refuge there against the attacks of Garuḍa. Among these Nāgas he mentions Śaṅkha and Padma of which the latter appears to be identical with Mahāpadma the tutelary spirit of the great Vular Lake which occupies a central position in the Kashmir Valley. This lake, through which the Vyath (or Jehlam) flows, is mentioned in the ancient chronicles by its Sanskrit name 'Mahāpadmasaras' or 'Padmanāga-saras'. Two local legends in which the Nāga of the great lake figures will be related below. (Plate XXV*a*.)

The Lord of all Nāgas of Kashmir, and chief guardian of the Valley is, as the chronicle assures us, not Padma but Nīla who has his abode in the Nīlakuṇḍa or main source of the Vyath, the ancient Vitastā. This river, the Hydaspes of classical authors, flows through the broad and fertile valley which a French writer of the seventeenth century, François Bernier, has very appropriately styled 'le Paradis terrestre des Indes'.[2]

In his account of one of the early rulers of Kashmir, Jalauka, the son of Aśoka (here we meet with the name of the great Buddhist emperor of India), Kalhaṇa relates that the king used to be carried by a Nāga, whose benevolence would not allow him to ride in stages with horses. The same king, so the story says, entered the lakes of the Nāgas by arresting the water, and dallied with the beauteous Nāga maidens.[3]

In the days of Abhimanyu I, thus Kalhaṇa relates [4], the Buddhists, headed by Nāgārjuna, became all-powerful and these enemies of tradition (*āgama-dvishaḥ*) cut off the rites prescribed in the *Nīla-purāṇa*. Now, when the prescribed customs were neglected and the oblations omitted, the Nāgas, not receiving their due offerings, caused the destruction of the people by sending down heavy falls of snow. So deep was the snow, that during the six months of the cold season the king was obliged to reside in Darvābhisāra, the country in the lower hills between the Vitastā and Chandrabhāga rivers. Fortunately, through miraculous influence, the Brahmins who offered the customary oblations (*bali-homa*), escaped imminent death, whereas the wicked Buddhists perished. Then a certain Brahmin, Chandradeva by name, a descendant of Kaśyapa, practised austerities to propitiate Nīla, the lord of the Nāgas and the warden of the land. Nīla showed himself to him, revealed anew the rites in his own Purāṇa and removed the calamity of excessive snow.

The *Nīlamata*, which is referred to in this passage, deserves some further notice. It

[1] *Rājat*, ii, 28–31, Stein's transl., vol. i, dp. 5 f.

[2] Bernier's *Travels in the Mogul Empire* (ed. by A. Constable and V. A. Smith), pp. 393 ff.

[3] *Rājat*, i, 111, and 114; Stein's transl., vol. i, pp. 21 f.

[4] *Rājat*, i, 177–84; Stein's transl., vol. i, pp. 32 f.

was first described by Dr. Bühler [1] after his visit to Kashmir in the year 1875. An edition of it, printed at Lahore, has appeared recently.[2] The work announces itself as a *Purāṇa* (it is conceived in the form of a dialogue between the Sage Bṛihadaśva and Gonanda, one of the early kings of Kashmir), but can more appropriately be said to belong to that class of devotional literature which is usually designated by the name of *Māhātmya*. It has been rightly described by Bühler as " a real mine of information regarding the sacred places of Kashmir and their legends."

For our present purpose the legends are undoubtedly the most valuable portion of the work. There is in the first place the legend of the creation of Kashmir, to which Kalhaṇa only very briefly refers.[3] We find it also mentioned by François Bernier at the beginning of his account—the first description by a European—of the Happy Valley. " Les Histoires des anciens Rois de Kachemire," that author writes, " veulent que tout ce Pays n'ait este autrefois qu'un grand lac, et que ce fut un certain Pire ou Saint Vieillard nommé Kacheb qui donna issuë aux eaux en coupant miraculeusement la Montagne de Baramoulé."

The legend is related at great length in the *Nīlamata*. The Saint of whom Bernier speaks is Kaśyapa, at whose request the gods come to Kashmir to fight the water-demon who infests the big lake and causes great trouble to the people of the surrounding countries. It is Baladeva who at the behest of his brother Vishṇu cleaves the Himālaya with his weapon, the plough-share, and thus drains the valley. Then the wicked demon is slain by Vishṇu. The place where according to popular belief the mountain was pierced by Baladeva is not Bārāmūla, as Bernier was told by his informants, but a spot near Vernāg at the opposite side of the valley.[4]

A Buddhist version of the legend has been preserved by Hiuen Tsiang. Here the hero of the story is the Arhat Madhyāntika who by means of a stratagem (similar to that employed by Vishṇu against the Asura Bali) rescues the land of Kashmir from the water-demon who in the account of the Chinese pilgrim is called ' a dragon-king ', or, in other words, a Nāga-rāja.

Both the legends will be given below. It is curious that in Nepal we find a very similar tradition. There, too, it is believed that the country was originally an enormous lake

[1] *Detailed Report of a tour in search of Sanskrit MSS. made in Kashmir*, etc. (*Jl. Bombay Branch, R.A.S., extra number*), Bombay, 1877, pp. 37 ff.

[2] *Nīlamata-purāṇam* (ed. by R. L. Kanjilal and Pt. J. Zadoo), Lahore, 1924. Besides the printed text we have consulted a MS. in Nāgari belonging to Sir Aurel Stein and deposited in the Indian Institute at Oxford. The Lahore edition consists of 1,613 verses, the MS. of 1,404 verses.

[3] *Rājat.*, i, 26–7 ; Stein's transl., vol. i, p. 5.

[4] *Nīlamata* 430 (MS. 331) *yasmin deśe tv Anantena halaṃ pūrvam niveśitaṃ tatra Nīlasya vasatiḥ pūrvam eva subhāvitā.*

inhabited by Nāgas, and therefore called 'Nāga-hrada' or 'Nāga-vāsa'. By divine agency the mountains to the south were pierced and the water rushed out carrying the Nāgas along with them. The deity who thus delivered the country was Mañjuśrī, or, according to another version, Vishṇu.[1] Here, too, there remained a lake of moderate dimensions and this was assigned to the Nāga Karkoṭaka (the only one who had stayed) for his habitation.

The *Nīlamata* next relates in what manner Kashmir became inhabited. At first, after it had been desiccated, human beings could live there only for six months. The remaining half of the year it was occupied by Piśāchas or goblins under their ruler, Nikumbha. At the beginning of spring when the snow had melted away the Piśācha king with his whole army left the country and went to fight the goblins that live in the 'Ocean of Sand', viz. the great desert of Central Asia. Then the human inhabitants came to live in Kashmir during the summer, but when they had gathered their harvest and the winter approached, the Piśāchas returned and no human being could abide owing to the excessive cold. Thus it continued during four Yugas. Then it happened that an old Brahmin, Chandradeva by name, stayed behind and found a refuge in the subterranean palace of Nīla, the king of the Nāgas. Not only did he find shelter here against the cold but the serpent-king consented to his wish that in future the people should be allowed to dwell in the country the whole year round. Moreover, Nīla imparted to his guest the rites which should be observed by the inhabitants of Kashmir. From that time onwards the people were no longer troubled by the Piśāchas, and there was no heavy fall of snow, as long as they observed the rites revealed by the Nāga king.

The rites ordained by Nīla occupy about two-thirds of the extant text of the *Nīlamata*. It must not be supposed, however, that because they are presented as a revelation of the serpent-king they supply a great deal of information regarding Nāga worship. In this respect they are somewhat disappointing, although they contain much that is of interest for a knowledge of popular worship in ancient Kashmir. They describe, for instance, two festivals which are closely connected with the legend of the Piśāchas and their occupation of Kashmir. The full moon day of Chaitra, the first month of spring, is the day on which Nikumbha and his host of goblins were wont to leave the country. On that date it is ordained that people should make a clay image of Nikumbha and pay reverence to it. The night should be passed with music and the next day the people should ascend the hills to say farewell to Nikumbha.[2]

The return of the Piśācha army is commemorated on the full moon day of Āśvina or

[1] Sylvain Lévi, *Le Népal*, vol. i. pp. 320 f.
[2] *Nīlamata*. 781–9, (MS. 670–9).

Aśvayuj, the first month of autumn. On this day too the image of Nikumbha is worshipped. People must place an oil-lamp outside their houses during the night, a custom still observed in Kashmir.[1] Obviously these two festivals celebrate the advent of spring and of winter.

Another feast which has a seasonal character is celebrated at the first fall of snow, for which, of course, no exact date can be fixed. On this occasion the Himālaya must be worshipped, and the two cold seasons Hemanta and Śiśira. It can be no matter of surprise that Nīla, too, partakes of the worship, considering that the snow-fall is attributed to the agency of the Nāgas. He is, indeed, to be presented with offerings of flowers and fruit and with incense of bdellion (*guggulu*). A *bali* of gruel is to be given and the Brahmins are to be fed with gruel and ghee. The day should be spent joyfully with music and dancing.[3]

The festival of the first fall of snow is associated with another solemnity peculiar to Kashmir, which, as Dr. Bühler observed, would rather shock the feelings of the orthodox Brahmins in the plains of India. It is the drinking of the new wine (*navamadya-pāna*).[2] On this occasion the goddess Śyāmā receives special worship in the form of offerings of flowers, incense, ointments, food, fruit, and roots. The people of Kashmir don their heavy winter clothes and with their friends, relatives, and servants sit out in the fresh snow and amuse themselves with songs and music and the dancing of nautch girls.

Another festivity in which Nīla and the Nāgas participate is celebrated in the month of Chaitra, " when Nikumbha hath gone out of the country." [4] It is called *Irāmañjarī-pūjā*, and has the character of a spring festival. Irā, so we are told, was an *apsaras* or heavenly nymph, she was cursed by Indra and turned into a plant, which grows in the Himālaya. On the occasion of her fête the people accompanied by their wives, children, and friends, all in festive dress, and in merry mood, go out to the *irā* gardens, and adorn themselves with the flowers and give them to the women-folk. Offerings of *irā* flowers are also to be presented to the gods Vishṇu, Rudra, Brahmā, the Prajāpatis, Indra, the Sun, the Moon, and the goddess Durgā. But the Nāgas, too, receive their share. Says Nīla : " The *irā* is dear to the Nāgas [5] and to me she is dear in particular, therefore it is by means of the *irā* flower that a wise man must worship the Nāgas together with me. Whosoever payeth worship unto me with *irā* flowers, with him I am well pleased."

[1] *Nīlamata*, 483–505 (MS. 378–99).
[2] *Nīlamata*, 579–83 (MS. 464–68).
[3] *Nīlamata*, 584–7 (MS., 469–72).
[4] *Nīlamata*, 790–803 (MS., 680–91).
[5] Such, at least, is the reading of the MS. (verse 690) : *irā nāgeshu dayitā dayitā me viseshataḥ*. The printed text (verse 802) has : *irā nārīshu dayitā*.

At first sight it may seem strange that in the *Nīlamata* no mention is made of the 'Nāga-pañchamī', the great feast of Snakes, which is celebrated all over India down to the present day. Among the annual festivals, however, described in that text there is one called 'Varuṇa-pañchamī', which takes place on the fifth lunar day of the waxing moon of Bhādrapada, the second month of the rainy season.[1] On this date, Nīla declares, the lord of waters (i.e. Varuṇa) is to be worshipped, the goddess Umā, and in particular Dhanada, 'the Giver of Wealth.' Now it appears from the text that this name indicates here not Kubera the god of wealth but the mountain Dhanada under which the serpent king Nīla is believed to dwell. The following prayer he enjoins the faithful to address to the wealth-giving mountain. "King amongst mountains, homage be unto thee that art beloved by Nīla and dear to the good. Thou art praised by us with devotion: do thou grant unto us whatsoever be our desire."

As in some parts of India the Nāga-pañchamī is celebrated on the fifth day of the Hindu month of Bhādon (Bhādrapada), we may perhaps assume that the Varuṇa-pañchami described in the *Nīlamata* is in reality identical with the festival of the Nāgas. It will be remembered that Varuṇa in his capacity of god of the ocean is regarded as the overlord of the Nāgas, and in consequence is sometimes himself called a Nāga.

We have seen that the *Mahābhārata* and the *Purāṇas* contain extensive catalogues of Nāgas. Such a list is also inserted in the *Nīlamata*.[2] Although it only professes to give the names of the principal Nāgas worshipped in Kashmir, it surpasses in length all lists known from Sanskrit literature. It comprehends not less than 527 names of Nāgas, thirty of which are said to occur twice and two thrice (which probably means that the Nāgas in question are worshipped in two or three different localities). We consequently arrive at a total of 561. When the Sage Bṛihadaśva has come to the end of this lengthy catalogue, he says in conclusion to king Gonanda: "Now, O king, the principal Nāga chiefs have been mentioned by me. As regards their followers, and their sons, sons' sons, and so forth, it would not be possible for me, O King, to enumerate them even in hundreds of years. All Nāgas have their virtues (*puṇyāni*) and their dwelling-places (*bhuvanāni*). All Nāgas are bestowers of boons, all are obedient to Nīla, all are exceeding dear to the great Vāsuki".[3]

Whether the long catalogue of the *Nīlamata* actually acquaints us with the names of the chief Nāgas worshipped from of old in the Kashmir Valley or whether it simply

[1] *Nīlamata*, 896–902 (MS. 772).

[2] *Nīlamata*, 1051–1113 (MS., 901–65). An alphabetical list of the chief Nāgas of Kashmir is reproduced in the Lahore edition as Appendix B. Neither the text nor the Appendix are free from errors. The well-known Elāpattra figures in both as Ailāputra, and Śaṅkhapāla as Saṃvarapāla in the Appendix.

[3] *Nīlamata*, 113–15 (MS. 966–8).

reproduces Puranic lists with more or less fanciful amplifications, it will be very difficult to decide. It is certainly remarkable that quite at the outset we meet here with the same pairs of names, such as Kambala-Aśvatara, Karkoṭaka-Dhanañjaya, Nanda-Upananda, which regularly occur in the lists of the Great Epic and the Purāṇas. We must, of course, admit the possibility of the cult of these Nāgas having penetrated into Kashmir. But it is also quite possible that these names were included in the roll of the *Nīlamata* simply because they figure constantly in the earlier lists. It is also significant that a Nāga Piṇḍāraka, of whom we know for certain that he had his sacred pool in Kashmir (he figures in a legend preserved by Kalhaṇa which will be found below), is absent from the list of the *Nīlamata*.

After enumerating the principal Nāgas, the Sage Bṛihadaśva acquaints us with the names of the four 'Guardians of the Quarters' or Dikpālas of Kashmir.[1] They are the following: Bindusara (or Bindusāra) in the east, Śrīmāḍaka (M. S. Śrīmāḍhaka) in the south, Elāpattra in the west, and Uttaramānasa in the north. The last-mentioned name occurs also in the *Rājataraṅgiṇī* to designate 'the sacred Gaṅga lake situated below the eastern glaciers of Mount Haramukh and popularly known as Gangabal'.[2] In all probability the three remaining names, too, were associated with certain localities in the mountains around the Kashmir Valley. Anyhow, the Dikpālas in question are evidently Nāgas. This is a point of some interest in connexion with the ancient notion of four dragons presiding over the regions of the horizon, to which we have referred in the preceding chapter. Here, too, Elāpattra, the ancient serpent king Airāvata, belongs to the group.

The same idea seems to underlie the following legend which is current in Nepal.[3] In the days of King Guṇakāma, so the story says, the country of Nepal was visited by a terrible famine which lasted for seven years. Since all prayers were vain, the king had recourse to the great magician, Śāntikara. This master, while using the proper incantations, drew a magical eight-petalled lotus-flower, which he filled with gold and powdered pearl. Then he made therein the effigies of the nine great Nāgas, and by his spells induced them to occupy their proper places. Varuṇa, white of complexion, wearing a sevenfold, jewelled Nāgahood, and carrying a lotus and a jewel in his hands, took his position in the centre; Ananta, dark blue, in the east; Padmaka, with his five hoods and the colour of a lotus-stalk, in the south; Takshaka, saffron-coloured and nine-hooded, in the west; Vāsuki, greenish with seven serpent-heads, in the north; Śaṅkhapāla, yellowish, in the south-west; Kulika, white coloured, and provided with thirty hoods, in the north-west;

[1] *Nīlamata*, 1116–18 (MS. 969–70) and Appendix C. The *Nīlamata*, 928–9 (not in MS.), also refers to a festival of the Dikpālas, but it is not clear which Dikpālas are meant.

[2] *Rājat*, iii, 448; Stein's transl., vol. i, p. 111. See the translator's footnote.

[3] Sylvain Lévi, *Le Népal*, vol. i, pp. 322 f.

Mahāpadma, gold-coloured, in the north-east. Only Karkoṭaka, who was portrayed in blue colour like a human being with a snake tail, remained absent, as he was ashamed of his deformity and would rather expose himself to the deadly influence of the spells than appear in person.

On the advice of Śāntikara, the king himself went to secure the help of the obstinate Nāga and, notwithstanding his remonstrances, forcibly dragged him along by the hair. When the nine great Nāgas had thus been brought together, Śāntikara worshipped them and besought them to reveal unto him a remedy against the drought. Then they told him that he should paint their images with the blood of Nāgas, and for the purpose they offered him their own blood. As soon as the wizard had followed their instructions the sky darkened, clouds overcast the celestial vault, and heavy rain began to pour down. This is the rite known as 'Nāga-sādhana' which has been resorted to ever since when the country was threatened with famine. "The remedy," M. Lévi says, "has lost nothing of its credit and is practised in Nepal up to the present day."

Let us now return to Kashmir, and see whether it is possible to locate some of the principal Nāgas. Nīla, the lord paramount of the Nāgas of Kashmir, was believed from early times to dwell in the main source of the Vitastā. Hence this fine spring was known as Nīla-nāga or Nīla-kuṇḍa. "The deep blue colour of the water," Sir Aurel Stein observes,[1] "which collects in the spring-basin, may possibly account for the location of the Nīlanāga in this particular fountain. Kalhaṇa's reference to the "circular pond" from which the Vitastā rises, shows that the spring had already in early times an artificial enclosure similar to the present one."

In his subterraneous palace the serpent king dwells in his royal pomp, which is so well described in the *Nīlamata*. It was here that the Brahmin Chandradeva sojourned during the six months of the cold season and was initiated by his host into the sacred rites to be observed by those that dwell in Kashmir. The same text locates the abode of Nīla under the mountain Dhanada,[2] which, as we have seen, is associated with the rites to be observed on the 'Varuṇa-pañchamī'.

In later times the sacred fount of Nīla became known by the name of Vēr Nāg, which is derived from the district of Vēr (now the Shāhābād *parganā*) in which it is situated. This comparatively modern designation can be traced back to the reign of Akbar. His minister and historian, Abu'l-Fazl, says:[3] "In the Vēr tract of country

[1] *Rājat.*, transl., vol. ii, pp. 469 f. Cf. *Rājat.*, i, 28.

[2] *Nīlamata*, 432 (MS. 333). Mount Dhanada, according to a gloss in the Oxford MS., is a mountain at Bānihāl.

[3] *Āīn-i-Akbarī*, transl., vol. ii, p. 361.

is the source of the Bihat [= Vitastā]. It is a pool measuring a *jarīb*, which tosses in foam with an astonishing roar, and its depth is unfathomable. It goes by the name of Vēr Nāg and is surrounded by a stone embankment and to its east are temples of stone."

Akbar's son and successor, Jahāngīr, who was particularly fond of Kashmir, often speaks of Ver Nāg in his 'Memoirs'. "The source of the Bihat," he says,[1] "is a spring in Kashmir called the Vīr Nāg; in the language of India a snake is *vīr-nāg*. Clearly there had been a large snake at that place. I went twice to the spring in my father's lifetime; it is 20 *kos* from the city of Kashmir. It is an octagonal reservoir about 20 yards by 20. Near it are the remains of a place of worship for recluses; cells cut out of the rock and numerous caves. The water is exceedingly pure. Although I could not guess its depth, a grain of poppy-seed is visible until it touches the bottom. There are many fish to be seen in it. As I had heard that it was unfathomable I ordered them to throw in a cord with a stone attached, and when this cord was measured in *gaz* it became evident that the depth was not more than once and a half the height of a man. After my accession I ordered them to build the sides of the spring round with stone, and they made a garden round it with a canal; and built halls and houses about it, and made a place such that travellers over the world can point out few like it." The octagonal enclosure of the spring, the water channels and the garden made by order of Jahāngīr and mentioned more than once with evident pride in his 'Memoirs' are still in existence and have, indeed, since been visited and admired by many a distinguished traveller (Plate XXV*b*).

In the district of Nāgām (ancient Nāgrāma) which is watered by the Dūdh Gangā or 'Milk Gaṅgā', a small stream which joins the Vitastā at Śrīnagar, there is a small lake likewise known by the name of Nīla Nāg. It is situated in a valley between low spurs descending from the Pīr Pantsāl range. Abu'l-Faẓl refers to it at some length. "In Nāgām," he says,[2] "is a spring called Nīlah Nāg, the basin of which measures 40 *bigahs*. Its waters are exquisitely clear, and it is considered a sacred spot, and many voluntarily perish by fire about its border. Strange to relate, omens are taken by its means. A nut is divided into four parts, and thrown in, and if an odd number floats, the augury is favourable, if otherwise, the reverse. In the same way if milk thrown in sinks, it is a good omen, and if not, it is unpropitious. In ancient times a volume, which they call *Nīlmat*, arose from its depths, which contained a detailed description of Kashmir and the history and particulars of its temples. They say that a flourishing city with lofty buildings is underneath its waters, and that in the time of Badu Shāh a Brahmin descended into it, and returned after three days, bringing back some of its rarities and narrated his experiences." It will be noticed that by some curious misapprehension the legend of the Brahmin

[1] *Tūzuk-i-Jahāngīrī*, transl., vol. i, p. 92; cf. also vol. ii, p. 174.

[2] *Āīn-i-Akbarī*, transl., vol. ii, p. 363. Cf. Stein, *Rājat.*, transl., vol. ii, pp. 474 f.

(*a*) View of Vular Lake (Kashmir).

(*b*) View of Ver-nāg (Kashmir).

[*To face p.* 228

Chandradeva's visit to the mysterious abode of the serpent king has been transferred to the mountain lake of Nāgām.

Another source of the Vitastā, also situated in the district of Vēr (Shāhābād), some 8 miles to the west of the Vēr Nāg, is consecrated to the great serpent king Vāsuki. It does not seem ever to have been a *tīrtha* of any importance.[1]

The Nāga Ananta (or Śesha) has given his name to the town of Anatnāg (now Islāmābād), situated at the foot of the western extremity of the plateau of Mārtaṇḍ. The abode of the Nāga is a great spring which issues at the southern end of the town. To the north of the town and on the way to Bavan is the Gautama-nāga.[2] We know from various sources that from an early date Takshaka was worshipped in the country of Kashmir. In the long account of the chief places of pilgrimage (*Tīrthayātrā-parvan*) found in the Great Epic,[3] the river Vitastā in Kashmir is said to be the abode of Takshaka, 'which releases from all sin.' Fuller information is supplied by the local poets of the Happy Valley. Says the poet Bilhaṇa[4]: "At a distance of a *gavyūti* and a half from the capital Pravarapura [now Śrīnagar] lies a place with high-rising monuments (*chaitya*) called Jayavana, where a pool filled with pure water and sacred to Takshaka, the lord of Snakes, cuts like a war-disc the head of Kali bent on the destruction of Dharma."

Up to the present day Takshaka is worshipped in the large pool of limpid water at the village of Zevan (the ancient Jayavana), two miles to the east of the ancient capital Pāndrenṭhan (Skt. Purāṇādhishṭhāna). From the Nāga the cultivation of the saffron flowers which flourishes in the neighbourhood, is believed to have originated. This spring is also mentioned by Abu'l-Fazl, the famous minister of the emperor Akbar. "In the village of Zevan," he says,[5] "are a spring and a reservoir which are considered sacred, and it is thought that the saffron seed came from this spring. When the cultivation begins, they worship at this fount and pour cow's milk into it. If as it falls it sinks into the water, it is accounted a good omen, and the saffron crop will be plentiful, but if it floats on the surface it will be otherwise."

The Kashmirian chronicler, Kalhaṇa,[6] speaks of the annual festival in honour of the great serpent king, "frequented by dancers and strolling players and thronged by crowds of spectators." It took place on the 12th day of the waning moon of Jyaishṭha, the first month of summer.

[1] Stein, op. cit., vol. ii, p. 470.

[2] Stein, op. cit., vol. ii, p. 466.

[3] *M.Bh.*, *Vana-p.*, lxxxii, 90.

[4] *Vikramāṅkadeva-charita*, xviii, 70. We quote Dr. Bühler's translation.

[5] *Āīn-i-Akbarī* (transl. Jarrett), vol. ii, p. 358.

[6] *Rājat.*, i, 222, Stein's transl. vol. i, p. 37 Cf. the translator's interesting note at *Rājat.*, i, 220.

Takshaka figures in the fascinating legend of the destruction of Narapura which is narrated by Kalhaṇa in his *Rājataraṅgiṇī* and will be given below. But the Nāga who brings about the ruin of the wicked king and his capital is Suśravas whose original home was a lake near Vijayeśvara (modern Vijabror, vulgo Bij-behara). The story says that Suśravas " pained by remorse and wearied by the reproaches of the people " left his old habitation and moved to a far-off mountain where he created a lake of dazzling whiteness which is seen by the people on the pilgrimage to Amarnāth. This lake, which is still known by the name of Suśram Nāg (the other modern designation of Śesha Nāg is due to popular etymology) lies at the north foot of a great glacier descending from the Kohenhār Peak. Here a small rock-bound inlet is believed to be the dwelling of Suśravas' son-in-law, the Brahmin Viśākha, who by the miraculous power of the former became converted into a Nāga. On that account it is called Zāmatur Nāg (Sanskrit Jāmātṛi-nāga), or, 'the lake of the Son-in-law !'[1]

The sister of Suśravas, the Nāgī Ramaṇyā, who wanted to assist her brother in his work of revenge but came too late, dropped her load of heavy boulders among the villages. Thus the village-land became a stone waste known as Ramaṇyā's Wilderness (*Ramaṇyāṭavī*). This name is preserved in the Rembyār stream familiar to travellers who enter Kashmir by the Pīr Pantsāl route.[2]

The Nāga Karkoṭaka to whom the royal house of Lalitāditya ascribed its origin must also have had his special *tīrtha*. Its exact position can no longer be fixed, but it must have been somewhere near the mountain-ridge on the Tosha Maidān road, which is now known as Kākodar. This name is no doubt derived from Kārkoṭaka, whence the neighbouring watch-station and village were called ' Kārkoṭa-draṅga '.[3]

Abu'l-Fazl mentions some more Nāgs which were famous in his days on account of the miraculous faculties ascribed to them. After having spoken of the marvellous sacred pool of Sandhyā Devī (Sund Brār), one of the holiest of Kashmir *tīrthas*, which lies some 3 miles to the east of Vēr Nāg, he writes :[4] " In this vicinity also is a spring, which during six months is dry. On a stated day, the peasants flock to worship and make appropriatory offerings of a sheep or a goat. Water then flows forth and irrigates the cultivation of five villages. If the flush is in excess they resort to the same supplications, and the stream subsides of its own accord. There is also another spring called Kokar Nāg, the water of which is limpid, cold, and wholesome. Should a hungry person drink of it, his hunger will be appeased, and its satisfaction in turn renews appetite."

[1] Stein, op. cit., vol. ii, p. 409.
[2] Stein, op. cit., vol. ii, p. 415.
[3] Stein, op. cit., vol. ii, p. 399.
[4] *Āīn-i-Akbarī*, vol. ii, p. 356. Cf. Stein, op. cit., vol. ii, p. 469.

Immediately after the famous *tīrtha* of Ishabar (ancient Īśeśvara) on the eastern shore of the Ḍal lake, Abū'l-Faẓl mentions a spring, called Shakar Nāg, "which is dry all the year, but should the 9th of any month happen to fall on a Friday, it bubbles up and flows from morn till eve, and people flock to partake of its blessings." [1]

"In Devsar in the village of Balau is a pool called Balau Nāg, 20 yards square, in which the water is agitated: it is embosomed in delightful verdure and canopied by shady trees. Whosoever is desirous of knowing the prospects of the harvest, or whether his own circumstances are to be prosperous or unfavourable, fills an earthen vessel with rice, writes his name on its rim, and closing its mouth, casts it into the spring. After a time the vessel of its own accord floats on the surface, and he then opens it and if the rice be fragrant and warm, the year will be prosperous and his undertakings successful, but if it be filled with clay or mud and rubbish, the reverse will be the case." [2]

At the village of Trahgām (i.e. Trigām at the old junction of the Vitastā and the Sindhū) Abu'l-Faẓl finally notes a fountain of sweet water called Chatar Nāg and in the middle a stone building of great age. "The fish grow to great size, but whosoever touches them is afflicted by some calamity." [3]

The Nāgs mentioned by Abu'l-Faẓl are very few in number compared with the enormous number of serpent demons which were supposed to haunt the springs and lakes of Kashmir. "In seven hundred places," that author assures us, "there are graven images of snakes which they worship and regarding which wonderful legends are told."

In any case, we have every reason to be grateful to the great Vizier of Akbar for not having deemed it beneath his dignity to collect these curious notes regarding the worship and superstitions surrounding the ancient spring spirits of the Kashmir Valley. They clearly show how largely the hosts of Nāgas must have loomed in the imagination of the rural population. The animal sacrifices (still practised in other tracts of the western Himālaya), the sanctity ascribed to the Nāgs and extended to the fishes (we refer to the story of the Dard king from the *Rājataraṅgiṇī* given below), and the curious customs of divination associated with the sacred springs—all these various traits combined produce a faithful picture of this form of popular worship.

The information supplied by Abu'l-Faẓl takes us back to a period three centuries ago. But even at the present time the capricious spirits of the water appear to have lost little of their influence upon the minds of the agricultural population of the Happy Valley. We may quote one of the best authorities on all that regards the Kashmir of to-day,

[1] *Āīn-i-Akbarī*, transl., vol. ii, p. 361. Cf. Stein, op. cit., vol. ii, p. 455.

[2] *Āīn-i-Akbarī*. transl., vol. ii, p. 362. Cf. Stein, op. cit., vol. ii, p. 470.

[3] *Āīn-i-Akbarī*, transl., vol. ii, p. 365. Cf. Stein, op. cit., vol. ii, p. 479.

Sir Walter Lawrence. "It is dangerous," that author observes,[1] "to discuss so great a mystery as the Hindu religion, yet I cannot help noticing the important part which water-springs and snakes play in the Kashmir mythology." "The pretty springs of cold clear water so frequent throughout Kashmir are the abodes of the Nāgs, the old deities who were worshipped in ancient times. When the Nāg visits the world he leaves his home in the heart of some mountain, and creeping through sinuous passages like a snake emerges at the spring. Sometimes he comes with benevolent intent, sometimes on mischief bent, and all agree that he is powerful and to be propitiated. In all the village tales the serpent nature of the Nāg is prominent. When the Nāg assumes the human form he can be detected by the water that drips from his locks. If one has leisure to sit by a spring with the villagers many curious legends may be heard, often full of interest and beauty."

Some of the ancient Nāga legends of Kashmir which have been preserved in Buddhist and Brahmanical literature will find an appropriate place in the present chapter. In the first place we give the story of the settling of Kashmir according to two Buddhist versions in which a Buddhist saint or Arhat figures as the culture-hero of Kashmir. Then follow three extracts from the *Nīlamata*, two of which also refer to the same subject. It will be seen that in these stories the origin of human existence and civilization in Kashmir is ascribed to the Sage Kaśyapa and to his descendant, Chandradeva. The four legends which we have drawn from the *Rājataraṅgiṇī* show us the Nāgas in various aspects and excel by their refined literary form.

The Arhat Madhyāntika rescues the Land of Kashmir from the Nāga[2]

[We here give the Buddhist version of the legend regarding the origin of Kashmir.]

The history of Kashmir sayeth : This country was once a dragon-lake. In old times the Lord Buddha was returning to the Middle Kingdom (Madhyadeśa) after subduing a wicked spirit in Udyāna,[3] and when in mid-air just over this country [Kashmir], he addressed Ānanda in this wise : "After my Nirvāṇa the Arhat Madhyāntika will found a kingdom in this land, civilize the people, and by his own exertions spread the Law of the Buddha."

In the fiftieth year after the Nirvāṇa, the disciple of Ānanda, Madhyāntika the Arhat, heard of the prediction of Buddha. His heart was overjoyed, and he repaired to this country. He was sitting tranquilly in a wood on the top of a high mountain-crag, and exhibited great spiritual changes. The dragon beholding it was filled with a deep faith,

[1] Walter R. Lawrence, *The Valley of Kashmir* (London, 1895), pp. 295 and 299.

[2] *Si-yu-ki* (transl. Beal), vol. i, pp. 149 f. Watters, op. cit., vol. i, pp. 265 f.

[3] Presumably the Nāga Apalāla is meant. Cf. pp. 121 f.

and requested to know what he desired. Then the Saint said : " I beseech thee to give me a spot in the middle of the lake just big enough for my knees."

Thereupon the dragon withdrew the water so far, and gave him a spot. Then by his spiritual power the Arhat increased the size of his body, whilst the dragon-king kept back the waters with all his might. So the lake became dry and the waters exhausted. On this the Nāga, taking his flight, asked for a place to live in.

The Saint then spake : " To the north-west of this is a pool about 100 *li* in circuit ; in this little lake thou with thy posterity mayest continue to dwell." Quoth the Nāga : " The lake and the land being mutually transferred, let me then be allowed to make my religious offerings to thee." " Not long hence," Madhyāntika rejoined, " I shall enter on the Nirvāṇa ; albeit I should wish to allow thy request, how can I do it ? " The Nāga then pressed his request in this manner : " May five hundred Arhats then ever receive my offerings till the end of the Law. After which I ask to be allowed to return to this country to abide in it as a lake." Madhyāntika granted his request.

The Arhat Madhyandina rescues the Land of Kashmir from the Nāga [1]

[A more detailed and very vivid version of the Buddhist legend is preserved in the Chinese *Vinaya* of the Mūla-Sarvāstivādin sect. In this form of the story the Buddhist Saint (here named Madhyandina) is credited with having settled the country of Kashmir and introduced the saffron cultivation for which it is famous all over India. The following rendering is based on the French translation published by M. J. Przyluski.]

After having subdued Apalāla, the dragon of Gandhāra, the Buddha had foretold that a hundred years after his Nirvāṇa, one of his Bhikshus would convert the venomous dragon Hu-lu-tu [2] in the land of Kashmir and that thereafter that country was to become a great seat of the Good Law.

Now the venerable Madhyandina remembered the prophecy of the Master and understood that the time had come to accomplish the Word of the Lord. Then he betook himself to the kingdom of Kashmir and seated himself cross-legged. Now this kingdom was guarded by a dragon which was hard to tame. Then the Venerable One, entering into ecstasy, made the ground tremble in six different manners. The dragon, seeing that the earth trembled, hurled thunder and lightning and caused torrents of rain to fall in order to frighten the Venerable One. Thereupon the Venerable One entered into the ecstasy of benevolence. Albeit the magical power of the dragon was great, he could not even move

[1] *J.A.* for the year 1914, pp. 535 ff. Cf. also pp. 64–7 and 74–7.

[2] The name Hu-lu-tu or Hu-lung, by which the dragon of Kashmir is here indicated, is probably the Chinese transcription of Holaḍā, the ancient name of the Vular *pargana*. Cf. Stein, op. cit., vol. ii, p. 460.

the lappets of the Bhikshu's robe. Then the dragon let loose a shower of hail above the Venerable One. But the hailstones changed into celestial flowers which fell down in dense profusion. The dragon, roused to fury, sent down a shower of knives, hatchets, and all sorts of weapons, but these were all changed into white lotus-flowers which filled the air around the Saint.

Through the power of the ecstasy of benevolence neither fire, nor iron, nor poison could do him any harm. The which seeing, the dragon greatly marvelled. Betaking himself to the spot where the Venerable One was seated, he spake these words: "O Saint, what is required?" The Venerable One made answer: "Do thou grant me a place for dwelling." Quoth the dragon: "That is difficult." Then the Venerable One said: "The Lord hath commanded me to abide in this place. He hath declared withal that in the kingdom of Kashmir a cell and a couch are easy to find, and that, as regards ecstasy (*samādhi*) and mystic union (*yoga*), it standeth foremost amongst all countries." Asked the dragon: "Is this a prophecy of the Buddha?" "Yes, verily." "Then how much land needest thou?" "As much land as will enable me to sit cross-legged." Said the dragon: "I grant it unto thee." Thereupon the Venerable One, seating himself with crossed legs, obstructed the issues of the nine valleys. "O Venerable Sir," quoth the dragon, "how many will be thy disciples?" The Venerable One, by entering into ecstasy, understood that 500 Arhats would settle in this country. "Let it be so," the dragon spake, "but if a single one out of the number be wanting I will take the land back." "Very well," the Venerable One said, "wherever there shall be a recipient there will be a benefactor, too. Now I will that a multitude of men come and inhabit this place." Said the dragon: "Let it be according to thy wish."

Then men came from the four quarters, and the Venerable One received them and himself measured out the towns and the villages. When they were settled, the men gathered and spake to the Venerable One: "Being settled here, we have found peace. But in what manner will there be provision for our sustenance and for our livelihood?" Thereupon the Venerable One, through the power of his supernatural penetration, led the multitude of men to the Gandhamādana Mountains, saying: "Do ye tear out all saffron bulbs." At that time there were great dragons in the Gandhamādana Mountains. When they saw how the fragrant plants were eradicated, they became incensed with a violent anger and wished to fling lightning and hail. Then the Venerable One calmed them, and explained the whole matter unto them. "O Venerable One," the dragons said, "for how long a time will the doctrine of the Buddha endure?" The Venerable One made answer: "It will endure in this world for a thousand years." Then the dragons spake: "Let us together make a covenant on oath. For as long as the doctrine of the Buddha will endure in this world, you will be allowed to use the produce of these mountains." Then together with his followers he gathered the roots of the fragrant plant. And having returned to Kashmir they sowed it, planted it, and made it multiply. And as long as the doctrine of the Buddha will endure this culture will not disappear thence. Thereupon, after having well settled the men of the four quarters, the Venerable One made manifest in all ways the effects of his supernatural penetration in such wise that the munificent householders as well as the ascetics all rejoiced. Like a fire that is extinguished, he entered Nirvāṇa whence there is no return. Then the people cremated his remains with costly sandalwood and buried his bones. And on that spot they constructed a *stūpa*.

How the Land of Kashmir was rescued from the Wicked Demon 'Waterborn'[1]

[At the time of the Deluge the goddess Satī changed herself into a ship in order to save Manu. This ship was drawn by Vishṇu in the shape of a fish and at last it landed in Kashmir on the top of a mountain which thenceforward is called Naubandhana or 'Ship-binding'. Then Satī became land, but in the middle there remained a large lake, six *yojanas* long and three *yojanas* wide.

Now when Garuḍa stole the *soma* from Indra,[2] he had received as a boon that the Nāgas should be his food. Therefore Vāsuki, the serpent-king, appealed to Vishṇu for protection of his tribe, and the god, being won over by his praise, appointed the great lake of the Land of Satī for a dwelling-place of the righteous Nāgas. There they would be safe from the onslaughts of their hereditary enemy. At the same time he ordered Vāsuki to annoint Nīla as chief of all Nāgas of Kashmir.]

At that time it happened that a demon, named Saṃgraha, tried to ravish Indra's wife, Śachī, but after a fight which lasted a full year he was slain by Indra. From Saṃgraha's seed, however, which had fallen into the lake, a child was born. It was brought up by the Nāgas and, as it was born in the water, they called it Jalodbhava or 'Water-born'. This Jalodbhava obtained from Brahmā a triple boon: magical power, unparalleled prowess, and immortality as long as he remained in the water. Then, puffed up with pride, he began carrying off and devouring the inhabitants of Darvābhisāra, Gandhāra, Jālandhara, and other neighbouring countries. The surviving people fled in fear of their lives and the land became desolate.

Now Nīla, the lord of the Nāgas, learnt that his father, the Sage Kaśyapa, was performing a pilgrimage to the principal *tīrthas* of Bhārata. So setting out to meet him he

[1] *Nīlamata*, 111-304 (MS. 71-227). A résumé of the passage was given by Dr. G. Bühler in his *Detailed Report*, pp. 39 f., and by Sir Aurel Stein in his *Rājat.* transl., vol. ii, pp. 388 f.

[2] Here the myth of the wager of the two sisters Kadrū and Vinatā is briefly related.

found him at Kanakhala, and, after respectful salutation, he mentioned his name. His father received him with gladness and smelled the head of his son. When they both were seated Nīla spake: "Thou hast visited many holy places in the East, the South, and the West. Now do thou also visit those that are in the North." Having said this he enumerated at length the places of pilgrimage along the rivers Vipāśā, Irāvatī, and Chandrabhāgā. Then Kaśyapa, attended by his son, crossed the divine Yamunā and the sacred Sarasvatī, and after visiting Kurukshetra (the which pious people resort to whenever the Sun is seized by Rāhu) he also crossed the Śatadru and blessed Vipāśā. In this wise being come to the land of Madra, and seeing that country desolate and depopulated, he questioned his son why a tract so rich and fertile were void of people. Thereupon Nīla, having related in what manner Jalodbhava abused the boon granted by Brahmā, besought his father most earnestly to devise a means of chastising the wicked demon.

Kaśyapa having consented, they both ascended to the heaven of Brahmā, and after a reverential welcome proffered by the gods, the sage and the serpent-king related all the villainous conduct of 'Waterborn'. Thereupon, being summoned by Brahmā, all the gods betook themselves to Naubandhana: Vishṇu, seated on Garuḍa, Śiva with Devī on his bull, Brahmā on his goose, and all the other gods accompanied by the hosts of heaven and all the fluvial goddesses, each of them riding on her peculiar animal. Whenas they had alighted on the mountain tops of Kashmir, Śiva took his stand on Mount Naubandhana, Vishṇu on the southern peak, and Brahmā on the northern peak.[1] But the cunning water-demon, hearing the tumult of the celestial army and knowing himself invulnerable within his own element, did not issue forth from the great lake. Then Vishṇu, addressing his brother Ananta (Baladeva) spake: "Do thou cleave the Himālaya by means of thy plough, and thereby quickly cause this divine lake to become waterless." Ananta did as he was bidden, and the water rushed out with tremendous speed. The demon, seeing the water wane, had recourse to magic and created a dense darkness, whereby the world became invisible. But Śiva seizing the Sun and the Moon in both his hands, within a moment the light prevailed again and the darkness vanished. Then Vishṇu assumed another form, and in that form he fought the demon, whilst in his primary form he witnessed the scene. It was a terrible fight in which they freely

[1] "Proceeding westwards from Bānahāl we come to a group of three snowy peaks reaching above 15,000 feet. With their bold pyramidal summits they form conspicuous objects in the panorama of the range as seen from the Valley. Kashmir tradition locates on them the seats from which Vishṇu, Śiva, and Brahmā, according to the legend already related, fought Jalodbhava and desiccated the Satīsaras. The westernmost and highest of these peaks (15,523 feet) forms the famous Naubandhana Tīrtha." Stein, *Rājat.*, transl., vol. ii, p. 393.

used trees and mountain-tops as weapons, but in the end Vishṇu cut off the demon's head with his discus and Brahmā rejoiced.

When thuswise 'Waterborn' had been slain, the mountain tops whereon the three gods, Brahmā, Vishṇu, and Śiva had first taken their stand, were named after them and declared sacred. The other deities, too, as well as the sages, selected spots which were to be sacred to each of them in the land which now had become dry. The same did the divine rivers.

Now, while the gods, sages, and serpents were present, Kaśyapa addressed Vishṇu, saying: "This land is fit to be inhabited by human beings, and thus it will be lovely and blessed." But when Kaśyapa had said this, the Nāgas spake: "We refuse to dwell together with human beings, O excellent Sage." Then quoth Kaśyapa, the Patriarch, waxing wroth: "Sith, disregarding my word, ye speak evil, therefore, in sooth, ye shall dwell together with the goblins." Upon these words Nīla, folding his hands, rejoined: "Those that are in the power of wrath, know not what they say." "In the midst of the Ocean of Sand," Kaśyapa said, "there is an island, six *yojanas* in length, wherein dwell very cruel goblins that side with the Daityas. In order to chastise them the mighty over-lord of the goblins, Nikumbha by name, goeth forth in the month of Chaitra with numerous goblins, five crores in number, and for six months he fights the wicked goblins which like-wise count five crores. After which Nikumbha returns with his army on the fifteenth day of the waxing moon of the month of Aśvayuj and abides in the Himālaya for six months. Henceforth this land is granted to him, and for six months ye will have to stay together with him and his army. But during the six remaining months, when Nikumbha hath gone forth, ye shall dwell together with men."

Being thus addressed, the righteous Nīla said again to his father: "Let us dwell together with men; let us not dwell together with cruel goblins."

When the serpent-king Nīla had spoke thus, Vishṇu quoth: "It must be according to the word of the sage, O Nīla, during four æons. Thenceforward ye shall dwell together with men. That Nāga, at whose abode men will dwell, him they will worship with flowers, incense, and ointment, with sundry food-offerings, lamps, and very exquisite shows (?). Those persons that will observe the good rites revealed by thee, in this land they will be rich in cattle, corn, sons, and sons' sons. Inasmuch as this country hath been created by the patriarch Kaśyapa, it will be known by the name of Kashmir. Vāsuki will take up his abode in it. Him thou shalt worship, for he is a portion of myself, and he is the king of kings of the Nāgas."

Having spoken thuswise, Vishṇu went whither it pleased him to go, and the gods, sages, serpents, and heavenly musicians went as they had come. From that time onward, the land was inhabited for six months by men that were come from sundry countries, and for six months it was occupied by flesh-eating goblins. The men, having gathered their harvest of grain, went forth from the country and in the month of Chaitra they alway returned.

How Kashmir was settled[1]

During four æons it remained the custom in Kashmir that the human inhabitants, after having stayed in the country for six months, and having gathered their harvest, went away at the end of the month of Aśvayuj. Now it happened that an old Brahmin Chandradeva by name, who was descended from Kaśyapa, being weary of life, did not leave the country. And the goblins of Nikumbha, on their return, caught him and played with him, as children are wont to play with a bird tied to a string. Being thus oppressed by the goblins and benumbed by the excessive cold, he was overcome by the utmost despair, and, roaming about in great perplexity of mind, he came to the abode of the Nāga-rāja Nīla. On the very spot where Ananta had first fixed his plough,[2] there Nīla had taken up his abode.

Now, at that time Nīla, the lord of the Nāgas, being worshipped by the great goblin Nikumbha and by the huge and terrible Nāgas, sat reclining on a couch under the mountain, Great Dhanada. The Nāgas and the Nāga maidens that have made their abode in Kashmir, waited in vast numbers upon the great Nāga king. Some amongst them praised the righteous king, others fanned him, and others, again, standing around his throne, ministered unto him. In their midst Nīla, resembling a mass of black antimony, shone forth by his ear-rings and by his diadem of sun-like splendour. He was adorned with a garment shining like lightning and with a silk upper garment. Being seated under a variegated canopy decorated all around with rows of little bells, he was distinguished by seven hundreds of terrible snake-hoods, radiant with jewels, and was surrounded by the effulgence spread by costly lamps.

Chandradeva, beholding him, thought: " This must be Nīla, the guardian of Kashmir and son of Kaśyapa." The twice-born Brahmin, approaching the Nāga and first uttering a benediction,[3] fell down on his knees, and then pronounced this hymn of praise: " Hail thee, O Nīla sovereign of the Nāgas, resplendent like the blue lotus-flower and resembling a mass of dark clouds, thou that hast made thy abode in the dark blue waves.[4] Thou shinest

[1] *Nīlamata*, 424–78 (MS. 325–73). Cf. Bühler, *Detailed Report*, p. 40 and Stein, *Rājat.*, transl., vol. ii, p. 389.

[2] Cf. above, p. 222.

[3] I read *svastyayanam*.

[4] The name *Nīla* means 'dark blue'.

ever, O Nāga, by thy hundreds of hoods, like the brilliant Sun-god by his rays. Thou, Nīla, that art enthroned like Vishṇu, art served with various rites by the Brahmins that know the sense of the Veda and duly perform sacrifices in worldly matters, and for the attainment of salvation. O Nīla, clad in blue raiment, the man that remembereth thee—the lord of spirits blue-eyed and like the ether all-pervading—albeit he be unrestrained of senses, he will be saved, O lord of Nāgas, by thy grace. O Nīla, the Vedas have sung thee that accomplishest the aims of lovers and art to be remembered by those that strive after salvation. Kadrū is adorned with a thousand sons, O monarch of the Nāgas, but by thee she shineth exceedingly even as Aditi by Vishṇu. For in thee there is right and truth and forbearance. In the encounters between the gods and the demons thou hast slain in hundreds and thousands those thorns in the side of gods and Brahmins. Thou excellent giver of boons and slayer of the hosts of thy foes, thou hast compassion on thy devotees and art devoted to Vishṇu, the god of gods. Exceeding dear thou art to Him, like the Nāga Vāsuki. The Wealth-giver [1] is alway the friend of thee, O Nāga, even as he is the friend of Śiva, and thou art thyself a giver of wealth to thy devotees, and thence thou art famed as 'Wealth-giver'. Thou art ever the refuge of the Nāgas even as Indra is of the gods. I am ever devoted to thee; this thou knowest, O Righteous One."

Then Nīla spake: "Welcome to thee, O most excellent amongst the twice-born, by good fortune art thou come into my presence. Worthy of worship thou art, O chief of Brahmins; I consider thee as my guest. Choose a boon, so it please thee, whatsoever be dear to thy heart. Behold my dwelling and abide therein at thy ease."

Quoth Chandradeva: "By all means thou must give me a boon, O best among Nāga lords. I choose a boon, O god, the which thou must give me. May the people dwell in Kashmir alway, O thou of terrible prowess; for the folk are vexed by continually departing and entering the country again, while leaving their dwellings and divers towns. May they then abide in the country constantly! This is the boon which I choose."

"Let it be so," Nīla said, "O most excellent amongst the twice-born, may the people abide here for ever and may they observe my word the which I have heard from Vishṇu."

Then, after conducting and honouring and entertaining him according to the rule, he revealed to the Brahmin the customs to be observed by those that dwell in Kashmir. For six months the Brahmin tarried at his ease in the abode of Nīla. Then, the month of Chaitra being gone by, the people returned from everywhere. So did the king, Vīryodana by name, escorted by numerous horse and elephants. Thereupon, being instructed by Nīla, the Brahmin, accompanied by a multitude of people, betook himself to

[1] Probably the mountain Dhanada is meant.

King Vīryodana. To him the Brahmin related all that had happened and the king related it to all the people. Thenceforward, the people that had settled rejoiced, and abode constantly in the country, while acting according to the word pronounced by Nīla. Having built towns and villages, *tīrthas* and temples, and divers dwelling houses, they abode there for ever. From that time onward there falls very little snow in this country, but the people constantly observe the rites prescribed by Nīla.

How the town of Chandrapura was submerged [1]

[The following legend, preserved in the *Nīlamata*, relates to the origin of the great Vular Lake, through which the river Vyath flows on its course through the valley. In normal years the length of the lake may be reckoned at about twelve and its width at six miles with an area of about seventy-eight square miles. But in years of flood it extends to thirteen miles in length and eight miles in width. From an early date various legends have clustered around this, the greatest of Kashmir lakes.]

In former times Garuḍa, the son of Vinatā, knowing that Mahāpadma the Serpent had made his abode in the Land of Satī, was wont to beset him sorely. Making an onslaught on his sons and dependents, the Giant-bird used to devour them in hundreds and in thousands. When his own people were devoured in this wise, Mahāpadma the Serpent betook himself hastily to the great Nāga Nīla for protection, and besought him for a dwelling in Kashmir. Then Nīla spake to Mahāpadma the Serpent: "Inasmuch as the Nāgas, O Tiger among the Serpents, have taken up their abode everywhere, there is no place where thou canst dwell, O most excellent of Nāga chiefs. Nor do I see any spot, howsoever small, O god-like Serpent, the which is not wholly occupied by Nāgas. By many followers thou art followed withal. Nevertheless, there is now a good vacant place left by 'Six-inch'. By me the Nāga 'Six-inch' hath been exiled from this country, for he formerly day by day ravished the consorts of men. Having banished him hence, I have given him a dwelling-place on the excellent Mount Uśīraka in the land of Dārva, O best of Serpents. I have duly settled him there as the guardian of the place, and, being worshipped by the people, 'Six-inch' abideth there at ease. At my request Vishṇu himself hath granted him security. On the ancient spot of 'Six-inch' King Viśvagaśva hath built his beauteous town, Chandrapura by name. Now the great Sage, Durvāsas, being come to that place in the disguise of a madman, found no shelter there. Then in his wrath he pronounced this curse: "May this town turn into a lake! This word of the *muni* is not known to any one, O Nāga; to me alone it is known through the favour of the *muni*.

[1] *Nīlamata*, 1125–59 (MS. 978–1004). Bühler, *Report*, p. 10. Stein, *Rājat.* transl., vol. ii, pp. 423 f.

Therefore, do thou quickly make thy dwelling in that spot, O Serpent. But first entreat King Viśvagaśva, the protector of the land, and put thou forth thy request by deceit, so that the king, being requested by deceit, will grant it out of greed. A king is apt to feel slightened in a matter beyond his control."

Being bespoken by Nīla in this wise, Mahāpadma the great Serpent, assuming the form of an aged Brahmin, went to the town of Chandrapura. There he visited King Viśvagaśva, the protector of the land, and seeing him, made his request to him, even as Vishṇu did to Bali. Quoth the Brahmin: "O gracious king, in thy bright town of Chandrapura thou must give me a dwelling which will suffice unto my large household." The king rejoined: "Let me give thee, O chief of Brahmins, a fine place in Chandrapura; do thou take as much as will suffice unto thee and thy household, O twice-born one."

When the king had poured out water into the recipient's right hand to confirm the donation and the solemn 'Hail thee' had been pronounced, the Serpent, assuming his Nāga shape, spake in the midst of the ministers: "Go thou forth from this town, followed by thy train of horse, elephants and chariots and surrounded by thy kinsmen and take withal thy whole wealth and property. Only thy whole town sufficeth unto me and my household, O monarch; quickly it will be turned into an extensive lake. Thereupon the righteous king, taking his whole wealth and property, went forth with his ministers from that town and at a distance of two *yojanas* to the west he built a town exceeding fair, the which is renowned in the world under the name of Viśvagaśvapura. There the king dwelt at ease honouring the Brahmins; but the ancient town was flooded by Mahāpadma the Serpent.[1]

THE DESTRUCTION OF NARAPURA [2]

Once upon a time there ruled in Kashmir a king, named Nara. On the sandy bank of the Vitastā he built a town which surpassed even Kubera's town by its wealth. In a neighbouring grove there was a pond of limpid and sweet water which was the abode of a Nāga, named Suśravas. Once it happened that a young Brahmin, Viśākha by name, fatigued by a long march, went at midday to the marshy bank of that pond to seek the shade. When he had refreshed himself and had started eating his porridge, he heard the sound of foot-rings and espied two sweet-eyed maids, wearing blue cloaks, who had stepped forth from a cluster of creepers. Then again taking a furtive glance, he saw the lotus-eyed ones eating the pods of wild pulse. "O shame, such food for such beauty." Thus he thought and invited them to partake of his meal. And fetching the pure and cold water

[1] "A recollection of this legend," Sir Aurel Stein remarks, "still lives in popular tradition, and the ruins of the doomed city are supposed to be sighted occasionally in the water."

[2] *Rājat.*, i, 201-73; Stein's transl., vol. i, pp. 34 ff.

of the pool which he made to form a cornet, he brought it for them to drink. When they had sipped the water and had thus become cleansed and had seated themselves, he, fanning them with leafy fans, bespake them in this wise: " Your humble servant having obtained the sight of you through some good works done in a previous birth, with the indiscretion wonted in a Brahmin would fain question you. Which blessed family is adorned by you lovely ones, and where did ye fall into so great misfortune that ye eat such tasteless food ? " One of them made answer : " Know us to be the daughters of this Suśravas. Not having got anything pleasant to eat, why should we not take to such food ? I that am promised by my father to the lord of the Vidyādharas, am named Irāvatī, and this is Chandralekhā, his younger daughter." Quoth the Brahmin again : " Whence then your wretched poverty ? " " Our father knoweth the reason," they rejoined, " him thou shouldest ask. Whenas he cometh to the festival of Takshaka in the month of Jyaishṭha on the twelfth day of the waning moon, thou wilt surely ken him by his hair-tuft dripping with water. At that time thou wilt also see us standing near him." Having thus spoken, the serpent-maidens forthwith vanished out of sight.

Then in due time came the great festival of Takshaka, frequented by dancers and strolling players, and thronged by crowds of pilgrims ; the young Brahmin, too, attracted by curiosity, moved among the spectators. Thus he came face to face with the Nāga Suśravas whom he kenned by the token which the girls had mentioned. The prince of Nāgas offered greeting to the Brahmin whom his daughters, standing at their father's side, had previously announced. In the middle of their discourse, when the Brahmin questioned him about the cause of his misfortune, the Nāga, heaving a sigh, made answer : " Wise men let their weal and woe wax old within their own heart, while life endureth and in the end the fire of the funeral pyre consumeth it. Who outside would notice the calamity which hath befallen people profound by nature, unless it were brought out by young children or servants ? Sith then this matter hath come to light through the childishness of these young girls, it would ill behove me to hide my secret before thee, O worthy one. That ascetic whom thou seest seated at the foot of the tree, with his head shaven and carrying only one tuft of hair, that is the field-guard who puts us to flight. As long as the fresh crop is not touched by those that watch the fields with their spells, the Nāgas, too, may not touch it. That one there does not eat it, and under that rule we are ruined. Do thou bring it about that this ascetic break his observance. We, too, know how to bestow a fit reward upon our benefactors."

The Brahmin promised the Nāga his assistance, and at last he succeeded in secretly dropping fresh corn into the food-dish of the field-guard. As soon as the latter took his food, the Nāga carried off the abundant harvest by sending down hail and heavy rain.

Freed from misery, on the next day he took the Brahmin into his own place. Honoured there by the two maids at their father's bidding, he enjoyed day by day pleasures which are easily obtained only by the immortals. When after some time he took leave from all, being ready to return to his own land, the Nāga promised him a boon, and he craved Chandralekhā, the younger daughter of his host. The serpent, obeying the commands of gratitude, imparted his daughter and great wealth to the Brahmin, albeit the latter was unworthy of such an alliance.

For a long time the young couple lived in undisturbed happiness and in never-ceasing festivities. Then it happened that the beauty of the Nāga daughter, the fame whereof had spread to the Court, excited the passion of the king. He alarmed the fair lady by sending messengers to seduce her, and, when she was not to be gained, he had the impudence to ask her from her husband, the Brahmin. Being repulsed more than once, he at last sent soldiers to carry her off by force. But while they attacked the house in front, the Brahmin left it with his wife by another way and fled for protection to the abode of his father-in-law. Blind with fury, the Nāga rose from his pool and, casting about dense darkness by thunder clouds, he burned the king with his town in a rain of fearful thunderbolts. Thousands of terrified people were burned in a moment.

The sister of Suśravas, the Nāgī Ramaṇyā, came forth to assist him from the depth of the mountains, carrying along masses of stones. But when at a *yojana's* distance from Narapura she learned that her brother had accomplished his work, she left the hail of stones among the villages. For five *yojanas* from that place the village-land became a waste buried under mighty boulders and known to this very day as 'Ramaṇyā's Wilderness' (*Ramaṇyāṭavī*).[1]

After completing this frightful carnage, the Nāga, pained by remorse and wearied by the reproaches of the people, left at day-break his habitation and moved to a far-off mountain. There he created a lake of dazzling whiteness, which up to the present day is seen by the people on the pilgrimage to Amarnāth. In the same locality there is another lake known as 'Son-in-law's lake' (*Jāmātṛi-saras*): it is the abode of the Brahmin who by his father-in-law's favour had been transformed into a Nāga.

How King Meghavāhana fettered the Nāgas [2]

Once when King Meghavāhana was disporting himself in the open he heard from afar the sound of loud cries raised by people in fright: "A thief! a thief!" Now, when the

[1] The name is preserved in the Rembyār stream. "Similar stories," Sir Aurel Stein remarks, "explaining the origin of stone-wastes, 'Murren' and other peculiar features of alpine orography, abound in the folklore of Switzerland, the Tyrol, Transsylvania, etc."

[2] *Rājat.*, iii, 16–26; Stein's transl., vol. i, pp. 74 f.

king in anger cried : " Who, oh who is there ? Let the thief be bound ! " then the loud cries for help ceased, but no thief came forth. Again, two or three days later, when he was gone out, two or three women of divine appearance presented themselves before him and besought his protection. The compassionate king having stayed his horse and consented to their wish, they with their folded hands touched the parting of their hair and bespake him in this wise : " Whilst thou of divine power upholdest the earth, who can, in good sooth, be in fear of any one else, O thou that art a vessel of mercy ? When our consorts, the Nāgas, once changing themselves into rain-showering clouds, obscured the celestial vault, the husbandmen, afraid of a sudden hail-storm and agitated in their mind by watching the luxuriance of the ripe crop of rice, cunningly made them, O Lord, the object of thy violent wrath. As soon as Your Majesty, hearing the piteous cry—" A thief, a thief ! "—had angrily ordered them to be bound, then at thy mere command they fell down bound in fetters. Now do thou have pity on us and show them mercy ! "

Hearing which the king, with mercy-brightened countenance, smilingly said : " Let all the Nāgas be freed from their fetters." Upon this order of the king the Nāgas shook off their bonds and after bowing down before his royal feet, they hastily departed thence together with their consorts.

The King, the Nāga, and the Magician [1]

[The following delightful Nāga legend relates to the reign of King Jayāpīḍa, one of the rulers of the Kārkoṭa dynasty. The Nāga Mahāpadma, whom we have already met, is the tutelary genius of the great Vular Lake of Kashmir.]

Once upon a time the king saw in his dream a person of divine appearance, who, folding his hands in supplication, addressed him after this fashion : " I am, O king, the prince of Nāgas, Mahāpadma by name, residing peacefully in thy domain, along with my kinsmen : to thee I apply for protection. A certain Dravidian sorcerer would fain lead me hence away, in order to sell me for money in a water-wanting desert tract. If thou, doing me so great favour, savest me from him, I shall show thee in thy own land a mountain which yieldeth gold ore."

The king, having learned this in his dream, sent out spies in all directions, and when that sorcerer had been found from somewhere and brought up, he questioned him regarding his intentions : " How canst thou drag out that Nāga of exceeding great might from the depth of the lake extending over many *yojanas* ? " " Unthinkable be the powers of magic," the wizard rejoined, " the which if thou wishest to see, come thou quickly and behold a marvel."

[1] *Rājat.*, iv, 592–617 ; Stein's transl., vol. i, pp. 174 f.

Then, followed by the king, he went up to the shore of the lake, and, having closed the quarters of heaven,[1] he caused the water to dry up by means of arrows discharged under proper spells. Thereupon the king beheld wriggling in the mud a human-faced snake, a span long, together with numerous small snakes. "Now let me seize him, O king," the sorcerer spake, "reduced as he is by my spells." But the king kept him back, saying: "Thou shalt not seize him." Quickly, upon the king's command, he withdrew the force of magic, and the lake assumed again its former state, extending in all directions. The king gave money to the Dravidian, and having dismissed him, he thought: "Should not that Nāga this very day give me the mountain containing the gold mine?"

Whilst he thought over this, the Nāga spake to him again in his dream, saying: "For what favour should the gold-bearing mine be shown unto thee? To thee I came for protection from fear of humiliation, but even thou, being my refuge, hast brought over me this disgrace. The subjects deem their master to be as unassailable as the ocean; what shame then can be greater for him than to be humiliated in their presence by others? How shall I in self-respect look upon the faces of those women who have seen me incapable of offering protection when another insulted them? However, what reason is there to marvel at the careless conduct of kings who be blinded by the intoxication of royalty and who act without previous consideration? The rulers of the earth think it a sport to humble lofty minds, whilst the latter, as long as their life endureth, deem it a living death. But even so the sight of us is not bare of profit; therefore a mountain abounding in copper ore will be shown unto thee."

Having thus spoken, the Nāga gave him such indications even in his dream that, when awaked in the morning, he found a mountain the which was a copper-mine. And from this mountain he drew copper sufficient to coin hundred crores less one *dīnārs* bearing his name.

The Dard Chieftain punished by the Nāga [2]

In the days when the great king Ananta ruled over Kashmir, it happened that the country was invaded by Achalamaṅgala, the chieftain of the Dards,[3] together with seven other barbarian princes who had been called in and were aided by some of the king's own barons.

Whenas that Dard ruler had reached the village of Kshīrapṛishṭha, the most valiant Rudrapāla,[4] eager for battle, went forth to encounter him. Now, when the two forces had covenanted to do battle on the morrow, the Dard lord, disporting himself, went to the pool

[1] Cf. above, p. 168.

[2] *Rājat.*, vii, 167–75; Stein's transl., vol. i, p. 281.

[3] The Dards still inhabit the valleys to the north of Kashmir.

[4] The exiled Shāhī prince from Gandhāra who stood in high favour at the Court of king Ananta.

which is the residence of a Nāga, called Piṇḍāraka. In his wickedness, albeit the bystanders endeavoured to restrain him, he fixed his dart in the body of a fish which was swimming there. Then the Nāga, assuming the shape of a jackal came forth from that pool, and the Dard chieftain eager for the chase threw himself after him. Now when the royal troops beheld him rushing up they deemed it to be an infraction of the covenant, and fearing an attack they moved out to do battle. Then there arose a battle-festival wherein brave men were wedded to the heavenly maids,[1] whilst the clash of the weapons seemed to kindle the nuptial fires. In that great tumult of warriors the head of the Dard lord was cut off, while the fame of Rudrapāla, that hero of awe-inspiring splendour, increased anew. In that battle the barbarian kings met either death or bondage, but the monarch of Kashmir gained gold and jewels and other treasures.

[1] The *Apsarases* who on the Indian battlefield fulfil the same function as the Valkyries of Norse mythology.

CHAPTER VII

The Nāgas as they survive in Worship and Legend

FROM the legends related in the preceding chapter, the general character of the Kashmir Nāgas is sufficiently clear. They are the water-spirits which dwell in springs, lakes, and pools, and which have power over rain, hail, and snow. The Nāga Mahāpadma, it is true, reveals himself to the king in the shape of a human-faced snake. But for the rest, these Nāgas have preserved little of their original serpent nature. How greatly do they differ from the savage and mordacious Nāgas of the Great Epic! It almost seems as if they had lost the power of using their poisonous fangs. Nowhere in the *Rājataraṅgiṇī* any mention of it is made. If roused to anger, they send down snow and hail. The Nāga Suśravas even annihilates a whole town along with its inhabitants. But his wrath is not without cause, and after the destruction of Narapura his remorse is so great that he refuses to stay on the spot which has witnessed his revenge.

It might be questioned whether, perhaps, the peculiar aspect under which the Nāgas appear in the Kashmir chronicle is to be accounted for from a personal propensity of its author. Is it merely the poetical vision of Kalhaṇa which we find here reflected? For such a supposition, however, there exists no foundation. On the contrary, there is good reason to assume that Kalhaṇa presents the Nāgas to his readers exactly as they lived in the imagination of the people of Kashmir. First of all, there are the legends, preserved by the Chinese pilgrims, which belong to the neighbouring country of Gandhāra. Apalāla the Nāga of the Swāt river, who causes disastrous floods and robs the produce of the fields, is closely allied with his brethren of the Happy Valley.

We may derive further corroborative evidence from the character of Nāga worship as it exists in the Western Himalāyas up to the present day. The rural population of the Panjāb Hills still worships the Nāgs, and—which is a point of great interest—the nature of these godlings agrees in all essentials with that of the Nāgas of the *Rājataraṅgiṇī*. On the whole, they are local deities, their worship being restricted to a special village or other locality. They are water-sprites, hence their capricious character: in worshipping them the alternately beneficial and destructive power of the water is propitiated. In order to win their favour, their worshippers endeavour to please them by means of music, offerings of flowers and incense and even by occasionally sacrificing a goat or a ram.

The Nāg temple is usually situated in a clump of cedar (*deodār*)[1] trees not very far from the village. Often it is associated with a spring or lake. The trees of the sacred grove may not be cut down and are regarded as the property of the deity residing in their midst. Sometimes the shrine is hidden within the interior of the forest or in some mountain ravine, standing quite by itself. The construction is extremely simple. The temple consists of a small square cella raised on a plinth of heavy timber, and built of rough stones alternating with wooden beams. This is covered in by a sloping or conical roof of slates or shingles, supported on wooden pillars, forming a verandah or procession path round the shrine. The woodwork and especially the roof naturally need periodical renewing, but the cella is seldom renewed, and is generally very old. This type of shrines which is connected with both Nāg and Devī worship represents the earliest style of temple architecture of the Himalāya.[2]

The timber-work, especially round the doorway, is often decorated with quaint carvings, in which rough effigies of snakes are most prominent. Horns of animals which have been offered in sacrifice are attached to the door-frame, which is often stuck full with votive offerings in the form of iron serpents and tridents.

A low doorway, over which a bell is suspended, gives access to the interior of the shrine. The clumsily fashioned stone idol which is enshrined within these primitive temples shows the god in the semblance of a human being bearing a snake-hood and usually attended by snakes. The temples dedicated to Bāski Nāg sometimes contain a second image said to represent the vizier of the Nāg king. (Plate XXVII.) An object seldom wanting in a Nāg or Devī temple is the *sangal*, or iron scourge, the use of which will be presently noted.

The attendants of the Nāg temples are a *pūjārī*, or priest, who is not necessarily a Brahmin but mostly belongs to the prevailing agricultural class, and one or more *cheḷās* (Skt. *cheṭaka*) or 'disciples' who may belong to any caste and, indeed, are sometimes low-caste people. According to popular notions the *cheḷā* is a more important personage than the *pūjārī*; for it is he who at the time when rain is needed becomes possessed by the deity who is supposed to prophesy through his mouth. The state of feigned or real ecstasy in which such predictions are uttered is indicated by the term *nāchnā* (Skt. root *naṭ*-), meaning 'to dance'.

" Seated at the door of the temple the *cheḷā* inhales the fumes of burning cedar wood from a vessel held before him, while he is fanned by a man standing near. The drums are

[1] The *deodār* (Cedrus Deodora), the *devadāru* or 'tree of the gods' of Sanskrit literature, grows in the Himālaya at an elevation of 6,000 to 10,000 feet above sea-level.

[2] *Chamba State Gazetteer*, p. 186 and *Kangra District Gazetteer* (Kulu, etc.), p. 37. Photographic views of a number of Nāg temples from the Panjāb Hills will be found in Brigade-Surgeon O. F. Oldham's book, *The Sun and the Serpent*.

PLATE XXVI.

Nāg temple at Chintā (Bhadarvāh).

[To face p. 248

beaten furiously—soon he begins to quiver and tremble, and this trembling increases till the entire body shares in the incessant motion, this being the recognized sign of the god having entered into him. Continuing to work himself into a frenzy he springs to his feet and dances madly, scourging himself all the time with the *sangal,* or the *tirsūl,* which he holds in his hand, sometimes with such severity as to draw blood. The harsh and discordant music gets louder and wilder, and others join in the dance, forming a circle with the *chelā* in their midst. A goat is then brought forward and presented to the god ; water is thrown upon it, and put into its ear, to make it tremble, this being the sign that the victim has been accepted. Forthwith the head is struck off and presented to the god, and in some cases the *chelā* drinks the warm blood as it flows from the quivering carcass. The dancing proceeds more wildly than ever till at last the *chelā* calls out that the god has come—all are then silent and questions are asked by the people and answered by the *chelā* as the mouthpiece of the god. Having done his part the *chelā* sinks on the ground exhausted, and is brought round by fanning and sprinkling water on his face and chest. The people then disperse to their homes." [1]

The *chelā* is usually very cautious in choosing the wording of his 'prophecies', so that it can never be said that they have not come true. Travelling in Kuḷū I once heard a *chelā* attached to a goddess (for the same institution is found in connexion with Devī worship in the Panjāb Hills), who towards the end of the hot season was consulted by the faithful on the all-important question whether the advent of the monsoon was soon to be expected or not. The *chelā*, or, rather, his mistress, the goddess, who spoke through his mouth (he took good care to use the feminine grammatical forms, e.g. *main pānī dungī*, instead of *dungā*) gave a reply in the following manner: "In the present Kali age all people, both Hindus and Muslims, give up their Dharm. If they continue in their evil ways I certainly shall not give rain. If, on the contrary, they will revert to the Dharm which they have forsaken, there will be rain very soon."

Usually each Nāg has his *melā* or annual fair, as is also the case with other *devatās,* such as Devīs and Rikhis (Skt. *ṛishi*). Then the villagers from the neighbourhood—men, women, and children, gaily dressed in festive attire—gather on the green in front of the temple and spend the day in dancing, drinking, and merry-making. Not only human guests come to pay their compliments to the Nāg on the occasion of his festival. The *devatās* of the neighbouring villages, too, carried on the shoulders of their worshippers and attended by musicians, make their appearance.

We have, no doubt, to think of such a *melā,* when Kalhaṇa in a few verses describes

[1] *Chamba State Gazetteer,* 1904 (Lahore, 1910), pp. 186 f. Cf. Oldham, op. cit., pp. 99 f.

the great *yātrā*-festival of Takshaka 'frequented by dancers and strolling players, and thronged by crowds of spectators'. The circumstance that the Nāga Suśravas with his two daughters mixes among the pilgrims is in perfect agreement with present usage.[1]

The Nāgs, who are nowadays worshipped in the Alpine Panjāb, have each a personal name, the origin and meaning of which are in most cases obscure. Sometimes they are named after the village to which their temple belongs. It but seldom happens that one meets with a name which is familiar from ancient literature. Thus Vāsuki, who in the *Mahābhārata* often figures as the king of serpents, is nowadays worshipped under the name of Bāski Nāg or Bāsak Nāg in various places of the Western Himālayas.

One of the tracts specially devoted to his cult is Bhadarvāh, the picturesque valley of the Nīrū, a tributary of the Chandrabhāgā or Chīnāb river.[2] In the *Rājataraṅgiṇī* (viii, 501) it is mentioned under the ancient name of Bhadrāvakāśa.[3] Once an independent principality ruled by its own line of Rājas, it became a bone of contention between its more powerful neighbours, and was finally absorbed by Jammu. It now forms part of the Jammu-Kashmir State. Bāski Nāg, who is regarded as the presiding deity of the valley, has temples in the little town of Bhadarvāh and in two villages—Bhejā Uparlā (i.e. Upper Bhejā, the lower village being called Bhejā Jaklā) and Nāltī.[4] Bāski is supposed to have two brothers, Mehal Nāg and Svār Nāg. The latter, who is the youngest brother and who is much dreaded for his bad temper, has a temple near Chintā picturesquely situated in the midst of stately *deodar*-trees (Plate XXVI).[5]

Nāg Pāl of Bhadarvāh

About the Bhadarvāh Rāja, Nāg Pāl, who must have been a contemporary of the great Akbar, some curious legends are told, in which Bāski Nāg plays a prominent part. It is said that Nāg Pāl's mother, who was a princess from the neighbouring principality of Kishṭavāṛ, became a widow six months after her marriage with Bisambhar Pāl. In order to avert the extinction of the ruling house, it was decided to resort to Bāski Nāg: the queen was left in the Nāg temple for one night and became pregnant. Now, as she was

[1] Cf. above, p. 242.

[2] Cf. my *Bhadravāh Notes* (*Annual Progress Report of the Superintendent of the Archæological Survey, Panjab and U.P. Circle, for the year ending* 31*st March*, 1904). The author's views on the character of Nāg worship have been considerably modified since his notes on Bhadarvāh were written.

[3] *Rājat.*, transl., Stein, vol. ii, p. 41.

[4] The *pūjārī* of Bāski Nāg is in each case a Brahmin; the *chelā* is either a Ṭhakkur or a Megh. The temples of Bhejā Uparlā and Nāltī are both built near a perennial spring. At the village of Satingal there is a shrine of Śāntan Nāg. Cf. Oldham, op. cit., frontispiece and plate facing, p. 114.

[5] Oldham reproduces a view of this temple under the name of 'Sabir Nāg' on the plate facing p. 66 of his book.

afraid that the legitimacy of her child would be doubted, she prayed Bāski Nāg to remove all suspicion. So it happened that the son she bore had a snake-hood issuing from his back and was therefore named Nāg Pāl.

Another legend holds that Nāg Pāl, when ruling chief, once betook himself to Delhi in the days of Akbar, the Great Mogul. There it happened that the Rāja's and the Emperor's water-carriers met at the same well, and each of them wanted to fill his *mashak* first. The end of the quarrel was that the imperial water-carrier was thrown into the well. Then Nāg Pāl was summoned before the Bādshāh, but he defended his servant's behaviour by saying that the water he wanted was intended for the worship of Bāski Nāg, and that it would have been polluted if the emperor's *māshkī* had been allowed to draw water first. Akbar asked him scornfully who this Bāski Nāg was, and called for a miracle from which it would appear that he was mightier than himself. The Rāja promised to show him one next day and when he appeared again before the Emperor, a five-headed snake issued from his turban and threatened to ascend the throne. Then Akbar became very much afraid, and promised him a boon, if he would take the snake back. So the Rāja did, and obtained the privilege of the royal drums (*naubat*), which up to the present day are beaten in the temple of Bāski Nāg at Bhadarvāh.

The destruction of Ḍughānagar

When visiting Bhadarvāh in the summer of 1903 I heard a local legend, which curiously recalls the ancient story of the destruction of Narapura preserved in the first book of the *Rājataraṅgiṇī*.[1] In days of old, before the present town of Bhadarvāh had been founded, the chief place of the valley was situated at the confluence of the Nīrū and the Haloṇ rivulet. That ancient capital, Ḍughānagar by name, met with a violent end in the following manner. It was in the time of a famine, so the story goes, that Bāski Nāg assumed the shape of a mendicant and went to Ḍughānagar, where he begged for food. But at every door he met with a refusal, till at last he came to the house of an old woman, who said : 'I have only a few herbs, but you are welcome to them.' Then, when she looked at him more closely, she noticed that water was dripping from his girdle, and she understood that her guest was not a mendicant, but Bāski Nāg. Seeing himself recognized, he warned his hostess not to speak to any one of his visit. Then he told her that within a few days the town would be destroyed, but that her house would be saved. After a few days a violent storm arose from the top of Kamalās,[2] and the whole town was flooded except the house

[1] Cf. above, pp. 241 ff.

[2] Mount Kamalās is a top 14,241 feet in height. The lake near the top (the 'Koond Kaplas' of the survey map) is one of the great *tīrthas* of Bhadarvāh. It is believed that Bāski Nāg who originally resided in Kashmir, found here a refuge from the attacks of Garuḍa.

of the old woman. The boulders which the angry Nāg hurled down still mark the place where once Ḍughānagar stood.

This legend, as noted above, has certain features in common with that of the destruction of Narapura by the Nāga Suśravas. There, too, the Nāga, though invested with human form, is recognizable by his hair-tuft dripping with water. And the origin of the stone waste along the Rembyāra river in Kashmir is explained from a similar cause as that on the confluence of the Nīrū and the Haloṇ in Bhadarvāh.

Bāski Nāg is also worshipped in the hill state of Chambā which comprises the Rāvī valley and a portion of the valley of the Upper Chīnāb. It is said that the cult of Bāski was introduced from Bhadarvāh in the beginning of the nineteenth century, because disease was prevalent among the cattle of the State. For some time the Nāg had a temple at the capital, likewise named Chambā, but unfortunately it was burned down. Evidently the means of his devotees were insufficient to have it rebuilt; the Nāg with his vizier found a refuge in a small shrine of the goddess Hiṛmā or Hiḍimbā which belongs to the ancient temple of Champāvatī Devī, the family goddess of the Rājas of Chambā. The shrine of Hiṛmā, as will be seen from the accompanying plate, is itself in a very delapidated condition (Plate XXVII). The boy, seated in the entrance is the *pūjārī*, who had recently succeeded his deceased father, the office being hereditary. The images of the two Nāgs were placed outside to be photographed. Bāski Nāg, the smaller one of the two, wears a royal crown surmounted by an eleven-fold hood. In his right hand he holds a sword marked with a snake, and in his left hand a *ḍamaru* or hand-drum. On each side of his feet there is a cobra in an erect attitude. The vizier, larger in size than his royal master, is shown holding a sword in his right, and a rosary (*akshamālā*) in his left hand. The persons attached to the service of Bāski are not Brahmins: the *pūjārī* belongs to the agricultural caste of the Ṭhakkurs or Rāṭhīs and the *cheḷā* is a Hālī, viz. a low-caste man. Bāski Nāg has also a temple at Himgiri.

There are a number of other Nāgs worshipped in various villages throughout the Chambā State, but it would serve no useful purpose to enumerate their names, which betray no connexion with any of the serpent-demons of ancient India. It has been asserted that one of them, called Indru Nāg, is the same as Nahusha whose story is told in the *Mahābhārata*,[1] but this assertion requires further confirmation. Indru Nāg is worshipped at several places:[2] at Kuārsī on the road to Dharmsālā, at Sāmrā in Ranhun Koṭhī, at Chinota, and in a cedar forest beyond Lāmū, between Chanota and Trehtā. A *melā* is held on the first of Bhādon. The *pūjārī* at each of Indru's temples is a Brahmin and the *cheḷā* a Hālī or a Gaddī (shepherd).

[1] Oldham, op. cit., p. 73.

[2] Indru Nāg has also a temple at Kanhiārā in Kāngrā. Cf. H. A. Rose, *Glossary of the Tribes and Castes of the Punjab*, vol. i, p. 154.

IMAGES OF BĀSKI NĀG AND HIS VIZIER (CHAMBĀ).

[To face p. 222

Among the numerous other serpent-gods found in Chamba we wish to mention only Mūl Nāg and Stūhr Nāg. The former has his shrine immediately above a very fine fountain at the village of Brehī. In his case the *pūjārī* is a *kumhār* or potter. Stūhr or Satūhr Nāg is worshipped at the village of Tur on the road to the Balenī Pass, by which the Dhaolā Dhār is crossed. The shrine of the Nāg contains two images, and, moreover, three snake-slabs of a type common in the Kāngṛā valley. The great number of votive offerings consisting of iron tridents, iron rods twisted into the shape of a snake, wooden swords, and little yokes of wood (given whenever a young ox is yoked to the plough for the first time), testify to the great popularity enjoyed by the Nāg and to the significance he has in the mind of the rural votaries. For the Nāg is the lord of the cattle, and when it happens that a calf has lost its way and gone astray and such an ex-voto is promised to his shrine, the lost animal is sure to come back to its owner. A defaced Gaṇeśa image is called the *gvālu* or cowherd of the Nāg. His *pūjārī* is a Rāṭhī and the *cheḷā* a Hālī.

The *pūjārīs* and *cheḷās* attached to the Nāg temples of Chambā commonly belong to the agricultural caste of the Rāṭhīs, but in a good many cases only the *pūjārī* is a Rāṭhī, the *cheḷā* being a Hālī. We have already met instances in which the *pūjārī* is a Brahmin, but it happens also that he belongs to the menial caste of the Hālīs.[1]

In the valley of the Chīnāb, too, Nāg temples are found. At Kilār in Pāngī there is a shrine of Det Nāg ; it is said that he was originally located in Lahul, and human victims were offered to him. " The lot had fallen on the only remaining son of a poor widow, and she was bewailing her misfortune when a Gaddī passed by, and, hearing the tale of woe, offered to take her son's place. He, however, stipulated that the Nāg should be allowed to devour him, and on his presenting several parts of his body in succession without result, he grew angry and threw the Nāg into the Chīnāb. The idol got out of the river again at Kilār and, being found by a cowherd, was carried up to the site of the present temple, where it fell down with its face on the ground. A shrine was erected and the image set up with its face looking inwards. A clump of cedar-trees at once grew up around the shrine."

" Kalihār Nāg, better known as Kelang (or Kailang), is believed to have come from British Lahul. Fifteen or sixteen generations ago cattle disease was prevalent at Kugti, and the people of that village vowed to hold a fair, it if abated. Tradition says that Kelang, in the form of a serpent, rode on the horns of a ram from Lahul, and stopped at Dūghi, two miles from the present temple. Remaining there for three generations, he went to Darūn at the source of a stream, a cold place difficult of access. So the people petitioned his *cheḷā* to remove lower down, and the Nāg through his *cheḷā* told them to cast a *bhānā*[2]

[1] For full particulars, cf. *Chamba State Gazetteer*, pp. 187 ff., and H. A. Rose, op. cit., vol. i, pp. 147 ff.

[2] A musical instrument consisting of a plate of metal which is struck with a stick.

from that place, and to build a new temple at the spot where it stopped. While digging the foundations, they discovered a three-headed image of stone, and on removing it a stream gushed forth. This happened many generations ago. Rāj Singh of Chambā (1844–70) presented a second image made of eight metals (*ashṭa-dhātu*), which shows the Nāg standing and holding a staff in his right hand. His head is surrounded with serpents. The shrine is closed during the winter months from the 1st of Māgh till the 1st of Baisākh. During the rest of the year worship is performed every Sunday, but only sheep and goats are accepted as offerings." [1]

I am much indebted to the Rev. Dr. A. H. Francke for the following legend which he recovered during his residence in British Lahul.[2] It refers to Tinan above the junction of the Chandrā and the Bhāgā, the two streams which form the Chandrabhāgā or Chīnāb river.

How the Nāgas provided Tinan with Springs

If it be asked in what manner the spring known as Chu-mig Zha-ra or 'the Blind Fount' took its origin, the following may be said. In former times a certain Lama from Tibet had sent many Nāgas in the hand of a man. When the latter had arrived at the place called Chu-mig Gyal-sa, they opened the casket and looked to see what would happen. Thereupon many Nāgas ran and leaped away and on the spot there issued forth many springs. These are called Chu-mig Gyal-sa. There was also a blind Nāga whom at first they had put aside. Now they took him and cast him away. Therefore but little water did issue forth on this spot. It was called 'the Blind Fount'.

In Chambā-Lahul on the left bank of the Chandrabhāgā there is a Buddhist temple in which a white marble image of Avalokiteśvara is worshipped under the name of Triloknāth. The village is known by the same name. The great annual festival, which takes place on the last day of Sāvan and is attended by large numbers of people, both Buddhists and Hindus, from the neighbouring hill-tracts, complies very little with the benign character of the Bodhisattva in whose honour it is supposed to be held. There is much drinking and dancing, and a ram is sacrificed. The main actors in the proceedings are not the Lamas who silently turn their prayer-wheels, but the *cheḷās* belonging to the Devī

[1] *Chamba State Gazetteer*, pp. 188 f.

[2] The above legend belongs to a collection of twenty-one texts in the local vernaculars which Dr. Francke collected and published in a limited number of autograph copies under the title *Die historischen und mythologischen Erinnerungen der Lahouler* (1907). The present legend is interesting in throwing light on such names as 'the blind Nāga', the 'one-eyed Nāga', 'the deaf Nāga', which are met with both in literature and folklore.

and Nāga cults.[1] On the day preceding the great *melā* a preliminary gathering takes place in the Hinsa Nālā above the village, where a ram, presented by the local Rānā, is sacrificed to the Nāg. The blood of the victim is poured into the spring of the rivulet at the foot of the glacier. This meeting is attended by the villagers of Hinsa, Shokole, and Tunde, which receive their water from this *nālā*. The water is said to remain always clear.

We now come to the fourth of the five great rivers of the Panjāb, the Biās (Sanskrit Vipāśā). The mountain region watered by this river once comprised three principalities—Kuḷū, Maṇḍi, and Kāngṛā—of which the last-mentioned State, the ancient Trigarta, was politically the most important. Kāngṛā and Kuḷū, however, have ceased to exist as independent States since the days of Sikh ascendancy, and Maṇḍi alone still survives as a principality ruled by its own line of Rajas.

Kuḷū, the ancient Kulūta, now forms part of the Kāṅgṛā district. It comprises four different tracts—Kuḷū proper on the upper Biās, Rūpī which comprises the valley of the Pārbatī an affluent of the Biās, Inner and Outer Sarāj, the latter bordering to the south on the river Satluj (*vulgo* Sutlej). These four tracts are again subdivided into *koṭhīs*, so named from the State granaries in which the grain and other tribute in kind was stored in the time of native rule.

The Chinese pilgrim Hiuen Tsiang in his account of Kulūta describes the inhabitants, as "coarse and common in appearance" and as "hard and fierce" of character.[2] The little kingdom situated at the outskirts of Aryan civilization has never been a centre of culture and learning, but it is of unusual interest for the study of folklore and primitive religion. Although Vishnuism was made the State religion by the Rajas of the seventeenth century, the great mass of the people still adheres to the worship of the old *deotas* which have their shrines each in his or her own village. These *deotas* belong to three different classes of supernatural beings—Devīs, Rikhis, and Nāgs—but, however different in origin they may be, the mode of religious worship is in general the same. Especially Devī and Nāg worship are very closely connected.

The Kuḷū valley is a great centre of Nāg worship. Here, too, Bāski or Bāsu, as the ancient serpent-king Vāsuki is commonly called by the Kuḷū people, is regarded as the chief of his tribe and as the father of the other Nāgs scattered over the various villages. There is a popular saying in Kuḷū: "*Aṭhārah Nāg aṭhārah Nārāyaṇ*," meaning "There be Nāgs eighteen and Nārāyaṇs eighteen." The term 'Nārāyaṇ' is employed in these hill-tracts

[1] In the year 1904, when I had the good fortune to witness the *melā* of Triloknāth for the second time, the officiating priests were the *chelās* of Mirkula Devī (a Brahmin), of Triloknāth (a Ḍāgī), and of the Nāg (a Rāṭhī).

[2] *Si-yu-ki* (transl. Beal), vol. i, p. 177. The want of intellectual culture among the Kuḷū people still finds expression in the popular saying *Jāegā Kuḷū hoegā ulū*, 'Whoever goes to Kuḷū will become an owl.'

to designate a being closely related to a Nāg. In the *Gazetteer* it is said that 'eighteen' is used to indicate a large number. It would perhaps be more correct to say that eighteen is considered an auspicious number.

How the eighteen Nāgs of Kuḷū were Born[1]

In times past, a little more than five thousand years ago, it happened in the village of Gośāl[2] in which the temple of Gotam Rikhi stands, that a certain peasant woman who was the wife of a man of the Kanet caste, having donned red clothes, went on to the roof of her house to have a look at the corn which had been placed there to dry; and on account of the cool breeze that woman fell asleep on the top of the roof. Now by chance, while she was sleeping, Bāski Nāg saw her and at once fell in love with her. Changing himself into the shape of a man, Bāski Nāg carried her off through the air and reached the upper regions. But he told her never to raise the hair of his head with her hand. Once when the Nāg had fallen asleep with his head resting on her lap, the woman, in spite of what he had told her, raised the hair of his head. At that moment the woman, looking down from the upper region, beheld her own house and fields and at that sight she began to weep. As soon as her tears fell on the face of Bāski Nāg he woke up. Then he made her his wife, and thereupon he said to her: "Whatsoever will be born from thy womb thou must worship." After he had spoken these words she found herself again on the roof of her own house.

Now, after nine months had gone by, once on a single day she gave birth to eighteen snakes. Those eighteen snakes the woman put in a large earthen pot of the kind which in Kuḷū they call '*bhāṇḍal*'. In that pot she made eighteen separate holes, and putting the milk of her own breast into a vessel, she nursed the snakes, each through his own hole, and for many days paid worship to them with incense. Now, after some four or five months it happened by chance that she had to go to the house of her parents. Then she said to her mother-in-law: "Do thou pay worship to these snakes during my absence." Having said this she went away to the house of her parents. After she had left, her mother-in-law on the next day put incense in a large iron spoon, placed fire on it, and went near the snakes to pay worship to them. On hearing her coming, the snakes thrust their heads through the holes. At the sight of the snakes the mother-in-law dropped the spoon containing the incense upon which fire had been placed in order to produce the smoke in such manner that the incense with the fire fell in the pot in which the snakes were kept. In consequence

[1] The legend in its present form was recovered by me *in loco*. For other versions, cf. *Kangra District Gazetteer* (Kulu), p. 62, and H. A. Rose, *Punjab Glossary*, vol. i, p. 167, and *N.S. Notes and Queries*, iii, § 196, No. 6.

[2] Also called Ghuśāl, north of Manālī.

TEMPLE OF GOTAM RIKHI (KULŪ).

(To face p. 256)

thereof the snakes escaped from the pot and fled in all directions. Out of the total number of eighteen snakes two went to Maṇḍi and Suket, and two appeared in the district of Lahul.

On this occasion, it is said, one of the Nāgs had one eye burned, and is therefore known as Kāṇā Nāg (*kāṇa* = 'one-eyed').[1] He remained on the spot and is still worshipped at the village of Gośāl in the temple of Gotam Rikhi, who, strange to say, is sometimes also described as a Nāg.[2] Kāṇā Nāg of Gośāl, perhaps in consequence of his bodily defect, is believed to be bad-tempered. If a cow passes his image, she is sure to give no milk that night. The vessel in which the offspring of Bāski Nāg were kept by their mother may still be seen in the temple of Gotam Rikhi. (Plate XXVIII.)

As to the names of the eighteen Nāgs, there is some difference of opinion among the Kuḷū people, but most accounts agree in including Sargaṇ (or Sirgaṇ) Nāg and Phāhal Nāg of *koṭhī* Jagatsukh, Dhūmal Nāg of *koṭhī* Baṛāgaṛh, Piyūlī (yellow) Nāg and Bāsu Nāg (considered as different from Bāski Nāg!) both of *koṭhī* Nagar, Kālī Nāg of *koṭhī* Rāisan, and Māhuṭī Nāg of *koṭhī* Kāis. Some authorities include three more Nāgs from *koṭhī* Kāis, namely, Ramnu (or Rumnu) Nāg, Sargun (or Sargaṇ) Nāg, and Śuklī Nāg. All the *koṭhīs* concerned belong to Upper Kuḷū, but it is said in the above legend that some of the eighteen found a refuge in the adjoining hill tracts.

Bāski Nāg has also a brother, Turu Nāg, who resides in a cave high up in the mountains. Like his brother this Nāg grants rains and prevents lightning. He also gives oracles as to rain, and when rain is about to fall, water flows out of his cave.[3]

The total number of Nāgs which are worshipped in the Kuḷū subdivision is considerably greater than eighteen, and, indeed, must come up to about four times that figure. According to a list which I owe to the kindness of Mr. H. L. Shuttleworth, I.C.S., late Assistant Commissioner of the Kuḷū subdivision, there are more than seventy places consecrated to various Nāg deities. Some Nāgs are worshipped at different localities, but usually each Nāg belongs to the particular village in the vicinity of which his temple stands. They are essentially local deities.[4] In some cases the Nāg has no shrine but a sacred lake high up in the mountains, where people go to bathe. Sometimes he has not even an individual name, but is simply indicated as 'Nāg'. It deserves notice that no Nāg

[1] The *Bhūridatta-jātaka* also relates of a Nāga who, owing to an accident in his early childhood, lost one of his eyes and in later life had a very irritable temper. Cf. above, p. 156. It is curious that Kadrū, the snake-mother, is also described as 'one-eyed'.

[2] A Nāga Gautama is known from literature and was worshipped in Kashmir.

[3] H. A. Rose, *Punjab Glossary*, vol. i, p. 170. We may compare Hiuen Tsiang's story about the Nāga Gopāla who likewise dwelled in a cave in the Kabul Valley.

[4] In several cases the Nāg is indicated by the name of the village to which he belongs, e.g. Bhalogū Nāg at Bhalogī, Māhuṭi Nāg at Māhoṭ, Karthā Nāg at Karthā, Bālū Nāg at Bālū, and Jibhi Nāg at Jibhi.

temples are found either at the capital Sultānpur or at any of the larger villages such as Nagar (the ancient capital) or Maṇikarṇ, famous for its hot springs. These places are now seats of Vishnuism.

As regards the attendants attached to the service of the Kuḷū Nāgs, in the great majority of cases both the *pūjārī* and the *cheḷā* belong to the agricultural caste of the Kanets. Sometimes, however, the former is a Brahmin ; in Inner Sarāj this is the rule, elsewhere it is an exception. The *cheḷā* seldom is a Brahmin, but it is not at all uncommon that he should be a member of the menial caste which is called 'Ḍāgī' in Kuḷū proper and 'Kolī' in Outer Sarāj. In one instance the *cheḷā* is a *lohār* or blacksmith. When the *pūjārī* is a Brahmin, the *cheḷā* is never a low-caste man. We may perhaps assume that in the cult of the Nāgs, the Brahmins have gradually usurped a position which originally was held by persons not belonging to the priestly caste.

Among the eighteen sons of Bāski we have mentioned Kālī Nag. Whether he is identical with the Nāga Kālika of the Buddha legend or with Kāliya the Nāga of the Yamunā who was subdued by Kṛishṇa it is impossible to say. This much is certain that Kālī Nāg takes rather a prominent place among his brethren and is worshipped in nine different localities of Upper Kuḷū and Rūpī. His temple at the village of Jari in the Pārbatī valley is a more pretentious sanctuary than the common type of village shrine. Besides the temple proper there are a number of subsidiary buildings : a *dharmsālā* or guesthouse, an open pavilion for the musicians, and a *bhāṇḍār* or granary for storing the grain-rents of the temple. The last-mentioned building, in appearance like a substantial dwelling-house, has not less than five stories, and is, indeed, the largest house of the village.

The temple itself, a quadrangular building with a veranda in front and a sloping roof, is built of pine wood, while the more durable cedar wood is used for some portions such as the door which is decorated with quaint carvings. On the left door we notice seventeen workmen and five bulls, said to have been employed in the building of the temple, the latter as beasts of burden (curiously recalling the legend of the cathedral of Laon). Raja Sidh Singh, the reputed founder of the temple, is also portrayed with his Rani and musicians on both sides. On the right doorwing there is the figure of a man being bitten by a snake as a punishment, it is said, for dishonesty, the snake having been sent by the Nāg to chastise him. The post between the two doorwings is carved with the effigies of Mahādeva on his bull and of Pārvatī on her tiger. The pillars supporting the veranda are carved with snakes curling, as it were, upwards along the shafts. Every full-moon a goat is offered to the Nāg.

" The most important outward and visible symbol of the god is his *rath*, not to be taken in its literal sense of a carriage, but in that of an ark or litter. It consists of two parts, the idol proper and the stretcher, on which it is carried. The latter is a high-backed chair without legs, attached to two long poles projecting for several feet at each end, and made of very flexible wood, usually silver birch. The idol proper is composed of a metal plate on which facial masks of gold, silver or brass are arranged in rows. On festive occasions when the god appears in his litter, the shield is placed in the stretcher and the whole is decorated with rich clothes, jewellery and flowers. Usually there is a canopy of long strips of cloth or of yak tails over the shield." [1]

In the case of Kālī Nāg the masks attached to the litter are said to represent the Nāg and his relatives, the two placed uppermost being Kālī himself and his brother Jvālā Nārāyaṇ. A second *rath* made of *deodār* wood is said to be employed exclusively to carry the Nāg to the big fair, which is held at the capital on the occasion of the Dasehra festival and which all *deotas* of Kuḷū have to attend. The temple contains also a big basket in which the Nāgs (represented by their masks) are taken to their real abode up the mountain—a sacred spring where they are placed in the running water.[2]

Nearly every hamlet in Kuḷū has at least one fair during the summer, and as some care seems to be exercised to prevent adjacent hamlets having their festivals on the same day, there is an almost continuous succession of fairs during the summer months. The idols are borne to the fair on the shoulders of their worshippers, each god being accompanied by his own band of musicians. The sign of animation by the spirit of the god is the oscillation of the *rath*. The bearers are under his influence, and their slightest movement is conveyed to the ark which dances up and down. Some of the worshippers are likewise seized with the divine afflatus, and tremble with possession or leap and shout before the idol.

" The first appearance of the *deota* is not earlier than the commencement of summer, about the beginning of Jeṭh (Skt. Jyaishṭha), when the first crop of wheat and barley is ready for the sickle and the young rice is getting big enough to be planted out in the fields. The idol is carried out of his temple by the priests and attendants, and his band of musicians accompanies, blaring uncouth music from drums, and cymbals, and trumpets. Thus the god is conveyed to the village green, where perhaps a few guests await him in the shape of idols brought from neighbouring villages with their escorts of attendants and musicians and worshippers. All the people are dressed in their best and profusely decorated with flowers ; shopkeepers have set up gay stalls for the sale of sweetmeats, toys, and knick-knacks ; and somewhere in the background (if the fair is in upper Kuḷū) will be found tents where *lugri* and country spirits can be procured. The *deota* dances, oscillated

[1] The description of the *rath* and of the appearance of the *deota* at the fair we have borrowed from Mr. H. W. Emerson's excellent account in the *Maṇḍi Gazetteer,* pp. 121 f., and from the *Kangra Gazetteer,* part ii, pp. 64 f.

[2] Cf. H. A. Rose, op. cit., vol. i, p. 147.

up and down in his chair by his carriers who, of course, are under his influence, and sometimes one of his guest gods or goddesses dances alongside of him, and the pair of them exchange grotesque bows and caresses. The contagion extends to the men in the crowd, or, at any rate, to such as are expert dancers ; they join hands and form a ring, the god and his musicians in the centre, and circle round with a graceful step, shouting the words of the airs which the bandsmen are playing on their uncouth instruments. Faster and faster grows the dance as evening approaches ; new dancers are always ready to take the place of those who drop out fatigued ; and the merry revel goes on from early afternoon till dusk when the idols return to their temples. The women with their gay head-dresses form bright groups of spectators on the hillside close to the green which is terraced into tiers of stone seats for their accommodation. In the Kuḷū *tahsil* they scarcely ever join in the dance, but in Outer Sarāj they form a ring separate from that of the men and in Inner Sarāj sometimes they join the men and dance in the same ring with them. But everywhere it is only the agriculturist classes, Brahmins and Kanets, who are admitted to the charmed circles, low caste people being strictly excluded. Sometimes outsiders, even of the higher castes, if not worshippers of the god, are not allowed upon the green."

It is the common practice that the *melā* of each particular Nāg temple takes place annually on a fixed date of the Hindu calendar. In a few cases, however, it is only determined that the annual festival is to be held in a specified month, the exact date being fixed each year by the Nāg himself through the agency of his *cheḷā*. In the case of Kālī Nāg of Shiraṛh (*koṭhī* Rāisan) the fair takes place every third year.

One would expect that the regular date for these festivals in honour of the various Nāgs of Kuḷū would be the fifth of the bright half of Sāvan, on which in the plains of India the Nāgapañchamī, the great feast of the serpents, is celebrated. This, however, is by no means the case.[1] It is even exceptional that the *melā* is held in Sāvan or Bhādon, the two months of the rainy season. This may be due to purely practical considerations, as the *barsāt* in the hills is mostly attended by a very heavy rainfall and consequently is little suited to festive gatherings as described above.

Usually the festivals held in honour of the individual Nāgs of Kuḷū are indicated by such names as *phāgalī* (or *phāglī*), *birshu*, and *śāyarī* (these are the three most commonly met), which are often combined with the name of the particular village to which the temple belongs. Thus the fair of Piyūlī Nāg of Baṭāhar (*koṭhī* Nagar) is called the 'Baṭāhar *phāglī*'. It may happen that two or three *melās* are annually held at one and the same temple. Dhūmal Nāg of Marjān (*koṭhī* Baṛāgaṛh), for instance, is in the habit of celebrating a *phāglī*, a *birshu*, and a *śāyarī* each year.

[1] Only in two villages of Inner Sarāj the *melā* of the local Nāg coincides with the Nāgapañchamī.

The *phāglī* is generally held in the month of Phāgun (Sanskrit Phālguna) preferably at the commencement of that month. Evidently the name of the festival is derived from that of the month ; and, as Phāgun is the last month of winter, we may assume that the *phāglī* is a feast celebrating the advent of spring. It is curious that in some cases the *phāglī* is fixed on the first of Māgh (the month preceding Phāgun), and again in other cases on the first of Chait (the month following Phāgun).

The *birshu*, evidently the same as the *bishu* of Maṇḍi and Sirmur,[1] is the festival of the Equinox ; the name is derived from Sanskrit *vishuva* ('aequinoctium'). In Kuḷū it appears to be observed on one of the first days of either Chait or Basākh (Skt. Chaitra, Vaisākha), and might perhaps be characterized as another Spring-festival.

The *śāyarī* or *sairi*, as it is called in the *Maṇḍi Gazetteer*,[2] celebrates the ingathering of the autumn harvest, and is held in Kuḷū on one of the first days of Asuj (Sanskrit Āśvayuja or Āśvina), which is the first month of autumn.

There are other names of festivals, e.g. *chachauhlī*, the nature of which we have not been able to ascertain.

In connexion with two Nāg temples in Kuḷū proper and Rūpī mention is made of a festival which is indicated by the name of *kāhikā*. This is no doubt identical with the *kaika* which Mr. Emerson has described in great detail as practised at the village of Hurang in Maṇḍi State.[3] "Its primary motive," that author says, "is the transference of sins or baneful influences to a human scape-goat and thus to allow both gods and men to carry on their affairs under the most favourable auspices." It would be interesting to know something about the *kāhikā* in Upper Kuḷū ; these festivals of the Western Himālaya all together are a fascinating subject which would repay a special study.

This much is certain, that, apart from the *kāhikā*, the festivals commonly celebrated in Kuḷū in connexion with the Nāg cultus have a seasonal character ; thus they, too bring out the close association which exists between this mode of worship and the agricultural pursuits of the rural population of that country.

With regard to the village gods of Maṇḍi State, Mr. Emerson remarks[4] that the majority of them belong to the serpent group. "This does not mean that they are necessarily called Nāgs ; the common title for the snake-gods is 'Nārāyaṇ'. Sometimes they masquerade under the names of Hindu divinities, but usually the legends connected

[1] *Maṇḍi State Gazetteer*, p. 124 ; *Sirmur State Gazetteer*, p. 63.

[2] *Maṇḍi Gaz.*, p. 124. "The first of Asauj, a day generally observed in the hills in thanksgiving for the autumn harvest (ibid., p. 131).

[3] *Maṇḍi Gaz.*, p. 124.

[4] *Maṇḍi Gaz.*, p. 120.

with them reveal their true nature. Even where the character of a god is open to doubt, an initial presumption arises that he belongs to the class of the serpent-gods." In Maṇḍi, too, they are venerated as the weather-gods, the guardian spirits of the springs, and the creators of the streams and lakes. The most popular amongst them is Kamru Nāg. Next to him comes Nārāyaṇ of Hurang. The large waterfall on the Pālampur road, about 16 miles from Maṇḍi, is the work of his hands. He lives in the deep valley below the Bhubu Pass, where he has his temple—a small *linga* shrine carved with the figures of serpents—in the midst of a dense forest of cedar, oak, walnut, and other trees, "the home of bears and monkeys which take heavy toll of the peasants' crops." The *kaika* or festival with its very curious rites which is celebrated at this mysterious fane every fifth year towards the end of July or in the first days of August has been described in detail by Mr. Emerson.[1]

In the lower Biās valley, the former principality of Kāṅgṛā, there are hardly any Nāg temples, but after the Dīvālī, about November, a festival, called Nāg-kā-pūjā is held to bid farewell to the snakes. On this occasion an image of the Nāg made of cowdung is worshipped, but any snake seen after it is called 'ungrateful' and killed forthwith.[2]

Further east, in the Satluj valley and in the Simla Hills, the Nāgs are prominent in folklore and popular religion. In a remote tract, called Tikrāl, which lies near the source of the Pabur, we meet with "a confederacy of five gods, called the Pānch Nāgs, who hibernate during the winter, going to sleep at the first fall of snow and only waking up again at the Phag, the festival which corresponds to the Holi of the Plains. The curious mode in which they are aroused by their worshippers by means of a furious attack with snowballs has been described by Mr. Emerson, to whose account we may refer for further particulars regarding this custom.[3]

Basheru of the Simla Hills[4]

[Another rain-god in the Simla Hills is Basheru, of whom the following legend is current.]

"Once a woman was cutting grass when her sickle struck a three-faced image of gold. She took it home and placed it in her cowshed, hoping that her herds would multiply. But next morning the shed was full of water and the cattle all drowned. So she gave it to a Brahmin, who put it in his granary. But next morning it, too, was filled with water, and so he set the people to build the image a temple a mile or two away, whence the god still controls the weather according to the wishes of his votaries. As he had no village green,

[1] Ibid., pp. 124 ff.

[2] *Kangra District Gazetteer*, 1904 (Lahore, 1907), p. 103.

[3] H. A. Rose, op. cit., vol. i, p. 145, n. 11, quotes Mr. Emerson.

[4] Ibid., p. 146.

he drained a lake by coming down in spate one night and cutting a deep channel. On this sward his festivals are now held. At the one in early spring the god is rejuvenated by being carried to his birthplace and there laid on his side so that he may be recharged, as it were, with the divine essence which still emanates from his natal soil. This process takes six or seven hours, during which time his bearers lie prostrate and his worshippers keep strict silence, but his musicians play to assist the ascent or transmission of the divine spirit, as well as to relieve the tedium of the god's inactivity." [1]

In the Plains of the Panjāb real serpent-worship must have existed in the time of Alexander the Great. It can still be traced as a survival in popular religion and folklore. If, for instance, we hear of a festival observed in the Gurdāspur district, and associated with the month Sāvan, at which the girls of every village go out together to some pond or stream, taking some sweetbread with them and there eat, sing, and swing, there is some reason to presume that this custom originates from the worship of the Nāgas at the commencement of the rainy season.[2]

We may also briefly refer to the cult of the 'Singhs' which belongs to the Panjāb and the western parts of the United Provinces. They are described as snake-gods who, although they cause fever, are not very malevolent, often taking away pain. They have great power over the milch cattle; the milk of the eleventh day after calving is sacred to them,[3] and libations of milk are always acceptable. As is also the case with certain Nāgas, they are generally distinguished by some colour, as indicated by their names—Kali 'black', Hari 'green', and Bhuri 'grey'. Often the diviner will declare a fever to be caused by some Singh whom no one has ever heard of before, but to whom a shrine must be built, and so they multiply in the most perplexing manner. They are the servants of Bāsak Nāg, the serpent-king.[4]

Much has been written about Gūgā, the deified hero, who is greatly venerated, especially by the lower classes in the Eastern Panjāb, the United Provinces, and Rajputana.[5] His legend shows infinite variation, but its close affinity with Nāga worship

[1] Cf. the custom in connexion with the masks of *Kālī Nāg* of Jari referred to above, p. 259.

[2] *Gurdaspur District Gazetteer*, p. 76.

[3] We may compare the singular custom in Pāngī and other parts of the Chināb valley, where for a fixed time in the month of Sāvan, and sometimes for the whole of that month, all the milk of the village is devoted to the local Nāg. Cf. *Chamba State Gazetteer*, p. 187.

[4] W. Crooke, *Popular Religion*, vol. ii, pp. 132 f. A few shrines of Bhure Singh are reported to exist in Dehra Dun.

[5] A. Cunningham, *A.S.R.*, vols. xiv, pp. 79 ff., and xvii, p. 159. *Ind. Ant.*, vols. xi, pp. 53 f., and **xxiv**, pp. 51 ff. D. Ibbetson. *Karnal Settl. Report*, 378. W. Crooke, *Popular Religion*, vol. i, pp. 211 ff. *Kangra District Gazetteer*, pp. 102 f. H. A. Rose, *Punjab Glossary*, vol. i, pp. 171 ff. *Maṇḍi State Gazetteer*, pp. 114 ff. *Chamba State Gazetteer*, pp. 183 f.

is evident. Sir Denzil Ibbetson wrote of him that "he is supposed to be the greatest of the snake-gods". This qualification perhaps refers more to the special benefits ascribed to his cult than to the traditions regarding the story of his life in which he has essentially the character of a knight and champion of the faith.

Gūgā, the ruler of the land of Bāgar, as the great prairies of Rajputana are called, is said to have been a valiant Rājput of the Chauhān clan and a contemporary of Prithī Rāj, the last Hindu king of Delhi. But according to another tradition he fell in battle with his forty-five sons and sixty nephews, while opposing Maḥmūd of Ghaznī. A third account places him in the time of Aurangzeb. Nothing, in fact, is known for certain about his history, but a vast body of folklore has clustered around his name. We hear how through the favour of the saint Gorakhnāth he was born of Rani Bāchhal in spite of the intrigues of her sister Kāchhal, how his treacherous twin cousins Arjan and Surjan attacked him, but were defeated and slain, how he was cursed by his mother in consequence and swallowed by the earth, and how after his death he was allowed to visit his wife at midnight. His faithful charger Javādiyā or 'Barley-born' takes a conspicuous part in his wonderful adventures.[1]

Most versions of his legend represent him as closely associated with the Nāgas. In Ludhiana it is even asserted that he was originally a snake and changed his form into that of a man in order to marry a princess. Afterwards he returned to his original shape.[2] Some say that in the cradle he was found sucking a live cobra's head. In most of his legends he is connected with the serpent-king Bāsak Nāg, who helped him to win his bride Siriāl (also called Surail, Surjila, or Chhariāl), who was the daughter of the Raja of Bundi.

When the Raja had broken his pledge and refused Gūgā the hand of his daughter, the hero went to the wood and by his flute-playing charmed the beasts and birds of the forest and also Bāsak Nāg, who placed the services of his satellite, Tātig Nāg, at his disposal. Gūgā then sent Tātig Nāg to Dhūpnagar in the country of Kārū, a land of great wizards. Here the Nāg, finding Siriāl in her garden, assumed his snake form and bit her while she was bathing in the tank. Again assuming the appearance of a Brahmin, he professed to be a snake-charmer. When ushered into the Raja's presence, Tātig Nāg exacted a promise in writing that the betrothal should be carried out if Siriāl recovered and then cured her, taking a branch of the *nīm*-tree, and using charms, but showing practical ability by sucking the poison down into her big toe. The king then fixed the

[1] In the Panjāb Hills the horse of Gūgā is known by the name of Nīlā. It was born on the same day as his master. This and some other details of his story seem to be reminiscences of Buddhist lore.

[2] *Ludhiana District Gazetteer*, 1904 (Lahore, 1907), pp. 88 f.

wedding seven days ahead, yet in spite of the shortness of time, Gūgā was miraculously transported to Dhūpnagar in time for the nuptials.[1]

According to the version of the legend current in Chambā, Bāsak Nāg was not Gūgā's ally and helper in his wooing, but his rival. When the hero set out with a large retinue for the capital of his prospective father-in-law (here the king of Bengal), he was opposed by Bāsak and his host, but the end was that the Nāg army was completely destroyed.[2]

Gūgā counts his devotees by the thousands in the Panjāb and the United Provinces.[3] He is especially worshipped in the Eastern Panjāb ; his shrines, called *maṛī* or *k͟hāngāh*, may be seen in almost every large village throughout the sub-montane tract and in the Kāṅgṛā Hills. Strange to say, this 'Cid Campador' of the Hindu faith is not only worshipped by all castes of Hindus, but also by Muslims on the strength of a tradition that Gūgā before his death became a convert to Islām and even made a pilgrimage to Mecca. He is known under a great variety of names—Gūgā Bīr and Gūgā Pīr, Zāhir Pīr and Zāhir Diwān, Bāgarvālā (from his reputed homeland), Rām Deva (in Hissār), and Mundlīkh (in Chambā).

His great popularity is no doubt largely owing to the belief that, when duly propitiated, he can save from snake-bite, and cause those who neglect him to be bitten. The attendants attached to his shrines adopt different cures ; some give the patient leaves of trees on the shrine to eat, others sprinkle holy water on the part affected. Snakes are part of the rude ornamentation of his shrine which usually contains a group of clumsily fashioned figures of stone or earth. Gūgā himself on horseback occupies the centre ; he holds a long staff or spear, above him two snakes meet, one being coiled round his staff. He is attended by his sister Gugṛī, his vizier Kailu Bīr, and his *guru* Gorakhnāth.[4]

In the Kāṅgṛā district Gūgā not only cures snake-bite, but also brings illness, bestows sons and good fortune. His offerings are first-fruits, goats, and cakes. He has a famous shrine at Barmar where the resident priests claim to cure the bites of snakes by making the patients eat of the sacred earth of the place and rubbing some of it on the wound. Pilgrims who often come from long distances also take away some of this earth as a protection.

At Chhappar, on the southern border of the Ludhiana district, there is a large shrine of Gūgā, and an annual fair is held in his honour on the Anant Chaudās, i.e. the 14th of

[1] R. C. Temple, *Legends of the Punjab*, vol. i, pp. 121 ff.

[2] According to a version current in Kuḷū, the bride of Gūgā, named Sūryar Nāgnī, was the daughter of Bāski Nāg.

[3] Some thirty years ago their number was estimated at 35,000 for the Punjab and 123,000 for the United Provinces.

[4] In the shrine of Gūgā at Sultānpur, the capital of Kuḷū, which I visited in 1904, Bāski Nāg in the form of a snake was shown issuing from the ground in front of the hero's horse.

the bright half of Bhādon. The fair, though a Hindu one, is attended also by Muslims; the average number of visitors is estimated at 50,000 people. The money and grain offerings made at the shrine, which are received by the resident Brahmins, amount to some Rs. 300 a year. People scoop out earth from a pond near the shrine seven times, and cattle are brought to it and kept for a night at the shrine to protect them from snakes. It is said that a person bitten will recover if put beside it.

Another *maṛī* or Gūgā temple of some repute is found at Raikoṭ in the same district; here, too, a *melā* is held on the Anant Chaudās. North of the town is a small tank called the Rattowānā. Here a mound of earth has from early times been used for Gūgā's propitiation, because close by is a large grove of *karīr* bushes, the haunt of snakes. The foundation of the *maṛī* was due to the appearance of a snake on the mound, which portent was interpreted by a Khatri girl (who was possessed by Gūgā) as an injunction that a shrine should be built on the spot. As many as 50,000 people used to frequent the fair, but Chhappar has supplanted it in popular favour. The *pūjārīs* are Brahmins.[1]

In many other places annual fairs are held in honour of Gūgā; the usual date of these gatherings, however, is not the Anant Chaudās, but the 9th of the dark half of Bhādon called the Gūgā-naumi. This date is said by some so be the date of his birth, and by others to be that of his wedding or of his death. On this occasion his *chhari* or switch, consisting of a long bamboo surmounted by peacock-feathers, a cocoanut, some fans, and a blue flag, is taken round by Jogis who ask for alms. In the Maṇḍi State his followers, mostly belonging to the caste of the Nāths, carry the images of Gūgā and his attendants with their canopies of cobra hoods, from house to house, singing songs in his honour and begging for alms.

In the Panjāb there are over 30,000 special votaries of the snake-godlings and in the United Provinces 25,000.[2] The great majority of them are, no doubt, to be found among the inhabitants of the Hill districts.

In Gaṛhwāl there exists a universal tradition that the Nāgas once resided in the valley of the Alaknanda. At the present day Śesh Nāg is honoured at Pandukeswar, Bhekal Nāg at Ratgaon, Sangal Nāg at Talor, Banpur Nāg at Margaon, Lohandea Nāg at Jelam in the Niti valley, and Pushkara Nāg at Nāgnāth in Nāgpur.[3]

In the Gangetic plains, too, there is evidence of serpent worship not only among the rural population, but also in the towns. It will suffice to quote two monuments found at Benares and Allahabad, well known as great centres of orthodox Hinduism.

In the north-western part of the city of Benares there is an ancient well, called Nāg

[1] *Ludhiana District Gazetteer*, 1904 (Lahore, 1910), pp. 88 f.

[2] W. Crooke, op. cit., vol. ii. p. 122.

[3] *Garhwal District Gazetteer* (1910), p. 112.

Kūān (Skt. *Nāga-kūpa*), which bears marks of considerable antiquity. It is dedicated to the Nāgarāja Ananta or Śesha, who is believed to have incarnated himself in Patañjali, the famous grammarian and author of the *Mahābhāsha*. On that account the grammarians of the city gather on the spot and discuss grammar on the 5th of the bright half of the month Sāvan. This is the date of the Nāgapañchamī or Festival of the Nāgas. On this occasion common folk, too, repair to the ancient well and make their offerings, the average attendance being estimated at 4,000 persons.[1]

Some fifty years ago a Hindu author called attention to the existence of a temple of Vāsuki at Prayāg or Allahābād, as it is nowadays commonly called. " The temple," he writes,[2] " is beautifully situated amidst a grove of trees, overlooking the Ganges, which flows just under it. The scenery is charming. It is a massive building on an elevated terrace, and looks quite new, for we learn that a hundred years ago it was all repaired, and the *pakka* stone *ghāṭ* under it constructed by a millionaire of Daraganj, a detached village of Allahābād lying on the bank of the river. The image of the Nāga Vāsuki is carved out of a black stone set in the front wall of the temple, and is about a foot and a half high. It is neatly sculptured as a hooded snake standing erect when enraged. There are other idols of less note."

" A large fair is held on Nāgapanchamī, to which many of the Hindus from Allahābād and neighbouring villages come, to secure the double merit of bathing in the sacred stream and worshipping the serpent-god on the auspicious occasion. The temple is resorted to by every pilgrim to Prayāg, with whom it is a belief that the merit of bathing in the sacred confluence of Gaṅgā and Jamunā is not complete until he visits the temple of the king of serpents. Pilgrims to other sacred places in India take Ganges water from this place only, as it is considered purer than elsewhere in Prayāg."

Monier Williams, who personally visited the Vāsuki temple at Dārā Ganj notes that the priest attached to it was not a Brahmin but a man of low caste. " On my expressing a wish ", he adds, " for some memorial of the place, he tore off a rude drawing of a many-headed serpent, which was fastened to the door of the shrine, and presented it to me." [3]

In Bihār, according to Sir George Grierson,[4] the snake-god Nāg is generally worshipped by the agricultural population. " In Saon (Śrāvaṇa) crowds of women, calling themselves his wives (*nāgin*), go out begging for 2½ days, during which period they neither sleep under

[1] M. A. Sherring, *The sacred city of the Hindus* (London, 1868), pp. 86 f., and 220. For the above information the author is indebted to the Principal of Queen's College, Benares.

[2] *Ind. Ant.*, vol. ii (1874), p. 124.

[3] *Religious Thought and Life in India* (1883), p. 323.

[4] G. A. Grierson, *Bihar Peasant Life* (Calcutta, 1885), pp. 404 f.

a roof nor eat salt. Half the proceeds of the begging are given to Brahmins and the other half invested in salt and sweetmeats, which are eaten by the whole village. During the expedition several characteristic songs are sung."

From the various data we have been able to adduce it will be sufficiently clear that in vast regions of Northern India the Nāg still holds a prominent position in popular religion and tradition. Yet in those parts there is little evidence of real serpent worship, *viz.*, of the adoration of the live animal. Ophiolatry only survives either in the form of a worship proffered to certain gods and saints for protection against the dangerous reptiles (and in many cases these divine protectors themselves are or were originally conceived in the semblance of snakes), or, as is the case in the Alpine Panjāb, the ancient serpent-demons have developed into weather-godlings and are now essentially the spirits of the water.

Even in a tract like Kuḷū where the veneration of the Nāgs is so greatly in evidence, the live snake is hardly ever an object of veneration.[1] In fact, the hill people show very little reluctance in killing snakes if these come in their way. The Nāg temples are decorated with the effigies of serpents, but no instance is known of live serpents being kept or fed in those shrines. In some mountain tracts there is a certain species of snake only which is held sacred. In Maṇḍi it is a large grass-snake, light brown above and of light colour below, which is worshipped by the people. In Chambā it is a whitish-coloured species that frequents the walls of houses, and is said to drink milk. *Pūjā* and incense are offered to it, and its presence is regarded as a good omen.[2] It is not a little curious that in both these cases the sacred snake is indicated by the name of *nāg*. It must be remembered that the real *nāg* of the plains occurs only in the lower hills; in Maṇḍi it is said to be rare, in Kuḷū and the greater part of Chambā it does not occur.

In order to find real ophiolatry—the cultus of the live serpent—we must turn our attention to Western and Southern India, where up to the present day it exists in an undisguised form.

Kāṭhiāvāṛ, the peninsula or western portion of the province of Gujarāt, is a great centre of Nāg worship.[3] There are temples of Vāsuki and his brother Vanduk, locally called

[1] The only instance which has come to my notice is at the foot of the Rohtang Pass, leading from Kuḷū into Lahul. On my way from Rala to the Pass I noticed that one of the load-carriers, a Rājpūt by caste, gathered some flowers and making a *salām*, laid them in front of a hole under a large stone. There, he explained, lived a *Nāg deota* who had the shape of a snake, but did no harm to anybody. On my return I learnt that on this spot there really live a family of snakes described as being spotted and provided with thick heads. They are fed by the people. If food is placed by the hole, first a lizard comes out, who, judging from his white colour, is believed to be very old.

[2] *Maṇḍi State Gazetteer*, p. 13; *Chamba State Gazetteer*, p. 39.

[3] J. W. Watson, *Places of snake-worship in Kathiāwār*. *Ind. Ant.*, vol. iv, pp. 193 ff. Cf. also *Ind. Ant.*, vol. i, pp. 6 f., and vol. iv, p. 6.

Vāsangji and Bāndiā Beli respectively, at Thān and Mandhogaṛh. The two Nāg brothers are said to have settled here after having rid the country of a dangerous demon, Bhīmāsur, at the request of five famous Rishis. To the present day no one is allowed to cut a tree in the grove that surrounds Bāndiā Beli's shrine, and it is said that, should any one ignorantly cut a stick in this grove the snake appears to such a person in his dreams and orders him to return the stick, and should he fail therein, some great calamity shortly befalls him; and, in fact, in or near the grove may be seen many such logs or sticks accidently cut and subsequently returned.

The Vāsuki temple at Thān contains the image of a three-headed cobra with two smaller monocephalous ones—one on each side—carved on the same slab. Besides which there is a figure of the four-armed Vishṇu; while on and in front of the altar on which the images are placed are *śāligrām* stones and *śaṅkh* shells. A common votive offering at this shrine seems to be a representation of the three snakes in alto-rilievo on a flat earthenware tile.

Other Nāg shrines in Kāṭhiāvāṛ are that of Pratik at Talsānā in Jhālāvār, and that of Devānik Charmālia in the village of Chokṛi under Chuḍā. But the most famous snake-temple of Gujarāt is that of the celebrated Dharaṇīdhara or 'Earthholder', situated at the village of Dhemā, a few miles to the north-west of Tharād, in North Gujarāt. This shrine is visited by pilgrims from all parts of India. There is a well-executed image of a cobra in the temple of the Dhem Nāg, as the Dharaṇīdhara is locally called. There are many other local shrines in Gujarāt and Kaṭhiāwāṛ where the cobra is worshipped.

A curious case of serpent-worship was recorded in the year 1875 by Mr. C. E. G. Crawford.[1] While encamped at the village of Khās (*taluka* Dhandhuka), he noticed a *thānak* of Charmālia, a local name for the Nāga, which was not there the year before. On his making inquiries he was told the following story. "A woman in the neighbouring village of Alāu mortally wounded a cobra, and then, for fear of the Dhāndhal Kāṭhis [2] (who are the worshippers in particular of the cobra, the other branches preferring the Sun), got him conveyed on a cot to a field outside Khās, where he was found by the people in a dying state, but with hopes of reviving him, they carried him to the place where the shrine now is, and spread sand for him, and put a canopy over him to shield him from the sun.[3] But in two days he died. Then they bethought themselves of worshipping him. But others objected that, unless he rose from the dead, he could not be held to be a god to be worshipped. So

[1] *Ind. Ant.*, vol. iv, pp. 83 f.

[2] The tribe of the Kāṭhīs from whom Kāṭhiāwaṛ has received its name entered the peninsula from Cutch in the thirteenth and fourteenth centuries.

[3] Cf. above, p. 152.

they waited and were duly rewarded. For, they tell me, from a hole hard by came forth a fine *nāga* exactly like the deceased, and when it was said he must have a consort two *nāgans* followed him out in succession. Then they began to collect money to build the present shrine, which is still unfinished, not having a roof over it. It resembles a wide squat chimney, and contains, besides a live cobra wrapped in a blue cloth, a red-daubed stone said to resemble the hood of a cobra, which appears to be the actual object of worship, and a small pan for fire. This inner shrine is being encircled by four stone walls which are at present only breast-high. On its south-west corner was lying an earthen representation of the hood, coloured red, and much more like the original than the stone in the inner shrine. This shrine, though new, appears to be of high virtue, to judge from the number of strings which are hung on a horizontal rod above it, being—like a large heap of cocoanuts in one corner—the votive offerings of persons who have been cured of some pain, not necessarily snake-bite, on vowing to visit the shrine, and tying one of these strings round the place affected in token thereof."

In the whole of Southern India serpent-worship is prevalent.[1] It is especially the cobra which is held sacred. The higher castes consider it a sin to kill it, and believe that the man who does so will be stricken with all kind of misfortune.

The great popularity of this cult in the South is testified by the snake-slabs or Nāga-kals, which are usually found, sometimes in great numbers, at the entrance of a town or village. Groups of such stones may be seen in a corner of the courtyard of a temple, either Hindu or Jain, near a tank or under a sacred tree. They are mostly due to childless wives who make a vow to instal a snake-stone (*Nāga-pratishṭhā*) if they are blessed with offspring. The usual practice is to have a figure of a cobra carved on a small stone slab, to place it in a well for six months in order to imbue it with life (*prāṇa-pratishṭhā*) by means of *mantras* and certain ceremonies, and then to set it up under a *pīpal-* or *nīm*-tree.[2] These two trees are often planted together and ' married ', as the saying goes. A platform is built around and the trees receive the worship of Brahmins and members of other high castes. It is believed that a woman will obtain children if she walks round the trees 108 times daily for 45 days consecutively.[3] The Nāga-kals are preferably placed in the shade of a pair of such married trees. Serpent worship, as we find it here, is therefore closely associated with tree

[1] Cf. J. Burgess, *A.S.R.W.I.* (London, 1874), pp. 43 f., pl. lvi (ten specimens of Nāg slabs from Konur Huli, Sinde-Manauli, Badāmī, and Aivalli in the Belgām Kaladgi districts of Bombay. *Ind. Ant.*, vol. iv, pp. 5 f., and vii, pp. 40 ff., and *Annual Report Archl. Department, Southern Circle*, for 1914–15, pp. 34 ff.

[2] These two trees—the Ficus religiosa and the Melia Azadriachta—are the *aśvattha* and *nimba* of Sanskrit literature. The *aśvattha* is called *Nāga-bandhu*, i.e. " kinsman of the Nāgas."

[3] The number 108 ($2^2 \times 3^3$) is regarded as auspicious.

PLATE XXIX.

NĀGAKALS OF KIKKERI (MYSORE).

[To face p. 270

worship. Sometimes the snake is supposed actually to reside in the tree and in all probability was originally conceived as its spirit.

The Nāga-kals show a considerable variety of pattern. The simplest and perhaps commonest type of these snake-slabs exhibit a single cobra standing, as it were, on the tip of his tail and curling upwards with expanded hood. Sometimes the Nāga is a faithful effigy of the natural animal, but very often, presumably to emphasize his divine character, he is made polycephalous (Plate XXIX). The number of the heads varies between three, five, and seven, but apparently there exists a certain preference for the figure five. The number of heads, it will be noticed, is always uneven. In some specimens a miniature *liṅga*, evidently meant as a symbol of procreation, is carved on the expanded hood ; or an umbrella, emblematic of royalty, may be seen over the Nāgarāja. Usually the cobra is carved in relief on a stone slab, some four feet in height. But at Adichanallur in the Tinnevelly district there is a large group of Nāga-kals [1] which show this peculiarity that they are carved in the round. The snakes are either single-hooded or many-hooded, and several of the latter have a little human figure seated on the coils and overshadowed by the serpent's hood. This figure is said to represent Kṛishṇa, but possibly has at the same time some reference to the wish for offspring which generally prompts the devotees of the Nāg to erect these stones.

A somewhat more elaborate type of Nāga-kals shows a pair of cobras intertwined in caduceus fashion, apparently in the act of copulation. Usually both snakes are monocephalous. If carved in profile, the animals sometimes are provided with a protuberance on the top of the head. It has somewhat the appearance of a crest or a pair of ears, but perhaps is meant to indicate the legendary jewel which the Nāg is supposed to wear on his head. In some other specimens which show the hooded snake facing, the jewel is very clearly marked.

In some cases the intertwined snakes are very artistically treated, as in a specimen from a village in the Belgām district (Bombay). Here only one of the two cobras, presumably the male, is shown with expanded hood. This is also the case with a snake-stone from Sinde-Manauli on the Mālaprabhā. One of the Nāga-kals from the Brahmeśvara temple at Kikkeri (Mysore) shows the same peculiarity. (Plate XXIX.) The circular spaces formed by the two interlaced serpents are very often filled with ornamental rosettes. The uppermost field, immediately beneath the snakes' heads, sometimes contains a miniature *liṅga*.

[1] In his *Progress Report*, for 1914–15, pl. xi, Mr. A. H. Longhurst has reproduced a number of these stones. He observes that the Nāga-kals of this type, especially when viewed from the back, represent in form the phallic emblem of Śiva.

Finally we must notice a type of snake-stones in which the serpent-deity appears as a hybrid being, its upper half being human and the lower half serpentine. This hybrid is a female and in all probability represents the serpent-goddess who in Southern India is known by the name of Mudama. Over her head she wears the usual hood combined of three, five, or seven snakes' heads. She holds both hands joined in front of her breast, and in each arm she has a baby snake. These representations of the serpent-deity, however interesting in connexion with popular religion, are not very pleasing from an aesthetic point of view. The thick and short-set snake body combined with the woman's bust gives these sculptures a singularly ungraceful appearance.

Two remarkable stones of this class were discovered by Mr. Longhurst at Hampi in the ruins of the ancient capital Vijayanagar. The one shows the snake-mother holding two little snakes in her arms in the usual manner, while two more stand at her sides. The other specimen is a very elaborate sculpture surmounted by a *makara-toraṇa* ; the Nāgī with her two little ones is attended by two human satellites of small size, both female, standing at each side of her.

Among a collection of more than twenty Nāga-kals set up in a garden near an ancient tank at the town of Anekal (some 20 miles south-east of Bangalore) there are three of the type last described ; the rest are ordinary slabs carved with one or two cobras (Plate XXX).

In the district of North Kānara, in the Kumpta *taluka*, at a place called Nāga-tīrtha, there is a well-built tank around which are small artificial caves containing thousands of serpent images.

In the South Kānara district on one of the highest mountains of the Western Ghāṭs, named Subrahmaṇya, there is one of the most famous serpent-temples of India.[1] The mountain, which is two-pointed, precipitous, and of peculiar shape, is one of the most prominent heights in these parts, resembling, as seen from Mercara, a gigantic bullock hump. Its elevation is 5,626 feet above the level of the sea. The locality is extremely wild and full of fever, excessively so during the cold and dry seasons ; nevertheless, great numbers of pilgrims resort thither especially during the December festival. The temple has no architectural pretensions, being, indeed, mostly constructed of laterite, the sanctuary in the centre is of granite, and contains the idol Subbaraya (= serpent-king) said to be a shapeless block. The shrine is square in form with an open cloister running round the four sides, and numbers of the ' coiling folk ' reside in it in holes and crevices made for them.

[1] M. J. Walhouse, *Ind. Ant.*, vol. vii, p. 42. According to the *Imperial Gazetteer*, new ed., vol. xxiii, p. 115, the correct name of the mountain is Pushpagiri. The name Subrahmaṇya, applied to the village at the foot of the mountain is in reality an appellation of the serpent-king Śesha, used in Southern India. It is well known that it is also another name of Kārtikeya or Skanda.

GROUP OF NAGAKALS AT ANEKAL (MYSORE)

[To face p. 27]

The annual festival takes place on the sixth day of the bright half of the month of Mārgaśīrsha (November-December); it is known as Subrahmanya-shashthī or Subbaraya-shashthī or Kukka-shashthī. Thousands of Brahmins are feasted on this occasion. At the same time a cattle fair is held at the foot of the mountain. Lepers and persons believed to be under the influence of evil spirits are brought to be cured by the miraculous power of the serpent-deity. People anxious to obtain offspring make a vow at this shrine which consists in fasting on the day of the festival and rolling in the remains of food left on the dishes spread before the Brahmins. Numerous devotees who have made a vow roll and wriggle serpent-fashion round the temple, and some will even roll up to it from the foot of the mountain, a mile distant.

A person supposed to be possessed by the spirit of Subrahmanya, dances at the temple, and is believed to have the power of foretelling the future. On the day of the *melā* one of the priests puts a leather bag on one of his hands, and, with the hand thus protected, takes out some handfuls of earth from the holes inhabited by the snakes. This earth is distributed to the assembled worshippers as a mark of the deity's favour. It is believed to cleanse from leprosy if rubbed on the parts affected and to remove the stigma of barrenness from women if a little be daily put in the mouth.

In the jungle surrounding the shrine of Subrahmanya there grows a species of cane, known as *Nāga-veta*, or ' Nāga-cane '. A walking-stick of this cane is considered to afford protection against the poison of snakes.

The serpentine body-rolling described here, which is called *anga-pratachinam* (Skt. *anga-pradakshina*), is practised also further south, where small snake-temples, called *Nāga-kovil* in Tamil), are not infrequent. Not far from the town of Madura, on the bank of the Vaigai river, there is such a shrine where men for payment will perform any number of rollings round as proxies for persons who have vowed them. These rollings are done very rapidly, with great fury and vociferation.

Other famous serpent-temples are reported to exist at Nāgapatnam (or Negapatam), the well-known ancient seaport on the coast of Coromandel and at Bhomaparanden in the Hyderabad State. The shrine at the former place is dedicated to the serpent-deity under the name of Nāganātha. Inside the temple near the image there is a white-ant hill, to which large offerings are made in honour of the serpent-god.

The Malabar coast is a great seat of the serpent cult. " Usually a clump of wild jungle trees luxuriantly festooned with graceful creepers is to be found in the south-west corner of the gardens of all respectable Malayali Hindus. The spot is free to nature to deal with it as she likes. Every tree and bush, every branch and twig is sacred. This is the Nāga-kotta (' Snake-shrine '). There is mostly a granite stone carved after the fashion of a cobra's hood set up and consecrated in this waste spot. If the shrines are not respected it is supposed to have a bad influence on human beings. Leprosy, itch, barrenness in women, deaths of children, the frequent appearance of snakes in the garden, and other diseases and calamities supposed to be brought about by poison, are all set down to the anger of the cobras. If there is a Nāga-shrine in the garden, sacrifices and ceremonies are resorted to. If there is none, then the place is diligently dug up, and search is made for a snake-stone, and if one is found it is concluded that the calamities have occurred because of there having previously been a snake shrine at the spot, and because the shrine had been neglected. A shrine is then at once formed, and costly sacrifices and ceremonies serve to allay the Nāga's anger. In this district the Nāga is the tutelar deity of the house, and god and shrine are conveyed with the property and frequently specified in deeds of transfer. *Pūjā* is offered at least once a year, often by a Brahmin; and the serpents are periodically propitiated by songs and dances, called 'Nagam-pattu'. The performance of such songs in private houses is supposed to be effective in procuring offspring. The high priest of the serpent cult in Malabar is the Pāmbanmākkād Nambūdiri, who lives in the town of Ponnāni in a house full of cobras which are said to be harmless to his family." [1]

In South Kānara two curious rites are known to exist in connexion with serpent-worship; they have been described as follows: [2] "Three afflictions are looked upon as due to the wrath of serpents for having killed a snake in a former life, namely leprosy, childlessness, and sore eyes. People so afflicted often perform costly ceremonies to remove the curse, which are superintended by the Mādhava Brahmins, originally fishermen, and not acknowledged as Brahmins out of Kānara. There are two ceremonies in ordinary use. The first, generally performed by a childless man, is *Sarpa-samposhkara,* or 'the serpent's funeral'. The fifth, sixth, fifteenth, or thirtieth of the month is chosen, and the family priest called to preside. The childless or afflicted penitent bathes and dresses himself in silk or linen attire, a spot in the house is chosen and the priest sprinkles some consecrated rice about it, to drive away any lurking devil, and then he and the penitent sit side by side on two wooden stools, kneading rice or wheat flour into dough. He then makes the figure of a serpent, and with many muttered holy *mantras* is believed to animate the figure and transform it for the time into a live serpent. Milk and sugar are then offered to it, and it is worshipped as a deity. After this other *mantras* are said, undoing the spell previously wrought, and taking away the life that was given. The serpent being dead, the penitent assumes the garb of mourning, and shaves off his beard and moustaches. He then carries

[1] *Malabar District Gazetteer* (1908), vol. i, p. 155.

[2] *Ind. Ant.,* vol. vii, pp. 42 ff.

the figure on his head to the bank of a river, where he reverentially places it upon a pile. The figure is then fenced round with chips of sandalwood and camphor, and melted butter poured over it. The pile is then lit with fire brought by the penitent from his own house with a vow that it shall be used only for the burning of the serpent-god. When burnt, the ashes are thrown into the river. The penitent is considered unholy and must not be touched for three days. On the fourth day the funeral of the serpent-god ends with an entertainment to eight unmarried youths below the age of twenty; they are held to represent eight serpents, and are treated with the utmost respect. This curious symbolical ceremony evidently denotes penitence and amends for the supposed killing of one of the sacred creatures in a former life, and the temporary ascription of serpent-nature to the young men seems a trace of the very ancient and widespread idea of the transformation of men into serpents, and serpents into men, which appears almost extinct in Lower India."

"The second ceremony, called *Nāga-maṇḍala*, is resorted to when that first described has failed in producing the hoped-for results. The penitent gives a great feast to his caste-men and unmarried youths, who are again supposed to personate serpents. In the evening bruised rice is scattered over a spot previously selected and the figure of a great serpent traced out in it. The figure is then worshipped, and a band of musicians summoned and well primed with toddy to sustain them in their work. They dress themselves in women's clothes and put on jewels, drumming and piping go on furiously, and the leader imitates the deity, reeling and writhing about frantically, and at times uttering words which are devoutly attended to as though spoken by the deity; yet the musicians are low-caste people. The wild discordant music is often prolonged throughout the night." [1]

In Kānara the persons supposed to be possessed by the serpent-deity are known by the title of Nāga-pātrī ('Vessel of the Nāga'). They are Brahmins and used to enjoy great repute. Disputes were referred to them for settlement, and their word was law. A summons from one of the Nāgapātrīs to a litigant was almost instantly obeyed. It appears, however, that the influence of these priests has considerably declined.

The great festival in honour of the serpents is the Nāgapañchamī, which, as the name indicates, is celebrated on the fifth day of the bright fortnight (the period of the waxing moon) of the month of Sāvan (Skt. *Śrāvaṇa*), the first month of the rainy season. This is early in August, about the middle of the rainy season. The rites to be observed on that day are laid down in a Sanskrit work, called *Vratarāja*, which appears to be extracted from

[1] The rite described here with the inspired priest regarded as the mouthpiece of the serpent-deity, and the wild music produced by low-caste musicians recalls the similar customs in vogue at the Nāg and Devī shrines in the Western Himālaya.

Hemādri.[1] Here follows the passage in question in translation : " In the month of Śrāvaṇa, on the fifth day of the bright fortnight, the poisonous ones must be drawn with cowdung on both sides of the door. This hath been declared to be a very holy day ; worship is to be performed on the fifth during twelve years. On the fourth (i.e. the preceding day) people must take only one meal and on the day itself only at night. One should make a Nāga of gold (?), silver, wood, earth, turmeric, or sandal or cause five serpents to be drawn. On the fifth day they should be worshipped with devotion ; the Nāgas are said to have five hoods. The five Nāgas must be worshipped according to the rule with parched grain (*lāja*), and with the five nectars,[2] with the flowers of the oleander, the ' hundred-leaf ',[3] the jessamine, and the red lotus, likewise with powdered sandal and other incense. Thereupon Brahmins ought to be fed with ghee, milk-rice, and sweetmeats. Ananta, Vāsuki, Śesha, Padma, and Kambala, and even so the Nāga Karkoṭaka, and the serpent Aśvatara, Dhṛitarāshṭra, Śaṅkhapāla, Kāliya, and likewise Takshaka, and the great Nāga Piṅgala are lauded month by month. At the end of the observance (*vrata*) there should be a *pāraṇa* (i.e. a meal to break the fast) with milk, and Brahmins are to be fed. A Nāga of gold (?), and a cow, as well as garments ought to be given to Vyāsa of immeasurable glory. In this wise one should ever worship the Nāgas with devotion, in particular on the fifth day, with milk and milk-rice. There should be no digging of the earth either by day or by night."

The festival as practised in the Konkan is described by a Hindu scholar, Rao Sahib V. N. Mandlik, in the following terms.[4] " On this day, early in the morning, each family brings an earthen representation of a serpent, or paints a family of five, seven, or nine serpents with rubbed sandalwood or turmeric. The vessels used in performing the worship are placed in front. Flowers, rubbed sandalwood, turmeric, parched rice, and beans or parched gram, and jowari (*holcus sorghum*) are offered to the serpents thus painted. Lamps are lighted and waved ; incense is offered ; and food and fruits are placed before them. On this day, only boiled food is partaken of by the people, and the dishes prepared are generally of a coarser kind than on other holidays. After the morning meal a lamp is generally kept lighted throughout the day by the side of the painting or image, and milk and edibles are also placed close by. In the afternoon people go to some place, generally an ant-hill,

[1] The passage in Sanskrit and English translation is given by Rao Sahib V. N. Mandlik in *Jl. Bombay br., R.A.S.*, vol. ix, pp. 174 f. The rites to be observed at the Nāga-panchamī are also described in Puranic literature, e.g. in the *Bhavishyat-purāṇa*.

[2] Milk, curd, ghee, honey, and sugar.

[3] Mr. Mandlik renders *śatapattra* by lotus, but as the lotus (*padma*) is mentioned subsequently, it is probable that some other flower is meant.

[4] Op cit., pp. 170 f.

where serpents are said by local tradition to reside. Here, generally, snake-charmers may be seen with live serpents to which offerings are made by the multitude. Even in Bombay these men take snakes round to the houses of the people in the native town, and all classes of the inhabitants amuse themselves by giving them different kinds of edibles. In the evening flowers and incense are again offered, lights waved, and edibles placed before the image or painting as the case may be, and one or more lamps are kept burning." The worshippers sit up all through the night, this watching being called by some keeping the serpents awake. The worship is mostly performed by the female members of the household, and at the conclusion all the ladies and children gather and the eldest of the former repeats the following *kāhāṇī* or story.

The Festival of the Nāgas

" Oh God! Nāgas, hear. There is a city, called Māṇikpura [or Maṇipura]. In it lived a Gāvaḍa (Gauṛ ?) Brahmin. He was ignorant of the Nāga-pañchamī. And he did not know that on that day there should be no ploughing, no digging, no picking and plucking, no burning and roasting. He went, therefore, to plough the land in his field on that day as usual. Now, there was in one place in the field a hole of a Nāgiṇa (a female cobra), and in it were her young ones, and they died by the striking of the plough. The Nāgiṇa who had gone out returned, and finding that all her young ones were dead, she grew enraged and set out to ascertain who it was that had killed them. Thus she came to the house of the Brahmin and seeing that blood had stuck to his plough, she decided that it was he who had killed her young ones. She, therefore, bit the Brahmin and all the members of his household who had gone to sleep, and killed them. And in order that his whole family might become extinct, she went to bite his daughter who had been married in another village. But the daughter had painted the Nāgs, and having worshipped them and given them offerings, had placed before them at night, frankincense and other fragrant things, lamps, edibles, etc. On seeing this the Nāgiṇa enjoyed the good things that had been placed there, and being pleased, said to the girl: ' O daughter, thy father killed all my young ones to-day, while ploughing the field. After having, therefore, killed all the persons in thy maternal home, I had come to bite thee, too, but as thou didst remember me and worship me, I am pleased and, therefore, I do not bite thee.'

" On hearing this, the daughter said: ' Thou hast killed all the persons in my maternal home; tell me some remedy by which they may come to life again. Thereupon the Nāgiṇa said: ' Do thou take this nectar and sprinkle it over their bodies, and thereby they will be restored to life.' Meanwhile the people in that Brahmin's village began to inquire why it was that the Brahmin had not yet arisen, and opening his door found that all the persons in the house had died. Just then the daughter arrived and sprinkling upon them the nectar given by the Nāgiṇa, restored them to life. Then she told her father all that happened, and added: 'Now from this day, when the month of Śrāvaṇa cometh, thou shouldst worship the Nāgs on the fifth day in the bright fortnight according to the rites laid down, and should place before them at night frankincense, lamps, and food. And on that day thou shalt not dig, neither shalt thou kill anything on that day.'

"From that day onwards the Brahmin began to act accordingly: the Nāgapañchamī became known to all the men in the village, and all proceeded to observe the festival of snakes. As the Nāgs were pleased with the daughter of the Brahmin, so may they be pleased with us and with you. O Nāgas, may your story of sixty sentences told in five be productive of good fruit to the narrator as well as to the hearer thereof."

At the time of repeating the above story, the reciter and her female hearers each take a few grains of rice in their hands, and at the conclusion they are partly exchanged and partly stuck to their foreheads."

In Northern India, too, especially in the Gangetic plains, is the Nāgapañchamī observed.

In Bengal the date of this festival is the fifth lunar day of Śrāvaṇa (July–August), but the observance of the rites is continued up to Bhādrapada (August–September). On these days a milky hedge-plant (*Euphorbia lingularum*) is planted on a raised mound of earth in the courtyard of the house, and in the form of this plant the goddess Manasā is worshipped. A person whose father, mother, or any relative happens to have died by snake-bite is specially enjoined to perform this ceremony, part of which consists in offering milk with the object of propitiating them. The people repair to places where snakes, especially cobras, are generally known to remain concealed and make offerings to them of milk, plantains, etc.

The goddess Manasā who is worshipped in connexion with the festival is identified with the sister of the serpent-king Vāsuki who was married to the hermit Jaratkāru and became the mother of Āstīka who, according to the ancient saga, related in the *Ādi-parvan*, was to save the Nāgas from being exterminated at the serpent sacrifice of Janamejaya.[1] Manasā is believed to afford protection against snake-bite, and is hence called Vishahari, 'poison-destroyer'. She is represented as a handsome female of a golden colour, sitting on the water-lily and clothed with snakes.[2]

[1] Cf. above, pp. 59 f.

[2] On the worship of Manasā, cf. J. Murdoch, *Hindu and Muhammadan festivals* (1904), p. 55; B. A. Gupte, *Hindu holidays and ceremonials* (1919), pp. 146 ff.; *Hindu and Muhammadan Feasts* (1914), pp. 57 f.

In Bihār the women mark their houses with lines of cowdung, and worship Śesh Nāg with milk and parched grain. On the Gobar Pāñche, which falls on the fifth of the dark half of the same month (late in July), the same god is often worshipped in Patna instead of on the former festival. This is called Behra Pañche in South Bhāgalpur.[1]

In the United Provinces the usual custom is for the head of the family to bathe on the morning of the feast, to paint on the wall of his sleeping-room two rude representations of serpents, and to make offerings to Brahmins. People pray to the eight chief Nāgas; girls throw some playthings into the water, and labourers take a holiday and worship the tools of their craft. Seven days before the festival people steep a mixture of wheat, gram, and pulse in water. On the morning of the feast they take a wisp of grass, tie it up in the form of a snake, dip it in the water in which the gram has been steeped, and offer it with money and sweetmeats to the serpents. In the eastern districts milk and dried rice are poured into a snake's hole. In some parts of the province it is the custom that girls let dolls float in the water of some convenient river or tank, and the village lads beat the dolls with long switches cut for the purpose. To account for this rite a legend is told which is an amplification of the saga of Janamejaya and the Nāgas.[2]

In Gaṛhwāl the ground is freely smeared with cowdung and mud, and figures of five, seven, or nine serpents are rudely drawn with sandalwood powder or turmeric; rice, beans, or peas are parched; lamps are lighted and waved before them; incense is burnt and food and fruit offered. These observances take place both morning and evening, and the night is spent in listening to stories in praise of the Nāga.[3]

In the Mirzapur district the Nāg Deotā is worshipped especially by the Kols on the occasion of the Nāgapañchamī, and at the villages of Bhainsia Tola and Tarkapur fairs are held which have an average attendance of a thousand people. The date of these fairs, however, appears to be the 11th of the bright half of Sāwan.[4]

In some parts of the United Provinces the Nāgapañchamī is celebrated in Bhādon (Skt. *Bhādrapada*),[5] but for several districts the date is stated to be the fifth of the bright half of Sāwan, which, as we have seen, is the day generally observed in the Deccan.

In Nepal the festival of the Nāgas is held on the fifth of the dark half of Sāwan. This day is locally believed to commemorate a fearful fight between Garuḍa and the Nāgas. The image of Garuḍa at Changu-Nārāyaṇ is reported regularly to perspire on the

[1] Grierson, *Bihar Peasant Life*, p. 400, § 1445.

[2] W. Crooke, *Popular Religion*, vol. i, pp. 138 f.; *Hindu and Muhammadan Feasts* (1914), p. 59.

[3] Atkinson, *Himalayan Gazetteer*, vol. ii, p. 836.

[4] *Mirzapur District Gazetteer*, p. 101.

[5] Mr. Crooke, op. cit., vol. ii, p. 137, says that the Nāga-pañchamī is held on the fifth day of Bhādon, but does not specify the *paksha*.

anniversary of that dreadful struggle. The priests wipe the idol with a handkerchief which is sent to the king. A single thread of the precious linen, if soaked in water, transforms it into an infallible remedy against snake-bite. The rites proper are celebrated at the confluence of two streams under the superintendence of a Nevar. After an ablution in the early morning attended by various ceremonies, he takes a dish on which he places rice, vermillion, milk, water, rice-flour, flowers, ghee, spices, sandal-powder, and incense. While burning the incense, he chants a benediction upon the Nāgarājas and prays that they may bless the crop.[1]

In the Panjāb, on the day of the Nāgapañchamī, a figure is drawn in black on the house-wall. It represents the snake-god in his dwelling-place and is believed to prevent the house from being infested with snakes.[2]

Although there may be variations in the date and in the local traditions and modes of observance, the Nāgapañchamī is still celebrated in large portions of India according to the ancient rites. Thus it continues to testify to the feelings of awe and veneration which the serpent evokes in the minds of the population since the earliest times we have cognizance of. These feelings are, perhaps, nowhere better expressed than in a poem by a poetess of modern India which will form an appropriate conclusion to the present volume.

The Festival of Serpents

Shining ones awake, we seek your chosen temples
In caves and sheltering sandhills and sacred banyan roots ;
O lift your dreaming heads from their trance of ageless wisdom,
And weave your mystic measures to the melody of flutes.

We bring you milk and maize, wild figs and golden honey,
And kindle fragrant incense to hallow all the air,
With fasting lips we pray, with fervent hearts we praise you,
O bless our lowly offerings and hearken to our prayer.

Guard our helpless lives and guide our patient labours,
And cherish our dear vision like the jewels in your crests ;
O spread your hooded watch for the safety of our slumbers,
And soothe the troubled longings that clamour in our breasts.

Swift ye are as streams and soundless as the dewfall,
Subtle as the lightning and splendid as the sun ;
Seers are ye and symbols of the ancient silence,
Where life and death and sorrow and ecstasy are one.

Sarojini Naidu, *The Bird of Time* (1919).

[1] Sylvain Lévi, *Le Népal*, vol. ii, p. 50. The Nevars are the old population of Nepal conquered by the Gurkhas in 1768.

[2] *Hindu and Muhammadan Feasts* (1914), pp. 58 f.

ADDITIONAL NOTES

Page 7 *n.*—The double meaning of the word *nāga* ('serpent-demon' and 'elephant') appears frequently to have led to confusion. It accounts for the two forms of the legend regarding the *Stūpa* of Rāmagrāma (pp. 127 ff.). Again, when (p. 63) Indra explains that the bull on which he was riding is Airāvata 'the Nāga-rāj', it is impossible to decide whether we have to think of a serpent-demon or of an elephant.

If the word *nāga* is in reality related to the English word 'snake', it follows that the original meaning must be 'serpent'. It deserves notice that in epical and classical literature (in Vedic writings the word occurs only in a few isolated cases) it is never used to denote the snake as an animal, but always designates either a serpent-demon or an elephant. In the older literature the divine snakes are called *sarpa.*

It has never been satisfactorily explained in what manner the word came to be applied to an elephant, an animal which bears very little resemblance to a snake. The explanations mentioned in the Petersburg Dictionary are ingenious but little convincing. Or are we to think of the Latin compound *anguimanus*, 'with serpent-hand,' found in Lucretius? But an equivalent compound, e.g. *nāgahasta*, does not occur in Sanskrit literature. Besides, as we have said, the word *nāga* never indicates the animal snake. Nor does it occur among the twenty-five synonyms for a snake in the *Amarakoṡa*. The modern form *nāg*, besides denoting the serpent-demon, is applied to one species of snake, viz. the cobra. On pages 210 f. we have suggested an interpretation on a mythological basis.

Page 23.—With reference to the name Nāgārjuna we may call attention to the frequent occurrence of the word 'Nāga' as the first member of personal names both in literature and in inscriptions. This alone would suffice to demonstrate the importance of the deified snakes in ancient India. Cf. the Index of personal names accompanying Professor Lüders' *List of Brāhmī Inscriptions. Ep. Ind.*, vol. x, pp. 193 f.

Pages 28 ff.—The close connexion between the cobra and the ant-hill is also exemplified in the *Vammīkasutta*, No. 23, of the *Majjhima-nikāya*, ed. Trenckner, pp. 142 ff., and *Further Dialogues*, transl. by Lord Chalmers, London, 1926, vol. i, pp. 100 ff., under the title "The Smouldering Ant-Hill". It is an allegory in which the ant-hill represents the human body, at the bottom of which lies concealed the cobra, symbolizing "the Almsman in whom the Cankers are no more". (*Nāgo ti kho bhikkhu khīṇāsavass' etaṃ bhikkhuno adhivachanam.*) The *sutta* contains the exhortation: "Leave the cobra alone; do not harm the cobra; pay homage to the cobra." (*Tiṭṭhatu nāgo, mā nāgaṃ ghaṭṭesi, namo karohi nāgassāti.*)

Pages 31 f.—On the cave of Namuchi cf. Bloomfield, *J.A.O.S.* for 1891, pp. 143 ff. An Asura cave at Rājagṛiha is noticed by Hiuen Tsiang (transl. Beal, vol. ii, p. 156).

Page 39.—The Bharhut bas-relief referring to the Nāgarāja Airāvata or Elāpattra is also illustrated in the *Cambridge History of India*, vol. i, pl. xvi, fig. 45.

Pages 40 f.—In dealing with the examples of theriomorphic Nāgas in Græco-Buddhist art, we are now able to add a bas-relief, recently acquired for the Peshawar Museum. It represents the Bodhisattva's first bath administered by the two Nāgas Nanda and Upananda. The latter are shown in serpent form hovering over the head of the new-born Bodhisattva.

Pages 41 f.—A statuette (height 10½ inches) of the Nāga Dadhikarṇa, inscribed with his name, was recently recovered at Mathurā from the river Jamnā and has now been added to the local collection. The Nāga Dadhikarṇa is mentioned in the *āhnika-mantra* in the *Harivaṃśa* and also in the list of Nāgas quoted by Hemachandra in his own commentary on the *Abhidhāna-chintāmaṇi*, verse 1311. Cf. *Ind. Ant.*, vol. xxxiii (1904), p. 103 and *A.S.R.* for 1908–9, p. 161.—We may also call attention to another inscribed sculpture in the Mathurā Museum representing a Nāgarāja canopied by a sevenfold serpent-hood and attended by two Nāgīs of smaller size. In the inscription which is dated in the 8th year of Kānishka (here apparently spelled Kāṇikkha) the Nāga image is dedicated together with a water-tank and a garden (Skt. *ārāma*). For further particulars we refer to Mr. Y. R. Gupte's article, *Ep. Ind.*, vol. xvii, pp. 10 ff. with plate. The inscription appears to mention the Nāga under the name of 'Svāmi-Nāga' (not 'Bhūmi-Nāga'), meaning "the Lord Nāga". The lettering is somewhat indistinct.

Page 42.—With regard to the attitude of the Nāga image of Chhaṛgaon standing with his right hand raised as if ready to strike, it deserves notice that exactly the same attitude characterizes the figure of the *chakravartin* or Universal Monarch surrounded by 'the Seven Jewels', as shown in Amarāvatī sculpture (J. Fergusson, *Tree and Serpent Worship*, plates lxxix, 2; xci, 3 and xciii, and J. Burgess, *The Buddhist Stūpas of Amarāvatī and Jaggayyapeta*, plates v, 2, and xxxiii, 3). Burgess (op. cit., p. 109; pl. xv, 3) reproduces also a bas-relief from Jaggayyapeta, carved in a more primitive style, which shows the *chakravartin*. Here the meaning of the gesture is evident. The *chakravartin*, as Dr. Burgess has rightly observed, causes a shower of money (square coins!), to descend from the clouds which are plainly visible over his head. We may perhaps assume that the pose of the Chhaṛgaon Nāga has the same significance. But in his case it is not, of course, a rain of coins which he is supposed to bring down on the heads of his devotees, but a shower of real rainwater. The Chhaṛgaon image is also reproduced by K. de B. Codrington, *Ancient India from the earliest times to the Guptas*, London, 1926.

Page 42.—At the village of Baldeo on the left bank of the Jamnā river, some 8 miles south-east of the city of Mathurā, there stands a temple dedicated to Baladeva, which attracts many votaries. The stone idol of Baladeva worshipped in this temple is undoubtedly an ancient

Nāga image. It is said to have been recovered from a neighbouring tank. The image is nearly life-size and has the characteristics of the Nāga figures of the Kushāṇa period. Cf. *A.S.R.* for 1908–9, p. 161.

Page 43.—On his visit to Sankīsā (Skt. Sāṃkāśya) Hiuen Tsiang notes a Nāga tank to the south-east of the great *Stūpa*. " He [the Nāga] defends the sacred traces with care, and being thus spiritually protected, one cannot regard them lightly " (transl. Beal, vol. i, p. 205). In his account of the site of Sankīsā, Sir Alexander Cunningham remarks: " The only spot that can be identified with any certainty is the tank of the Nāga, which still exists to the south-east of the ruins, in the very position described by Hwen Thsang. The name of the Nāga is Kārewar, and that of the tank Kandaiya Tāl. Milk is offered to him during every day of Vaisākh, and on the Nāg-panchamī of Srāvana, and at any other time when rain is wanted ". (*A.S.R.*, vol. i, p. 274). The earlier pilgrim Fa Hien (transl. Beal, vol. i, pp. lxi f.) has the following: " There are perhaps [at Sāṃkāśya] a thousand male and female disciples who have their meals in common. They belong promiscuously to the systems of the Great and Little Vehicle, and dwell together. A white-eared dragon is the patron of this body of priests. He causes fertilizing and seasonable showers of rain to fall within their country, and preserves it from plagues and calamities and so causes the priesthood to dwell in security. The priests, in gratitude for these favours, have erected a dragon-chapel, and within it have placed a resting-place for his accommodation. Moreover, they make special contributions, in the shape of religious offerings, to provide the dragon with food. The body of priests every day select from their midst three men to go and take their meal in this chapel. At the end of each season of rain, the dragon suddenly assumes the form of a little serpent, both of whose ears are edged with white. The body of priests, recognizing him, place in the midst of his lair a copper vessel full of cream; and then, from the highest to the lowest, they walk past him in procession as if to pay him greeting all round. He then suddenly disappears. He makes his appearance once every year."

Another curious instance of Nāga worship associated with Buddhism we quote from Hiuen Tsiang's account of Kauśāmbī (transl. Beal, vol. i, p. 237):—" To the south-west of the city 8 or 9 *li* is a stone dwelling [cavern ?] of a venomous Nāga. Having subdued this dragon, Tathāgata left his shadow here; but though this is a tradition of the place, there is no vestige of the shadow visible. By the side of it is a *stūpa* built by Aśokarāja, about 200 feet high. To the north-east of the Nāga-dwelling is a great forest."

Page 46.—The serpent-carrying figures on the Nāga shrine of Panataran are supposed to represent priests holding bells. The theriomorphic Nāga is also frequently met with on the ancient monuments of Eastern Java and in the religious and domestic architecture of the Isle of Bali. The upper terrace of the main temple of Panataran is decorated with winged Nāgas and Siṃhas. Nāgas are also employed to embellish the flights of steps leading up to the terrace of East-Javanese shrines. Fine specimens occur on a small subsidiary temple belonging to

Chandi Tigawangi near Kĕdiri. At the entrance of Chandi Kidal near Malang we noticed two detached Nāga heads of a highly fantastical type which must once have served to adorn the flight of steps. They bear some resemblance to *makaras* and are characterized by ram's horns, four fangs, a jewel on the top of the head and a lotus-flower (?) hanging down from their mouth. Nāgas of the same type are found at Chandi Samentar. In the modern temple architecture of Bali the Nāga finds frequent employment. It is a common device that the temple—either a *meru* with a high, pagoda-like roof or a *padmāsana* dedicated to the Sun-god —is supposed to rest on a tortoise whose head, four legs, and tail are shown emerging, as it were, from the basement of the building. This animal represents the 'Fire Tortoise' called Kūrma Gni (Skt. *agni*), Bedawang Gni or Bedawang Nala (Skt. *anala*), on which the earth is supposed to rest. It is composed of fiery substance and by its movements is believed to cause the earthquakes and volcanic eruptions which often visit the Isle of Bali. The 'Fire Tortoise' in its turn is said to be enveloped by a gigantic Nāga who controls and counteracts its too violent movements. The latter animal, evidently the old world-serpent, is also represented in conjunction with the tortoise around the basement of the Balinese shrines. The *meru* of Pura Batur at the foot of the great volcano has two such Nāgas. For the mythological interpretation here given I am indebted to Dr. V. E. Korn, of the Civil Service of Netherlands India.

Page 49.—The idea of the Sun's chariot being drawn by Nāgas also occurs in the *Vishṇu-purāṇa*, ii, x, where it is said that his car is presided over by Ādityas, Ṛishis, Gandharvas, Apsarases, Yakshas, Nāgas, and Rākshasas, one member of each class doing duty in every month of the year. The Nāgas mentioned in this connexion are Vāsuki, Kachchhanīra(?), Takshaka, Nāga (?), Elāpattra, Śaṅkhapāla, Dhanañjaya, Airāvata, Mahāpadma, Karkoṭaka, Kambala, and Aśvatara. The rendering of Wilson "the serpent harnesses his steeds", although based on the commentary, does not agree with the text which says *vahanti pannagāḥ*.

Pages 51 f.—On the myth of 'the Rape of the Soma by Garuḍa' according to the version of the Old-Javanese *Mahābhārata* cf. H. H. Juynboll, *De geschiedenis van Garuḍa*. (*Gedenkschrift Kon. Inst. v.d. T.L. and V. v. Ned.-Indië*, 1926, pp. 156 ff.) The two plates accompanying Dr. Juynboll's article reproduce Balinese illustrations of the Garuḍa myth.

Page 56.—Another ancient temple, named Chandi Kidal, near Malang in Eastern Java, is adorned with three Garuḍa figures occupying the centre of each of the three walls outside. The Garuḍa on the north is shown carrying a female probably meant for Vinatā, that on the east a vessel of ambrosia, and that on the south side three Nāgas. Cf. N. J. Krom, *Inleiding tot de Hindoe-Javaansche Kunst*, 2nd ed., vol. ii, p. 60, and *Publicaties Oudh. Dienst*, vol. i (1925), pp. 12 ff., pl. vii, figs. *a–c*.

Page 56.—According to the *Mahābhārata* (*Ādi-parvan*, xxix) the elephant and the tortoise were in reality two *ṛishi* brothers, named Vibhāvasu and Supratīka, who quarrelled about a heritage and cursed each other. The episode of the elephant and the tortoise occurs also in the *Kathāsaritsāgara*, xii, 138–43.

Page 60.—Another example is the story of King Parīkshit of Ayodhyā and the frog-princess Suśobhanā, the daughter of the frog-king Āyu. She marries him on the condition that he will not show her any water. The pact being broken, she becomes a frog. *M.Bh.*, *Vanaparvan*, cxcii.

Page 79.—The curse pronounced by Arjuna recalls the words spoken by Vālmīki to the Nishāda hunter, "Mayest thou not, O Nishāda, find a resting-place (*pratishṭhā*) in eternity, because out of a pair of curlews thou hast killed one that was confused with love." (*Rām.*, *Bāla-k.*, ii, 15.) The curse of the Sage probably refers to the wandering habits of the Nishādas.

Page 85.—"Where in a former creation the wheel of the law was set into motion, there in the Naimisha Forest on the bank of the Gomatī lies a town named after the Nāga(s)." In the *Rāmāyaṇa* (*Uttara-k.*, xcii) the Naimisha Forest is the scene of Rāma's horse-sacrifice, where Vālmīki's poem is recited for the first time by Kuśa and Lava, the two sons of Rāma. Can it be that the name of the forest has something to do with Nemisa or Nemesa (also called Naigamesha and -meshin), the goat-headed deity who presides over childbirth ?

Page 91.—The spot where Kṛishṇa subdued Kāliya Nāg is pointed out at Bindrāban at the outer *ghāṭ* on the river Jamnā where a little shrine contains a figure of the Nāga. Apparently this image is nothing but a fragment of a pillar, on the top of which a number of imitations of cobra-heads have been fixed. Kṛishṇa is shown standing on the top of the Nāga so-called between two female figures said to represent Nāgīs, and a figure of Baladeva is in front of it. These four figures are dressed up in the usual fashion.

Pages 95 f.—As noted above, a Græco-Buddhist bas-relief has been lately recovered, showing the Bodhisattva's first bath administered by the Nāgarājas Nanda and Upananda who here appear in animal shape. The scene of the first bath is often represented in the art of Gandhāra, but with the exception of this unique piece of sculpture, the school invariably introduces the gods Brahmā and Śakra, who usurp the office of the two Nāga-kings in laving the new-born Bodhisattva. Cf. Foucher; *L'art gréco-bouddhique du Gandhāra*, vol. i, pp. 308 f., figs. 156–7.

Pages 99 ff.—The birds performing the *pradakshiṇā* round the Bodhisattva are also mentioned by Hiuen Tsiang (transl. Beal, vol. ii, p. 124). The meaning of the birds shown on the Amarāvātī pillar in the British Museum was correctly interpreted by the translator in his footnote 73. We recognize them on two other sculptures from Amarāvatī which were reproduced by Fergusson, *Tree and Serpent Worship*, plates lxvii and lxxvii (= Burgess, op. cit., pl. xxxvii, 2).

Pages 102 ff.—On Muchilinda, cf. Hiuen Tsiang, op. cit., vol. ii, p. 128.

Pages 108 ff.—On the conversion of the Kāśyapas cf. Hiuen Tsiang, op. cit., vol. ii, pp. 130 f. For the Amarāvatī sculpture representing the scene we refer to Foucher, op. cit., pp. 455 f., fig. 228.

Pages 121 f.—On the legend of the Nāga Apalāla cf. *Travels of Sung-yun* (*Si-yu-ki*, transl. Beal, p. xcv). After referring to the legend, the pilgrim says: "To the west of the river is a tank occupied by a Nāgarāja. By the side of the tank is a temple served by fifty priests and more. The Nāja-rāja ever and anon assumes supernatural appearances. The king of the country propitiates him with gold and jewels, and other precious offerings which he casts in the middle of the tank; such of these as find their way out through a back exit, the priests are permitted to retain. Because the dragon thus provides for the necessary expenses of this temple (clothes and food), therefore men call it the Nāga-rāja temple."

Page 129.—On the Sanchi bas-relief representing Aśoka's visit to the *Stūpa* of Rāmagrāma cf. J. H. Marshall, *Guide to Sanchi*, p. 47. We may also refer to an Amarāvatī sculpture reproduced by Fergusson, op. cit., pl. xcviii 2, where we see two men evidently in the act of opening a *Stūpa* being prevented in their purpose by the interference of a majestic Nāgarāja.

Pages 144 f.—Perhaps we may recognize the *Vidhurajātaka* in an Amarāvatī sculpture reproduced by Burgess, *Amarāvatī*, pl. xxii 2. The stone, which is evidently part of the coping, has suffered much from exposure, so that the details are by no means distinct. We recognize, however, the Yaksha general on his prancing horse, the wise Vidhura holding on to the tail.

Page 150.—There can be little doubt that the Kaṇṇapeṇṇā (*variant* Kaṇṇavaṇṇā) is identical with the Kistnā or Kṛishṇā, the great river of Southern India. In Sanskrit inscriptions this river occurs under the name of Kṛishṇavarṇā. Cf. Dr. L. D. Barnett's note in *Ep. Ind.*, vol. xii, p. 145. In the *Saṅkhapāla-jātaka* the Kaṇṇapeṇṇā is located in the kingdom Mahiṃsaka which is the same as the Andhra country.

Pages 176 f.—The story of Udayana and the wonderful lute is well illustrated in a series of highly artistic bas-reliefs which once adorned the cistern of Jalatunda (Djalatoenda), situated in the middle of the forest some 10 kilometres from Trawas, Eastern Java. They are labelled by means of two short inscriptions in old-Javanese which read: *Udayana* and *Mṛigayavatī* and bear the date [Śaka] 899 corresponding to A.D. 977.—One of the panels which is now preserved in the Batavia Museum, shows the prince meeting the Śabara snake-charmer. Cf. Krom, *Inleiding*, 2nd ed., vol. ii, p. 37.

Pages 187 ff.—The legend of the young Nāga is related at great length by Hiuen Tsiang (transl. Beal, vol. i, pp. 63 ff.) who locates it in Kapiśa. The story is here continued after the death of the Novice who, reborn as a Nāgarāja, causes great destruction, and opposes King

Kānishka when the latter wishes to build a convent and *Stūpa* "at the foot of the Snowy Mountains". The Nāga assuming the appearance of an aged Brahmin shows himself to the King and endeavours to dissuade him from his undertaking. "We Nāgas," he says, "are only brutish creatures. Nevertheless among lower creatures the Nāga possesses great power, which cannot be resisted. He rides on the clouds, drives the winds, passes through space, and glides over the waters; no human power can conquer him." In the conflict which follows the king invokes the full power of all his religious merit with the result that "from both his shoulders there arose a great flame and smoke". At last the Nāga submits, but is still afraid that by chance an angry heart may rise in him. So he concludes by saying: "Each day let the king send a man to observe the mountain-top; if it is black with clouds, then let him sound the bell (*ghaṇṭā*) loudly; when I hear the sound, my evil purpose will subside." Then the building of the convent and of the *Stūpa* was brought to completion.

Pages 196 ff.—Śesha is also introduced in a well-known episode of Kṛishṇa's childhood. When Vasudeva carries his new-born son across the Jamnā river to bring him into safety, it is said that "Parjanya [the Rain-god] rained while thundering in a low voice, and Śesha followed, warding off the water by means of his hoods". (*Vavarsha Parjanya upāṃśugarjitaḥ Śesho'nvagād vāri nivārayan phaṇaiḥ*, *Bhāg. P.*, x, 3, 49).—Rai Bahadur D. R. Sahni informs me that he has recognized this scene in an early piece of sculpture found somewhere near Mathurā and now preserved in the local museum.

Page 203.—We find Takshaka combined with *Vaiśālā (Pali *Vesālā*) in a passage in the *Mahāsamaya-suttanta, Dīghanikāya*, xx, 9 ff. (Pali Text Society, pp. 257 f.), which contains an enumeration of deities, including Nāgas.

Page 221.—With reference to the Kashmir tradition regarding King Jalauka being carried by a Nāga we may quote the following passage from Hiuen Tsiang's account of Kucha (transl. Beal, vol. i, p. 20): "To the north of a city on the eastern borders of the country, in front of a Deva temple, there is a great dragon-lake. The dragons, changing their form, couple with mares. The offspring is a wild species of horse ('dragon-horse'), difficult to tame and of a fierce nature. The breed of these dragon-horses became docile. This country consequently became famous for its many excellent horses. Former records [of this country] say: "In late time there was a king called 'Gold Flower', who exhibited rare intelligence in the doctrines [of religion]. He was able to yoke the dragons to his chariot. When the king wished to disappear, he touched the ears of the dragons with his whip, and forthwith he became invisible."

Page 230.—The name Kakodar is also applied to a mountain-range.

It is curious that the word *kākodara* as an appellativum occurs among the twenty-five synonyms denoting a snake which are enumerated in the *Amarakośa*. The grammarians, no doubt, took the word to be a compound of *kāka* ('crow') and *udara* ('belly'), but in reality it is probably a Prākrit equivalent of Karkoṭa.

Pages 233 f.—We may compare the following passage from Fa-Hien: " In Ts'ung-ling there are poison-dragons who, when evil purposed, spit poison, winds, rain, snow, drifting sand, and gravel stones; not one of ten thousand meeting these calamities, escapes." (*Si-yu-ki*, transl. Beal, p. xxix).

Pages 258.—The name Maṇikarṇ by which the village in the Pārbatī valley is known, suggests that the locality with its hot springs was originally sacred to a Nāga Maṇikarṇa. We have noted (p. 218) that the word *maṇi* is often found in Nāga names. It is curious that the name 'Maṇikarṇikā' is also applied to one of the most important *ghāṭs* of Benares where a sacred well is the centre of religious worship. May we assume that here too the local deity was originally a Nāga?

Page 267.—The great centre of Nāg worship at Benares is the Nāg Kuān or Snake-well. Four flights of steps, numbering altogether forty steps, lead down to a large circular well which is considerably below the level of the street. There is a stone slab with a Nāgārī inscription let into the wall. The *pūjārī* declares that the well gives access to Pātāla or the Nether World, the abode of snakes. A snake image is said to exist inside the well below the water level. Besides there are snake stones let into the well. At this well thousands of people are said to assemble on the occasion of the Nāgapañchamī.

Above the Chaukī Ghāt a number of snake-stones are found under a large *pīpal* tree at the head of the steps. They were noticed by Mr. E. B. Havell and will be found reproduced in his book on Benares.

The temple of Ādikeśava stands in a very fine position above the junction of the Ganges and the Barnā. In a room belonging to this temple medicines are kept for distribution to the poor. It is designated by the name of *aushadhālaya*. On both sides of the doorway there is a mud image of a cobra, painted, which is said to be worshipped on the day of the Nāgapañchamī.

INDEX

U